Pan-Africanism
or
Communism

GEORGE PADMORE

DT 31
P3
1971

Pan-Africanism
or
Communism

GEORGE PADMORE

FOREWORD BY
RICHARD WRIGHT

INTRODUCTION BY
AZINNA NWAFOR, Ph.D.
Professor of Political Science
Harvard University

DOUBLEDAY & COMPANY, INC.
GARDEN CITY, NEW YORK 1971

FEB 11 '72

166309

Library of Congress Catalog Card Number: 71-164438
Introduction Copyright © 1971 by Azinna Nwafor
All Rights Reserved
Printed in the United States of America

Dedicated to the Youth of Africa—
the Torchbearers of Pan-Africanism

TO FIGHTERS FOR FREEDOM

'Through the troubled history of man comes
sweeping a blind fury of destruction and the
towers of civilization topple down to dust.

In the chaos of moral nihilism are trampled
under foot by marauders the best treasures of
man heroically won by the martyrs for ages.

Come, young nations, proclaim the fight for
freedom, rise up the banner of invincible faith.

Build bridges with your life across the gaping
earth blasted by hatred, and march forward.

Do not submit yourself to carry the burden of
insult upon your head, kicked by terror, and dig
not a trench with falsehood and cunning to
build a shelter for your dishonoured manhood;
offer not the weak as sacrifice to the strong to
save yourself.'

—RABINDRANATH TAGORE

CONTENTS

ACKNOWLEDGMENTS

I am deeply indebted to a number of colonial nationalists in Britain who encouraged me in the writing of this historical account of the struggles of Africans and peoples of African descent for Human Rights and Self-Determination in the modern world.

I take this opportunity of thanking them all for the willing aid and co-operation they have given me, in particular, Mr Abu Mayanja of the Uganda National Congress and Mr Hugh Scotland, secretary of the Coloured Peoples' Association, who have devoted so much of their valuable time to reading the manuscript and have offered many constructive criticisms and suggestions. However, I am alone responsible for the views expressed throughout the book.

My thanks must also go to my distinguished colleagues, Mr J. A. Rogers, the Afro-American historian, for allowing me to quote extensively from his biographical work, *World's Great Men of Colour*, and Dr W. E. B. DuBois, that Grand Old Man of the Negro race, whose brilliant autobiography, *Dust of Dawn*, is an invaluable source of information on the early history of Pan-Africanism.

Acknowledgment is offered in generous measure to the late Marcus Garvey, whose writings and speeches, edited by his widow, Mrs Amy Jacques Garvey, of Jamaica, under the title *Philosophy and Opinions of Marcus Garvey*, are indispensable as a source of original material on the Back to Africa Movement and the rise of Black Nationalism between the two World Wars. Also to the following for permission to use various copyright passages: Oxford University Press for a quotation from Lord Hailey's *An African Survey*; Messrs Hamish Hamilton Ltd for a quotation from John Gunther's *Inside Asia*; Messrs Lawrence & Wishart Ltd for a quotation from Stalin's *Marxism and the National and Colonial*

Question; Messrs William Collins & Sons Ltd and Miss Julia Monteath, trustee of Sir Reginald Coupland's estate, for quotations from *Wilberforce;* and I must beg forgiveness from anyone whose rights have been overlooked in this list. Finally, I must thank my wife for so generously aiding me in my researches and for typing the draft manuscript, correcting proofs, preparing the index, and sustaining my efforts throughout the writing of the book.

G.P.

AUTHOR'S NOTE

Since the end of the Second World War it has become notorious, both in the press and in certain political circles of the Western world, to ascribe every manifestation of political awakening in Africa to Communist inspiration. This is gross hypocrisy, part of the cold war propaganda designed to discredit African nationalists and to alienate from their movements the sympathy and support of anti-colonial elements within Labour and progressive organizations, which, while friendly towards the political aspiration of the colonial peoples, are hostile to Communism.

The facts revealed in this book will prove the falsity of this smear campaign and pinpoint the danger to the Western peoples of allowing the policies of their Governments to destroy the latent friendship and goodwill of the Africans; policies which may well force Africans to seek allies among the Communists in their efforts to gain their independence.

At the moment none of the African independence movements is influenced by Communism. Indeed, this book will show that the struggles of Africans and peoples of African descent began with their endeavours to establish a 'National Home' on the West African coast nearly a century before Communist Russia emerged as a power in world politics. As a matter of fact, much of the first Back to Africa efforts belongs to the period of the Abolitionist movements in Britain and America. At that time, the Russian peoples themselves were living very close to slavery under the yoke of Czarist serfdom.

In order to place this phase of African nationalism in its true historical perspective, I have found it necessary to survey in broad outline the progress of the colonization of Sierra Leone and Liberia and to trace their constitutional and political development.

The main purpose of the book, however, is to record the rise and growth of the contemporary Negro political movements: 'Pan-Africanism' and 'Garveyism' or 'Black Zionism'. The latter was, primarily, an attempt to revive the nineteenth-century Back to Africa movements which inspired the foundation of Sierra Leone and Liberia.

During the nineteen-twenties, Black Zionism as expounded by its founder, Marcus Aurelius Garvey, was the most militant expression of African nationalism. As affirmed by C. L. R. James, the West Indian historian, the name of Garvey 'rolled through Africa. The King of Swaziland told a friend some years after that he knew the names of only two black men in the Western world, Jack Johnson and Marcus Garvey.'[1] Though Black Zionism did not sustain itself as an organized movement, 'one thing Garvey did do. He made the American Negro conscious of his African origin and created for the first time a feeling of international solidarity among Africans and people of African descent.'

Both Garveyism and Pan-Africanism, which originated about the same time, have much influenced the present generation of nationalists, but neither movement has drawn inspiration or support from Communism. On the contrary, the philosophies and programmes of both movements have been bitterly assailed by the Communists. For instance, the Sixth Congress of the now defunct Communist International declared open war upon the Garvey movement when the leaders refused to allow white Communists to exploit their organization in the service of Soviet foreign policy. In its directive to American Communists the International declared that 'Garveyism, which was formerly the ideology of the masses, like Gandhism, has become a hindrance to the revolutionization of the Negro masses. Originally advocating social equality for Negroes, Garveyism subsequently developed into a peculiar form of Negro "Zionism", which, instead of fighting American imperialism, advanced the slogan "Back to Africa". This dangerous ideology, which bears not a single democratic trait, and which toys with the aristocratic attributes of a non-existent "Negro Kingdom", must be strongly resisted, for

[1] C. L. R. James: A History of Negro Revolt, p. 68.

it is not a help but a hindrance to the mass Negro struggle for liberation against American imperialism'. Pan-Africanism, too, was branded as 'reactionary petit-bourgeois nationalism', and its founder, the distinguished Afro-American scholar, Dr W. E. B. DuBois, was denounced as 'a betrayer of the Negro people'.

When, therefore, Western imperialists and their apologists in the Labour movement credit the Communists with inspiring emerging African nationalism, they are either being deliberately misleading or self-deceiving. The dynamic forces of post-war anti-colonialist movements which are challenging the political and economic domination of the West are the spontaneous expression of the hopes and desires of the Africans, looking forward to a place as free men in a free world. Africans do not have to wait for Communists to 'incite' them. The realities of their status have infused their determination to be free. And they prefer to attain freedom under the standard of Pan-Africanism, a banner of their own choosing.

For if there is one thing which events in Africa, no less than in Asia, have demonstrated in the post-war years, it is that colonial peoples are resentful of the attitude of Europeans, of both Communist and anti-Communist persuasion, that they alone possess the knowledge and experience necessary to guide the advancement of dependent peoples. Africans feel that they are quite capable of leading themselves, and of developing a philosophy and ideology suited to their own special circumstances and needs, and have come to regard the arrogance of white 'loftiness' in this respect as unwarranted interference and unpardonable assumption of superiority. Africans are quite willing to accept advice and support which is offered in a spirit of true equality, and would prefer to remain on terms of friendship with the West. But they want to make their way under their own steam. If, however, they are obstructed they may in their frustration turn to Communism as the only alternative means of achieving their aims. The future pattern of Africa, therefore, will, in this context, be in large measure determined by the attitudes of the Western nations.

Recognizing the oneness of the struggles of the Coloured
World for freedom from alien domination, Pan-Africanism
endorses the conception of an Asian-African front against
that racial arrogance which has reached its apogee in the
Herrenvolk philosophy of *Apartheid*. Pan-Africanism, moreover, draws considerable inspiration from the struggles of
the national freedom movements of the Asian countries, and
subscribes to the Gandhian doctrine of non-violence as a
means of attaining self-determination and racial equality. It
rejects the unbridled system of monopoly capitalism of the
West no less than the political and cultural totalitarianism of
the East. It identifies itself with the neutral camp, opposed to
all forms of oppression and racial chauvinism—white or
black—and associates itself with all forces of progress and
goodwill, regardless of nationality, race, colour, or creed,
working for universal brotherhood, social justice, and peace
for all peoples everywhere.

Africans, like Asians, have a vested interest in *Peace*, since
only in a world, ordered and free from violence and war can
they hope to create a new life for themselves and make their
positive contribution to modern civilization.

Pan-Africanism recognizes much that is true in the Marxist
interpretation of history, since it provides a rational explanation for a good deal that would otherwise be unintelligible. But it nevertheless refuses to accept the pretentious
claims of doctrinaire Communism, that it alone has the solution to all the complex racial, tribal, and socio-economic
problems facing Africa. It also rejects the Communist intolerance of those who do not subscribe to its ever-changing
party line even to the point of liquidating them as 'enemies of
the people'. Democracy and brotherhood cannot be built
upon intolerance and violence.

In their struggles to attain self-government and self-
determination, the younger leaders of Pan-Africanism have
the task of building upon the ideological foundations laid by
Dr DuBois, the 'father' of Pan-Africanism. The problems
facing these men are very much more varied and complex
than those which beset the founders of the Sierra Leone and

Liberian settlements. They are under the necessity to evolve new political means and organizational techniques adapted to African traditions and circumstances. They also have to work out a social philosophy which will integrate and uplift peoples making the transition from primitive tribal forms of society to modern industrialized states with the speed demanded by present-day pressures.

So that the reader may appreciate some of the difficulties facing emerging African nationalism, I have given a brief review of political evolution in the Gold Coast and Nigeria since the end of the Second World War. In these West African colonies political advance has been along constitutional lines, in contrast to Kenya, where the tensions in multi-racial society have erupted in Mau Mau conflict and bloody violence. A comparison of British colonial policies in West and East Africa will enable the reader to appreciate better the explosive effects which the denial of racial equality in a plural society can have. The problem of European settlements in East, Central and Southern Africa can be solved only by the creation of *a common citizenship for all the races—indigenous and immigrant—on the basis of absolute equality for Africans in Church and State*. There is no other solution, since Africans are not going to tolerate being treated as inferiors in their own lands.

In the hope of throwing some light on to the conflicting and bewildering medley of colonial systems in Africa, I have attempted to define and interpret the political and social status of Africans living under the rule of the different European powers which exercise dominion over the continent. Africa is, without doubt, the continent, *par excellence*, of administrative anarchy. Each of the ruling powers pursues its own particular form of government; some even pursue two or three conflicting policies at one and the same time.

For instance, while British policy in East, Central, and Southern Africa is to support white colonization and European domination, in West Africa, Colonial Office policy is based upon the principle of national self-determination for Africans by process of gradual constitutional reform. If this policy were only honestly and vigorously pursued by the British Government, irrespective of the party in office, it would be the most effective bulwark against Communism, the spectre haunting the white settlers and British colonial officials. For African nationalists will only turn to Communism when they feel frustrated in their aspirations and become resentful of what they consider to be a betrayal of the professions enunciated by the Western democracies in the Atlantic Charter.

Our criticism of British colonial policy is not in what it professes to stand for—'self government within the Commonwealth'—but the failure to make good this promise unless actually forced to do so by the colonial peoples. It has always been a case of 'too little and too late'. The result is that the dependent peoples, who would otherwise be Britain's friends and allies, become her implacable enemies. What British colonial policy needs to do today is to make open recognition of awakening African self-awareness, and instil its own acts with boldness and imagination. Deeds and not vague promises are what is wanted.

For their part, the African nationalist leaders must resolve their own internal communal conflicts and tribal differences, so that, having established a democratically elected government, the imperial power will find less danger in passing power to the popularly elected leaders than in withholding it. Once a colonial people have achieved freedom, as the history of the recently emerged Asian nations has so well illustrated, they will know how to defend it against those subversive elements within their midst who seek to make them pawns in the power politics of the cold war belligerents.

In the coming struggle for Africa, the issue, as I have already inferred, will be between Pan-Africanism and Communism. Imperialism is a discredited system, completely rejected by Africans. As for white colonization, it can maintain itself only with outside military support. The white man in East and Central Africa has forfeited the loyalty and goodwill of the Africans, who no longer have illusions about professions of 'trusteeship' and 'partnership'. These British settlers, to say nothing of the fanatical racialists and rabid defenders of *Apartheid* in South Africa, have made it abundantly clear to the Africans that they regard them merely as hewers of wood and drawers of water in their own countries.

As to Communism, Africans have no reason to be scared

of the red bogey as long as their political leaders remain true
to the ideals and principles of Pan-Africanism. For politically, Pan-Africanism seeks the attainment of the government of Africans by Africans for Africans, with respect for
racial and religious minorities who desire to live in Africa
on a basis of equality with the black majority. Economically and socially, Pan-Africanism, subscribes to the fundamental objectives of Democratic Socialism, with state control
of the basic means of production and distribution. It stands
for the liberty of the subject within the law and endorses the
Fundamental Declaration of Human Rights, with emphasis
upon the Four Freedoms.

The post-war happenings in Asia have shown that forms of
government are not of paramount importance to the masses
of the people. Their interest is in the satisfaction of their
elemental needs. Communism exploits misery, poverty, ignorance and want. The only effective answer to Communism,
therefore, is to remove these conditions by satisfying the
wants and material needs of the common people, which re-
volve primarily round food, clothing, and shelter. Any honest,
incorruptible government seeking to do this will provide the
best guarantee against Communism. Hence, Pan-Africanism
sets out to fulfil the socio-economic mission of Communism
under a libertarian political system.

Finally, for Pan-Africanism, the self-determination of the
dependent territories is the prerequisite to the federation of
self-governing states on a regional basis, leading ultimately
to the creation of a United States of Africa. For there is a
growing feeling among politically conscious Africans throughout the continent that their destiny is one, that what happens
in one part of Africa to Africans must affect Africans living
in other parts. As far back as forty years ago, Dr DuBois, in
his book, *The Negro*, pointed out a truth which, if anything,
is even more pregnant today. '*There is slowly arising not only
a curiously strong brotherhood of Negro blood throughout the
world, but the common cause of the darker races against the
intolerable assumption and insults of Europeans has already
found expression. Most men in the world are coloured. A
belief in humanity means a belief in coloured men. The fu-*

ture world will, in all reasonable possibility, be what coloured men make it.'

This is the inescapable challenge of the second part of the twentieth century.

GEORGE PADMORE.

London
July, 1955

FOREWORD

Concerning George Padmore I am biased, for he is my friend. Yet, despite a personal relationship, I think that I can be objective about him. My admiration for him is evoked not only by his undeniable qualities, but by the objective position which he occupies in the minds of black people throughout the world.

George is, in my opinion, the greatest living authority on the fervent nationalist movements sweeping Black Africa today. Not only does he know those movements intimately, not only does he understand them in terms of their leaders, aims, structures, and ideologies, but George and his life *are those movements, aims and ideologies*. His activity has, for more than twenty-five years, helped to shape and mould those movements in all of their bewildering complexity. George has ranged from the Kremlin to the African bush, from that asylum for ex-slaves called Freetown (Sierra Leone) to the multi-racial societies of the West Indies, from the lonely black men lost in the white London fogs to the store front churches in the Black Belts of America. Indeed, George is the veritable ideological father of many of the nationalist movements in Black Africa, having been the mentor of scores of African nationalist leaders who now hold or will soon hold power. By his background, his training, and his experience, he possesses a wealth of knowledge which he has selflessly poured into the minds of his black brothers.

George lives in a small apartment near Mornington Crescent in London and I have often been a guest in his home. I have seen him labour day in and day out, to the exclusion of all other interests, upon the one thing that really matters to him: freedom for black people. The kitchen in that apartment is George's office and workroom and through that kitchen have trooped almost all of the present day leaders of

Black Africa. They came seeking information, encouragement, and help, and George gave of his days and hours to expounding the intricacies of politics to nationalists like Wallace Johnson, Nkrumah, Kenyatta, Azikiwe, Joe Appiah, Musazi, Mayanja, and the Sudanese leaders, Abdulla Khalil, Mahgoub, Osman, etc. George is an ascetic, loving ideas more than public display, valuing scrupulously political facts and social processes.

The present volume represents the ripe wisdom of a great and tireless fighter. Mellowed, balanced, conversant with the ideologies and personalities of colonial struggles, he now feels that he can point out the road to freedom for Black Africa and indicate how that road should be travelled.

This book is uniquely valuable in that it relates, for the first time, the history of black nationalist movements from the establishment of the first Negro settlement in Sierra Leone in 1787 up to and including the period (1920-56) of the abortive attempts of the Communist International to capture those movements. (It may surprise many people to learn that Black Nationalism is far older than International Communism!) This book also contains an account of why and how black nationalists feel that Western imperialists sought to capture those movements . . . What? Negroes view both Communists and Imperialists as having an element in common?

At long, long last it may be possible to spell out something to European and American readers and to the men in the Kremlin about how black people feel . . . Black people primarily regard Russian Communists as *white* men. Black people primarily regard American, British and French anti-Communists as *white* people . . . Is that surprising? It ought not to be. If this comes as a shock to those interested in this problem, it simply means that they have never understood the Colour Problem. The black man's is a strange situation; it is a perspective, an angle of vision held by oppressed people; it is an outlook of people looking upward from below. It is what Nietzsche once called a 'frog's perspective'. Oppression oppresses, and this is the consciousness of black men who have been oppressed for centuries,—oppressed for so long that their oppression has become a tradition, in fact, a kind of culture. This elementary fact has baffled white men, Communist and non-Communist alike, for more than fifty years. The Negro's outlook is basically determined by his economic and social position, by his colour, and racial oppression. The Negro did not create the issue of colour, or race, or the condition in which he lives, but he has been moulded and influenced by them. The Negro's fundamental loyalty is, therefore, to *himself*. His situation makes this inevitable. [Am I letting awful secrets out of the bag? I'm sorry. The time has come for this problem to be stated clearly so that there is no possibility of further misunderstanding or confusion. The Negro, even when embracing Communism or Western Democracy, is not supporting ideologies; he is seeking to use *instruments* (instruments owned and controlled by men of other races!) for his own ends. He stands outside of those instruments and ideologies; he has to do so, for he is not allowed to blend with them in a natural, organic and healthy manner.]

There will be Negroes who will rush indignantly forward to decry what I have just said. The higher their position of trust in France, England or America, the more vehemently they will deny what I am saying, for they will be ashamed to let their white neighbours or friends know how they really feel. It is most amazing that society can induce in people basic feelings which those people are ashamed to own!

In these pages George gives us a graphic exposition of the relationship of International Communism to African, West Indian and American Negro mass movements, and I can say flatly that no man living is better qualified to write that exposition than George Padmore, for, from the Comintern itself, he helped to shape much of the later phases of that relationship. But, when George discovered that, beyond doubt, Stalin and his satraps looked upon black men as political pawns of Soviet power politics, to be manœuvred in Russian interests alone, he broke completely with the Kremlin. BUT HIS BREAKING DID NOT MEAN THAT HE THEN AUTOMATICALLY SUPPORTED THE ENEMIES OF THE SOVIET UNION. AND HIS REFUSAL TO SUPPORT THE ENEMIES OF THE SOVIET UNION WAS NOT DICTATED BY ANY LOVE FOR STALIN. NO! HE CONTINUED HIS WORK ALONE, STRIVING TO ACHIEVE THROUGH HIS

OWN INSTRUMENTALITIES THAT WHICH HE HAD WORKED FOR WHEN HE WAS IN THE COMINTERN HIERARCHY. THAT IS, FREE-DOM FOR BLACK PEOPLE. I have laboured this point, for there is a great danger that any struggle conducted by Negroes will be branded as Red-inspired, and people must open their minds and understand the historic background of Negro struggle, or, truly, tragedy will engulf Africa.

That the Africans, West Indians and American Negroes have flirted with Communism is undeniably true, but just as true is the sad fact that in almost every instance the black victim discovered that he was not serving his own interests when he was caught in the Stalinist coils. Today nobody is more immune to the call of Communism than black men who found, to their bitter sorrow, that they were being used for ends that were not theirs.

This book recounts the great saga of the rise of black people from slavery to freedom on an intercontinental scale and brings us to the crucial crossroads—a hopeful resolution for black freedom and a partnership of races purged of terror, lynching and colour lines, etc., or a continental mass struggle conducted by Africans in Africa, a struggle that will duplicate the tragic upheavals in Asia. It is not up to black men to say how this issue will be resolved; but make no mistake: the black man will cling tenaciously to his dream of freedom!

If my words carry any weight, I commend this volume for close study to the white governmental officials of the Western world, to white churchmen, Catholic and Protestant alike, and equally to the dour and brooding white rulers in the Kremlin. I would urge them to read it and get a true, human perspective of the hopes, fears, struggles and hard-bought progress of the Negro in the modern world.

I, for one, salute and congratulate George Padmore for his having kept the faith and fought the good fight.

PARIS, *March* 2, 1956.   RICHARD WRIGHT

THE REVOLUTIONARY AS HISTORIAN: PADMORE AND PAN-AFRICANISM

A Critical Introduction to George Padmore: PAN-AFRICANISM OR COMMUNISM

George Padmore's *Pan-Africanism or Communism* shares the distinction—common to most great works of historical writing as with Thucydides, Machiavelli, and Trotsky's *History of the Russian Revolution*—of being the creation of a participant as historian. For next to the colossal figure of W. E. B. DuBois, Padmore—the political revolutionary—holds an exalted position in the pantheon of Pan-Africanism; and in his chef d'oeuvre he has presented us a most vivid account of that movement in which he played so exemplary a role. Indeed there was in Padmore an admirable double-faceted *vis historica*: the revolutionary's desire to make history and the writer's impulse to describe it and grasp its meaning.

Born Malcolm Nurse in the West Indies, the name George Padmore by which he goes down in history is a *nom de guerre* which he adopted when he joined the Communist Party. As he explained in a letter to a friend, 'all revolutionaries are compelled to adopt false names to hide their identity from the Government'. He later rose to become the foremost black figure in the Communist International—the Comintern—culminating in his receiving appointment as a colonel in the Red Army. He travelled extensively in Africa in an effort to create the nucleus for a Comintern-directed African leadership. Subsequently, as head of the African Bureau of the Comintern in Germany he organised an International Conference of black workers at Hamburg.

Padmore's experiences with the Comintern were marked

by accumulating episodes of wide fluctuations in the various policies pursued by the established Stalinist bureaucracy. Lacking any consistency from the perspective of the glorious ideals underlying the triumphant revolution, the seemingly irrational vicissitudes of these policies were in fact dictated and rationalized by the exigencies of what were perceived to be the national interests of the young Soviet Republic for survival. In this the struggle of the African peoples for liberation constituted only one strategy in the struggle against Western imperialism. An instance is the Comintern's proposal for the establishment of 'Black Republics'. This was required by a policy of anti-imperialism as also by the phenomenal success of Marcus Garvey's 'Back to Africa' mass movement, which led the Communist Party to seek accommodation and alliance with Garvey. But when the tide turned and an alliance was forged with the imperialists against the Axis powers, the policy was accordingly altered. Moreover, the imperviousness of Garvey to any kind of alliance or pursuit of a common front with the Communists had been painfully disillusioning. Garvey could form an alliance in the course of a common interest with the ultrareactionary and racist KKK, but he discerned no common interests whatsoever with the Communists. But as long as it seemed possible to the Comintern that some of Garvey's followers could be converted from Garveyism to Communism by satisfying the nationalist aspirations for a 'National Home' which Garvey had promised, they too seriously advanced the policy of a Black Republic. In this the Comintern offered black Americans a state of their own in the Black Belt, that is in 'that strip of territory in the heart of the Southern part of the USA extending south and southwest from the eastern part of Virginia to the border of Texas, in which the black population exceeds the white'.

Thus the doctrine of self-determination, with the right of secession, and the establishment of an independent black nation was declared applicable to blacks in the Southern United States, as also with the similarly proffered 'Native Republic' in South Africa. This piece of Stalinist sophistry was severely criticised by many blacks in the United States as well as those in South Africa. Those protesting the decree

were, naturally, denounced and expelled as 'right-wing deviationists'. Padmore called the 'Black Republic' thesis a
'fantastic scheme'. As he commented: 'The blacks wanted to
know how they, a poor down-trodden and unarmed racial
minority group, were to establish an autonomous self-
governing "Black Belt State" within the Republic of the
United States. But even assuming that it was possible, a territory inhabited exclusively by blacks would be no different
from Dr Malan's *Apartheid*, which aims at segregating the
Africans in the Union of South Africa into an all-black
"Bantu State"—a sort of glorified Native Reserve.' This criticism was as valid and perspicacious when it was initially
made, as it is today when directed against certain sections
of contemporary black nationalism for whom the establishment of autonomous Black Republics has become a favourite
battle cry. The analogy with the Bantustans which the South
African Governments have set up in which to incarcerate
Africans and thus be better enabled to control them is a
particularly precise analogy. It is an instance whose significance for the prospect of black liberation still needs to be
digested by the merchants of Black Republics. One encounters here a demonstration of the conservative world view on
which the black nationalist ideology rests. Slavery, repression,
and defeat have driven the black nationalist into a kind of
social *Apartheid*. As Tom Nairn so judiciously observed of
the British working class: 'Such "apartheid" was the necessary pre-condition of the conservative class-hierarchy. It was
only the systematic fostering of this sense of irremediable
and inherited difference, of social exclusion felt (even if not
intellectually asserted to) as a fact of nature. This was one
of the most powerful weapons any conservative regime has
ever had in its hands, worth any number of policemen. A
conservative totality, and the broad distribution of property
and power it represents, is bound to be safe as long as the
various subordinate sectors of it have a consciousness of
themselves as different and separate, as mere "sectors" in the
social space allotted to them. Such a sectional or corporate
self-consciousness is the essence of social conservatism.' It
is relatively irrelevant that it should be accompanied by a
sense of grievance or injustice, by demands that wrongs be

righted. What matters is that the wrongs and rights are apprehended as those *of* the class, as opposed to the moments in history where a class desires to escape altogether from its *Apartheid* and identifies its rights with those of society as a whole. The reflex of class hierarchy in a conservative totality is the consciousness of oneselves as an 'estate', a separate nation within a nation. Black nationalists should ponder the implications of this perspective or they would merely serve to encourage postponement of black liberation to the Greek kalends. Of course, with the Comintern, as we have noted, this was merely a strategic position in another struggle. And when it turned out an inconvenient policy, it was accordingly abandoned.

Furthermore, during the heady days of the German-Soviet non-aggression pact the official party line proclaimed that it was an 'imperialist war', but as soon as Soviet Russia was forced into the theatre of war it became immediately transformed into an 'anti-fascist war of liberation'. In Africa the policy dictated by the vagaries of this official view varied from promoting anti-imperialist offenses against Britain and France to discouraging them. When, for instance, the Franco-Soviet Pact was signed in 1935, the Comintern instructed its Africa Bureau to 'go easy' on French colonialism. The depressing catalogue of Machiavellian cynicism underlying Soviet policy finally induced Padmore's resignation from the Comintern and also from the Communist Party. As he complained after his resignation: 'The Russians like the British ruling class have "no permanent friends, nor permanent enemies but only permanent interests"—namely, the survival of the Soviet Union.' One recalls the very similar judgment of the bureaucratic deformation of the Russian Revolution which Aimé Césaire made when he too broke with the Communists twenty-five years later. As he stated then: 'It's neither Marxism nor Communism I repudiate; the use certain people have made of Marxism and Communism is what I condemn. What I want is that Marxism and Communism be harnessed into the service of coloured peoples, and not coloured people into the service of Marxism and Communism. That the doctrine and the movement be tailored to fit men, not men to fit the movement. And—of course—that goes for others besides Communists.' In fact, had they known it, Padmore and Césaire could, with perfect justice, have quoted to the Russians the severe censure which Albert Sorel in *L'Europe et la Révolution Française* made of the French Revolution at the onset of its bureaucratic degeneration: 'The French republicans believed themselves to be cosmopolitans, but they were that only in speeches; they felt, they thought, they acted, they interpreted their universal ideas and their abstract principles in accordance with the tradition of a conquering monarchy. . . . They identified humanity with their homeland, their national cause with the cause of all the nations. Consequently and entirely naturally, they confused the propagation of new doctrines with the extension of French power, the emancipation of humanity with the grandeur of the Republic, the reign of reason with that of France, the liberation of peoples with the conquest of States, the European revolution with the domination of the French revolution in Europe. . . . They established subservient and subordinate republics which they held in a sort of tutelage. . . . The revolution degenerated into an armed propaganda, then into conquest.' One needs only substitute Russian for French for an appreciation of a comparable degeneration which bureaucratic Stalinist orthodoxy inflicted on the Russian Revolution.

This situation forced Padmore to break with the Communists. But in severing connections with them, Padmore did not join the frenzied ranks of the professional anti-Communists in remorseful contrition and fulminations over the god that failed them. Nor did he reconcile himself to imperialism and the oppressions of African peoples, with the soothing accompaniment of Wordsworth's famous formula of reconciliation with which that ex-revolutionary reconciled himself to Pitt's England: 'Far, far more abject is thy enemy.' Such a formula did not suit Padmore. There was in him, on the other hand, a need to intensify the struggle against imperialism as also against that Communism which has been polluted by the exigencies of Stalin's balance-of-power political struggles with the Western countries. Arthur Koestler once wrote that 'if we survey history and compare the lofty aims in the name of which revolutions were started, and the sorry end to which they came, we see again and again how a *polluted civilization pollutes its own revolutionary offspring*' [italics added]. Such an observation would lead—as, curiously, it did not lead Koestler—to the conclusion that if indeed the 'revolutionary offspring', Communism, has been 'polluted' by the civilization against which it has revolted, the struggle against this pollution becomes at once and simultaneously the struggle against the polluted offspring as also and inevitably against the source of that pollution. Padmore drew this conclusion. For though conceived by him as a bulwark against Communism, yet 'Pan-Africanism recognizes much that is true in the Marxist interpretation of history, since it provides a rational explanation for a good deal that would otherwise be unintelligible.'

In his enduring and lifelong involvement with Pan-Africanism, it becomes for him a tool for combatting both imperialism and Communism. One implication of this view is that since, for Padmore, 'Communism exploits misery, poverty, ignorance and want', Pan-Africanism sets out ultimately 'to fulfil the socio-economic mission of Communism under a libertarian political system.' Pan-Africanism as the only effective weapon against imperialism and Communism is admirably suited to the era of the cold war during which most African countries emerged into independence. Thus we find in Padmore the intellectual forerunner of the theories of 'non-alignment' and 'positive neutrality' which the emergent countries of Africa and Asia universally adopted in their foreign policy declarations and in their involvement in world affairs. Attaining independence within the context of a world divided between two powerful and opposed blocs of nations: West and East, capitalist and Communist, principally between the ideological and material polarities of the United States and the Soviet Union—arriving at independence in a world so structured, they proclaimed their determination not to be drawn into any commitments or alliances with either camp. Instead, their policy positions would be determined by a commitment to certain basic principles such as justice, equality, the principles of fundamental human rights, and respect for international obligations deemed necessary and essential for the maintenance of peace and world order. In general, these new nations believed that their most important contribution to world politics would be, as President Nyerere once stated, 'in the effort to judge issues on their own merits and to take our stand accordingly'. Needless to add, such a policy was of necessity anti-colonial and anti-imperialist in character. It strengthened their jealous regard for the preservation of their newly-won independence, and as they 'would not have British masters, so would [they] not have Russian masters either'. It is important to recognise the historical justification and progressive standpoint of this policy. As Jack Woddis has noted, such a policy 'corresponds to the stage of development these states have reached, helps to weaken the positions of imperialism and makes a valuable contribution to the cause of anti-colonialism and world peace'.

Padmore's 'historical account of the struggles of Africans and peoples of African descent for Human Rights and Self-Determination in the modern world' begins, appropriately, by situating Pan-Africanism in its origin in exile. Pan-Africanist movement was for a long period a movement outside Africa before it became a movement within Africa:

"For the dim regions whence my fathers came
My spirit, bondaged by the body, longs."

It begins thus in exile where the slaves, torn from Africa, were deposited and dispersed. It is from this mystic geography of the dispersion that the exiled African begins the recognition of himself and of Africa: 'of Africa,' as Sartre has apostrophized, 'the last circle, navel of the world, pole of all black poetry; Africa, dazzling, incendiary, oily as the serpent's skin; Africa of the fire and the rain, torrid and suffocating, phantom Africa, vacillating as a flame, between being and non-being, more true than the "eternal boulevards and their legions of cops", but yet remote, disintegrating Europe by its black invisible lines; Africa beyond reach, *imaginary* continent.' Padmore marvellously and succinctly sums up this eccentric origin of Pan-Africanism through the dialectical poles of those giants of Pan-Africanism: Marcus Garvey and W. E. B. DuBois.

Marcus Garvey, whose phenomenal 'Back to Africa' movement mobilised massive popular support amongst the

wretched of the American society on a scale that has never
been equalled in the history of this country, yet who also
possessed an intellectual and political universe deeply anti-
thetical to that of Padmore. For Garvey's fulminations were
directed, not against the fact of imperialist domination and
colonialism in itself, but rather against European, *white*,
domination. Indeed, were Africa held under the imperial subjugation of black ruling classes as opposed to whites, Garvey
would have been unruffled by such a situation; for he was a
true believer in and firm advocate of capitalism, which he ex-
tolled as the agent of progress in the world. 'Why,' he asked
in *Philosophy and Opinions*, 'should not Africa give to the
world its black Rockefeller, Rothschild and Henry Ford? Now
is the chance for every Negro to make every effort toward a
commercial, industrial standard that will make us comparable with the successful businessmen of other races.' This is
as bankrupt an understanding and analysis of the black pre-
dicament in American society as are its present-day descendants: President Nixon's 'black capitalism' projects. Needless
to say, Garvey did not much care for socialism, which he
pronounced was 'the greatest abomination ever inflicted upon
mankind'.

For that formidable figure, W. E. B. DuBois, Back-to-
Africa movements were harebrained, 'bombastic' schemes—
'utterly impracticable'. This true begetter of Pan-Africanism
sought, on the other hand, the attainment of self-government
and independence for Africans in Africa on the foundations of
socialist societies and cooperative economies that would have
no place for Garvey's or anyone else's millionaires—of whatever complexion. In DuBois' scheme of things, Pan-
Africanism would be raised on the solid structures of individual liberty, national self-determination, and democratic
socialism.

There is truly an elective affinity between DuBois and
Padmore, and the admirable pages which Padmore devotes to
the indefatigable struggles of DuBois on behalf of Pan-
Africanism are as much a glowing tribute in celebration of
the sagacity and foresight of the Great Man as they are
revealing of the author. Padmore painstakingly reconstructs
the various Pan-African Congresses held under the inspira-

tion and direction of DuBois, against the illuminating background of the problems which he encountered in the process:
the opposition of the United States Government; his efforts to
involve Africans in this all-too-African movement; the failure
to generate a mass movement in sharp contrast to Garvey's
success; and, not least, the opposition of the various European Governments to permitting any of the meetings to convene in Africa. There is surely an element of the grotesque
in the formulation of the French refusal to the convening of a
projected conference in Tunis. The French, DuBois reported,
'politely but firmly informed us that the Congress could take
place at Marseilles or any French city, but not in Africa'.

Yet for all these weighty obstacles in the path of the Pan-
Africanists, what one finds most astonishing is the myopia
of the colonial authorities, in the light of the very moderate
demands made by these African intellectuals. From the very
outset we encounter over and over again in the resolutions
of these conferences the demand only that Africans must
have *the right to participate* in their governments, not that
the colonialist structure be dismantled. They also accepted
the invidious ethnocentric distinctions between civilized Africans and the uncivilized, and merely sought in the various
resolutions colonialist 'recognition of civilized men as civilized, despite their race or colour'. What makes critical judg-
ments of these demands as being essentially moderate most
damaging is that they are sustained not from the advantage
conferred by historical hindsight, but from the perspective of
the era of the Congresses. Consider, for an instance, what
would constitute radical demands at this stage. These were,
after all, the historical moments when the Bolsheviks had
just triumphed in Russia and were exhorting all subject and
colonial peoples to rise and overthrow their oppressors, their
respective feudal and imperialist regimes, and to 'expropriate
all the expropriators'. Such revolutionary principles and appeals were the real radical demands of the epoch—and not
a wind of these blew through the civilised halls of the Pan-
African Conferences. Instead one encounters the omnipres-
ent and rather naïve belief that the colonialists could be ra-
tionally argued out of their possessions in Africa. These
'thinking intelligentsia of the Negro race', as they once desig-

nated themselves, hardly recognised that imperialism is an
irrational system that is impervious to civilized, non-violent
discourse. For as Fanon and others have lately emphasized,
colonialism is a system that is erected on violence and maintained on a violent pattern of relationships, and which only
understands the dialectics of violent discourse. But the Pan-
Africanists were soon to be disillusioned. Slowly, but im-
perceptibly, they came to recognise that being black and
being colonised they would continue to be treated as uncivilized, however civilized they might be. In short, that in
the Manichean colonial situation there are fixed, unalterable
barriers between the vanquished subjects and their rulers,
and that the system blindly refuses to permit any breaches
of its 'natural laws'—precisely because it collapses when it
makes concessions. This consciousness, of course, contained
within it the roots of radicalism.

The turning point came with the very significant Fifth
Pan-African Congress, which met in Manchester, England,
in 1945—held against the back cloth of the recently concluded
World War. At this session, though now in the background,
DuBois had finally succeeded in bringing African nationalists
to the foreground of the Pan-African movement. Among the
active participants in this session were Kwame Nkrumah,
Jomo Kenyatta, Peter Abrahams, amongst an illustrious
luster of men that later filled the Cabinet posts of independent African countries. George Padmore himself was the
organising genius directing the session. The resolutions passed
at this Congress take on an increasing stridency of tone and
content. They were no longer content with civilized blacks
and Africans being treated as civilized whatever their colour,
but instead issued a call to mobilise the masses. In one resolution, they 'condemned the monopoly of capital and the rule
of private wealth and industry for private profit alone. [They
welcomed] economic democracy as the only real democracy.'

Furthermore, they 'expressed the hope that before long the
peoples of Asia and Africa would have broken their centuries-
old chains of colonialism. Then, as free nations, they would
stand united to consolidate and safeguard their liberties and
independence from the restoration of Western imperialism, as
well as the dangers of Communism.' As to the means to adopt

towards gaining their liberation, they were now prepared, for the first time, to resort to violence should it become necessary and unavoidable: 'If the Western world is still determined to rule mankind by force, then Africans, as a last resort, may have to appeal to force in the effort to achieve freedom, even if force destroys them and the world.' Or again: 'We say to the peoples of the colonies that they must fight for their freedom by all means at their disposal.' Their *Declaration to the Colonial Peoples* is a remarkable call to arms.

Pan-Africanism or Communism? This is the theme which Padmore so questioningly explores in his book. And his answer is unequivocal. As he defines it, 'Politically, Pan-Africanism seeks the attainment of the government of Africans by Africans for Africans, with respect for racial and religious minorities who desire to live in Africa on a basis of equality with the black majority. Economically and socially, Pan-Africanism subscribes to the fundamental objectives of Democratic Socialism, with state control of the basic means of production and distribution. It stands for liberty of the subject within the law and endorses the Fundamental Declaration of Human Rights, with emphasis upon the Four Freedoms.' This defines also the challenge of Pan-Africanism. Thus in the 'struggle for national freedom, human dignity and social redemption, Pan-Africanism offers an ideological alternative to Communism on the one side and tribalism on the other'.

Since, besides, 'the Communists' strength lies in the knowledge that Western democracy is caught in its own dilemma when confronted with the fulfilment of its own professions to the darker peoples,' Pan-Africanism is conceived as a strand of that 'dynamic nationalism based upon a socialist programme of industrialization and cooperative methods of agricultural production,' which is 'the only force capable of containing Communism in Asia and Africa'. Indeed, 'Doctrinaire Marxism, especially as propagated by the British Communists, who have made not one single original contribution to the practical application of Leninism, has no particular appeal for colonial nationalists. As no self-respecting African wishes to exchange his British masters for Russian ones, Africans only lend ear to Communist propaganda when they feel betrayed and frustrated.' Thus Pan-Africanism forms part of a universal rejection of colonialism and domination of all subject peoples, so that if the Western countries were at all aware of their genuine interests, they must suitably adjust their goals to these prevailing winds the better to preserve their influence and tutelage of the emerging nations. The change in relationship is unlikely to be very painful to the West. 'First, it is necessary to keep one step ahead of the Communist by removing the grievances of the so-called backward peoples, which the Communists everywhere seek to exploit for their own ends. Secondly, the colonizing Powers must be prepared to fix a date for the complete transfer of power—as America did in the Philippines—and to give every technical and administrative assistance to the emerging colonial nations during the period of transition from internal self-government to complete self-determination.' The latter prescription, at any rate, was universally adopted by the colonial powers in the decolonising process of the winds of change. And indeed Padmore's admonition does sound all too reminiscent of British Prime Minister Harold Macmillan's 'winds of change' speech. There Macmillan had warned his audience that 'the growth of national consciousness is a political fact' which 'our national policies must take account of'.

From our present perspective Padmore's thesis appears rather quaint, for in fact neither the Pan-Africanist movement nor Communism offered a revolutionary alternative to the liberation of the African continent. The Russian Communists quickly surrendered their revolutionary heritage with the ossification of the Stalinist bureaucracy and the triumph of the non-Marxist doctrine of Socialism in One Country. Concomitant with this circumstance was, as we have seen, the pursuit of the politics of expediency in which all policy was subjected to the determining national interest of the Soviet Union, and which, in general, placed at the service of the victorious revolution the methods of the *ancien régime*. Padmore remained faithful to the revolutionary ideal of the liberation of subject peoples from the stranglehold of imperialism, and soldiered on in the cause of Pan-Africanism.

This was a lifelong mission in which he lived to accomplish spectacular and enduring achievements in the decolonization of Africa.

Still, the limitations of this current of Pan-Africanism must at once be stated. Padmore argued that if the Colonial Office policy 'based upon the principle of national self-determination for Africans by process of gradual constitutional reform' were only 'honestly and vigorously pursued by the British Government, irrespective of the party in office, it would be the most effective bulwark against Communism'. This issue of African nationalism or Communism which contributed the primary preoccupation of the cold-war era diplomacy in fact appears to be a red herring to divert attention from the real needs of the colonised peoples of Africa and elsewhere. The real issue, it would seem, is not whether despite winning important political concessions up to and including independence, they are to be still held firmly in the grip of imperialist forces, of those of the United States and of the former colonial powers; but whether the African territories and people are to acquire and enjoy genuine independence, complete sovereignty over their own policies, resources, economy, culture, and their military dispositions. In other words, whether Africa will continue to exist in a state of refurbished servitude, or whether it will definitively rise to break its chains of subjugation and thence emerge as an independent actor in world affairs. This alone constitutes the real revolutionary alternative for the liberation of Africa.

Measured in these terms, Pan-Africanism did not offer a revolutionary choice to the emancipation of Africa from its centuries of conquest, domination, and colonial exploitation. The necessarily progressive role which the movement played in the evolution of Africa to independent status should not be underestimated, but the severe limitations of the scope and method are such that it contributed in no small degree to the disarray of the contemporary African scene and the general disenchantment with the fruits of political independence. It would seem that the storm centres of popular uprising for African emancipation were in fact headed off with the aid of Pan-Africanists, who represented themselves to the colonial authorities as the only forces capable of curbing the violence of the masses. We have already noted Padmore's admonition to the imperialists that they would be better able to preserve their interests in Africa by granting political independence to the African nationalists. Indeed the colonialists anticipated such views in decolonising their empires.

This is the sum-total of the sixties' phenomenon of formal political independence in black Africa which has involved nothing more than an empty ceremonial hauling down of flags. This had in fact been the intent. Harold Macmillan, in that famous 'winds of change' speech in South Africa, had left no doubt on this score. For as he reminded his hearers, the political independence of India, far from having wrought any great hardship on Britain and the Commonwealth, had actually strengthened and stimulated their economic and social associations. Such political sagacity and sleight of hand highly recommended itself to Africa. It is a development which has left the African masses utterly disillusioned and dejected, for in reality, their independence has brought no change in the structure of their societies, nor has it affected the pattern of relationships which existed prior to the attainment of independence. Under the symbolic direction of African Presidents and Prime Ministers, the business of exploiting and running Africa for the benefit of the European interests has continued—as always—to be pursued with aggressive rapacity.

I believe that the designation of this decolonising process as the 'winds of change' is highly significant. They certainly were not storms of change or 'tempests dropping fire'. The difference in the status of independent Africa is as appropriately designated by 'winds of change' as the different status achieved by revolutionary China in 1949 is brilliantly anticipated by *Storm over Asia*, the title of Pudovkin's famous film, complete with the mushroom clouds and revolutionary forces marching to victory, reminiscent of the forces that accomplished the triumph of the Chinese Revolution. In short, to a connoisseur of words and ideas such as was Mr Macmillan, the originator of winds, the happy choice is not merely fortuitous, but is fully charged with metaphorical significance. The lasting effects left by a storm or a hurricane are devastating and thoroughgoing, not so with the soothing,

difficult-to-notice aftereffects of winds. Winds do not por-
tend earthquakes, as do hurricanes—and nothing short of an
earthquake can transform moribund Africa for the benefits
of its impoverished inhabitants for whom

'.................................Yet ever more
Sterile, like the Furies, remain the toil of the Poor.'

Padmore, who ended his career as Special Adviser on African Affairs to Kwame Nkrumah, devotes a chapter, 'Pan-
Africanism in Action,' to Nkrumah's struggles for African
emancipation which ended successfully in his leading the
first black African country to self-government and independence. In many respects this is most appropriate, for
Nkrumah's Ghana is a supreme exemplar of that phenomenon which Fanon has well formulated: 'Before independence,
the leader generally embodies the aspirations of the people
for independence, political liberty and national dignity. But
as soon as independence is declared, far from embodying in
concrete form the needs of the people in what touches bread,
land and the restoration of the country to the sacred hands of
the people, the leader will reveal his inner purpose: to become the general president of that company of profiteers impatient for their returns which constitutes the national
bourgeoisie.' Indeed it is a sobering statistic that when the
British authorities threw Nkrumah into jail for his anti-
imperialist activities, the masses showed impressive confidence in him by voting him and his party into office with
staggering majorities, forcing the authorities to take him from
the prison to head of government. Yet, when in a military
coup d'état a decade later he was ignominiously ousted from
office by an ill-assorted band of playboys, there was no demonstration of popular support, and no farewell. It is a crushing
judgment. Moreover, it would seem, if we are to believe Peter
Abrahams in his ambiguous tribute: A *Wreath for Udomo*,
that by the end of his life, Padmore himself had become a
political embarrassment to Nkrumah and his 'Gab Boys'.

George Padmore died in a London hospital in September
1959, four years before the Addis Ababa Conference which
inaugurated the Organisation of African Unity. In many respects the OAU is the culmination and embodiment of that
Pan-Africanism which Padmore has chronicled. Starting as a

political movement in exile, and handed on to a group of aspiring and dedicated African leadership who led their several countries to political independence, Pan-Africanism had been a movement carried out over the heads and at the expense of the African peoples themselves. At Addis Ababa this breed of African leadership determined to constitute itself as a new kind of Holy Alliance to preserve the existing status quo which they had inherited from their colonial masters. Their abhorrence of political revolution is total. As one of them stated, with brutal frankness: 'Speaking for ourselves, we prefer things as they are.' A first reckoning: Behind the minds of Africans whenever they contemplate the future of their continent there looms the awesome image of the U.S., the U.S.S.R., and lately of China. Yet, seldom is it recognised and assimilated by them that these enormous aggregations were the political decisions of revolutionary peoples before they became mighty realities of social power and material wealth. It would seem that the Africans expect the processes of history to be suspended for them, expecting to reap the advantages of the social content of a liberating revolution whilst shrinking back from the severity of revolutionary methods.

The OAU does not even make the pretense of speaking to the African peoples and on their behalf. The Preamble to the Charter of the OAU is an invocation presented on behalf of 'We, the Heads of African and Malagasy States and Governments'. Contrasted to this traditional diplomatic style of the ancient cultures of contempt, the United Nations Charter is in a very revealing light more populist in its being presented on behalf of 'We, *the Peoples of the United Nations Determined* to save succeeding generations from the scourge of war, which twice in our lifetime has brought untold sorrow to mankind . . .' Here is a significant fact that the UN Charter is being presented in the name of the *Peoples* of the United Nations. Not only does the UN Charter lay claims to speak on behalf of the people of the world, but is also in fact addressed to them: to their fears and their hopes—their fears of another carnage such as they had just witnessed in the Second World War, and their hopes that an international instrument should be launched that is powerful enough to prevent any future outbreaks, or any recidivism into similar barbarism.

The OAU, on the contrary, is not addressed to the fears and hopes of the African peoples. The concept of African unity which it represents is a synthetic unity imposed on the Africans, dictated by the interests for self-preservation of African Heads of States, or, as revealed in a recent African conflict, by the interests of United Petroleum, as opposed to the interests for genuine unity of the African peoples generated from the base like a tidal wave—a unity of the peoples which issues from real struggles for complete emancipation of the continent and the explosive release of its formidable potentialities. President Nyerere must have had this circumstance in mind when he admonished his fellow Heads of State at an OAU meeting in September 1969. There he had warned: 'The OAU was established by the Heads of African States. But it is intended to serve the Peoples of Africa. The OAU is not a trade union of African Heads of States. Therefore, if it is to retain the respect and support of the People of Africa, it must be concerned about the lives of the People of Africa. We must not just concern ourselves with our own survival as Heads of States; we must even be more concerned about peace and justice in Africa than we are about the sanctity of the boundaries we inherited.'

In his withering attack on the concern of the OAU Heads of States for the sanctity of inherited boundaries, Nyerere was exploding one of the sacred cows of the organisation. It would seem that this issue exercised a marked obsession over the assembled Heads of States, for we encounter provisions stipulating 'respect for the sovereignty and territorial integrity of each member-state' in the Preamble to the Charter as well as in two other of its operative articles. The delegates agreed in effect that the African unity which they sought could only be attained within the framework of the existing colonial boundaries bequeathed them by their colonial masters. As one of them stated: 'It is no longer possible, nor desirable, to modify the boundaries of Nations, on the pretext of racial, religious or linguistic criteria. . . . Should we take [these] as criteria for setting our boundaries, a few states in Africa should be blotted out from the map.'

Perhaps a few states in Africa should be 'blotted out from the map', or how else can the OAU reconcile its bundle of explosive contradictions? On one level it is established as an organisation to promote continental African unity, and on the other it fears that in the process 'a few states in Africa [would] be blotted out from the map'. It would seem that in their jealous regard for the preservation of colonial boundaries, the Heads of African States met belatedly in Addis Ababa in 1963 to draw up a Charter that would retrospectively ratify the Treaty of Berlin of 1885 by which the continent was shared out between thirteen European countries without anyone consulting African opinion. Such a situation well argues the incompleteness of the African liberation. Universally, the colonialists have succeeded in handing over power to the Africans best suited to preserve their interests, and the Africans still have to seize their independence. As Sartre has splendidly summed up the current scene: 'The imperialists no longer hold command but have continued to control. Whereas Africans are now in power, but exercise no command.' This is why the Africans must still have to seize their independence for a revolutionary social transformation of their societies. Goethe's view commands assent,

'He only earns his freedom and his life
Who takes them every day by storm.'

But that would constitute the consuming subject of another book and of a drama yet to be enacted. For the meantime, the publishers are to be highly commended for this reissue of Padmore's work, which has for long enjoyed the status of a rare book. It appears at an opportune moment when Pan-Africanism of a sort is once more flourishing in exile, in America. It deserves to be widely read.

Azinna Nwafor
Harvard University
27 January, 1971

Pan-Africanism
or
Communism

I

BACK TO AFRICA MOVEMENTS

NATIONAL HOME FOR NEGROES IN SIERRA LEONE

Nearly a century and a half before the Jamaican visionary, Marcus Aurelius Garvey, proclaimed himself Provisional President of Africa and announced his intention of leading the Negroes of the Western World back to the land of their forefathers, British humanitarians had successfully established a 'National Home' for Negroes in Sierra Leone, on the coast of West Africa. But this was not the Black Zion envisaged by Garvey. It was a white man's scheme to get rid of unwanted blacks.

These Negro repatriates, popularly known as Creoles, were the descendants of African slaves in Britain who were liberated before the Emancipation of 1834, ex-slaves settled in Nova Scotia, and others rescued from transatlantic slave ships following the abolition of the slave trade in 1807. The Sierra Leone settlement—the first experiment of its kind—pioneered the way for the establishment of Liberia, the first independent black Republic in Africa.

The Sierra Leone colonization project was sponsored by private initiative. It was only after it had proved a success that the British Imperial Government assumed responsibility for its protection and administration.

Sierra Leone can truly be described as the child of English philanthropy and enlightened humanitarianism; the greatest living monument to the memory of the Abolitionists. For it was they who had the vision and the courage to embark upon this enterprise in the face of the greatest difficulties and hardships.

This African community occupies a unique place in the history of the British Empire. It was inspired by confidence in the potentiality of Negroes to assimilate Western civilization. The founders were not concerned with trade and commerce and the exploiting of Africans. They wanted to give the black race, which had suffered untold cruelties at the hands of the so-called civilized white nations during centuries of slavery, an opportunity to build for themselves a modern democratic society on their ancestral continent. They also wanted to demonstrate that racial partnership, based upon the recognition of universal human dignity as opposed to domination, was the only lasting basis of friendship between Europeans and Africans. Sierra Leone was not only to be an asylum for ex-slaves, but an agency for the civilizing of Africa. Its citizens were to be trained to spread both the Gospel and modern knowledge to the surrounding barbarism.

'The design is noble,' wrote the great Abolitionist, William Wilberforce, 'and I trust it will please God to bless the undertaking.'

While Wilberforce took a keen and lively interest in the Sierra Leone adventure, the main credit belongs to his good friend, Granville Sharpe, whose moral courage and bulldog tenacity forced the Lord Chief Justice Mansfield to declare that 'as soon as any slave sets his foot on English ground he becomes free'.

SLAVES IN BRITAIN

At the time of the Somerset case, slavery was legal not only in the colonies but also in England. 'It was held in 1677 that Negroes being usually bought and sold among merchants, so merchandise, and also infidels, there might be property in them. In 1729 the Attorney General ruled that baptism did not bestow freedom or make any alteration in the temporal condition of the slave; in addition the slave did not become free by being brought to England, and once in England the owner could legally compel his return to the plantations.' Thus writes the distinguished West Indian historian, Dr Eric Williams,[1] who also points out that 'so eminent an authority as Sir William Blackstone held that with respect to any right the master may have lawfully acquired to the perpetual service of John or Thomas, this will remain in the same state of subjection for life, in England or elsewhere'.

Since slavery was recognized as a legal institution and upheld by the Courts of England, despite the poetic licence of William Cowper that 'slaves cannot breathe in England',[2] Africans were freely bought and sold in London, Liverpool, Bristol and other British seaports. Apart from those transported to America and the West Indies, it was fashionable in British aristocratic circles to keep black retainers.

'In the reign of the Georges, Negro and mulatto slaves and servants were common in the homes of the nobility and the rich. Royalty, itself, set the fashion. George I had two Mohammedan Negroes, Mustapha and Mahomet, of whom he was very fond. They attended to his personal needs, and dressed him, much to the discontent of certain dukes, whose prerogative dressing the King was.' Dr Samuel Johnson also had a Negro servant and favourite, Francis Barber, to whom he left some of his property, and who was very popular with the women. Johnson said of him, 'Frank has carried the empire of Cupid further than most men . . .' Another black Don Juan of the period was Joubise, son of a Negro slave from St Kitts, who was adopted by the rich Marchioness of Queensberry.[3]

The descendants of many of these Negro favourites of the

---

[1] Eric Williams: *Capitalism & Slavery*, p. 45 (University of North Carolina Press).

[2] William Cowper's attack on the slave trade in *The Task*, and his famous poem *The Negro's Complaint*.

[3] J. A. Rogers: *Sex & Race*, Vol. I, pp. 201-2—Race Mixing in the British Isles; published in New York.

aristocracy married into well-known English middle-class families and as time went on the African strain became completely absorbed.

In addition to Negroes living permanently in the British Isles as house servants, large numbers of them accompanied their masters to England from the West Indies every year.

During the eighteenth and early nineteenth century, the West Indian sugar planters and merchants constituted the wealthiest section of the capitalist class. They dominated English society. None but the very rich could vie with them in luxurious living. Among such families were the Beckfords, whose palatial homes, Fonthill Mansion in Wiltshire and Fonthill Abbey, were among the most magnificent homes in the land; the Longs, one of whose members, Lord Farnborough, built Bromley mansion in Kent; the Codringtons; John Gladstone, father of the famous Victorian statesman—all made their fortunes out of slavery. They not only built magnificent houses, but endowed churches and colleges out of the labour, toil, and tears of the blacks.

It was against this powerful and well entrenched middle-class, connected by blood and economic interests with those in governing circles, that Granville Sharpe had to fight a single-handed battle for years before he succeeded in getting Lord Chief Justice Mansfield to deliver his famous judgment.

THE SOMERSET CASE

Let us review briefly the events leading up to this famous victory. It was the year 1772. James Somerset was a Negro slave bought by a West Indian planter named Charles Stewart, who proposed to transport him to Jamaica on the ship *Anne and Mary*. Due to the timely intervention of Granville Sharpe, the Negro was rescued before the ship sailed out of London. The owner, relying upon the early decisions of King's Court that a Negro, being private property, could be recovered, brought an action to recover his slave seized by Granville Sharpe, on a writ of *habeas corpus*.

Mr Sharpe not only engaged counsel, Francis Hargrave, to

defend the right of the Negro to be free, but actually prepared the line of defence, and won. Lord Mansfield's judgment, proclaiming that 'as soon as any slave sets his foot on English ground he becomes free', not only affected the man Somerset, but guaranteed the liberty of some 14,000 Negroes then living in Britain. However, slavery was still to exist for more than sixty years in British possessions overseas, but from that moment it ceased to exist on the soil of England.

This sudden emancipation brought new problems for the Negroes, who either deserted their masters or were driven into the streets of London and other cities. What was to become of them? As slaves, they were housed, fed, and clothed by their masters, however badly. But now as freedmen, who would employ them? How were they to live? Unlike today, there were no Public Assistance Boards to which they could turn. Granville Sharpe, ever enterprising and courageous, soon found a solution to this socio-economic problem.

THE CLAPHAM SET

With the support of a group of friends and co-workers in the cause of Negro Emancipation, popularly known as the Clapham Set, Mr Sharpe set about to formulate plans to rescue the Negroes, called the 'black poor' of London. Among the most distinguished members of the Clapham Set—so-called because most of the Abolitionists lived around the London suburb of Clapham—were William Wilberforce, James Stephenson, father of the famous Colonial Secretary; Edward Eliot, Henry Thornton, Rev John Venn, Dr Lushington, William Smith later Lord Teignmouth, Charles Grant, Rev James Ramsey, William and Thomas Clarkson, Gisborne Babington, and his brother-in-law Zachary Macaulay, father of the great historian, Thomas Babington, Lord Macaulay. Several of the Clapham Set were members of Parliament. But whether independent-minded Tories or Whigs, they were all fanatical Abolitionists, fervent Evangelists and great humanitarians. Their all-absorbing passion in life was the abolition of slavery and the salvation of the African race from the accursed slave trade.

In all this Granville Sharpe was the organizing genius—the patriarch of the Clapham Set—'It was a remarkable fraternity—remarkable above all else, perhaps, in its closeness, its affinity. It not only lived for the most part in one little village; it had one character, one mind, one way of life.'[4] Such were the men who constituted the coterie nicknamed the 'Saints'. In commenting upon the life work of the Clapham Set, Professor Coupland says, 'It was, indeed, a unique phenomenon—this brotherhood of Christian politicians. There has never been anything like it since in British public life.'[5]

THE SIERRA LEONE COMPANY

In his *obiter dictum* in the Somerset case, Lord Chief Justice Mansfield remarked that 'slavery . . . is so odious that nothing can be suffered to support it, but positive law . . . and therefore the black must be discharged'. Lord Mansfield, however, warned about the social consequences of the sudden emancipation of the 14,000 or 15,000 slaves then in England. But, added the Chief Justice, *fiat justitia ruat cœlum*—justice be done whatever the consequences.

The Clapham Set, especially Granville Sharpe, assumed the moral responsibility of providing aid and assistance to destitute Negroes. Sharpe was himself not a rich man, but his colleagues, in particular Henry Thornton, the banker and philanthropist, gave generously out of their incomes to relieve the sufferings of the Negroes, many of whom had been reduced to actual beggary. Charity, however, was no solution to the problem and the Government took no interest in finding employment for the destitute blacks.[6] Something drastic

---

[4] Reginald Coupland: *Wilberforce*, p. 204 (Collins).

[5] Ibid., pp. 204-5 (Collins).

[6] The Poor Law Authorities regarded this new class of pauper without enthusiasm, and a charitable society especially formed for the relief of the Black Poor found itself in the same difficulties as

had to be done—and done quickly—to save these unfortunate Negroes from death by starvation and cold, for their numbers were increasing from year to year by the influx of runaway slaves from ships calling at English ports. A solution presented itself in 1786, fourteen years after Lord Mansfield's judgment.

Among newcomers to the Clapham Set was a Dr Smeathman, a naturalist who had spent a number of years collecting butterflies in Sierra Leone. The doctor suggested that Sierra Leone would not only provide an ideal home for destitute Negroes, but that such a settlement along the West African coast would also be a base 'for the purpose of checking and putting down the slave trade, and of diffusing the principles of Christian religion among the natives'. The idea was welcomed with enthusiasm by Granville Sharpe, who set about to organize a committee for relieving the 'Black Poor'. Public appeals were made and soon sufficient funds were available to send out a mission to negotiate the purchase of land along the Sierra Leone coast as an asylum for the destitute Negroes. The original grant of land covering twenty square miles was obtained from a Temne ruler, Chief Tom, who was a vassal of the powerful King Naimbanna, the overlord of the peninsula. It was named Granville Town in honour of Sharpe, who succeeded in getting the Government to provide transportation and supplies for the first batch of repatriates.

On February 22, 1787, about 400 Negroes, accompanied by an English chaplain and 60 white prostitutes, collected from the streets of London, embarked at Portsmouth under command of a naval officer, Captain Thompson, for West Africa. It is only fair to say that Granville Sharpe and his colleagues knew nothing of the deportation of these women who had been made drunk by the authorities and decoyed on board the ships. The expedition arrived at Sierra Leone in May. 'By September their numbers had fallen to 276 and by the following March only 130 were left alive.'[7] Their numbers had dwindled as a result of diseases and climatic conditions.

Despite this tragic beginning, Mr Sharpe persevered in his

Granville Sharpe, writes Edward Lascelles: *Granville Sharpe*, p. 81 (Oxford University Press).

[7] Edward Lascelles: *Granville Sharpe*, p. 83.

efforts to keep alive what he referred to as 'my poor ill-thriven swarthy daughter, the unfortunate colony of Sierra Leone'. Fresh Negroes were sent out; the settlement was reorganized and provisions regularly supplied by the British Government. Gradually, things began to straighten out. Permanent houses were built and agriculture established. Education and religious life were not neglected. But no sooner had the colonists got on their feet than another disaster overtook them. The settlement was invaded by the warriors of King Jimmy, a neighbouring chief, who burnt the colony down as a reprisal for an attack upon his town by Captain Savage of H.M.S. *Pomona*. It appears that Captain Savage had suspected King Jimmy of supplying contraband slaves to certain British and other slave traders.

Another start had to be made. The original St George's Bay Association which was responsible for initiating the Sierra Leone scheme was reorganized in 1790 as the Sierra Leone Company. Through the influence of William Wilberforce, the Company secured a Royal Charter—the first of the African chartered companies. But, unlike those which were to appear later on the African scene, the principal aim of the Company was not money-making but the civilizing of Africa and the abolition of the slave trade.

To help the company to carry out its humanitarian objectives, the English public contributed about £240,000—a considerable sum in those days. Many difficulties still had to be faced and surmounted before the colony was firmly established. Following the destruction of Granville Town by King Jimmy's men, a new settlement was built and named Freetown. By 1792 nearly all the 'Black Poor' in England had been transported to this part of the coast, where they were joined by other Negroes repatriated from Nova Scotia and the West Indies.

THE NOVA SCOTIAN SETTLERS

The Nova Scotians were originally slaves in the southern states of America who ran away from their masters. Most of them were rescued by the 'Underground Railway' and found asylum in the free territories of the northern states and Canada.

During the American War of Independence many of these runaway Negroes enlisted in the Royalist armies against the colonists, who, while proclaiming that 'all men are created equal', favoured the maintenance of slavery. The British, on the other hand, promised the Negroes not only freedom, but land. After the war, those who survived were transported to Nova Scotia. There they suffered great hardships from the cold climate. They were also disappointed with the treatment they received at the hands of the British authorities in Canada, who failed to provide them with land and financial assistance in order to establish them in their new home.

Unable to get their grievances redressed on the spot, the ex-servicemen elected a leader by the name of Thomas Peters, who was sent to England to present their case to the British Government. On his arrival in London, Peters immediately established contact with the Abolitionists who undertook to make representations to the Prime Minister, William Pitt, to rescue the Nova Scotians and settle them in Sierra Leone.

In this Granville Sharpe was ably assisted by his friend, Thomas Clarkson, who, says Dr Eric Williams, 'was one of those friends of whom the Negro race has had unfortunately only too few'.[8]

Arrangements with the British Government having been completed, an expedition of sixteen ships of the Royal Navy, under the command of Lieut Clarkson (the brother of the Abolitionist), transported 1,131 Nova Scotians from Halifax in Canada to Sierra Leone. All but 63 arrived safely in March 1792 and were settled in villages around Freetown, which had become the centre of a thriving and expanding community.

Having had military training, the Nova Scotians were, on the whole, a disciplined lot. Many of them had acquired some education and an acquaintance with skilled trades and house-building, and were able to make a valuable contribution to the life of the new colony at a time when such tech-

[8] Eric Williams: *Capitalism & Slavery*, p. 179.

nical knowledge was badly needed. Thomas Peters, their
leader, became one of the most prominent citizens of Freetown and a trusted adviser of Lieut Clarkson, who was appointed the first Governor of the colony. Unfortunately, relations between the Nova Scotians and some of Clarkson's
successors was not so good. Rebellion broke out in 1800 in
protest against the Company's officials who had imposed a
ground rent or quit tax on the farms of the settlers. The Nova
Scotians claimed that the land had been granted to them
by the Crown. The revolt was suppressed with the aid of
550 Maroons who arrived in Sierra Leone shortly before the
disturbance broke out.

THE WEST INDIAN SETTLERS

These Maroons, or West Indians, constituted the third
group of Sierra Leone immigrants. They were Negro slaves
who had revolted against their Spanish and British masters in
Jamaica and set up self-governing settlements on the island.

Sociologically, these West Indians are the most interesting
of the foreign communities transplanted on the West African
coast. The term Maroon, derived from the Spanish *Cimar-
rones*, meaning mountaineers, was applied to the blacks who,
after deserting from the plantations in the plains, took refuge
in the mountain fastness. They were mostly descendants of
tribes from the Gold Coast and Nigeria, and were considered
the most martial and independent Negroes. They refused to
accept their status as slaves, and for a hundred and fifty
years were the chief source of trouble to the plantation owners. They were the inspirers of every slave revolt in the island.
During the early period of the British occupation of Jamaica,
the Maroons carried on constant guerilla warfare against the
English settlers; making periodical raids upon the sugar plantations and retiring into their mountain strongholds, where
they inflicted defeats on the military sent against them. To
help the militia hunt them down, the Jamaica Government
imported special dogs 'much resembling shepherds' dogs in

Great Britain, and being no larger, but possessing the keen scent of the bloodhound, the greyhound's agility, and the bull-dog's courage.'[9] With the aid of these animals, several puni-tive expeditions were carried out against the Maroon settle-ments. These self-governing communities were administered according to African tribal laws and customs under recog-nized chieftains, such as the famous Captain Cudjoe, Captain Accompong, Captain Kofie, Captain Quako and Captain Johnny.

In order to bring an end to the state of unrest and lawless-ness which was having an adverse effect upon the sugar in-dustry—the economic backbone of the colony—the Governor, Sir Edward Trelawney, despatched the officer commanding the Jamaican militia, Colonel Guthrie, on a peace mission to Captain Cudjoe, the most renowned of the Maroon leaders, offering to recognize their independence and guaranteeing them security of the lands forming their villages, free of taxa-tion in perpetuity. Describing the meeting of the British Mis-sion and Captain Cudjoe at the Peace Settlement in 1738, Captain R. C. Dallas, a British officer on Colonel Guthrie's staff, writes:

'Colonel Guthrie advanced unmolested with his troops through situations in which the Maroons might have greatly annoyed him even with the large force he then had under him. Making, however, the best disposition of his troops that the nature of the ground would permit, he marched on with confidence, and judging of the distance he was from the Maroons by the sound of their horns, he continued advanc-ing till he thought he could make them hear his voice that he was come by the Governor's orders to make them an offer of peace which the white people sincerely desired.

'An answer was returned declaring that the Maroons wished the same and requesting that the troops might be kept back.

'Several Maroons now descended and among them it was difficult to discover the Chief himself. Cudjoe was rather a short man, uncommonly stout, with very strong African fea-tures and a peculiar wildness in his manners. He had a very large lump of flesh upon his back which was partly cov-

9 Sir Harry Johnson, *The Negro In The New World*, p. 243.

ered by the tattered remains of an old blue coat of which the skirts and sleeves below the elbow were wanting . . .

'Around his head was tied a scanty piece of white cloth, so very dirty that its original colour might have been doubted. He wore no shirt, and his clothes, such as they were, as well as that part of his skin which was exposed, were covered with the red dirt resembling ochre. He had a pair of loose drawers which did not reach to his knees, and a small round hat with rim pared so close to the crown that it might have been taken for a calabash. Such was the Chief, and his men were as ragged and as dirty as himself: all were armed with guns and cutlasses. Cudjoe constantly cast his eyes towards the troops under Colonel Guthrie. He appeared very suspicious and asked Dr Russell many questions before he ventured within reach.

'At last Dr Russell offered to change hats with him as a token of friendship, to which he consented and was beginning to converse more freely when Colonel Guthrie called aloud to him, assuring him of a faithful compliance with whatever Dr Russell promised. He said that he wished to come un-armed to him with a few of the principal gentlemen of the island, who should witness the oath he would solemnly make to them of peace on his part with liberty and security to the Maroons on their acceding to it.'[10]

When the news of the peace settlement was announced, the planters, who had sent their wives and children to England for safety, were overjoyed. Their families could now return. Peace reigned for over half a century after the settlement was signed. But when news of the Haitian Revolution reached Jamaica through the white French settlers of San Domingo, who came seeking refuge on the British island, the Maroons broke into revolt in 1796. The Maroon leaders, inspired by the struggle of the Haitian slaves to win their freedom, called upon the blacks in Jamaica to do the same. Maroon bands once more came down from the mountains to incite the plantation slaves to rise in rebellion.

After bitter fighting the Maroons were driven back into the

[10] J. A. Rogers: *World's Great Men of Colour*, Vol. II, pp. 461-2 —Life of Captain Cudjoe.

mountains. Those who surrendered were pardoned and allowed to retain their lands and liberty. Their descendants still live in small communities known as Moore towns in the Jim Crow mountains to the extreme north-eastern part of the island and around Accompong in the cockpit country of the Parish of St Elizabeth.

On the other hand, the ringleaders and several hundreds of their followers who were captured were placed under arrest and deported to Nova Scotia. They were later transported to Sierra Leone. According to Sir Harry Johnson, the distinguished British colonial historian: 'There was a remarkable spirit about the Maroons which, in spite of occasional episodes of cowardice or treachery, seems to have inspired a liking and respect in the minds of British officers fighting against them, the sympathy felt for the first-class fighting man. So much so, that when the Assembly of Jamaica decided to transport a third of the Maroons to Nova Scotia (and thereby rid the colony of the terror they had inspired for a hundred and fifty years), Major General Walpole, the principal officer commanding the troops engaged in suppressing the Maroon rising, declined to accept the sword of honour voted him by the House of Assembly.'[11] The West Indian immigrants in Britain are the descendants of these slaves.

THE CREOLE COMMUNITY

Having succeeded in establishing an African asylum for ex-slaves rescued in Britain and the New World, the Abolitionists concentrated their efforts first upon ending the transatlantic slave trade, before tackling the more difficult problem of complete emancipation in the West Indies and other British colonies. This phase of the anti-slavery campaign fell largely upon the shoulders of those members of the Clapham Set who were Members of Parliament. Thanks to their devoted service to the black race, their leader, Wilberforce, then

[11] Sir Harry Johnson: *The Negro In The New World*, p. 247 (Methuen).

the Member for Hull and Yorkshire was able to win the sympathies of his intimate friend, William Pitt, the Prime Minister, for the anti-slave trade crusade.

The first resolution to bring an end to the trade was introduced by Wilberforce in May 1789, but the opposition of the West Indian plantocracy, shipping, and mercantile interests in London, Liverpool and Bristol was still strong enough to defeat its adoption. His persistent efforts, however, were rewarded when, on March 16, 1807, the House passed a Bill without division, declaring it illegal to transport African slaves in British ships. The question that remained was: How was this Act of Parliament to be made effective? To enforce such a law required naval supervision in the Atlantic. With this object in view, the British Government negotiated an agreement with the Sierra Leone Company for the handing over of the West African settlement to imperial authority. The transfer was effected in 1808, and Freetown was converted into a maritime base of operation for the ships of the Royal Navy engaged in intercepting vessels with illegal cargoes of 'black ivory' destined for West Indian ports.

'Henceforward the resources of a great nation were to be devoted to making the colony what it was designed to be— namely, an establishment for the suppression of the slave trade, and the religious and moral improvement of the natives,' wrote Dr Blyden, the African diplomatist. He went on to remark that 'It is a very interesting fact that on the spot where Englishmen first began the work of African demoralization, Englishmen should begin the work of African amelioration and restoration. England produced Sir John Hawkins, known to Sierra Leone by his fire and sword policy. Two hundred years later, England produced Granville Sharpe, known by his policy of peace, of freedom, and of religion. The land of Pharaoh was also the land of Moses. Alone amid the darkness of those days, stood Sierra Leone—the only point at which the slave trade could not be openly prosecuted —the solitary refuge of the hunted slave.'[12]

It is estimated that between 1819 and 1828 the British cruisers captured and landed at Sierra Leone 13,281 slaves,

12 E. W. Blyden: *Christianity, Islam and the Negro Race*, p. 223.

an annual average of about 1,400. Between 1828 and 1878 an approximate 50,000 Negroes released from slave ships were disembarked here.

These Negroes came from territories all along the Guinea coast—from Senegambia to Angola. As a rule, the slaves were captured by tribal chiefs who had a monopoly of the hinterland trade and sold into bondage to European sea captains, who tried to smuggle their contraband cargoes across the Atlantic.

Like the Nova Scotians and West Indian Maroons, the Africans rescued from the slave ships were settled in and around Freetown. These villages bore the historical names of Wellington and Waterloo, Hastings and Kent, Wilberforce and Bathurst, Gloucester and York. The repatriated blacks were given the generic description of 'Creole' to distinguish them from the indigenous Negroes, who belong largely to the Mende and Temne tribes. By the time complete emancipation of slaves throughout the British Empire was proclaimed in 1834, the Creoles were considered the most civilized communities in Africa. Their numbers were increased by discharged soldiers of the West Indian Regiment during the latter part of the century.

Regrettably, Wilberforce did not live to see the crowning glory of his labour of a lifetime. He died a month before the Emancipation Bill was signed by good Queen Victoria. But his memory, like that of John Brown's body, lives on, for ever cherished in the hearts of Africans and peoples of African descent.

The Abolitionist Movement, which centred around the Clapham Set, was indeed 'a unique phenomenon—this brotherhood of Christian politicians'.

The long and arduous struggle on behalf of the Negroes from the Somerset case to Emancipation constitutes one of the most glorious chapters in British social history. These noble and selfless fighters for right against wrong, for freedom and justice for the black man, removed the greatest blot from their country's escutcheon and placed Britain in the forefront of the humanitarian nations. This is the finest legacy which the Clapham Set could have bequeathed to their country. The memory of the Abolitionists will always live in the minds and hearts of the descendants of those whom they fought to set free. British Socialists, who should have been the heirs of this rich legacy, have squandered in large measure the goodwill of the Africans. If England can again produce such men as 'the Saints' wedded to honourable principles rather than to opportunism and expediency, she can recover her moral leadership of the world, in spite of her political and economic decline.

MISSIONARY INFLUENCE AMONG CREOLES

After the Sierra Leone settlements had been taken over by the British Imperial Government, Freetown and the surrounding areas were declared a Crown Colony. This designation has distinguished the coastal region from the interior, which was only proclaimed a Protectorate in 1896, based on treaty agreements signed between the British and the chiefs of the hinterland tribes.

Here we are only concerned with the political and constitutional evolution of the coastal area known as 'the Colony'. Under the benevolent protection of the British Crown from external intervention on the one hand, and the sympathetic guidance and devoted labour of German Protestant missionaries on the other, the Creoles of the Colony rapidly became the first Westernized community in Africa. Drawn as they were from heterogeneous elements, cut adrift from their ancestral cultures, traditions and customs, the repatriates intermarried and adopted the English way of life. The Queen's language became their normal medium of communication. As time went on, however, they evolved a *lingua franca*, known as *Krio*, which has become the popular tongue among both the Colony people and the indigenous tribes settled in and around Freetown.

This Creole language is one of the most fascinating to be heard in any part of Africa. 'The speech of the Sierra Leone streets, cannot be called a patois of English. It is not the pidgin English of China nor the unintelligible lingo of the West Indies. It is not the dialect of Quashee nor the humorous slang of Uncle Remus. It is a transfusion, so to say, of numerous African idioms and phrases. Words from the Timneh, Eboe, Aku, Mandingo, Foulah, Soosoo and Arabic, are blended with words from the English language, which is itself a mixture—so that the proper designation of the Sierra Leone vernacular would be—"mixture of mixtures, all is mixture". It has become something more than the only medium of communication known to the masses. It has acquired a sacredness of its own. There are certain ideas which have been expressed in it—certain images created—which lose their full flavour if rendered into other words . . .

'Its idioms are oriental. It has grown up of itself. It has had no grammarian to formulate its rules, nor can it be known how the common agreement among the people was attained. But the fact remains that it exists, and it will linger long among them. It is the language of the domestic life, of courtship, of marriage, of death, of intensest joy and deepest grief. The people will not consent to speak of the private matters of the heart—to discuss matters affecting their domestic wellbeing in any other tongue, any more than they would discuss such things in company with strangers. To those acquainted with it, it has a convenient flexibility, and certain picturesque aspects. It is easily acquired by natives from the interior, and forms a convenient bridge from their dialects to the English language.'[13]

Because the soil around Freetown was not suitable for prosperous agriculture, the Creoles soon gave up farming and became the artisans, the professional middle class and the traders, while the aborigines of the surrounding country, such as the Sherbros, Mendes and Temnes, were the agricultural producers. Those who drifted into Freetown provided the unskilled labour.

The social stratification in Sierra Leone was the inevitable result of the kind of early education implanted by the missionaries. It was of a purely literary kind, which did not fit the educated Creoles for anything but clerical work. This education was readily assimilated by the repatriates, who, for

[13] E. W. Blyden: *Christianity, Islam and the Negro Race*, pp. 244-45.

a long time, enjoyed a monopoly of the professions—the ministry, law, medicine, teaching, and clerical work in Government
and commercial establishments, not only in Sierra Leone but
also in many of the neighbouring coastal territories.

The educational system began in the early years of the nineteenth century, following the founding of the first missionary
schools by the Church Missionary Society, with which the
Abolitionists, especially Wilberforce and Fowell Buxton, were
closely associated. 'We desire to make Western Africa the
best remuneration in our power for the manifold wrongs,'
declared the Society, which took the initiative in establishing
Fourah Bay College in 1827. It was the first institution for
higher education in tropical Africa, and was placed under the
auspices of Durham University. This work of educating and
Christianizing the Negroes also owes much to the Wesleyan
Methodists, who began in 1811, seven years after the first
Anglican missionaries arrived in Freetown.

Each succeeding generation of Creoles became more and
more Europeanized. Many of their ancestors had already
assumed the patronymics of the Abolitionists and the early
German and English missionaries as their own family names.
Thus we find today well-known Creole families with such
Germanic surnames as Metzger, Renner, During, Hansel,
Beckhauer, Scholding, Kissling, Frey, Gollmer, Decker, as
well as British ones like Horton, Thompson, Cummings,
Hughes, Boston, Weeks, Betts, Morgan, Vaughan, Tubb,
Humphrey, Tates, Miller, Rhodes, Townsend, Taylor, Ma-
caulay, etc. These were the names of CMS missionaries who
worked and died in Sierra Leone.

FIRST AFRICAN BISHOP

Year after year, educated Creoles trained in the missionary
schools and at Fourah Bay College went out to various parts
of West and Central Africa, spreading Christianity and enlightenment among the heathen Africans. The most famous
of these black pioneers was Dr Samuel Adjei Crowther, the
first African bishop. He had been rescued from a slave ship

as a boy and brought to Freetown, where he received his early education and training for the ministry. After his ordination in England in 1843, Dr Crowther returned to West Africa and started to preach the Gospel among the people of Yorubaland, where he was born. He subsequently transferred his activities to the Niger Delta, where he established the Church of England Mission, assisted by other Creole pastors and catechists recruited from Sierra Leone and, later, the West Indies.

Forty years after Dr Crowther had been rescued, he was consecrated bishop at Canterbury Cathedral—the first black Prince of the Church. By the time he died in 1891, the Cross had been firmly planted among the heathen tribes of South-eastern Nigeria.

Other distinguished Creoles were Sir Samuel Lewis, Q.C., K.C.M.G., Attorney-General of Sierra Leone, and the first full-blooded African to act as Chief Justice in a British colony; Dr James Africanus Horton, Surgeon-Major in Her Majesty's Armed Forces in West Africa; Isaac Pratt and John Artagpah Macaulay, Members of the Legislative Council; Dr E. Taylor Cummings, several times Mayor of Freetown.

CONSTITUTIONAL DEVELOPMENT IN SIERRA LEONE

Sierra Leone was the first West African territory in which the Crown Colony form of government was established. It was introduced in order to provide a form of administration suitable to the Westernized Creoles who, without tribal moorings, had no system of indigenous government to which they could adhere. Never numbering more than 30,000 souls out of a total population of nearly two millions, the Creoles, willy-nilly, have become the torch-bearers of British parliamentary institutions. On the other hand, until 1953, the indigenous natives of the Protectorate have been administered through their traditional tribal system of chieftaincy. Now both communities—Creoles and Protectorate natives—participate in the Central Legislative Council. And although the Sierra Leone settlement started before Liberia, the Americo-Liberians have overtaken and surpassed the Creoles in the art of independent self-government.

Constitutional development during more than one hundred and forty years of Colonial Office rule has been made at a very slow pace. Three years after the Sierra Leone Company surrendered its charter to the British Crown in 1808, the Imperial Government set up an advisory council to assist the Governor in administering the Crown Colony. The Advisory Council consisted of the Chief Justice, the Colonial Secretary, and one unofficial member. The Council was not only responsible for the affairs of Sierra Leone but until 1843, for the administration of Gambia, and in 1850 that of the Gold Coast. After these colonies were detached from Sierra Leone, the Advisory Council was replaced by a Legislative Council in 1863, to which a Creole, Mr Ezzido, was appointed for the first time. An Executive Council was also established at the same time. The Creole representation on the Legislative Council varied from time to time, but they were always appointed by the Governor until 1924, when the system of elected representation was first introduced.

Under the reformed Constitution of 1924 provision was made for three elected African members on the Legislative Council, which then consisted of ten unofficial members and eleven officials. Apart from the three elected Negro members, three others were nominated by the Governor from the Creole community to the unofficial side of the Council. However, it was not until 1943 that the Creoles got on the Executive Council, when two of the unofficial Negro members of the Legislative Council were appointed to serve with four European officials. The first significant change from paternalistic Crown Colony administration to limited internal self-government occurred in 1951, with the coming into being of the present Constitution. It brought about a revolutionary change in the political relationship between the Colony Creoles and the Protectorate tribes, who until then had been divorced from direct participation in the machinery of Central Government.

Since the merging of the Colony and Protectorate areas into a single Sierra Leone administration, the indigenous tribes, who constitute the overwhelming majority of the population, have swamped the Creole representation in the Legislative Council. The Council consists of the Governor as President and a Vice-President, with fourteen members elected by tribal councils acting as electoral colleges, to represent the Protectorate. Only in the Colony, which is divided into seven constituencies, does direct voting obtain. The present electoral arrangement should be discarded and universal adult suffrage should be introduced throughout the entire country.[14] This will stimulate the growth of the party system on a non-tribal basis and hasten the liquidation of the out-of-date administrative division of Sierra Leone into Colony and Protectorate, and pave the way for the integration of the two artificially created areas into one united country.

Meanwhile, with Protectorate representation in the ascendancy as a result of the present unsatisfactory system of voting, the political leadership which the Creoles enjoyed for over a century has passed into other hands. Consequently, five of the six African Ministers in the Executive Council represent the Protectorate. The four other members of the Council—a sort of embryonic Cabinet—are British officials.

Dr M. A. S. Margai, the chairman of the majority Sierra Leone's People's Party in the Legislative Council, is officially designated Chief Minister.

The original Sierra Leone settlement has developed considerably since the first seeds of civilization were planted by the Abolitionists and nurtured by the missionaries. One can only hope that it will be the dedicated aim and determination of the present-day descendants of the Creoles to join forces with the progressive and educated indigenous elements emerging in the Protectorate, to complete the vision of Granville Sharpe, whose confidence in the potentialities of the black race inspired the efforts of the Clapham Set to found the colony as a 'National Home' for the descendants of Negro slaves.

[14] An Electoral Reform Commission appointed in 1954 under the chairmanship of Mrs Byron Keith-Lucas, Senior Lecturer in Local Government at Oxford, has recommended the introduction of universal adult suffrage after 1960. In the meantime, the franchise will be based upon a small income or property qualification.

II

FOUNDING OF LIBERIA

Inspired by the achievements of the British Abolitionists in rescuing the 'Poor Blacks' of England and ex-slaves in British territories in the New World, American Quakers and other supporters of the Anti-Slavery Movement in that country decided that they too would establish a 'National Home' for free Negroes on the West African coast. Underlying the idea was also the thought that Christianized Negroes would be better missionaries for spreading the Gospel among the heathen tribes of Africa than white Americans. A combination of black colonization and missionary work in Africa would enable America to get rid of free Negroes, whose presence was an incitement to those still held in slavery to attempt their escape. At the same time it would put a stop to slave trading among the chiefs of coastal tribes by converting them to Christianity.

The American Colonization Society, the counterpart of the Sierra Leone Company, was established in 1817 under the presidency of Bushrod Washington, the brother of General George Washington, father of American Independence. Bushrod Washington was a judge in the State of Virginia. He was succeeded by the distinguished Maryland lawyer, John Latrobe, under whose leadership the colonization scheme made most progress.

A NEGRO PIONEER

African colonization also found enthusiastic support among certain free Negroes in the New England States of America, who believed that the black race would never receive justice and social equality at the hands of the whites as long as they remained in America. Prominent among these Negroes was Paul Cuffe, a wealthy Massachusetts sea captain and ship owner.

'Very early in his life he developed an interest in commerce, and at sixteen years of age, in 1775, he secured employment on a whaling vessel. In the following year, during his second voyage, he was captured by the British and detained in New York for three months. During the War (of Independence) he and his brother refused to pay taxes in Massachusetts on the grounds that they had been denied the franchise. Shortly thereafter, Massachusetts passed a law allowing free Negroes liable to taxation all the privileges belonging to other citizens. In 1780 Cuffe began to build ships of his own and to engage in commerce. As the profits mounted, he expanded his seagoing activities and built large vessels. He began with a small open boat of less than ten tons. By 1806 he owned one large ship, two brigs, and several smaller vessels, besides considerable property in houses and land. After joining the Society of Friends he became deeply interested, along with many other Quakers, in the welfare of Negroes and wanted to engage in some activity that would improve their lot. In 1811 he went to Sierra Leone in his own vessel to investigate the possibilities of taking free Negroes back to Africa. The war with England in the following year prevented him carrying out his plans. In 1815, however, he took thirty-eight Negroes to Africa at an expense of three or four thousand dollars to himself. He learned, as colonizationists of a later date were to learn, that the expense

of taking Negroes back to Africa was so great as to be prohibitive.'[1]

Captain Cuffe's expedition stimulated great interest in the
'Back to Africa' movement, and two years later the first American Colonization Society was organized to carry on the work
he had commenced. Later on, these societies sprang up in a
number of American States. Funds were contributed from
public sources to defray the expenses of transporting free
Negroes back to Africa.

FREE NEGROES OF AMERICA

At the time of Paul Cuffe's voyage to West Africa, the
position of the Negro in the Southern States of America was
fundamentally different from his status in England. As a
result of Lord Mansfield's decision in the Somerset case, all
blacks living in Britain were automatically set free. This was
not the case in America. There, slavery was still legal and the
rights of the owners in their slaves were enforceable by law.
However, in certain States, especially in the North, there were
a considerable number of free people of colour. Of the million
odd Negroes in the United States in 1800, about 200,000
were freedmen, either as a consequence of manumission by
their masters, who were often fathers of children by slave
women, or Negroes who had purchased their freedom.

While they had more rights than bondsmen, their status
was inferior to that of poor whites. It was to these Negroes
that the leaders of the American Colonization Society made
their appeal. The prospect of having their own government,
under which they could enjoy in safety and tranquillity their
natural rights and the blessings of life, found a ready response
among the free Negroes. They little realized at the time the
difficulties and hardship which had to be overcome in trans-
lating their dreams into reality.

[1] John H. Franklin: *From Slavery to Freedom*, p. 158 (A. A.
Knopf, New York).

EARLY AFRO-AMERICAN SETTLERS

Drawing upon the experiences of the Sierra Leone Company, the sponsors of the American Colonization Society secured a charter from the United States Government in 1819 giving the Society the right to set up a free State for Negroes in West Africa. To prepare the ground, the Society despatched two white men, Samuel J. Mills, one of the original founders of the Society, and Ebenezer Burgess, to negotiate the purchase of land from African chiefs as a suitable site for settlement. On the advice of the British Governor of Freetown, they secured land on Sherbro Island off the Sierra Leone coast, and the first contingent of eighty-eight Negroes under the Society's agent, Dr Samuel A. Crozer, was transported in 1820. Within a few years most of them died. Those who survived moved to Freetown and joined the British Colony.

Disappointed, but not discouraged, the Society made a second attempt to get a foothold on the Guinea coast. This time twenty-one Negroes, under the leadership of John B. Russwurm[2] and Ephraim Bacon, sailed further south and secured land from an African chief at a place now known as Cape Montserrado, in 1821. This small group was later joined by others who came out under Dr Edi Ayers, another agent of the Colonization Society, and Captain Robert Stockton, the commander of an American warship which brought supplies provided by the United States Government.

Despite many deaths among the colonists and conflict with European sea captains engaged in illegal slave trade, the settlers gradually established themselves. These were the first beginnings of the Black Republic, which the Negroes named Liberia—the land of the free. As a gesture of gratitude to James Monroe, the then American President, who gave the

[2] Russwurm was a native of Jamaica and the first Negro to graduate from an American University.

'Founding Fathers' his protection, the capital was called Monrovia.

Encouraged by the success in overcoming tremendous initial difficulties and hardships, other settlements were made at different places along the Liberian coast, under the auspices of various colonization societies which sprang up in many States of the American Union.

Since all of these societies had one common objective, namely, the creation of an independent sovereign State for Negroes on the African continent, the various settlements were encouraged to amalgamate to form a Commonwealth. In this respect, the American philanthropists differed radically from the British Abolitionists, who were only concerned with establishing a colonial asylum for rescued slaves. They never conceived of Sierra Leone becoming an independent self-governing nation, but always thought of it as remaining under the protection of the British Crown. The Americans, on the other hand, were republicans and anti-colonialists. Having only recently won national independence from the British, they looked upon the Liberian enterprise as a foster child of the revolutionary tradition of 1776. The American Colonization Society was merely the instrument through which the nationalistic aspirations of the Negroes were to be realized. As soon as the opportunity presented itself which would give concrete expression to their dreams, plans were set in motion to unite the settlements under a single republican Government, free and independent of American control.

After securing the approval of the directors of the American Colonization Society, twelve Negro representatives from three of the four[3] existing settlements—Montserrado, Grand Bassa and Sinoe—assembled in convention at Monrovia on July 26, 1847, to sign the Declaration of Independence, and adopt a Constitution which was modelled after that of the U.S.A.[4] The convention also adopted a national flag consisting of six red stripes with five white stripes alternately displayed longi-

[3] The fourth settlement, Maryland, founded by the Colonization Society of the State of Maryland, maintained a separate existence from its foundation until 1857, when it came into the Liberian Commonwealth.

[4] See Appendices I and II.

tudinally. In the upper angle of the flag, next to the flag pole, a square blue ground covering in depth five stripes. In the centre of the blue, one white star. Liberians popularly called their flag *The Lone Star*. And the black Pilgrim Fathers took as the motto for the new State the significant words: 'The Love of Liberty brought us here'.

The total population of repatriates at the time of independence was not more than three thousand.

This eloquent declaration of freedom proclaimed by men who had but recently emerged from the degradation of slavery, is a document worthy to take its place among the great charters of liberty.

The Convention also adopted a Constitution, embodying the fundamental articles of Government covering the rights of Citizenship; Legislation; Executive and Judicial powers.

The Legislature consists of two chambers—a House of Representatives and a Senate. The former comprises thirty-one members, representing the five counties of Montserrado, Grand Bassa, Sinoe, Grand Cape Mount, and Maryland; Eastern, Western and Central Provinces and Marshall Territory, the principal administrative regions of the Republic. Representatives serve a period of four years.

There are ten Senators, two from each of the five counties, who serve for a period of six years.

Supreme executive power is vested in the President, who is elected by the people. Originally the President held office for two years only, but the term was increased to four years in 1907, following an amendment to the Constitution. In 1938, the Constitution was again amended to make the presidential term eight years. As this excluded a holder of the office from re-election, the law was amended once more in 1948. As it now stands, a President's first term of office is eight years and he is eligible for re-election, but cannot serve more than another four years.

The Cabinet is appointed by the President and holds office at his pleasure. It includes the Secretary of State, the Secretary of the Treasury, the Attorney-General, the Postmaster-General, Secretary of War, Secretary of the Interior, Secretary of Public Instruction, Secretary of Public

Works and Utilities, and Secretary of Agriculture and Commerce.

The Judiciary consists of the Chief Justice and four Associate Judges of the Supreme Court.

THE BILL OF RIGHTS

The fundamental rights of citizenship are embodied in the Bill of Rights which declared that 'the end of the institution, maintenance, and administration of government is to secure the existence of the body politic, to protect it, and to furnish the individuals, who compose it, with the power of enjoying in safety and tranquillity their natural rights and the blessings of life; and whenever these great objects are not obtained the people have a right to alter the government and to take measures necessary for their safety, prosperity and happiness'.

The enunciation of such liberal principles is all the more remarkable when we recall the fact that the Liberians had had no previous experience in political democracy. Indeed, in America, from whence they came, Negroes were still held in slavery, and serfdom still prevailed in many parts of Europe. Yet it is fashionable in certain negrophobist circles to sneer at Liberia and ridicule the Negroes for wanting to live under their own flag. But Liberians certainly have nothing to be ashamed of. Despite their country's backwardness in terms of industrialism, the Republic was conceived in Liberty and dedicated to the promotion of Freedom.

Judging Liberia in the context of contemporary history, her Constitution was one of the most liberal and democratic in the world at the time it was promulgated. A year after Liberia was declared a free democratic Republic, a wave of revolution overswept Europe, in which the middle classes strove to obtain the minimum of constitutional government. In Paris, the people drove Louis Philippe out of France and set up a provisional republican government, which only paved the way for Louis Napoleon, first as President and finally as Emperor Napoleon III. In Germany, the pedantic, muddle-headed, loquacious representatives of the German bourgeoisie assembled at Frankfurt to draw up a liberal constitution. But by the time this 'Assembly of old women', as Marx described them, had summoned the courage to offer the Emperorship to Frederick William IV, King of Prussia, the counter-revolution had been prepared, and the Junker monarch contemptuously declined to accept 'a crown picked up out of the gutter'. And that was the end of constitutional democracy in Germany.

The same year witnessed the suppression of the Hungarian revolt under Louis Kossuth, which was drowned in a sea of blood by General Huynea, called the 'hyena'. The same tragedy overtook the uprisings in Vienna, Bohemia, Milan and Venice. As a result, the Magyars had to wait until 1867 before getting national independence within the dual monarchy of the Austrian-Hungarian Empire. It was then that Hungary was given a parliament and government of its own.

Italian unification came five years earlier in 1861, under the inspired leadership of Garibaldi and Mazzini and the statesmanship of Victor Emmanuel and Cavour. In the United States, it took a bloody civil war to bring slavery to an end in 1863.

Conversely, from the onset of Liberian nationhood, the Negroes, who so short a time before had known the sting of the slave master's whip, proudly proclaimed to all the world that *there shall be no slavery within this Republic. Nor shall any citizen of this Republic or any person resident therein deal in slaves either within or without this Republic, directly or indirectly.*

III

BIRTH PAINS OF BLACK NATIONHOOD

The immediate problem which confronted the newly-created State of Liberia was to secure recognition from the Great Powers. It was relatively easy for twelve Negroes representing about 3,000 ex-slaves settled in three communities along the West African coast to get together in Monrovia and proclaim themselves a free, independent sovereign nation. It was quite a different proposition to get the European Powers to recognize them as such and to admit the new Republic into the comity of nations, especially as the United States, from whence they had come, withheld official recognition.

To overcome the formidable difficulties which presented themselves in the diplomatic sphere, the first President of Liberia, the Hon Joseph Jenkins Roberts, himself undertook the task of presenting his Government's case before the crowned rulers of Europe and other heads of State.

President Roberts, a highly cultured mulatto born in Virginia in 1809, had immigrated to Liberia at the age of twenty. He was endowed with a fine personality, and outstanding administrative and diplomatic abilities. Soon after his inauguration, in 1848, the President set out on his mission accompanied by his wife, an octoroon lady, who was the image of Queen Victoria. The President's first visit was to Britain, where he was cordially received in official circles. Lord Palmerston signed a treaty of amity and commerce which placed the Liberian Republic on a footing of the most-favoured

nation. The President was also received in audience by Queen
Victoria, who expressed her personal interest in the Negro
State. The impression he made was deep enough to elicit
from the British Lords of the Admiralty the presentation of a
naval sloop and a coastal vessel to assist the Liberian Government in policing the 350 miles of coast against illegal slave
traders and smugglers.

With the blessing of Queen Victoria, President Roberts
proceeded to France, where he was also cordially received by
Louis Bonaparte, later Napoleon III, who granted recognition to Liberia. The President next visited Leopold I, King
of the Belgians, and from Brussels he went to Holland, Denmark, Lübeck, Hamburg, and Prussia, with equal success.
He returned home in 1848. By the end of his term of office,
Liberia was recognized not only by the great European Powers
but also by Norway, Denmark, Sweden, Spain, Portugal,
Brazil, Haiti, and other nations of the New World. American
recognition was obtained only in 1862, after the outbreak of
the Civil War, which ended slavery in the United States.
Until then, the influence of the slave-owning South was so
powerful in the Federal Government in Washington, D.C.,
that American officials in the State Department doubted
whether the Senate would ratify a treaty made with a Government controlled by former American Negro slaves. So strong
was colour prejudice that 'it was feared if Liberia was recognized as an independent State, the United States would have
to receive at Washington a man of colour as the Liberian
envoy to the great Republic'.[1] Liberia was not always served
by such able statesmen as President Roberts, who held office
for three terms.

Having secured recognition for his country, his successors
were able to devote themselves to the equally important problems of defining the boundaries of the Republic and establishing friendly relations between the settlers and the indigenous
tribal chiefs.

[1] Sir Harry Johnson: *Liberia*, Vol. I, p. 228.

DR BLYDEN'S DIPLOMATIC MISSION

The responsibility for regularizing diplomatic relations between the young Republic and the British Government was
assigned to the most brilliant Liberian diplomatist and
scholar of the day, Dr Edward Wilmot Blyden. He was appointed the first Liberian Minister Plenipotentiary and Envoy
Extraordinary to the Court of St James in 1877, and was
received by Queen Victoria at Osborne on July 30, 1878,
being introduced by the Marquis of Salisbury, then Secretary
of State for Foreign Affairs.

Dr Blyden was a full-blooded Negro, whose Ewe ancestors
had been brought as slaves from the Gold Coast to the Dutch
West Indian island of St Thomas, where he was born in 1832.
In 1847 he sailed for New York, hoping to get a higher education, but because of the hostility towards men of colour in
America, he was unable to find a place in any institution of
learning. The Colonization Society of New York offered him
a free passage to Liberia, where he landed in January, 1850.
There he secured a classical education, and developed linguistic talents of a very high order. He became editor of the
Liberian Herald at the age of nineteen, and was subsequently
teacher, professor and president of Liberia College. He occupied many responsible positions in the Liberian Republic.
He was several times Secretary of State for the Interior, and
served twice as Liberian Ambassador to the Court of St
James.

During his diplomatic missions abroad, Dr Blyden received
many academic and other distinctions. Several universities
conferred upon him the honorary degree of Doctor of Laws.
In 1880 he was elected Fellow of the American Philological
Association, the first Negro to receive the distinction. He was
elected honorary member of the Society of Science and Letters of Bengal in 1882, and two years later was made Vice-
President of the American Colonization Society. He was also
the first African to be elected an honorary member of the
Athenæum Club, in recognition of his contributions to

Islamic scholarship. He was at one time adviser to the Government of Sierra Leone on Mohammedan education, and in 1872-73 was employed by the British Government on a diplomatic mission to negotiate a peace settlement between warring Muslim rulers in the interior of Sierra Leone before this part of West Africa was declared a British Protectorate. Dr Blyden was also the author of a number of books.[2]

FRONTIER PROBLEMS

At the time Liberia secured recognition, Africa was still considered the 'Dark Continent'. Few had penetrated into its interior, and fewer still were interested in staking out territorial claims. Here and there along the coast European nations exercised spheres of influence, relics of the earlier slave trade period. But none showed any interest to acquire extensive areas away from the sea coast. In fact, a Select Committee of the House in 1865 advised the Liberal Government of Lord John Russell to abstain from acquiring territories in West Africa and to abandon those already under British control, except Sierra Leone, which occupied a special place in the imperial scheme of things, having been founded as an asylum for Negroes under British protection.

Lying between Sierra Leone on the east and the French colony of the Ivory Coast on the west, with French Guinea to the north, Liberia covers an area of 43,000 square miles, but at one time was larger. As long as Britain and France maintained an anti-colonialist attitude, Liberia's territory remained secure. But sandwiched between the colonial possessions of France and Britain, she suffered from their depreda-

[2] *Liberia's Offering; From West Africa to Palestine; The African Problem and other Discourses Delivered in America in 1890; Christianity, Islam and the Negro Race; The Negro in Ancient History; Liberia: Its Status and Field; Islam and Race Distinction; Africa and the Africans; A Voice of Bleeding Africa.* In pamphlet form, Dr Blyden published *Aims and Methods of a Liberal Education for Africans; Origin and Purpose of African Civilization* (correspondence between E. W. Blyden and Sir J. Pope-Hennessey, C.M.G.).

tions once her powerful neighbours embarked upon territorial aggrandisement in Africa. Her trouble started with the scramble for colonies which followed the Berlin Conference of 1885. Even before the Conference gave formal sanction to the carving up of the Continent between the European Powers, Britain and France began annexing Liberian territory as they advanced the frontiers of their respective colonies of Sierra Leone and Ivory Coast from the Atlantic into the interior.

After the Berlin Conference, the French, operating from the Ivory Coast, grabbed so much of Liberian territory that the British Foreign Secretary, Lord Salisbury, was obliged to induce France to restrain her aggression within reasonable limits.

The Liberians protested in vain against the spoliation, but received no assurances of support from either the United States or Great Britain. British encroachment took the form of supporting claims of British traders for 'protection' against hostile tribes. On the excuse of maintaining 'law and order' among the frontier tribes, the British annexed a considerable part of Liberian territory adjoining Sierra Leone. The Black Republic lost all the territory between Sherbro and the Mano River, which the Liberian Government had purchased from native chiefs. British encroachments on the western frontier continued from year to year, until the Sierra Leone boundaries were finally determined by an Anglo-Liberian commission in 1903.

FINANCIAL PROBLEMS

Liberia has been equally unfortunate in her financial dealings with foreign countries. From the very earliest days of independence until quite recently, she was saddled with a heavy national debt.

In contradistinction to Sierra Leone, where the Negro settlers have always had the benefit of financial support and guidance of the British Colonial Office, the Liberian colonists had no external source to which they could appeal for financial assistance in the early days of the Republic. Consequently, from the very beginning, the Liberian Government was obliged to borrow money from foreign bankers at exorbitant rates of interest in order to meet internal and recurring expenses in setting up and maintaining civil and military establishments. All these establishments called for large sums of money. Yet, as late as 1884, the annual revenue was only £25,000, derived from customs import and export duties, tax on real estate at ½ per cent of the assessed value, poll tax on all the country's inhabitants at one dollar per head, and military fines. Sierra Leone's revenue in the same year was £62,282. Moreover, Liberia's national welfare was not always well served by some of her early officials. For example, a special committee on public accounts appointed in 1864 to investigate into the Republic's financial affairs, revealed an alarming state of corruption in which even President Roberts' successor, Mr Stephen Benson, was involved. The Committee found that public funds had been used for private speculation for the benefit of President Benson.

Another President, Edward J. Roye, was impeached and deposed from his office in 1871 for conspiring with the British Consul in Monrovia and two Liberian officials to misappropriate part of the first foreign loan of £100,000 borrowed from London bankers. Of this amount, it is said that only £27,000 actually reached the Liberian Treasury, the rest was split up between Roye and his confrères. Roye was drowned in Monrovia harbour while attempting to escape with part of the loot. Saddled with these worthless bonds, Liberia had to agree to pay between £70,000 to £80,000 as principal at a progressive rate of interest of from 3 to 5 per cent. Payments were made from 1896 to 1913, when the debt was refunded by a new loan of 1912.

Without capital to develop the country's agricultural and mineral resources and thereby increase the Republic's revenue, the Government was forced to live upon borrowed monies. The second loan was also for £100,000 at 6 per cent interest. It was raised through a British company interested in developing rubber in Liberia. This time the Liberian Government was completely swindled by the British operators. After breaking off relations with the speculators, the

British Government intervened on their behalf and forced the
Liberians to accept certain demands, among them the appointment of British customs officials, an English officer in
command of the Liberian Frontier Force, and reform of the
treasury and courts. To escape from becoming a British colony
like Sierra Leone, the Liberian Government had to accept the
British *diktat*.

In his report to the 29th Legislature of the Republic in
December 1904, President Arthur Barclay, who was born a
British subject in the West Indian island of Barbados in
1854 and emigrated with his father to Liberia in 1865,
warned his countrymen of the danger of foreign intervention.
Things had changed since the Republic was established in the
middle of the nineteenth century. The anti-colonialist policies
of the great European Powers had, after the Berlin Conference of 1885, given place to active imperialist expansion.
By the end of the century, the Europeans had already annexed practically all of Africa, and Britain and France had
their eyes on Liberia as the only country on the West
Coast which had escaped their control.

'Nations, like individuals, must live within their income
or else go into bankruptcy and so lose control to a very great
extent of their affairs', declared the President, who then proceeded to review the country's financial position as it was in
1904 when he first assumed office.

'The Foreign bonded debt amounts to £96,997. We are
paying interest on £78,250 at the rate of 3½ per cent and
the charge on the revenue for sinking fund and interest will
be $16,000 for the next three years. The internal bonded
debt amounts to $133,557, of which $36,000 bears interest
at 6 per cent and balance at 3 per cent. The annual charge is
about $5,000.

'The floating debt is estimated at under $200,000, less than
one year's average income. It consists of currency, audited
bills and drafts on the Treasury.

'About $150,000 of this sum is held by foreign merchants.
It forms the principal embarrassment of the Treasury, since
it is being constantly liquidated out of current revenue. To
meet the deficit and pay current expenses of government,
the Treasury has constantly to ask for advances from the

merchandise holders of this debt. For this accommodation it is paying interest at the rate of from 25 to 33 per cent.

'The total debt of the country is about $800,000, of which the English 1871 7 per cent loan is the largest item. The debt would be covered by about three years' revenue.

'For the last ten years, 1893 to 1903, the revenue from all sources is returned at $2,243,148. The disbursements were $2,177,556, showing a balance in favour of the country of $65,592.'

During the period under review, the annual salary of Liberian Cabinet Ministers was £120. The Vice-President, the Secretary of State and Chief Justice got £200 each, while the President received £700! At times the Government was unable to find the money to meet these obligations.

Faced on one side with the constant threat of bankruptcy, and on the other, with the danger of intervention by foreign governments on behalf of European merchants and bondholders, all the energies of Liberian statesmen were concentrated upon safeguarding the independence of the Republic. This called for the most skilful diplomatic manœuvring between the French and British, whose colonial territories bounded Liberia on the east and west.

In all this, President Arthur Barclay played a most important role. He was elected for two years in 1904, and in 1907 was re-elected for two terms of four years each. During his second term of office he was able to introduce drastic fiscal reforms. This enabled the administration to stabilize the situation temporarily and ward off a threatened financial collapse.

FOREIGN INTRIGUES

In 1908, President Barclay made an appeal to the United States Government for financial assistance to ease off the pressure of Great Britain, but the Foreign Office in London opposed American financial assistance on the ground that British officials were already in control of the Liberian customs service and Frontier Force. Things looked bad for the Negro

Republic. European Powers were no longer prepared to tolerate the existence of an independent black nation in the midst of their colonial dependencies. Liberia's very existence was a bad example to the Africans living under white domination. The days of philanthropy and sentimentality towards Negroes were over. Imperialism was in its heyday; the 'White Man's Burden' was in the ascendent. Liberian statesmen realized all this. Their own hope lay in disagreement among the great Powers, which alone could save the Republic from absorption between Britain, France, and Germany, the great rivals in the scramble for territories in West Africa. The fears of the Liberians were not exaggerated. The year after President Barclay warned his countrymen to be on the alert against the danger of foreign intrigues and intervention, a mutiny broke out among the Frontier Force composed mostly of Sierra Leonians under the command of a British officer, Colonel R. Macay Cadell. Cadell had been made to resign and hand over his command to a Liberian officer after certain information had reached the President regarding a plan to stage a *coup d'état*. About the same time, 'the British Foreign Office received a cable from an Englishman at Monrovia saying that such a mutiny might take place and asking for protection. The day before the mutiny, a British gunboat appeared in the harbour of Monrovia. It was afterward learned that a British regiment in Sierra Leone was under orders to go to the same destination. A mutiny actually took place on February 1, 1909. But the Liberian Government quickly suppressed it by calling out the militia.'[3]

After the failure of the mutiny, the British Government agreed to withdraw its opposition to American assistance to Liberia. In a note to the United States Government, the British Foreign Secretary, Sir Edward Grey, let it be known that his Government 'would support any scheme for a loan which would put Liberia's finances in shape, provided that the preferential rights and privileges of British bondholders of the present customs loan were maintained and that provisions were made in the scheme for the payment of outstanding British claims.'[4]

[3] R. L. Buell: *The Native Problem in Africa*, Vol. II, p. 788.
[4] Ibid., p. 802.

Shortly after the February incident, President Theodore Roosevelt despatched an American commission to Liberia to investigate the country's resources. The commissioners noted the strained Anglo-Liberian relationship and remarked that 'if Liberia is to be dismembered, France wants a share in it'. The report also stated that 'it is generally believed in Liberia that Germany has been biding her time till she could undertake with good grace an intervention in Liberian affairs'.

Commenting on the abortive mutiny, the American investigators pointed out that 'but for the prompt and judicious action of the Liberian Executive, aided by the American Minister Resident, the following would presently have been the situation: a British gunboat in the harbour, a British officer in command of the frontier force and a large number of British subjects among the enlisted men, a British officer in charge of the Liberian Customs, a British Officer in charge of the Liberian gunboat *Lark*, a British regiment in the streets of Monrovia . . .'

The commission likewise declared: 'There is a widespread belief among them (the Liberian people) that this was a plot on the part of British subjects in Liberia to make it appear that the Government was tottering to its fall and bring about the British occupation of Monrovia.'[5]

Liberians had every reason to be distrustful of their powerful British and French neighbours. For over ten years, from 1912 until 1925, France kept up frontier pressure upon Liberia to force the Negro Republic to surrender the Zinta area, which she wanted to incorporate into the Ivory Coast colony. Despite the intervention of the United States Government to save Liberia from foreign occupation, in April 1925, French troops invaded Liberia and occupied ten villages. In desperation the Liberian Government again appealed to the United States for protection. But in order to secure American aid against France, the Liberian Government had to grant a vast rubber concession to the Firestone Company. At the time 'many Liberians believed that it was only by securing the investment of American capital in Liberia that the Government could count on the continued support of

[5] Ibid., p. 788.

the United States.'[6] In this they were right, for after the Liberian Government signed the Firestone Agreement, which we shall discuss later, the French agreed to frontier rectification. Since then they have stopped annexing Liberian territory.

The American commission recommended American assistance in adjusting frontier disputes between the Liberians and the British, and in paying off Liberia's foreign debts; and otherwise to aid the black Republic to maintain its independence.

On the basis of the report, the U.S. Government announced in July 1910 that it would take charge of the finances, military organization and boundary questions in dispute between Liberia and her powerful neighbours. This was agreed to by Britain, France and Germany, who were invited to share in the financial arrangements. This was concluded in 1912 when a private loan of $1,700,000 at 5 per cent was subscribed by British, French, American, Dutch, and German banking houses. For this financial assistance, Liberia had to place the collection of her revenue in the hands of an American Receiver-General appointed by the United States Government, assisted by British, French, and German sub-Receivers. This arrangement continued until the First World War when America assumed full control over the finances of the Republic. The constabulary was also placed under American control.

As on previous occasions, the Liberian Government received very little actual cash, as the greater part of the bonds were issued directly to creditors in payment of claims. Bonds to the amount of $225,000 were delivered in Germany, $715,000 in London, $460,000 in Amsterdam, and $158,000 in New York.

After redeeming the country's outstanding debts, the Liberian Government was just as badly off as ever. There were no monies in the Liberian Treasury to use for economic development or social services, such as education and public health. To make matters worse, the first charges on the stagnant revenue were interest and sinking fund on the inter-

---

[6] R. L. Buell: Ibid., Vol. II, p. 793.

national loan and salaries for the foreign customs Receivers, who often quarrelled among themselves over the allocation of payments.

Instead of assisting Liberia's economic and social progress, in fact every new loan got the country more and more into the clutches of international finance, represented by J. Pierpont Morgan and Company, Kuhn Lobb & Co., the National City Bank and First National Bank of New York; Robert Fleming & Co. of London; M. M. Warburg & Co., of Hamburg; Hope & Company of Amsterdam, and the Banque de Paris et des Pays Bas, of France.

Dependence upon foreign finance had, in turn, its disastrous consequences on the country's internal affairs. The Government was very often unable to pay the salaries of public servants, and police, in consequence of which 'law and order' was often threatened. Exploiting the weakness of the Government, which was still largely based on the few thousand civilized Negroes settled along the coastal area, unscrupulous European traders engaged in smuggling often incited native tribes to revolt against the authority of the legitimate Government. Arising out of one such disorder in Grand Bassa county in 1912, the property of some German traders was damaged. The German Government, therefore, despatched the warship *Panther* to Liberia and issued an ultimatum to the Government of the Republic. Thanks to the good offices of the U.S. Government, the situation was saved. The President apologized, and agreed to pay compensation to the German merchants.

No sooner was this German threat over than the Liberian Government was faced with a serious revolt by the Kru tribe who besieged Sinoe in 1915. The situation was again saved by the timely intervention of America. The United States cruiser *Chester* was despatched to Monrovia, with arms and other military supplies for the Liberian frontier force. Some years later Colonel Charles B. Young, who was then the highest ranking Negro officer in the United States Army, was loaned to the Liberian Government to reorganize the defence forces of the Republic.

How long could Liberia maintain its independence? This was the question facing its leaders when the first World War broke out. British shipping, which played a large part in keeping open the trade and commerce of Liberia with the outside world, was withdrawn, and the German merchants were expelled upon Liberia's entry into the war on the side of the Allies. By 1917, Liberia's financial position had become so desperate as a result of the fall in trade, that the Government had great difficulty in collecting enough revenue to meet its monthly salary bills. On many occasions advances had to be made to the Government by the British-owned Bank of British West Africa to save the situation. For this good turn the bank was well compensated in the form of commission on its advances. The bank debt was finally liquidated in 1923 out of reparations money received from the sale of German properties in Liberia. But these assets were not enough to make any appreciable contribution to the relief of the country's foreign indebtedness. The Government therefore had to seek other avenues of assistance to get out of the grip of the international financiers.

Despite renewed appeals to the U.S. Government, under whose influence Liberia had declared war upon Germany following America's entry into the war in 1917, financial aid was withheld. In a memorandum addressed to the American President on January 10, 1918, the Liberian Government stated that 'in the opinion of the Cabinet, the dangers threatening the Republic were so imminent as to warrant a strong and candid appeal to the United States for a loan of five million dollars with which to cancel the 1912 loan, to establish a receivership entirely under American control, to take up its internal debt, and to develop the country'.

After much haggling, the American State Department gave its approval in 1919. When the conditions attached to the loan were disclosed to the Liberian people, they protested so strongly that their Government had to cancel it although the then Liberian Secretary of State, Mr C. B. D. King, had already given his approval. In return for the loan of five million dollars, the Liberian Government had agreed to place not only the Customs but the internal revenue under the control of the General Receiver, who would be assisted by three Receivers and an Auditor. To govern native tribes, a Commissioner General of the Interior, four or more District

Commissioners, and three or more officials, would all be designated by the President of the United States. The General Receiver would approve the budget before transmission to the Liberian Legislature, and control the amount of the Customs duties to be paid over to the Liberian Government for its current administrative expenses. After paying interest on the loan, administrative expenses, and other charges, the Receivership would pay one-half of the Surplus Account under the sole order of the Republic and the other half to the Improvements Account to be expended on education and public works with the consent of the Receiver. No concession could be granted by the Liberian Government to foreigners without their first being favourably reported upon by the Financial Adviser.[7]

In trying to impose a policy of dollar dictatorship upon Liberia, one thing the U.S. State Department forgot was that poor as the Liberians were, the love of liberty brought them to the coast of West Africa. They were not prepared to exchange their new-found freedom for American dollars. Poor, yet proud and independent, they have always been suspicious of the white men who would seek to reduce them to the same colonial status as the Negroes settled in the neighbouring colony of Sierra Leone.

To break the stalemate caused by the people's rejection of the American terms, the Liberian legislature authorized the Government to secure more satisfactory conditions. Negotiations were re-opened in Washington in 1921, but when the Liberian negotiators returned to Monrovia with the new terms, opposition broke out again. Many Liberians believed that the acceptance of this agreement meant the end of Liberia's independence. While Mr King, who had by that time assumed the presidency, was prepared to override public opinion and ratify the agreement, the U.S. Senate refused to give its approval. 'The proposed Liberian loan had met its death, and there was general rejoicing in Liberia.'[8]

[7] R. L. Buell: Ibid., Vol. II, p. 813.
[8] R. L. Buell: Ibid., Vol. II, p. 816.

DOLLAR IMPERIALISM TAKES OVER

But this popular rejoicing did not last long. For what the American Government failed to get the Liberians to accept voluntarily, was to be achieved by private enterprise disguised as 'philanthropic' capitalism. Briefly, the story is this.

After the First World War, America found herself confronted with a British rubber monopoly. As rubber is an indispensable product in the motor car industry in the United States, a conference was called by the rubber manufacturers, in which the United States Government participated. At this conference it was agreed that the United States Government would actively co-operate with the industrialists in providing a tropical sphere of interest in order that they might produce their own supplies of raw rubber.

Ex-President Hoover was then the Secretary of Commerce. He was the official spokesman of the U.S. Government and the principal supporter of this imperialist project. At that time Mr Hoover was the most bitter assailant of the Stevenson Plan, which created a monopoly for British and Dutch rubber dealers who were restricting the production and marketing of rubber from Malaya and the East Indies in order to control prices on the world market. About 75 per cent of the world's supply at that time was under British control. America, on the other hand, was the largest consumer. This dependence of American motor car manufacturers upon British rubber producers did not suit Wall Street. A way had to be found to get out of the grip of the British. And Liberia provided the solution. It was at this stage that the Firestone Rubber Company appeared upon the Liberian scene.

Backed by American diplomatic pressure on the Liberian Government, Mr Harvey Firestone succeeded in getting President King to accept the very terms formerly proposed by the U.S. State Department but rejected because of popular disapproval. The Liberian Government was caught between two evils: American economic imperialism versus European political imperialism.

During the negotiations between the representatives of the Firestone Company and the Liberian Government, the French were again threatening to invade Liberia as a result of a frontier dispute. 'France may overrun Liberia like Germany did Belgium, and Liberian soil will become the battleground of contention and struggle for decision as to who shall be the dominating power in Africa, France or England', wrote *The Liberian Star*.[9]

The U.S. Government endorsed the view that the French had designs on Liberian territory and that border incidents had been deliberately created to give French troops an excuse to occupy the hinterland of Liberia. To avoid trouble with her powerful neighbour, the Liberians hoped that by acceptance of the Firestone terms, the Republic would secure American protection against France. In the circumstances, the Liberians had no choice. The Firestone agreement was therefore signed in 1926. Under its terms, the American company was granted a concession of one million acres of land for the cultivation of rubber at an annual rent of six cents per acre. In return, Liberia was offered a loan of $5,000,000 at 7 per cent, advanced through the Firestone Corporation of America, a subsidiary of the Firestone Rubber Company. But only half was subscribed up to 1945.

The Liberian Government was able to use part of the money—$1,180,669—to liquidate the principle and accumulated interest in the 1912 loan, and the balance to carry out certain internal administrative and fiscal reforms, with the aid of an American adviser. Under the terms of the loan Firestone stipulated that the office of Receiver of Customs was to be abolished and a Financial Adviser appointed, who alone would be responsible for disbursement of funds stipulated for public works, including sanitation. The Firestone loan came just in time to save Liberia from being placed under international trusteeship of the League of Nations.

To provide labour for the rubber plantations, the Liberian Government had to agree to facilitate the recruiting of native tribesmen from the interior of the Republic. 'In the spring of 1926 the Government established a Labour Bureau at the

9 *The Star*, Monrovia, March 31, 1926.

head of which it appointed a Commissioner, under the control of the Secretary of the Interior. According to this Commissioner, the Bureau will supply annually a total of 10,000 men to the Firestone plantations—two thousand men from each county.[10] By June, 1926, the Bureau already had supplied the plantations with six hundred men. It sent out requisitions to each Native and District Commissioner who in turn divided up contingents among the chiefs. According to the Commissioner the Firestone plantations paid the chiefs one cent a day for each boy and the same sum to the Government bureau.

'Thus, under this system, which is similar to that which has produced wholesale compulsory labour in other parts of Africa, the Firestone Plantation Company is making it financially worthwhile for the Government and the chiefs to keep the plantations supplied. The concession Agreement Number Two imposes on the Government the obligation to co-operate in securing these men. As Liberian officials and chiefs are already accustomed to imposing compulsion whether in securing men for road work or for Fernando Po, there is no reason to believe they will employ different methods in obtaining labour for the Firestone Plantations'.[11] In 1954 the Goodrich Rubber Company also secured a 600,000 acre concession.

LEAGUE OF NATIONS ENQUIRY

In 1930, the League of Nations appointed an international commission to enquire into charges of forced labour and slavery levied by Mr Roland Faulkner, a Liberian Senator, against President King's administration. Incidentally, the British Supreme Court in the neighbouring colony of Sierra Leone was still upholding the legality of chattel slavery as late as 1927.[12] The Commission consisted of Dr Cuthbert

[10] R. L. Buell: Ibid., Vol. II, p. 834.

[11] The Firestone Company was employing about 25,000 in 1954 at a daily wage of 30 cents. The company provides housing, medical service and other forms of social welfare. G.P.

[12] See the case of Rex v. Salla Silla and Rex. v. Mfa Nanko and

Christy, an Englishman, representing the League of Nations; Dr Charles S. Johnson, an Afro-American, representing the United States, and the Hon Arthur Barclay, a former President of Liberia, representing the Republic. The Commission confirmed the charges and made a number of recommendations in its report. The most important were: (1) that Liberia abandon the policy of the 'closed door'; (2) the re-establishment of the authority of the chiefs; (3) the appointment of Americans to administrative positions in the Government, such as Commissioners and District Officers; (4) declare domestic slavery and pawning illegal; (5) stop the shipment of labourers to Fernando Po and other places outside Liberia; (6) increase discipline over the military forces and (7) encourage emigration from the United States.

The Liberian Government accepted the recommendations which were set in operation by Mr Edwin Barclay, who succeeded Mr King, following his resignation, to the presidency in December 1930. Building upon the reforms started by President Barclay, his successor, President William S. Tubman, has been able to make use of the increased revenue derived from the export duty on rubber shipped to the United States during the war years, to put Liberia on the firmest financial foundation it has known since the establishment of the Republic. Mr Tubman was first elected for a term of eight years in May 1943, at the age of 48, was re-elected for a second term of four years in 1951, and for a third term in 1955.

RENASCENT LIBERIA

In his inaugural address to the Legislature in 1952, the President was able to announce that the Republic had no foreign or domestic debts. The national revenue had increased from $2,041,999 in 1945, the first term of the President's

---

others quoted in *Slavery*, by Lady Kathleen Simon, pp. 74-80 (Hodder & Stoughton). Mr L. S. Amery, who was then Colonial Secretary, ordered the liberation of 214,000 slaves in the Protectorate in 1928.

office, to $12,830,685 in 1951. During that period, which coincided with the centenary of Liberia's independence (1947), a number of large-scale public works projects were carried out, all of which contributed substantially to the country's financial stability. Apart from a number of motor roads and a 45-mile railway line from Monrovia to the Bomi Hills, the most important public works project was the construction in 1947 of a modern harbour at Monrovia, able to accommodate the largest liners.

The capital of $20,000,000 was provided by the United States Government in the form of a loan under the Mutual Aid Agreement. Because of Liberia's strategic position, facing South America, she received considerable assistance of a permanent kind from the United States during the war. In March 1942, the two Republics signed an agreement under which the United States Government constructed a modern airport at Roberts Field on the Farmington River and a seaplane base at Fisherman Lake in the county of Grand Cape Mount. America also paid for the building of several hundred miles of road for military purposes. In 1938, the country had only 200 miles of motor road. By 1952, this mileage had increased to over 1,000. During a visit to the United States in the latter part of 1954, President Tubman negotiated a loan of fifteen million dollars for 20 years at 4¾ per cent from the U.S. Import-Export Bank to be spent on road building and bridges. The postal service and tele-communications have also been expanded under the stimulus of American aid.

At the request of the Liberian Government, the United States sent a public health and economic mission to West Africa in 1944. The United States Government has also contributed $1,400,000 to pay salaries of experts in the fields of agriculture, nursing and education under the United Nations Point Four Programme, while the Liberian Government has contributed $2,000,000 towards financing the projects. As a result of a geological survey carried out by Americans, large deposits of iron ore, estimated at 15 million tons, have been discovered at a place known as Bomi Hills, 40 miles from Monrovia. Bauxite, platinum, manganese, corundum, gold and diamonds have also been found.

In 1946, President Tubman granted a concession of 25,000

acres to an American financier, Lansdell K. Christie, of New York, to exploit the iron deposits for a period of eighty years against payment of certain rents and royalties. As in the case of the Firestone concession, there was strong popular opposition to the Christie concession. The President has been heavily criticized not only for the generous terms granted Mr Christie, but for ignoring the constitutional procedure in such matters and adopting a dictatorial attitude to those opponents who petitioned the legislature not to ratify the agreement. The Bomi Agreement was revised in 1952 at the request of the Liberian Government. Under the new arrangement, the Christie Liberia Mining Company, with which is associated the Republic Steel Company of America, will pay the Government a larger percentage in royalties and will share profits on a fifty-fifty basis, beginning in April 1957, and before that date if certain outstanding Government debts are settled. This will substantially increase the Government's revenue, to which the Firestone Company already contributes 25 per cent of its gross profits.

The political record shows that, despite charges of dictatorship against the President by his opponents, Mr Tubman has been making a genuine attempt to democratize the régime. The first National Executive Council to link the tribal chiefs with the Central Government was convened in May 1954 and presided over by the President. In this connection, credit must be given to him as the first head of the Executive to grant the suffrage to women and to extend representation in the legislature to the indigenous peoples of the hinterland still living under tribal law and custom. The task of integrating the *indigènes* into the modern state is a formidable one, and can only be achieved by raising their standards of living and closing the cultural gap between them and the Westernized Negroes.

Apart from having maintained their national independence against great odds for over a century, the Westernized Negroes living along the coast have succeeded in establishing closer links with native tribes of the interior than the Creole aristocracy of Freetown have done with the indigenous tribes living in the Protectorate of Sierra Leone. However, the present administration still has much to do to disprove the charges from opponents of sharp practice in the implementation of the electoral system, which is based upon adult suffrage from the age of twenty-three.

Theoretically, the party system exists, but the True Whig Party is the only one with a popular mass basis. Repeated attempts have been made to form opposition parties but without success. Mr Tubman's opponents claim that anyone criticizing the President and the True Whig administration is subject to severe punishment under the draconian Sedition Law of 1933,[13] which was enacted under the administration of President Barclay and given greater strength by President Tubman in 1945. Mr Barclay opposed Mr Tubman as the candidate of the Independent True Whig Party for the Presidency in 1955, but was defeated by 223,166 votes to 851. The Independent candidate, Mr W. O. Davies-Bright, only got 17 votes.

Most educated Liberians are very sensitive to any form of criticism against their country. This is quite understandable, for they have had to face and overcome difficulties which few white people engaged in nation-building have had to contend with. Throughout her history, the Black Republic has been the object of the ridicule and contempt of the White World. It has also been an object of aggression by the great European Powers, especially Britain and France, during their period of territorial expansion in West Africa. The young Republic was preyed upon and exploited by international bankers and moneylenders, while denied the technical assistance and scientific aid of international agencies until quite recently. Liberia's enemies even tried to use the League of Nations to abolish her independence. After the League's Commission reported, R. C. F. Haugham, C.B.E. a former Consul-General in Liberia declared: 'That Liberia should longer be permitted to remain an independent Republic is neither more nor less than a scandal which the League should lose no time in bringing to an end. It may safely be said that Liberians as

[13] Shortly before the presidential election in May 1955, the Government fined Mrs Bertha Corbin, the editor of the *Independent Weekly* five thousand dollars for criticizing certain actions of the Tubman Administration. The newspaper supported the candidature of former President Barclay.

a whole cannot be entrusted with the governance of between one and two millions of helpless Africans, nor should a division of the West African coast lands, situated between two progressive colonies, be permitted longer to stagnate in their unworthy, incapable hands. That being the case, the administration of the country should be removed from their control, and handed to the League, under Mandate, to one or other of the great colonizing Powers.'

Endorsing the proposal to liquidate Liberia's independence, Sir Alfred Sharpe, K.C.M.G., a former Governor of Sierra Leone said that, 'There is only one remedy, and that is for Liberian territory to be taken over by one of the white nations and put in proper order. Who is to do this? It comes down to a question of America or England. There is only one other nation which might be said to be interested, individually, in Liberia, and that is France, for the reason that she would like to have a right of way from her hinterland of French Guinea across Liberian territory to a port on the Liberian coast. America is interested, firstly, from the fact that the United States was responsible for the creation of this black republic, and secondly, owing to their large financial interests there, the Firestone Rubber Company, and the loans made from America.'[14]

Despite these open threats to her independence, Liberia has been able to earn for herself the right to nationhood. Starting from the very bottom of the ladder, the small communities of ex-slaves dumped down on the hostile West African coast without capital, technical knowledge or experience in government, have shown a capacity to survive which deserves the admiration of all men of peace and goodwill.

'The struggles of the early Liberian colonists against the ignorant opposition of their own untutored people, stimulated by slave-traders, have a species of pathos and romance to which the struggles of the first colonists in America offer nothing similar', writes the famous African statesman, Dr Blyden. 'The battles of the African pilgrims were not for empire over an alien race; not for power or dazzling wealth; but for room in the land to which they had a hereditary right, *de*

---

[14] *West African Review*, August, 1931.

vita et sanguine certant. The pathetic aspect of their position was, that they had to confront a ferocity, not natural, but generated under the dark influence of incarnate fiends—to fight against a people allied to them by blood, and probably identical in their antecedents, who would gladly have welcomed them but for the malevolent interference of those supreme criminals of humanity—*hostes generis humani*—who had ruthlessly robbed their fathers of their homes.

'We could here recite—if this were the place for it—the thrilling hardships and heroism, of their hunger and thirst and nakedness, of their chills and fever; of their confronting, with axe in one hand and gun in the other, the illimitable forests and the malarious swamps; of the devotion and bravery of their women, by whose unswerving fidelity and magical inspiration, one was made to chase a thousand, and two were able to put ten thousand to flight. But it is enough to say that they were triumphant over all obstacles, and succeeded in laying in suffering and sorrow, and in indomitable faith, the foundation of a State.'[15]

With its financial position stronger than at any period in its chequered history, Liberia is, for the first time since its founding, in a position to carry out the ideal of her founders —the building of a National Home for the descendants of former Negro slaves on the continent of their ancestors.

Men like Dr Blyden, President Arthur Barclay and his brother, Secretary of State Ernest Barclay, having pioneered the way, quite a number of other West Indians emigrated to Liberia during the period between the two World Wars. They have, on the whole, made good citizens. Some have done well in trade and agriculture, while a few have occupied prominent positions in the Government and public life.

Liberia, with just two million inhabitants, is still underpopulated. The Government might find it feasible to promote a scheme of planned immigration of Negroes from the Western Hemisphere, who either have capital to establish productive enterprises or professional training or technical skills which could be utilized in the development of the Republic.

[15] E. W. Blyden: *Christianity, Islam and the Negro Race*— 'African Civilization', pp. 411-12.

Doctors, dentists, engineers, veterinaries, stock breeders, agronomists, chemists, surveyors, etc., might be encouraged. There will probably be no need of lawyers, as Liberia already has enough. The present Government has already indicated its intention to improve the living standards of the people. A considerable proportion of the national revenue is already being spent on carrying out an extensive public health and sanitation programme drawn up by a team of experts of the World Health Organization. The educational system is also being reformed and expanded, especially in the field of technical training. Liberia College, the oldest institution of higher learning, has been raised to university status.

In the sphere of external affairs, Liberia has widened her diplomatic relations abroad by establishing missions in several countries. Since 1947, the Republic has despatched Negro Ambassadors to London, Paris and Washington, and appointed Ministers in Madrid, The Hague, Vatican City, Brussels, Beirut and Port-au-Prince, capital of the Negro Republic of Haiti. In addition to embassies and legations, the Liberian Government has established fifteen Consulates-General and thirty-four Consulates in various parts of the world.

All these post-war reforms constitute a significant achievement on the part of the Tubman administration and reflect great credit upon the financial stability of the Republic. For prior to the Second World War, Liberia could not afford to maintain diplomatic missions abroad and was represented in London and a few other foreign capitals by white men who acted in an honorary capacity as Ministers and Consuls.

PART TWO

IV

AFRICA: PAWN IN EUROPEAN DIPLOMACY

During the period between the founding of the Liberian Republic in 1847 and the Conference of Berlin in 1885, most of the so-called Dark Continent continued to be ruled over by native kings and chiefs. But after 1885, the great Western Powers intervened and started to share the continent out among themselves. From then on, Africa became a mere pawn in European diplomacy, and her people, the defenceless victims of unregulated exploitation.

Before the period of colonial expansion, the relationship between Europe and Africa was different. In the earlier centuries, Europeans were not concerned with territorial annexation. They only wanted cheap labour for their New World colonies, and as Africa provided a vast reservoir of slaves, the whites bought the blacks and transported them to the Western Hemisphere. After the abolition of the Slave Trade in 1807, European interest in Africa declined. Apart from a few coastal regions in the north and south of the continent, settled by white colonists, such as the French in Algeria and the Dutch (Boers) and English in the Cape, Africa was allowed to remain under native tribal rulers.

Interest in Africa only revived in the latter part of the nineteenth century, when economic rivalries among the Western Powers gave rise to imperialistic expansion. This was dictated by the need for overseas markets, sources of raw materials, national prestige and fresh outlets for the profitable investment of capital. Until these desires arose, even Britain, the leading nation in the world, had but limited territorial interest in Africa. So little, in fact, that until a decade before the Berlin Conference, colonial annexation was by no means a popular external policy in British governing circles. Rather, the prevailing sentiment was definitely anti-Colonialist. As long as Britain was considered the workshop of the world she had little to fear from foreign competition. 'For approximately three-quarters of the nineteenth century English industry was as mighty as Gulliver in Lilliput. Even as late as 1870 Great Britain was smelting half the world's iron and more than three times as much as any other nation; she was making almost half of the world's cotton goods; her foreign commerce was more than twice that of any foreign rival.'[1]

BRITAIN LEADS THE WAY

England got all the food and raw materials she required from abroad, and sold the world all the goods and services she could supply. Why then bother about colonies; especially in 'darkest' Africa, where the natives would have to be taught to want Western commodities before a market could be created. Even Disraeli, who was later to become the most ardent imperialist, at that time described colonies as 'millstones around our neck'. As late as 1865, a Select Committee of the House of Commons recommended the abandonment of all British spheres of influence in West Africa, except Sierra Leone, for which the Liberal Government of Lord John Russell felt a special obligation to the repatriated Negroes settled there. Yet within a few years a new imperialist movement arose in Britain around the Royal Colonial Institute, which was founded in 1868 to combat the 'Little England' policy of the Liberals. From then onwards, colonial expansion became a political slogan among Tory imperialists. Leading the imperial vanguard was Joseph Chamberlain, the one-time radical mayor of Birmingham, who deserted the

[1] P. T. Moon: *Imperialism and World Politics*, p. 25 (Macmillan).

Liberals and as Colonial Secretary played an active part in
the forward march on Africa.

'It is the duty of the State to foster the trade and obtain
markets for its manufactures,' declared Chamberlain. How
did this need for markets arise? Here we must retrace our
survey of colonization in Africa and examine the economic
challenge which Britain was facing from her foremost commercial rival, Germany. The outcome of this competition was
destined to have disastrous consequences for Africans, Asians
and other darker races.

FRANCE FOLLOWS BRITAIN

After the Franco-Prussian war of 1870, Prussia, under Bismarck's leadership, took the initiative offered by the unification of the German Empire. There followed a period of
intensive industrialization. By the end of the nineteenth century, Germany emerged as Britain's greatest competitor.

The economic growth of the new Reich first found an outlet
in the home market. But as the end of the century approached,
Germany, too, began to seek a place for herself in the African
sun. She, too, had need to secure overseas markets and
sources of raw materials to accommodate her ever-increasing
industrial expansion and outlets for capital investment, as
well as coaling stations for her ever-growing merchant fleet.

A similar movement for overseas expansion was going on
in France. In her case, it was stimulated not so much by
industrial needs as by national egotism resulting from her
defeat in 1870 and the loss of Alsace and Lorraine. To divert
France's attention from a revengeful policy against Germany,
and help restore her *amour propre*, the German Chancellor
encouraged French statesmen to turn their attention to Africa.
There, France could find new territories to annex in compensation for the lost provinces. Bismarck, incidentally, also
hoped that colonial expansion would bring France into conflict with England and cause her to dissipate her energies
outside of Europe.

The Bismarckian policy of diverting France overseas was

diplomatically successful for some time. Eleven years after the Franco-Prussian war, France annexed Tunis, which act of aggression brought her into conflict with Italy. This threw Italy into the camp of the Dual Alliance, Germany and Austria. This in turn brought the Triple Alliance into being.

Even Britain became suspicious of the rapid rate of French penetration into Africa and was on the look-out for allies to checkmate Gallic colonialism. Therefore, when Bismarck considered the time appropriate to support the Hamburg and Bremen merchants and charter companies in their ambitions to share in the African loot, the Iron Chancellor sent his son, Herbert Bismarck, on a secret mission to London in 1884 to explain Germany's colonial aims. Young Bismarck met with enthusiastic support in Tory imperialist circles, for Britain was then without a friend in Europe. At home, the Liberal Government of Gladstone was under heavy attack from the Tories, led by the third Marquis of Salisbury, who later succeeded Mr Gladstone as Prime Minister. Even Gladstone welcomed Germany's entry into Africa. In a speech delivered to the House of Commons on March 12, 1885, the 'Little Englander' declared: 'If Germany is to become a colonizing power, all I can say is, God speed her. She becomes an ally and partner in the execution of the great purpose of Providence for the advancement of mankind.'

THE BERLIN CONFERENCE

Thanks to the diplomatic success of young Bismarck's mission, the German Chancellor convened the Conference in Berlin in November 1884, at which the powers with colonial ambitions in Africa were invited to regulate their claims peacefully. After the General Act of the Berlin Conference was signed on February 26, 1885, the three great Western European Powers—Britain, France and Germany—started in real earnest to annex colonies and protectorates all over the continent. At the end of the century, Britain had acquired in addition to Sierra Leone, Gambia, Gold Coast, and Nigeria in West Africa; part of Somaliland, Uganda and Kenya in the

East; Nyasaland, Northern and Southern Rhodesia in the Centre; and Bechuanaland, Basutoland, and Swaziland in the South. British settlers had already established colonies in the Cape and Natal. Sudan was held in Condominium with Egypt after its conquest by Lord Kitchener in 1898.

France, already established in Algeria and Tunis, added the following territories to her empire: Mauritania, Upper Volta, Sudan, Niger, Guinea, Ivory Coast, and Dahomey in West Africa; Gabon, Middle Congo, Ubangi, Chari and Chad in Equatorial Africa; Somaliland, and the island of Madagascar off the East Coast of Africa.

Germany, although a late-comer, got 1,026,229 miles with a population of 16,687,000, covering Togoland and the Cameroons in West Africa; the entire South-West Africa extending from Portuguese Angola to the Union of South Africa as well as Tanganyika on the east coast.

Spain and Portugal, although considerably shrunken in status to third-rate Powers, were allowed to remain in possession of their ancient colonies. The former retained Rio de Oro, Ifni and Spanish Guinea along the west coast, and the island of Fernando Po. The Portuguese Empire comprises Mozambique on the east coast, Portuguese Guinea and Angola on the Western mainland, with the islands of Sao Thomé and Principe off the coast.

Italy, having suffered a series of defeats in her attempts to grab Ethiopian territory, first by the Tigreans at Dogali in 1887, and most disastrously by the Emperor Menelik at Adowa in 1896, had to content herself with a slice of Somaliland and Massawa, which she acquired from the Khedive of Egypt in 1885, with the connivance of the British.

The vast and rich colony of the Congo in Central Africa, which was granted to the Belgian King, Leopold II, as his personal property, was taken over by the Belgian nation in 1908, following exposures of slavery, forced labour and other atrocities against the natives. These revelations were made by Sir Roger Casement, the British Consul in the Congo, and the famous English anti-Imperialist, E. D. Morel, the great champion and defender of the black race.

The policy of nineteenth century British colonization was pioneered by chartered companies. The Imperial Government assumed direct control when the agents of these chartered companies came into conflict with their French rivals on the one hand, and African chiefs who resisted their encroachments on the other. Although the Conference of Berlin laid down certain rules for the 'peaceful' partitioning of Africa, rivalry and jealousy quickly manifested themselves among those participating in the scramble. There were incidents which nearly led to war.

Italy, for instance, resented the occupation of Tunisia by France in 1881. To find compensation, she was encouraged to encroach upon Ethiopia, then the only independent kingdom, apart from Liberia, left in Africa. But Italy was too weak to carry out her imperialistic ambition of becoming a great colonial Power. It was only in 1912 that she acquired Libya, with an Arab population of only 793,325. Because most of the country is waterless desert, Italian colonization was greatly handicapped. Libya was only able to absorb 95,176 Italian immigrants, compared with 300,000 French settlers in Tunisia, which is only 48,300 square miles, and French Morocco's 153,870 square miles with a European population of 367,815.

Italy's failure to find accommodation for her surplus population in the African sun has always been a source of rancour between herself and other imperialist Powers with vast colonial empires. But Italy was not the only nation whose diplomacy was influenced by events in Africa between the Berlin Conference and the First World War.

ANGLO-FRENCH CONFLICT OVER FASHODA

In 1898, France and Britain nearly came to blows over Fashoda in the Sudan, and other minor incidents such as Waima in Sierra Leone and the Upper Niger. France, in order to secure the friendship of England for her policy of *revenge* against Germany, ordered the withdrawal of Captain Marchand from the Nile Valley. In recognition of the Sudan as an extension of Britain's sphere of influence over Egypt,

England agreed to allow France to annex Wadi and to have a free hand in Morocco.

The Moroccan Question had a most far-reaching effect on European diplomacy in the years immediately preceding the First World War. France not only had to secure Britain's support before establishing a protectorate over Morocco in 1912, then recognized as part of the Sultan of Turkey's dominion in Africa, but she had to square matters with Italy who was still resentful of her annexation of Tunisia, and also with Spain. Theophile Delcassé, the French Foreign Minister who was responsible for solving the Fashoda crisis, undertook the task of isolating Germany before pouncing upon Morocco.

'If I conclude my agreement with England, Italy and Spain, you will see Morocco fall into our garden like a ripe fruit,' he declared, adding: 'But believe me, I shall not stop there. This liquidation shall lead us to a practical alliance with England. Ah, my dear friend, what beautiful horizons would open before us! Just think! If we could lean both on Russia and on England, how strong we should be in relation to Germany.'[2]

Delcassé's diplomacy succeeded, and Morocco fell into the French Empire 'like a ripe fruit' in 1912, eight years after signing an alliance with Britain—the *Entente Cordiale*. To round off his colonial foreign policies, Delcassé agreed to let Spain have a coastal strip in Morocco, and Italy was given a free hand to annex Tripoli and Cyrenaica, two North African provinces of the Turkish Empire.

ANGLO-GERMAN RIVALRIES IN EAST AFRICA

Anglo-German relations also passed through a period of crisis during the years under review. England was not only alarmed by the rate of German economic development and commercial competition, but by Germany's growing naval power. The honeymoon period between the two countries,

[2] See G. P. Gooch: *Before the War: Studies in Diplomacy*; E. D. Morel: *Morocco in Diplomacy*.

fostered by the pro-German Tories, was fast coming to a close. After dropping the old pilot, Bismarck, the Kaiser declared that 'German colonial aims can only be secured when Germany has become the master of the ocean . . . The trident must pass into our hands.'[3]

This was a definite challenge to Britain, then the mistress of the seas. Until then, Tory statesmen had been pursuing a policy of appeasing the Kaiser, in the hope of bringing about an alliance with Germany. In furtherance of this policy of friendship, Britain had ceded Heligoland to Germany as a naval base in 1890, in exchange for the withdrawal of her claims to parts of Uganda, Zanzibar and Pemba, put forward by the notorious Dr Karl Peters, agent of the German East Africa Company. Dr Peters had acquired Tanganyika for the German fatherland. Eight years later relations between Britain and France were strained to breaking point over Fashoda and the rivalry between the agents of the Royal Niger Charter Company and the French, who were trying to sign treaties with Fulani chiefs in Northern Nigeria. Britain then entered into a secret agreement with Germany to divide up the Portuguese colonies, giving Germany the lion's share.

Mr Arthur James Balfour, the Foreign Secretary who initialled the agreement with Count Hatzfelt, was hoping that this would satisfy the Kaiser's colonial appetite and stop his naval rearmament programme. Unfortunately, for the promoters of the scheme, the secret leaked out before the bargain was consummated. The Portuguese, who were supposed to be 'Britain's oldest allies', naturally protested, but they could do no more. As France had been left out of the projected share-out, she too objected, and the project was allowed to drop.

To reassure Portugal that England and Germany were not taking advantage of her financial difficulties, Britain signed the Treaty of Windsor in 1899, 'guaranteeing' the Portuguese Colonial Empire. Yet the threat to her African possessions, acquired in the fifteenth century under the Bull of Pope Alexander VI, was not entirely removed. Despite the Treaty of

[3] Mary Townsend: *The Rise and Fall of Germany's Colonial Empire*, Ch. VII—Colonial Policy and Weltpolitik.

Windsor, in 1913 Sir Edward Grey, the Liberal Foreign Secretary, in an effort to satisfy Germany's demands for a larger stake in Africa, made a secret deal with Prince Karl Lichnowsky, the German Ambassador in London. Sir Edward agreed to support Germany's pressure on Portugal, which was then passing through a period of political unrest, to cede Angola, the islands of San Thome and Principe and the northern portion of Mozambique.

The outbreak of the First World War saved the Portuguese Empire from disruption. Had the Anglo-German agreement been consummated, Germany had intended to carry out a policy of Mittel-Afrika by joining up the newly-acquired portion of Mozambique on the Indian Ocean with Angola on the Southern Atlantic, driving a wedge between British southern and central Africa, and thereby isolating the Union of South Africa from the British territories to the north of the Union. Diplomatic documents have since revealed that to consolidate this grandiose scheme, Germany also intended to acquire the Belgian Congo as part of her Mittel-Afrika empire. Even as late as the spring of 1914, Gottlieb von Jagow, the German Foreign Secretary, informed the French Ambassador in Berlin that his Government was prepared to do a deal with France in support of his country's annexation of the Belgian Congo. 'Only great powers,' declared the German Minister, 'have the strength and resources for colonization. Small powers must disappear or gravitate into the orbit of the great.' But the European crisis over Serbia had already gone too far for France to accept von Jagow's gesture. The outbreak of war that summer saved the Belgian Congo from passing out of the hands of a 'small' power into those of a 'great' one.[4]

FROM MANDATES TO TRUSTEESHIP

Germany lost her African empire with the 1914-18 war. Her colonies of Togoland, Cameroons, South-West Africa

[4] See Prince Lichnowsky's Memorandum in *International Conciliation*, No. 127, pp. 58-65.

and Tanganyika were detached and shared out among the victorious Allied Powers.

As the war had been fought for 'democracy' and 'the right of self-determination' of peoples, it was necessary to deceive world public opinion about the new status of the former German colonies. It was made out that these colonies were not being annexed, but were being held in trust in the interest of the native inhabitants. To achieve this perfidy, General Smuts, in a pamphlet entitled *The League of Nations— Practical Suggestions*, formulated the principles of the Mandatory system, which were subsequently embodied in Articles 119 of the Treaty of Versailles and 22 of the Covenant of the League of Nations.

It stated that 'To those colonies and territories which as a consequence of the late war have ceased to be under the sovereignty of the States which had formerly governed them and which are inhabited by peoples not yet able to stand by themselves under the strenuous conditions of the modern world, there should be applied the principle that the well-being and development of such peoples form a sacred trust of civilization and that securities for the performance of this trust should be embodied in this Covenant.'

This was precisely the same hypocritical promise made by the signatories of the General Act of the Berlin Conference of 1885, which, as we saw, regulated the carve-up of Africa. There it was stated that the motive of the imperialists in colonizing the continent was 'to protect the natives in their moral and material well-being, to co-operate in the suppression of slavery and the slave trade, to further the education of the natives; to protect missionaries, scientists and explorers . . .' . The mandatory system was, in fact and in reality, a continuation of the old Berlin fraud draped in the veil of morality.

The German African colonies were placed under two categories of Mandated *B* and *C*. The former consisted of Tanganyika, which was handed over to Britain, with the exception of the province of Ruanda-Urundi. This was given to Belgium in compensation for the devastation she suffered from German occupation. Togoland and the Cameroons were each divided into two parts and assigned to Britain and France.

South-West Africa was placed in category C and awarded to the Union of South Africa, whose troops had invaded and occupied the territory during the war.

Italy, who in a secret treaty between herself and the Allies in 1915 had been promised a share in the colonial loot as a reward for having deserted the Central Powers, was left out.

To those who have much, more shall be added. And to those with little, even that shall be taken away. After the Second World War, Italy suffered the same fate as Germany after the First. Her African Empire, which covered 889,152 square miles, with an African population of 2,425,025 and 151,844 white settlers, was confiscated. Eritrea was federated to Ethiopia; Italian Somaliland was placed under United Nations Trusteeship, and Libya was declared a so-called independent kingdom under British tutelage.

The old German colonies were converted from Mandates into Trusteeship territories under British, French and Belgian administration. South-West Africa has been openly annexed and incorporated into the Union of South Africa by Dr Malan, despite the protest of the African inhabitants and the United Nations' objection.

The end of the First World War found Africa in the same dependent status to which it had been reduced after the Berlin Conference. With the exception of Egypt, Ethiopia, Liberia, and the South African Union, all the territories were under some form of foreign domination.

Before the continent had passed completely under European control, it was possible to repatriate Negroes from the western hemisphere and settle them along the coast of West Africa. As we saw, all the Sierra Leone Charter Company, and later the American Colonization Society, had to do was to purchase land from the native chiefs, in order to provide settlements for the black immigrants. But once the European Governments had taken possession of the African coast line and installed themselves as sovereign rulers throughout the continent, Negro colonization projects could only be carried out with their consent and active support. And obviously, having established themselves as masters of Africa, they were not prepared to help to promote a Black Zionist Movement which might one day challenge their over-lordship.

V

BLACK ZIONISM OR GARVEYISM

Black Zionism among American Negroes was inspired by the Universal Negro Improvement Association and African Communities Imperial League, founded by Marcus Aurelius Garvey, the greatest black prophet and visionary since Negro Emancipation. Under the slogan, 'Africa for the Africans at home and abroad', Garvey, a past master in the art of mass-psychology and impassioned demagoguery capitalized on the racial disabilities of the Negroes in America. He exploited the disillusionment which affected peoples of African descent everywhere after the First World War, in which they had fought in order 'to make the world safe for democracy', and 'the right of self-determination'.

Within very few years of launching his Back to Africa campaign in 1920, Garvey succeeded in organizing the biggest mass movement of protest ever witnessed in the United States. By 1923 the U.N.I.A. claimed over 6,000,000 members, though many of his opponents maintain that it never had more than half that number. That is as may be. By 1925, however, the movement began to disintegrate and Garvey died an exile in London in 1940, poor but not forgotten. The rise and fall of this Negro Moses had been meteoric.

Garvey was born of African parentage in the West Indian island of Jamaica on August 17, 1887. He was a full-blooded Negro of Koromantee stock, a fact of tremendous importance, as it coloured his whole outlook and relationship with American Negro leaders, many of whom were of mixed blood. It influenced, too, the policies of the movement which he founded to give expression to his racialistic philosophy and nationalistic ambitions.

Writing of his early life, the future Provisional President of Africa tells us why he decided to build a strong and mighty black nation.

'I asked: Where is the black man's government? Where is his King and his kingdom? Where is his President, his country, and his ambassador, his army, his navy, his men of big affairs? I could not find them, and then I declared: I will help to make them.'[1]

Jamaica, he realized, was too small a place in which to act out the great destiny he had assigned himself, so he transferred his activities to the United States in 1916.

Frequently Garvey's utterances had a bombastic sound, but for all that he was no ignoramus. He had travelled widely in South and Central America observing the conditions of the coloured populations before paying his first visit to England. He spent several years in London working with a well-known Egyptian nationalist of Sudanese descent, Duse Mohammed Ali, the editor of an anti-imperialist magazine, *African Times and Orient Review*. As an ardent supporter of Zaghloul Pasha, the leader of the Wafd Party in Egypt, Duse Mohammed Ali indoctrinated Garvey in nationalism and inspired him to take up the cudgel on behalf of the Negro. While in London, Garvey was a regular visitor to the British Museum, where he read extensively. Throughout his life, his favourite books were the Bible, Shakespeare and Plutarch.

Napoleon was his greatest hero. In fact, Bonaparte seems to have been the only white man he considered his equal! For Garvey was a man of inordinate conceit. Yet there remains no doubt that he was one of the outstanding orators of his race and an equally able journalist. His greatest asset, however, was—his colour. Garvey was unmistakably black, with prominent negroid features. These physical characteristics gave him an advantage over his American Negro political opponents, most of whom were mulatto or near-white. Gar-

[1] Marcus Garvey: *Philosophy and Opinions*, edited by Amy Jaques Garvey, Vol. II, p. 126.

vey, like Dr Malan, believed in 'racial purity', the point of departure between them being that the Boer sought the purity of the white race, and the Negro that of the black.

'I believe in a pure black race just as how all self-respecting whites believe in a pure white race, as far as that can be.'[2]

THE NEGRO MOSES

Garvey thought of himself as the Moses of the Negro race, and since a chosen people cannot be undefiled, Marcus Garvey naturally pontificated that only those who were one hundred per cent negroid could hold office in the organization, and thus carried his all-black world to its logical conclusion—racial purity. Accordingly, he admonished both whites and blacks that the purity of the races was being endangered. 'It is the duty of the virtuous and morally pure of both the white and black races,' he declared, 'to thoughtfully and actively protect the future of the two peoples by vigorously opposing the destructive propaganda and vile efforts of the miscegenationists of the white race, and their associates, the hybrids of the Negro race.'

The fanatical racialism of Garvey brought him into head-on conflict with American Negro political, religious and social-uplift leaders, especially their *doyen* and leading propagandist, Dr W. E. B. DuBois. Dr DuBois was the 'father' of Pan-Africanism, the rival political ideology to Garvey's Black Zionism.

Rejecting co-operation with the light-skin American leaders, whom he denounced as 'the hybrids of the Negro race', Garvey, because of his racial doctrine, rather welcomed the aid of two notorious negrophobists, E. S. Cox of the Ku-Klux-Klan and John Powell of the Anglo-Saxon Clubs. They frequently addressed Garvey's meetings, extolling his Back to Africa Movement, with its emphasis on 'racial purity'.

These white men, who were then leading a campaign of terror against the Negroes in the Southern States, were bitter

[2] Marcus Garvey: *Philosophy and Opinions*, Vol. I, p. 37.

enemies of the programme of economic, political and social equality for coloured Americans advocated by Dr DuBois and other mulatto leaders of the N.A.A.C.P. The white racialists supported Garvey, as they hoped that his Back to Africa Movement would get rid of the Negroes in America and thereby solve the racial problem in the south.

On his side, Garvey welcomed their support, as it strengthened his position against his mulatto opponents. Answering their criticisms of his alliance with these white enemies of the Negro race, Garvey unashamedly admitted why he united with the Ku-Klux-Klan. 'The Klan was fighting to make America a white man's land, and he was fighting to make Africa a black man's one . . . He called what he and they were doing, "The Ideals of Two Races" . . .'[3]

Another reason was that 'Garvey had allied himself with these sinister organizations largely as one way of getting revenge on the American Negro leaders, nearly every one of whom were opposing him. In fact, he seemed to take a delight in opposing everything for which the American Negro leaders stood . . . His special target was Dr DuBois, who, in an article in The Crisis,[4] had called him a "little, fat, black man; ugly, but with intelligent eyes and a big head". The Klan and the Anglo-Saxon Clubs had promised him congressional support to get his followers to Africa, but used him only as a tool. Of course they were willing to give him a free hand in Africa where they had neither power nor interests in exchange for the substantial benefits derived from the exploitation of Negroes in America.'

Garvey hated mulattos even more than he hated white people. In his native Jamaica, where he had grown up, Garvey had seen how the men of mixed blood, popularly known as 'brown men', constituted themselves the middle class. This brown middle class formed a buffer between the poor blacks below them and the white upper class, composed of British civil service officials, planters, merchants, prosperous professional men and higher members of the clergy. Until recent years, the whites and mulattos exercised ab-

[3] J. A. Rogers: World's Great Men of Colour, Vol. II, p. 604.
[4] The official propaganda organ of the N.A.A.C.P., of which Dr DuBois was then the Director of Publications.

solute political and economic power, and had good reason to fear a challenge from the blacks.

Such positions as the whites did not want went to the 'brown men', products of white and black mixture. The blacks formed the despised mass, the lower class of urban workers, sugar plantation labourers and peasants. In a country where 'white' is synonymous with power and wealth, it was inevitable that gradations of colour were of paramount importance, and that the poorest were the blackest—like Garvey. The 'brown men' strenuously kept out those who strove to enter their ranks from below. The blacks regarded them as the gendarmes of white privilege and power. They aped the white folk, and the black folk hated them. That was the pattern in Jamaica in Garvey's day.

The situation in America is entirely different. There the white majority has no need of the services of the mixed blood Negroes to keep the black masses 'in their place'. All Negroes —black and light skin—are the same. They are all 'just niggers' to the American white man. Consequently, American Negroes of both light and dark skin work together for the betterment of their race.

Conditioned to the prevailing pattern in Jamaica, Garvey transferred his prejudice against light-skin Negroes to the American scene, failing to understand that there was no cleavage between the different shades of Negroes. Thus, from the very outset of his activities in the United States, he alienated the sympathetic support of most of the recognized Negro leaders for his cause. It was a major mistake, and led finally to the failure of his Back to Africa Movement and his personal downfall and imprisonment.

Before the final crisis came, however, Garvey strutted, a principal figure, across the stage of Negro self-consciousness. He convened conventions; he organized a black national church. He established a Black Line Steamship Company, founded a newspaper. He sent delegations to the League of Nations and to foreign states. He created orders of chivalry. And he also declared himself Provisional President of Africa.

Such a consummate actor had never before been witnessed by the black world. Garvey was both hated and loved. Often he created enemies when he should have made friends. Never was he ignored.

BIRTH OF NEGRO EMPIRE

Marcus Garvey founded his Negro Empire in New York in the year 1920. Territory, it had none; but its subjects were counted by the millions and scattered throughout the world.

On August 1, 1920, Garvey convened his first Parliament in the form of an international convention. Representatives came from far and wide. The date was significant. Ever ready to exploit the sacred memories of his people, Garvey recalled that on August 1, 1834, the good Queen Victoria had set free the slaves. He, therefore, selected that date to summon their descendants to New York to proclaim the new struggle against the white man's oppression in Africa. 'Wake up, Ethiopia! Wake up, Africa!' Garvey thundered to the hysterical applause of the assembled delegates. 'Let us work towards the one glorious end of a free, redeemed, and mighty nation. Let Africa be a bright star among the constellation of nations . . .'[5]

This goal was envisaged in the declaration of aims and objects adopted by the Convention:

'The Universal Negro Improvement and African Communities League is a social, friendly, humanitarian, charitable, educational, institutional, constructive and expansive society, and is founded by persons desiring to the utmost to work for the general uplift of the Negro peoples of the World. And the members pledge themselves to do all in their power to conserve the rights of their noble race and to respect the rights of all mankind, believing always in the Brotherhood of Man and the Fatherhood of God. The motto of the organization is: One God! One Aim! One Destiny. Therefore, let justice be done to all mankind, realizing that if the strong oppresses the weak confusion and discontent will ever mark the path of men, but with love, faith and charity toward all, the reign

[5] Marcus Garvey: *Philosophy and Opinions*, Vol. I, p. 5.

of peace and plenty will be heralded into the world and the generation of men shall be blessed.'

The declared objects of the Association were:

'To establish a universal confraternity among the race; to promote the spirit of pride and love; to reclaim the fallen; to administer to and assist the needy; to assist in civilizing the backward tribes of Africa; to assist in the development of independent Negro nations and communities; to establish a central nation for the race; to establish commissaries or agencies in the principal countries and cities of the world for the representation of all Negroes; to promote a conscientious spiritual worship among the native tribes of Africa; to establish universities, colleges, academies and schools for the racial education and culture of the people; to work for better conditions among Negroes everywhere.'[6]

'Emperor' Garvey held many such conventions at Madison Square Gardens, the great New York boxing stadium, and at Liberty Hall, the Harlem headquarters of the U.N.I.A. These conventions opened with great spectacle. There was a huge parade through the streets of Harlem in which banners were carried bearing such inscriptions as 'Africa must be free'; 'The Negro fought in Europe, he must fight in Africa'; 'Freedom for all'.

At the first convention, Garvey, who was then only thirty-three years of age, was unanimously elected Provisional President of Africa and President-General and Administrator of the Universal Negro Improvement Association. As head of the African empire-to-be, his official title was 'His Highness, the Potentate', and his honorarium $22,000. The eighteen members of the 'High Executive Council' or Shadow Cabinet, received from $3,000 to $10,000 a year. After the 'Provisional Government' had been approved and sworn in, Garvey conferred peerages and knighthoods upon them.

These black dignitaries, the first of the nobility of the 'Negro Empire', were graced with such high-sounding titles as Duke of the Nile, Earl of the Congo, Viscount of the Niger and Baron Zambesi. Others were made Knights of the Distinguished Service Order of Ethiopia, Ashanti and Mozam-

[6] Marcus Garvey: *Philosophy and Opinions*, Vol. II, pp. 37-38.

bique. Anticipating Sir Winston Churchill, Garvey even created an 'Overlord' of Uganda. They were all provided with magnificent robes and capes patterned after the British orders of chivalry, such as the Garter, the Bath, and the Thistle. The black nobility were even more gorgeously attired than the white aristocracy. For Negroes dearly love gaudy costumes.

As Africa would first have to be liberated before Garvey's nobility and Provisional Government could take over, 'an army would eventually be needed to drive out the white usurpers: and so Garvey founded the Universal African Legion, the Universal Black Cross Nurses, the Universal African Motor Corps, the Juvenile, the Black Eagle Flying Corps—all with uniforms and officers. A steamship line also was needed: and so he sponsored the organization of the Black Star Line and purchased ships'.[7]

In the short space of four years from the time he left Jamaica, Garvey travelled fast and far. He came into the heyday of his success. An eye-witness gives this graphic account of the first convention. 'Noisy meetings at Liberty Hall were climaxed by a magnificent parade in which more than fifty thousand Garveyites marched through Harlem. His Excellency Marcus Garvey, Provisional President of Africa, led the demonstration bedecked in a dazzling uniform of purple, green, and black, with gold braid, and a thrilling hat with white plumes as long as the leaves of Guinea grass. He rode in a big, high-mounted black Packard automobile and graciously, but with the restraint becoming a sovereign, acknowledged the ovations of the crowds that lined the sidewalks.

'Behind him rode His Grace Archbishop McGuire, in silk robes of state, blessing the populace. Then, the Black Nobility and the Knight Commanders of the Distinguished Order of the Nile, followed, the hierarchy of state, properly attired in regalia drawn from a bold palette. Arrayed in gorgeous uniforms of black and green, trimmed with much gold braid, came the smartly strutting African Legion, and in white, the

[7] Gunnar Myrdal: *The American Dilemma*, Vol. II, p. 747 (Harpers).

stretcher-bearing Black Cross Nurses. Then came the troops of kilt-clad Boy and Girl Scouts, trailed by a multitude of bumptious black subjects. Harlem was spell-bound. For the first time white New York became aware of the proportions of the movement, its implications, and indeed its divertisse-ments. Marcus Garvey had become a world figure, and his movements and utterances were noted by every European power with possessions in Africa.

'He sent a goodwill greeting to Abd-el-Krim, the rebel leader of Spanish Morocco; and advocated unity with all darker peoples—in the Caribbean, Africa, India, China and Japan.'[8]

As a means of carrying his injunctions and directives to his millions of followers in all parts of the black world, Garvey founded the *Negro World*, which he edited himself. Week after week, His Highness the Potentate issued messages with the infallibility of papal encyclicals, whipping the faithful to action.

'Africa for the Africans', 'Renaissance of the Black Race', 'Ethiopia Awake'. These were the magic slogans which Garvey exploited to the delirious delight of his followers, to whom he was 'His Excellency'. Money poured in from all parts of the black world. A member of the new aristocracy, Sir Isaiah Emmanuel Morter, Knight of the Distinguished Service Order of Ethiopia, and 'Prince of Africa', living in Belize, British Honduras, bequeathed $300,000 to Garvey. But 'His Excellency' was double-crossed out of that by some of his 'rebellious subjects'. The matter even reached the Judi-ciary Committee of the British Privy Council, which decided against Garvey in favour of the rebels.

'Up, you Mighty Race,' he continued to roar. 'You can accomplish what you will. It is only a question of a few more years when Africa will be completely colonized by Negroes, as Europe is by the white race. No one knows when the hour of Africa's redemption cometh. It is in the wind. It is coming. One day, like a storm, it will be here.'

The Colonial Offices of the European States sat up and took notice. Garvey was becoming a definite menace to them.

[8] Roi Ottley: *New World A-Coming,* p. 76 (Dutton).

The Negro World, which was published in English, French
and Spanish, was declared a seditious publication and proscribed by several colonial governments. In certain places the
punishment to be seen with a *Negro World* was five years
hard labour, and in French Dahomey it was life imprisonment
. . . It was suppressed in such places as Trinidad, British
Guiana, Barbados, etc., in the West Indies and all French,
Italian, Portuguese, Belgian, and some of the British colonies
in Africa. Garvey was accused of alienating the loyalty of
the Negroes and inciting them against their white rulers.

BLACK CHRIST AND MADONNA

Although Garvey had been born a Catholic, he established
his own African Orthodox Church under a black Patriarch,
Archbishop Alexander McGuire, a brilliant West Indian
theologian. Yet the Black Moses was always a great admirer
of the power of the Roman Church, to which he returned before he died in 1940.

During the heyday of his political career, Garvey frequently expressed admiration for the universalism and
authoritarianism of the Vatican, which he held up as an example to the supporters of the U.N.I.A. 'Our union must know
no clime, boundary or nationality. Like the great Church of
Rome, Negroes the world over must practise one faith, that
of confidence in themselves, with one God, one Aim, one
Destiny— . . . the founding of a Racial Empire whose only
natural, spiritual and political limits shall be God and Africa,
at home and abroad.'[9] Challenging the authority of traditional Christianity in matters appertaining to the spiritual
life of the Negroes, Garvey adopted a 'Black Christ and Black
Madonna' as symbols of his African Orthodox Church. His
nationalistic psychosis knew no limits in his efforts to instil
racial pride and self-respect in his followers. 'You must forget the white gods,' he pontificated. 'Erase the white gods
from your hearts. We must go back to the native church, to

[9] M. Garvey: *Philosophy and Opinions,* Vol. II, pp. 415-16.

our own true God.' Garvey's doctrine influenced the spread of dissident nationalist churches in Africa.

'Many of the Garveyites compare Garvey with Hitler, to the latter's disadvantage. They say that Hitler's torrential flood of rhetoric, with its direct appeal to primitive mass emotions, is similar to Garvey's oratory, but that Hitler perverted Garvey's racial philosophy and proclaimed the superiority of the German over all other races, while Garvey tried to lift up and convince the Negro that it was basically the equal of other races.'[10]

Garvey admitted that his doctrine was based on racial fascism. 'We were the first Fascists. We had disciplined men, women and children in training for the liberation of Africa. The black masses saw that in this extreme nationalism lay their only hope, and readily supported it. Mussolini copied fascism from me, but the Negro reactionaries sabotaged it.'[11]

MISSION TO THE PROMISED LAND

Having aroused the hostility of European Powers with colonies in Africa, Garvey realized that the U.N.I.A. would enjoy no legality in these territories. He therefore turned his attention to Liberia, through which he hoped to get a foothold on the African Continent. As the United States was not a colonial power in Africa, Garvey appealed to his white Southern friends to support his Liberian colonization scheme. He assured them that his Back to Africa plan was the only solution to America's dilemma, how to remove the Negroes.

'Africa,' he declared, 'affords a wonderful opportunity at the present time for colonization by the Negroes of the Western World. There is Liberia already established as an independent Negro Government. Let white America assist Afro-Americans to go there and help develop the country. Then,

[10] Claude McKay: *Harlem; Negro Metropolis*, p. 179 (Dutton and Co., New York).

[11] J. A. Rogers: *World's Great Men of Colour*, Vol. II, p. 602 (New York).

there are the late German colonies,[12] let white sentiment
force England and France to turn them over to the American and West Indian Negroes who fought for the Allies in
the World War. Then France, England and Belgium owe
America billions of dollars which they claim they cannot
afford to pay immediately. Let them compromise by turning
over Sierra Leone and the Ivory Coast on the west coast of
Africa and add them to Liberia and help make Liberia a
state worthy of her history. The Negroes of Africa and
America are one in blood. They have sprung from the same
common stock. They can work and live together and thus
make their own racial contribution to the world.'[13]

Garvey was able to extract promises of support for his Back
to Africa scheme from several influential Southern politicians
who were anxious to get rid of the Negroes from America. For
example, 'Senator McCallum of the Mississippi Legislature
introduced a resolution in the House for the purpose of petitioning the Congress of the United States of America and the
President to use their good influence in securing from the
Allies sufficient territory in Africa in liquidation of the war
debt, which territory should be used for the establishing of
an independent nation for American Negroes.'[14]

In anticipation of United States official support, Garvey
despatched a mission to Africa in 1920 to negotiate with the
Liberian Government for a grant of land on which to establish
community settlements under the auspices of the U.N.I.A.
The mission was well received by President King and his
Secretary of State, Mr Edwin Barclay, both of West Indian
descent. Mr King's father was a Jamaican soldier who served
in the British West Indian Regiment in West Africa and later
settled in Sierra Leone. Mr Barclay's father hailed from Bar-
badoes and was Secretary of State of the Republic. His uncle
was the distinguished and able President Arthur Barclay. He
himself succeeded Mr King to the Presidency.

It is not surprising, therefore, that these men welcomed
the idea of providing new homes for Negroes from the Western Hemisphere. A committee of prominent citizens was

[12] Togoland, Cameroons, South-West Africa, Tanganyika.
[13] Marcus Garvey: *Philosophy and Opinions*, Vol. II, p. 40.
[14] Ibid., Vol. I, p. 68.

appointed under the chairmanship of Vice-President H. T. Wesley to select suitable sites and assist the U.N.I.A. in carrying out its colonization plans.

In 1924, Garvey sent out a second mission to complete arrangements. Under the terms of the provisional agreement reached between his representatives and the Liberian Government, the U.N.I.A. guaranteed the repatriation of between twenty and thirty thousand families in the first two years . . . the worth of each family would be roughly estimated at $1,500 each. The immigrants were to be provided free of charge with thousands of acres of fertile land on the Cavalla River in the Maryland County near Cape Palmas. They, in return, had to 'subscribe to an oath that they will respect the established authority of the Liberian Government.'[15]

The entire enterprise was to be financed by the U.N.I.A. at the cost of about $2,000,000. A fund for this purpose was immediately launched by Garvey and met with tremendous response. The organization undertook to erect public buildings—a hospital, town hall, court house, post office, police and fire stations, library, cinema, community and cultural centre, schools and technical colleges, electric and power plant, water filtration plant, sewerage system—and construct roads.

Although Garvey had assured the Liberian Government that he had no political designs upon the Republic, it later transpired that this was not quite true. According to his American Negro opponents, Garvey had got Mr Gabriel Johnson, the Mayor of Monrovia, and one George Osborne Mark, a Sierra Leone Creole who held the rank of General in the Liberian Frontier Force, elected Potentate and Deputy Potentate respectively of the U.N.I.A.

Garvey had also established direct contact with Chief Justice James Dorsen, the most influential Liberian at Cape Palmas, the capital of the county selected for the proposed U.N.I.A. settlements.

With the assistance of these prominent Liberians and the active support of his followers, it is alleged that Garvey was planning to break the power of the True Whig Party politi-

[15] Report of Liberian Committee appointed by President King, Document 3, Section E-1924.

cians, who had been in control of Liberian affairs ever since the inception of the Republic. Garvey himself admitted that the U.N.I.A. 'mission to Liberia years before had returned with two reports: one in glowing praise to be read to his followers; the other, a private one, painting an awful picture of the present regime, accusing it of corruption and slavery. One of Garvey's enemies, getting a copy of this secret report, had it sent to the Liberian President'.[16]

The effect was dramatic. President King cancelled the concession granted to the U.N.I.A. and ordered the seizure of all the goods, building materials and machinery, valued at hundreds of thousands of dollars, which Garvey had shipped out to Liberia for use in the construction of houses for the first contingent of his followers at Cape Palmas. Liberia was then passing through an acute financial crisis and the salaries of the Republic's officials were several months overdue. Part of the proceeds from the sale of the U.N.I.A. construction materials was used to pay them. The President also ordered the arrest and deportation of Negro surveyors, engineers and other U.N.I.A. building staff who had arrived in the country to supervise the work of construction. Thus came the tragic end of Garvey's Back to Africa movement.

Apparently, President King had been warned by neighbouring Powers that they would not tolerate the presence in Liberia of an organization working for the overthrow of European supremacy in Africa. At a dinner given in honour of President King in Freetown, in January 1925, the Governor of Sierra Leone, Sir Ransford Slater, declared: 'Lastly, may I say how warmly we in Sierra Leone appreciate your courage and applauded your statesmanship in taking such prompt and vigorous steps to show that Liberia would have nothing to do with any movement having as its avowed object the fomenting of racial feeling of hatred and ill-will. Your Excellency, by slamming the door on spurious patriots from across the Atlantic, men who sought to make Liberia a focus for racial animosity in this continent, deservedly earned the gratitude not only of every West African Government

[16] J. A. Rogers: *World's Great Men of Colour*, Vol. II, p. 609.

but of all who have the true welfare of the African at heart.'[17]

Apart from the financial ruin resulting from the Liberian bubble, the Black Star Line turned out to be a white elephant. In order to transport his followers back to Africa, Garvey had invested hundreds of thousands of dollars in establishing his steamship company, capitalized at $10,000,000. All of the ships were named after famous Negro leaders, and most of them turned out to be unseaworthy. There was the S.S. *Frederick Douglas*, bought for $165,000 and sold for junk at $1,600. The S.S. *Antonio Maceo*, formerly the private yacht of an American millionaire, cost $60,000 plus $25,000 for refitting. It fell to pieces off the coast of Cuba. Another ship, the S.S. *Phyllis Wheatley*, sank in the Hudson River at New York, while a fourth was seized for non-payment of debts resulting from bad management and outright dishonesty among his top-ranking officers.

END OF A UTOPIAN EMPIRE

While blackness of skin guaranteed a place in the U.N.I.A. hierarchy, it did not protect the movement from crooks. Many of the black 'nobility' had only joined the movement to prey upon it. As soon as it faced ruin, they deserted and joined forces with Garvey's enemies to send him to jail. The end came when he was convicted and sentenced to five years' imprisonment in 1925 for using the U.S. mails to defraud. Two years later he was granted a pardon by President Calvin Coolidge and deported back to Jamaica. 'There he entered politics and won a seat in the City Council, causing a considerable stir on the island by his article in his newspaper *The Black Man*. In a libel case he was cited for contempt of court and sentenced to three months' imprisonment and a heavy fine.'[18]

With Garvey removed from America, his main sphere of activity, the U.N.I.A. quickly disintegrated and broke up.

[17] R. L. Buell: *The Native Problem in Africa*, Vol. II, p. 733.
[18] J. A. Rogers: *World's Great Men of Colour*, Vol. II, p. 607.

Like the generals of Alexander the Great, Garvey's 'generals', with the support of their 'legionnaires' seized power over the various territorial units of the U.N.I.A. and converted the properties and funds of the organizations to their personal use.

Garvey, still obsessed with his prejudice against the Jamaican 'brown men', brought his activities to London, from where he attempted without success to stake a political 'comeback'. Dissension and disillusionment, however, had gone too far among his 'pure black subjects' to be able to resuscitate the once world-wide movement. Even in the United Kingdom he found the task beyond his capacity. In the first place, the Negro population at that time was too small to provide any substantial organizational strength and, more important as far as Garvey was personally concerned, they were too poor to contribute the funds he needed to revive the U.N.I.A. He spent his declining years addressing small crowds of English people in Hyde Park, boasting of his former glory.

The first 'President-Elect of Africa' died in 1940, an event completely ignored by the white world. But Garvey has not been forgotten by his own people. For fourteen years after his death, in August 1954, the members of the Jamaican House of Representatives voted to erect a monument to his memory. It was a fitting tribute by 'brown men' and blacks to their distinguished countryman.

Despite the failure of his Black Zionist project in Liberia, Garvey most definitely made a marked contribution to the struggle for African awakening, a fact recognized even by his bitterest opponents. For example, Dr DuBois, one of those 'light-skin Negroes' whom Garvey considered his greatest enemies, says of the Back to Africa Movement that 'it was a grandiose and bombastic scheme, utterly impracticable as a whole, but it was sincere and had some practical features; and Garvey proved not only an astonishingly popular leader, but a master of propaganda. Within a few years, news of his movement, of his promises and plans, reached Europe and Asia, and penetrated every corner of Africa.'[19]

[19] W. E. B. DuBois: *Dusk of Dawn*, p. 277 (Harcourt, Brace, New York).

Another famous American Negro leader, James Weldon Johnson, the former Secretary of the N.A.A.C.P., the rival organization of the U.N.I.A. says this of his contemporary, 'Garvey failed. Yet he might have succeeded with more than moderate success. He had energy and daring and the Napoleonic personality, the personality that draws masses of followers. He stirred the imagination of the Negro masses as no Negro ever had. He raised more money in a few years than any other Negro organization has ever dreamed of. He had great power and great possibilities within his grasp. But his deficiencies as a leader outweighed his abilities.'

What were some of these deficiencies? Nobody really believed that Garvey was an unscrupulous demagogue out to fleece the most primitive and ignorant elements of his race. He was born poor, lived moderately, and died even poorer than he was born. His faults were other than mercenary. He was vain, arrogant, and highly sensitive to criticism. He suffered from a persecution complex and resented advice from even his closest colleagues. He distrusted even the members of the 'shadow cabinet' of his provisional black government. Garvey was unable to co-operate with anyone who disagreed with him. In short, he was supremely egotistical. His egotism amounted to megalomania; and so the men surrounding him had to be for the most part cringing sycophants. His business ventures failed more from bad management than conscious dishonesty. His Liberian colonization scheme collapsed as a consequence of his own vanity. He was entirely without tact and diplomacy. While seeking the assistance of the Liberian politicians for his Back to Africa Movement, Garvey publicly abused and denounced the leaders of the Negro Republic as the 'dull, ignorant, selfish, narrow and racially unpatriotic group, headed by King and Barclay that run the country,'[20] when they discovered that he was aiming at their overthrow.

'Do you wonder why such Negroes want to keep Marcus Garvey and his aides out of Liberia?' he asked. We certainly do! No ruling class, white or black, is going to relinquish its power voluntarily. This is what the self-proclaimed Provisional

[20] Marcus Garvey: *Philosophy and Opinions*, Vol. II, p. 488.

PART THREE

VI

BACKGROUND TO PAN-AFRICANISM

During the period when Marcus Aurelius Garvey was at the zenith of his power, his chief antagonist, William Edward Burghardt DuBois was expounding ideas of Pan-Africanism which were to have a more permanent influence on African political awakening.

Pan-Africanism differed from Garveyism in that it was never conceived as a Back to Africa Movement, but rather as a dynamic political philosophy and guide to action for Africans in Africa who were laying the foundations of national liberation organizations. It must be remembered that at the time Communism and other radical currents of twentieth century Anti-Imperialist ideas had not penetrated into the African Continent and Pan-Africanism was intended as a stimulant to anti-Colonialism.

Garvey's fulminations were against European domination in Africa. He resented the monopoly which white imperialists had in the exploitation of Africa, even while he himself believed firmly in the capitalist system. 'Why should not Africa give to the world its black Rockefeller, Rothschild and Henry Ford? Now is the opportunity. Now is the chance for every Negro to make every effort toward a commercial, industrial standard that will make us comparable with the successful business men of other races.'[1] Garvey had no use for Socialism. And as for Communism—that was the greatest abomination ever inflicted upon mankind!

'Capitalism', he asserted, 'is necessary to the progress of

[1] Marcus Garvey: *Philosophy and Opinions*, Vol. II, p. 68.

the world, and those who unreasonably and wantonly oppose or fight against it are enemies of human advancement; but', he added, 'there should be a limit to the individual or corporate use or control of it. No individual should be allowed the possession, use, or the privilege to invest on his own account more than a million; and no corporation should be allowed to control more than five millions. Beyond this, all control, use and investment of money should be the prerogative of the State with the concurrent authority of the people.'[2] Garvey was never one to talk other than in terms of millions!

Here again was a source of conflict between Garvey and DuBois. Common ground between them, there was none. Their concepts of political philosophies and economic systems were diametrically opposed. Dr DuBois was not only firmly against transporting American Negroes back to Africa, but was a staunch advocate of complete self-government for Africans in Africa organized on the basis of socialism and co-operative economy which would leave no room for millionaires, black or white. National self-determination, individual liberty, and democratic socialism constituted the essential elements of Pan-Africanism as expounded by DuBois.

He was born on February 23, 1868, at Great Barrington, Massachusetts, into a comfortable middle-class family. His intellectual abilities manifested themselves at an early age, and from boyhood he was destined to become the most outstanding scholar of his race. He won academic distinctions from elementary school to university and beyond. Dr DuBois studied first at Fisk and then at Harvard Universities in the United States and later at the University of Berlin. Since then, academic degrees and other honours have been conferred upon him by several universities. He was the first Negro to be elected a Fellow of the National Institute of Arts and Letters of America.

Garvey, the agitator and organizer, was supreme as an orator. DuBois exercised his influence largely through his writings and the classroom.[3] For over half a century he has

[2] Marcus Garvey: *Philosophy and Opinions*, Vol. II, p. 72.
[3] Dr DuBois's writings include the following books: *Suppression of the African Slave Trade* (1896); *The Philadelphia Negro* (1899);

been in the forefront of every campaign for the advancement of the Negro peoples in America and elsewhere. In those long uphill battles for political, economic and social equality, DuBois has wielded a powerful pen to great advantage. A man of tremendous moral courage and integrity, DuBois has been the most prolific writer among the Negro intelligentsia. His works have covered poetry, fiction, sociology and history, apart from hundreds of learned articles on Negro and Colonial problems in outstanding sociological journals and leading magazines in many countries. But his chief medium of propaganda on behalf of the African peoples has been *The Crisis*, a magazine which he founded in 1910 and edited until 1932 as 'A record of the Darker Races'.

'His editorials in *The Crisis* stirred the spirit of manhood in those Negroes capable of being stirred and made them more militant. At the same time he drew the continuous fire of the white exploiters of the Negro in the South and their Northern sympathizers and even of those white liberals who felt that Negroes ought to be less insistent on their rights and be more grateful to white America for all the good it was believed it had done for them.'[4]

While Garvey opposed white race prejudice with black, DuBois combated racial arrogance and social chauvinism on both sides. This he did by making a scientific study of the so-called 'Negro Problem' and exposed the myth of 'racial superiority' expounded by such pseudo-biologists as Count Arthur de Gobineau, Houston Stewart Chamberlain, Madison Grant and Lothrop Stoddard, the ideological fathers of Adolf Hitler and the racialists of America and South Africa.[5]

By helping to eliminate the servile mentality and 'Uncle

The Souls of Black Folk (1903); *John Brown* (1909); *Quest of the Silver Fleece* (1911); *The Negro* (1915); *Darkwater* (1920); *The Gift of Black Folk* (1924); *Dark Princess* (1927); *Black Reconstruction* (1935); *Black Folk Then and Now* (1940); *Dusk of Dawn* (1940); *Colour and Democracy* (1945); *The World and Africa* (1946); *In Battle for Peace* (1952).

[4] J. A. Rogers: *World's Great Men of Colour*, Vol. II, p. 595.

[5] Count de Gobineau: *Inequality of Human Races*; Madison Grant: *The Passing of the Great Race*; Lothrop Stoddard: *The Rising Tide of Colour*; Chamberlain: *Foundation of the Nineteenth Century*.

Tom' attitude which were to be found quite widely among Negroes right up to the First World War, DuBois contributed in large measure to the awakening militancy of the coloured people, which Garvey took full advantage of when he arrived in America in 1916.

Dr DuBois was a brilliant teacher as well as a first-class publicist. Before leaving the cloistered atmosphere of academic life for the rough-and-tumble of politics, he held several professorships. During this early period of his life, he trained many of the younger coloured intellectuals who are now carrying on the struggle for Negro advancement in all spheres of American life. As Professor of Economics and History at Atlanta University from 1897 to 1910, he edited the Atlanta University Studies, which charted the course for the ideological battles in which he was to become involved against white racialists and Negro utopians. Thus, 'when he began active life, it was with greater intellectual preparation than any other Negro had yet acquired'.[6]

WASHINGTON—DU BOIS CONTROVERSY

But before joining issue with Garvey, DuBois had crossed swords with Booker T. Washington, the one mulatto leader whom Garvey admired. Dr Washington was the founder of the famous Tuskegee Institute in Alabama and the first Negro leader to enjoy nation-wide recognition from the white rulers of America. Without DuBois's scholastic training and broad culture, Booker T. Washington was, nevertheless, a man of great stature. But he was an adamant conservative who, like Garvey, believed in and accepted racial separation. DuBois stood four square for racial equality and integration which, in his interpretation meant not necessarily miscegenation, but political, economic and social justice and first-class citizenship for all Americans, regardless of race, colour or former condition of servitude. DuBois, in short, wanted the white people to resolve 'the American dilemma' by implementing the four-

[6] James Weldon Johnson: *Black Manhattan*, p. 134.

teenth and fifteenth amendments to the United States Constitution which guaranteed political equality to the Negroes.

Dr Washington was opposed to such a radical policy. Born into slavery in a log cabin in Virginia, he knew the white 'Bourbons' of the South much better than DuBois who was born in New England. Washington's mother was a black slave and his father a white slave-owner. By his own exertions he acquired an education and from the humblest beginnings was the first of his race to rise to a most eminent position in the nation.[7]

Dr Washington's racial philosophy was first publicly enunciated at the Atlanta Exposition of 1895, at which he was invited to speak on behalf of the Negro race as their officially recognized leader. The hatred and bitterness of the Civil War was still very much alive and black men in the South were living in fear of white terrorism exemplified in the Ku-Klux-Klan. The whites were bent on keeping them in a condition of virtual slavery in spite of constitutional guarantees. 'The situation called for rare diplomacy . . . To the liberal whites, North and South, Booker T. Washington appeared the man of the hour in this situation.' He could not afford to offend the prejudices of the whites while at the same time appearing not to have surrendered the rights of his people to the South. 'Skilfully avoiding any accusation against the whites, he painted a rosy picture of the future for the whites, and of the profit they would reap, provided they gave the Negroes a freer chance to develop themselves.'[8]

When he spoke, he assured the white people that 'in all things that are purely social we can be as separate as the fingers, yet one as the hand in all things essential to material progress'. The fairest leaders of Dixie rose to their feet and cheered. From that day to his death in 1915, the white ruling classes, north and south, acclaimed Booker T. Washington the one and only true spokesman for the Negro. President Grover Cleveland wrote him a letter of congratulation. Honours were poured upon him. Northern capitalist philanthropists gave money to his college. He was invited by President Theodore

---

[7] Washington's autobiography: *Up From Slavery* is one of the finest in the English language.

[8] J. A. Rogers: *World's Great Men of Colour*, Vol. II, pp. 581-82.

Roosevelt to dine at the White House, the first coloured man to be so honoured. Dr Washington was consulted by Presidents, Governors and Senators, and became the black adviser of the Republican Party in the dispensation of political patronage to Negroes. After his death, the farm on which he was born was purchased by public subscription and the log cabin restored as a national shrine. In 1940, the U.S. Government issued a postage stamp with his likeness to commemorate his life, and five years later his statue was erected in the Hall of Fame for great Americans.

Commenting on Washington's racial philosophy, Dr Du-Bois says that he 'did not advocate a deliberate and planned segregation, but advised submission to segregation in settlement and work, in order that this bending to the will of a powerful majority might bring from that majority gradually such sympathy and sense of justice that in the long run the best interests of the Negro group would be served; particularly as those interests were, he thought, inseparable from the best interests of the dominant group. The difficulty here was that unless the dominant group saw its best interests bound up with those of the black minority, the situation was hopeless, and in any case the danger was that if the minority ceased to agitate and resist oppression it would grow to accept it as normal and inevitable.'[9]

Dr DuBois attacked Dr Washington's doctrine of tame submission and carried the fight into the camp of the Negro conservatives who supported Washington. His first attack was made in an essay entitled 'Of Mr Washington and Others' in his book *The Souls of Black Folk*, which appeared in 1903.

'To gain the sympathy and co-operation of the various elements comprising the white South was Mr Washington's first task; and this, at the time Tuskegee was founded, seemed for a black man, well-nigh impossible. And yet ten years later it was done in the words spoken at Atlanta: "In all things purely social we can be as separate as the five fingers, and yet one as the hand in all things essential to material progress." This "Atlanta Compromise" is by all odds the most notable thing in Mr Washington's career. The South inter-

[9] W. E. B. DuBois: *Dusk of Dawn*, pp. 196-97.

preted it in different ways: the radicals received it as a complete surrender of the demand for civil and political equality;
the conservatives as a generously conceived working basis for
mutual understanding. So both approved it, and today the
author is certainly the most distinguished Southerner since
Jefferson Davis, and the one with the greatest personal
following . . .'

To counterpoise the 'Atlanta Compromise', Dr DuBois concluded that 'the black men of America have a duty to perform, a duty stern and delicate—a forward movement to
oppose a part of the work of their greatest leader. So far as
Mr Washington preaches Thrift, Patience, and Industrial
Training to the masses, we must hold up his hands and strive
with him, rejoicing in his honours, and glorying in the strength
of this Joshua called of God and of men to lead the headless
host. But so far as Mr Washington apologizes for injustice,
North or South, does not rightly value the privilege and duty
of voting, belittles the emasculating effects of caste distinctions, and opposes the higher training and ambition of our
bright minds—so far as he, the South, or the Nation, does
this—we must increasingly and firmly oppose them. By every
civilised and peaceful method we must strive for the rights
which the world accords to men, clinging unwaveringly to
those great words which the sons of the Fathers would fain
forget: "We hold these truths to be self-evident: That all men
are created equal; that they are endowed by their Creator
with certain unalienable rights; that among these are life,
liberty and the pursuit of happiness".'[10]

This exhortation of DuBois served as a rallying call to the
militants of the Negro race to come together. A Moses had
arisen to lead his people. To harness and direct the gathering
support, Dr DuBois and another Negro intellectual, the
famous journalist, William Monroe Trotter, who had graduated from Harvard University in the same year that Dr
Washington made his 'Atlanta Compromise', convened a conference in 1905. Compared with the conferences which Garvey was to stage later, it was a tame and colourless affair. It
was a gathering of the 'talented tenth'—the Negro intelligent-

[10] W. E. B. DuBois: *Soul of Black Folks*, pp. 42-43 and 58-59.

sia. Nevertheless, it brought together for the first time a group of radical middle-class Negroes, and provided them with a common platform based upon the following eight-point programme drafted by Dr DuBois:

(1) Freedom of speech and criticism.

(2) An unfettered and unsubsidized press.

(3) Manhood suffrage.

(4) The abolition of all caste distinctions based simply on race and colour.

(5) The recognition of the principles of human brotherhood as a practical present creed.

(6) The recognition of the highest and best known training as the monopoly of no class or race.

(7) A belief in the dignity of labour.

(8) United effort to realize these ideals under wise and courageous leadership.

THE NIAGARA MOVEMENT

The 1905 conference gave birth to a new protest organization known as 'The Niagara Movement'. In the following year, another conference was held at Harper's Ferry, the place where John Brown, the greatest American Abolitionist, was hanged for striking a blow against slavery.

In a manifesto, *An Address to the Country*, Dr DuBois, whose fame had by then become nation-wide as the first Negro to challenge Dr Washington's leadership, wrote: 'The men of the Niagara Movement, coming from the toil of a year's hard work, and pausing a moment from the earning of their daily bread, turn toward the nation and again ask in the name of ten million the privilege of a hearing. In the past year the work of the Negro-hater has flourished in the land. Step by step the defenders of the right of American citizens have retreated. The work of stealing the black man's ballot has progressed and the fifty and more representatives of stolen votes still sit in the nation's capital. Discrimination in travel and public accommodation has so spread that some of our weaker brethren are actually afraid to thunder against colour discrimination as such and are simply whispering for ordinary decencies.

'Against this the Niagara Movement eternally protests. We will not be satisfied to take one jot or tittle less than our full manhood rights. We claim for ourselves every single right that belongs to a free-born American, political, civil and social; and until we get these rights we will never cease to protest and assail the ears of America. The battle we wage is not for ourselves alone, but for all true Americans. It is a fight for ideals, lest this, our common fatherland, false to its founding, become in truth the land of the "Thief and the home of the Slave"—a by-word and a hissing among the nations for its sounding pretensions and pitiful accomplishment.

'Never before in the modern age has a great and civilized folk threatened to adopt so cowardly a creed in the treatment of its fellow citizens, born and bred on its soil. Stripped of verbiage and subterfuge and in its naked nastiness, the new American creed says: Fear to let the black men even try to rise lest they become the equals of the white. And this is the land that professes to follow Jesus Christ. The blasphemy of such a course is only matched by its cowardice.

'In detail our demands are clear and unequivocal. First, we would vote; with the right to vote goes everything: Freedom, manhood, the honour of your wives, the chastity of your daughters, the right to work, and the chance to rise, and let no man listen to those who deny this.

'We want full manhood suffrage, and we want it now, henceforth and forever.

'Second. We want discrimination in public accommodation to cease. Separation in railway and street cars, based simply on race and colour, is un-American, undemocratic, and silly. We protest against all such discrimination.

'Third. We claim the right of free men to walk, talk and be with them that wish to be with us. No man has a right to choose another man's friends, and to attempt to do so is an impudent interference with the most fundamental human privilege.

'Fourth. We want the laws enforced against rich as well as poor; against Capitalist as well as Labourer; against white as well as black. We are not more lawless than the white race, we are more often arrested, convicted and mobbed. We want justice even for criminals and outlaws. We want the Constitution of the country enforced. We want Congress to take charge of the Congressional elections. We want the Fourteenth Amendment carried out to the letter and every State disfranchised in Congress which attempts to disfranchise its rightful voters. We want the Fifteenth Amendment enforced and no State allowed to base its franchise simply on colour.

'The failure of the Republican Party in Congress at the session just closed to redeem its pledge of 1904 with reference to suffrage conditions in the South seems a plain, deliberate, and premeditated breach of promise, and stamps that party as guilty of obtaining votes under false pretence.

'Fifth. We want our children educated. The school system in the country districts of the South is a disgrace and in few towns and cities are the Negro schools what they ought to be. We want the national government to step in and wipe out illiteracy in the South. Either the United States will destroy ignorance, or ignorance will destroy the United States.

'And when we call for education we mean real education. We believe in work. We ourselves are workers, but work is not necessarily education. We want our children trained as intelligent beings should be, and we will fight for all time against any proposal to educate black boys and girls simply as servants and underlings, or simply for the use of other people. They have a right to know, to think, to aspire.

'These are some of the chief things which we want. How shall we get them? By voting when we may vote; by persistent, unceasing agitation; by hammering at the truth; by sacrifice and work.

'We do not believe in violence, neither in the despised violence of the raid nor the lauded violence of the soldier, nor the barbarous violence of the mob; but we do believe in John Brown, in that incarnate spirit of justice, that hatred of a lie, that willingness to sacrifice money, reputation, and life itself on the altar of right. And here on the scene of John Brown's martyrdom, we reconsecrate ourselves, our honour, our property to the final emancipation of the race which John Brown died to make free.'

FROM NIAGARA TO N.A.A.C.P.

The Niagara credo fell like a political atomic bomb upon the American nation. Never before had Negroes spoken so defiantly to white folk. The whole nation sat up and took notice. For DuBois and his friends had posed in uncompromising terms a challenge to white America. The white reactionaries, and the conservative Negro leaders, denounced the new movement of challenge from the house tops. But liberal-minded whites applauded the emergence of radical Negro leadership. The 'New Negro' had dethroned 'Uncle Tom'.

Five years after the inauguration of the Niagara Movement—so-called because its first conference was held in Buffalo within sound of the great Niagara Falls—a group of Northern liberals of abolitionist traditions threw in their lot with the 'New Negroes' to form the National Association for the Advancement of Coloured People. The new inter-racial N.A.A.C.P. organization adopted for its programme the aims and objects expounded by the earlier Niagara movement. Since then, it has sought to keep alive the spirit and tradition of the great Abolitionist Movement personified in William Lloyd Garrison. In fact, Garrison's grandson, Oswald Garrison Villard, the distinguished liberal journalist and philanthropist, took an active part in the creation of the N.A.A.C.P. Other white liberals who played a prominent part in the Negro emancipation struggle are John Dewey, the famous philosopher, William Dean Howells, the celebrated man of letters, Charles Edward Russell, Jane Addams, and Mary White Ovington. The N.A.A.C.P. continues to enjoy the support of many of America's best-known liberals and progressive whites. What is even more important, it has become the acknowledged defender and champion of Negro rights in the United States, fighting all forms of segregation through propaganda and publicity, legal and constitutional methods. Black folk owe an everlasting debt of gratitude to Dr DuBois, who, for over fifty years, has stood watch over their cause, and

whose steadfast courage and selfless devotion has helped to
make it possible for the N.A.A.C.P. to reach its present national and international status.

When the N.A.A.C.P. set up headquarters in New York
City in 1910, Dr DuBois resigned his professorship at Atlanta
University and took over the editorship of *The Crisis* as
Director of Publicity and Research for the organization. It
was due to his brilliance as a publicist that *The Crisis* soon
became the most widely read and politically influential journal among Negroes in America. Indeed, its influence extended
far beyond the shores of America, and it was extensively read
in all foreign lands peopled by coloured folk. By the end of
the First World War, the name of William Edward Burghardt
DuBois was highly respected and esteemed among Africans
and peoples of African descent throughout the world.[11] Having contributed to the founding of an effective propaganda
organization through which the struggle for Negro political,
economic and social emancipation in America could be conducted, Dr DuBois turned his attention to the African aspect
of the Colonial Question and the formation of the Pan-
African Congress.

[11] In 1920, Dr DuBois was awarded the Spingarn Medal in recognition of his outstanding contributions to the advancement of his
race. This medal was established in 1914 by the N.A.A.C.P. in
honour of the liberal Boston lawyer, Joel E. Spingarn, a forthright
American fighter for Negro rights. It is awarded annually to the man
or woman of African descent and American citizenship who, during
the year, has attained the highest achievement in any field of human endeavour. In 1924, Dr DuBois was appointed United States
Envoy Extraordinary and Minister Plenipotentiary to Liberia, on the
occasion of the inauguration of President King.

VII

ORIGIN OF PAN-AFRICANISM

Although Dr DuBois was not the first Negro intellectual to have visions of a Pan-African movement, the credit must go to him for giving reality to the dream and conserving its ideals until such time as it found acceptance as the basic ideology of emergent African nationalism. The idea of Pan-Africanism first arose as a manifestation of fraternal solidarity among Africans and peoples of African descent. It was originally conceived by a West Indian barrister, Mr Henry Sylvester-Williams of Trinidad who practised at the English Bar at the end of the nineteenth century, and beginning of the present. It appears that during his undergraduate days and after, Mr Sylvester-Williams established intimate relations with West Africans in Britain and later acted as legal adviser to several African chiefs and other native dignitaries who visited the United Kingdom on political missions to the Colonial Office.

Africa then, as now, was going through crises. The old Bantu nations in Southern Africa were faced with racial conflict. The ancestral lands of these Africans were being threatened by Boers and Britons. The South African Charter Company of Cecil Rhodes was extending its tentacles into Central Africa. Even in West Africa, the Governor of the Gold Coast, Sir William Maxwell, was attempting to turn Fanti tribal lands into Crown property.

To combat the aggressive policies of British imperialists, Mr Sylvester-Williams took the initiative in convening a Pan-

African conference in London in 1900, as a forum of protest against the aggression of white colonizers and, at the same time, to make an appeal to the missionary and abolitionist traditions of the British people to protect the Africans from the depredations of the Empire builders.

'This meeting attracted attention, put the word "Pan-Africanism" in the dictionaries for the first time, and had some thirty delegates, mainly from England and the West Indies, with a few coloured North Americans. The conference was welcomed by the Lord Bishop of London and a promise was obtained from Queen Victoria, through Joseph Chamberlain, not to "overlook the interests and welfare of the native races".'[1]

Unfortunately Mr Sylvester-Williams returned to the West Indies a few years later and died. The Pan-African concept remained dormant until it was revived by Dr DuBois after the First World War. Thanks to his devotion and sacrifice, he gave body and soul to Sylvester-Williams's original idea of Pan-Africanism and broadened its perspective.

Between 1919 and 1945, Dr DuBois was largely responsible for the organization of five international congresses and for formulating their programmes and strategy along the path of non-violent Positive Action. For more than thirty years, Dr DuBois watched over the gradual growth of the Pan-African Congress with the loving affection of a father until such time as his child had found a home on African soil. To-day, Pan-Africanism is becoming part and parcel of emergent African nationalism, serving as a beacon light in the struggle for self-determination, the prerequisite to regional federations of self-governing African communities which may one day evolve into a Pan-African Federation of United States.

Looking back at the age of seventy-two on this phase of his life's work, Dr DuBois tells us of the vision and need that inspired him to revive the Pan-African movement in 1919 and to give it a wider perspective than that conceived by Mr Sylvester-Williams. Eight years before he summoned the revived Pan-African Congress, Dr DuBois had been invited to address the World Races Congress of leading anthropolo-

[1] W. E. B. DuBois: *The World and Africa*, p. 7 (Viking Press, New York).

gists and sociologists in London on the American race problem. 'Contacts of Negroes of different origins and nationality, which I had then and before at other congresses and the Races Congress, were most inspiring. My plans, as they developed had in them nothing spectacular nor revolutionary. If in decades or a century they resulted in such world organization of black men as would oppose a united front to European aggression, that certainly would not have been beyond my dream. But on the other hand, in practical reality, I knew the power and guns of Europe and America, and what I wanted to do was in the face of this power to sit down hand in hand with coloured groups and across the council table to learn of each other, our condition, our aspirations, our chance for concerted thought and action. *Out of this there might come not race war and opposition, but broader cooperation with the white rulers of the world, and a chance for peaceful and accelerated development of black folk.*'[2]

Such is the modesty of the man and his realistic evaluation of the position of Africa in world affairs.

FIRST PAN-AFRICAN CONGRESS

Immediately the armistice was declared, Dr DuBois set out for Paris in the hope of petitioning the victorious Allied Powers to adopt a Charter of Human Rights for Africans as a reward for the services rendered by *black men* on the battlefields of Europe and elsewhere. 'My plan to have Africa in some way voice its complaints to the world during the Peace Conference at Versailles, was an ambitious project conceived in time of war, without political backing and indeed without widespread backing of any kind. Had it not been for one circumstance, it would have utterly failed; and that circumstance was that Black Africa had the right to send from Senegal a member to the French Government.'[3] The black deputy in question was the Senegalese Negro, Monsieur

[2] W. E. B. DuBois: *Dusk of Dawn*, pp. 274-75.
[3] Ibid., p. 261.

Blaise-Diagne, the most influential Colonial politician in France at the time. He was a close friend of Georges Clemenceau, and when France was faced with military disaster in 1917, the Prime Minister appointed Monsieur Diagne Commissaire-General for West Africa. Clemenceau charged him with the responsibility of recruiting African troops for the Western front to help stem the German offensive, at the Battle of the Marne in July 1918. The Afro-American historian, J. A. Rogers, who knew the African deputy quite intimately, says that 'Diagne accepted the post for two reasons. He knew that of the exploiting white powers in Africa, France showed the least colour prejudice; and he felt that if the blacks came to the rescue of France it would make her more liberal.

'But when he arrived in Africa he ran full tilt against colour prejudice. The white Governor of Senegal resented the holding of such a high post by a Negro. Instead of coming to receive him in person, as the occasion demanded, the Governor sent a minor official with a small detachment of black troops to do the honours. Diagne did not mind the slight to himself but feeling that it was the dignity of France, itself, that was being slighted, refused to go ashore, and sent a telegram to Clemenceau telling what had happened. Clemenceau replied with a sharp message to the Governor bidding him receive Diagne with full military honours or resign.

'Diagne on landing, plunged into the jungle and into the midst of the hostile blacks, with only a few friends. He soon won them over. Eighty thousand answered the call, more than twice the number Clemenceau had asked for. All had been done within three months and without friction. Clemenceau was overjoyed.[4]

'When Diagne returned to France, Clemenceau offered him the Legion of Honour. Diagne, declining, said that he had only done his duty and that that was reward enough. Such a thing was unheard of, the Legion of Honour being a highly

[4] 'During the first year of the war 70,000 black troops were raised in French West Africa. By 1918 Black Africa had furnished France 680,000 soldiers and 238,000 labourers in all. We have seen what we have never seen before, what enormously valuable material lay in the Black Continent,' declared General Smuts. G.P.

sought decoration. Even President Poincaré himself could not shake Diagne's determination to accept no reward . . . Diagne was not without his critics, some of whom were sincere and others motivated by jealousy. He was called by some a traitor for having brought the Africans to fight for France and a tool of the rich white colonial interests. Others, however, praised him as having done more than any other to strengthen the position of coloured peoples in the French Empire.[5]

'After the war, the West African deputy emerged as a leading parliamentarian and was made Under Secretary of State for Colonial Affairs in 1931. Diagne was one of the most effective speakers in parliament. His delivery was without pose; he spoke clearly and to the point in a French that was worthy of a member of the Academy. He was extremely popular in West Africa, so popular in fact, that many predicted he might become another Somory or Mahmadou Lamine.[6] In 1918, he was too ill to return to Senegal for elections. Nevertheless, he polled 7,343 votes of 8,000 cast in his district. The three greatest things in life, he once said, were Dignity, Love and Justice.'[7]

This was the African who came to the rescue of DuBois and got Clemenceau's permission to hold the first Pan-African Congress in Paris during the sitting of the Peace Conference. 'Don't advertise it,' said the Prime Minister to Diagne, 'but go ahead.'[8]

Paris at that time was flooded with American newspaper correspondents and reports of the proposed Congress got out before the delegates could assemble. The American officials in President Wilson's entourage were afraid that the Congress might discuss, among other things, the lynching of Negroes in the United States and the treatment of Afro-American

[5] J. A. Rogers: World's Great Men of Colour, Vol. II, pp. 416-19.

[6] Somory Toureh, a West African Mohammedan chieftain called the 'Napoleon of the Sudan', led guerilla warfare against the French in the territory of the Niger from 1881 until his surrender in 1898. Among his adversaries were Colonels Joffre and Gallieni, later raised to the dignity of Marshals of France.

[7] Ibid., p. 419.

[8] W. E. B. DuBois: The World and Africa, p. 10.

troops in France. The American statesmen had good reason to be alarmed, for apart from maintaining racial segregation between black and white troops serving under the Stars and Stripes, the U.S. Army authorities in France tried to impose their racial prejudices on the French people. Dr DuBois had exposed this attempt in *The Crisis* magazine which he then edited. He had secured a copy of a circular entitled *Secret Information Concerning Black American Troops*, which had been issued by U.S. Army authorities in Paris instructing French military missions how they should deal with Negro troops. There would be no 'intimacy between French officers and black officers,' it stated. 'We may be courteous and amiable with these last, but we cannot deal with them on the same plane as with the white American officers without deeply wounding the latter. We must not eat with them, must not shake hands or seek to talk or meet with them outside the requirements of military service.'

The directive also stated that 'We must not commend too highly the black American troops, particularly in the presence of (white) Americans. It is all right to recognize their good qualities and their services, but only in moderate terms, strictly in keeping with the truth . . .

'Make a point of keeping the native cantonment population from "spoiling" the Negroes. White Americans,' the document added, 'become greatly incensed at any public expression of intimacy between white women and black men.'[9]

To assure the American Peace Delegation that the Pan-African Congress had no intention of concerning itself primarily with the American Negro problem, which was being handled in the United States by the N.A.A.C.P., DuBois tried to get an interview with President Wilson, but only got as far as seeing his chief adviser, Colonel Edward House, 'who was sympathetic, but non-committal'.

On the other hand, Acting Secretary of State Polk assured the American people that 'the State Department had been officially advised by the French Government that no such conference would be held'. Negro delegates from America desiring to attend were refused passports.

[9] James Weldon Johnson: *Black Manhattan*, p. 245.

Undeterred by the unco-operative attitude of the American Government, DuBois, backed by Diagne, proceeded with the preparation of the Congress. It was a race against time, for at any moment the U.S. officials in Paris might have protested to the French Government against this, and have the Congress banned. To guard against this, DuBois secretly contacted a number of prominent Africans, West Indians and other colonials then in Paris and by the time the Congress convened, there was quite a representative gathering of black folk. There were fifty-seven representatives from various African colonies, the West Indies, and the United States. Although a modest gathering, it aroused considerable interest among the international delegations to the Peace Conference at Versailles, especially those with interests in Africa.

The Pan-African Congress was described by the Paris correspondent of the *New York Evening Globe* as 'the first assembly of its kind in history, and has for its object the drafting of an appeal to the Peace Conference to give the Negro race of Africa a chance to develop unhindered by other races. Seated at long green tables in the council room today were Negroes in the trim uniform of American Army officers, other American coloured men in frock coats or business suits, polished French Negroes who hold public offices, Senegalese who sit in the French Chamber of Deputies . . .' .

PETITION TO LEAGUE OF NATIONS

As the 'Father' of Pan-Africanism, it devolved upon Dr DuBois to make the principal report and draft the main resolution. After the various colonial representatives had spoken on the economic, political and social problems in their respective countries, the Congress unanimously adopted a petition requesting the victorious Allied Powers to place the former German African colonies of Togoland, Cameroons, South-West Africa, and Tanganyika under international supervision, to be held in trust for the inhabitants as future self-governing countries. This proposal, in a much diluted form, was subsequently embodied in the Mandates System of the

League of Nations, from which natives of the territories concerned were excluded. The Pan-African Congress also adopted a resolution embodying the following demands:

(a) That the Allied and Associated Powers establish a code of law for the international protection of the natives of Africa, similar to the proposed international code for labour.

(b) That the League of Nations establish a permanent Bureau charged with the special duty of overseeing the application of these laws to the political, social and economic welfare of the natives.

(c) The Negroes of the world demand that hereafter the natives of Africa and the peoples of African descent be governed according to the following principles:

   (i) *The Land.* The land and its natural resources shall be held in trust for the natives and at all times they shall have effective ownership of as much land as they can profitably develop.

   (ii) *Capital.* The investment of capital and granting of concessions shall be so regulated as to prevent the exploitation of the natives and the exhaustion of the natural wealth of the country. Concessions shall always be limited in time and subject to state control. The growing social needs of the natives must be regarded and the profits taxed for social and material benefit of the natives.

   (iii) *Labour.* Slavery and corporal punishment shall be abolished and forced labour except in punishment of crime; and the general conditions of labour shall be prescribed and regulated by the State.

   (iv) *Education.* It shall be the right of every native child to learn to read and write his own language, and the language of the trustee nation, at public expense, and to be given technical instruction in some branch of industry. The State shall also educate as large a number of natives as possible in higher technical and cultural training and maintain a corps of native teachers.

(v) *The State*. The natives of Africa must have the right to participate in the Government as fast as their development permits, in conformity with the principle that the Government exists for the natives, and not the natives for the Government. They shall at once be allowed to participate in local and tribal government, according to ancient usage, and this participation shall gradually extend, as education and experience proceed to the higher offices of state; to the end that, in time, Africa is ruled by consent of the Africans . . . whenever it is proven that African natives are not receiving just treatment at the hands of any State or that any State deliberately excludes its civilized citizens or subjects of Negro descent from its body politic and culture, it shall be the duty of the League of Nations to bring the matter to the notice of the civilized world.

These were the demands voiced by Africans as far back as 1919. Where was the Communist Movement then?

POST-WAR VIOLENCE IN U.S.A.

Having projected his Pan-African programme into the realm of international politics, Dr DuBois returned to America, from where he hoped to build a real organization capable of stimulating the national aspirations of the natives of Africa, and of securing wider support for the activities of the Congress. Unfortunately, he did not get the support he had expected from American Negro leaders, and had to pursue his plans almost single-handed.

The lukewarmness of the Afro-American leaders was not due to any lack of sympathy with the peoples of Africa. The years immediately after the First World War witnessed widespread violence against the coloured people in the Southern States of America and because of this, all the time, energy, and financial resources of the N.A.A.C.P., which was just about ten years old, were being used to combat the reaction and violence let loose against the defenceless Southern blacks.

'The facts concerning the year 1919 are almost unbeliev-able as one looks back upon them today,' wrote Dr DuBois. 'During that year seventy-six Negroes were lynched, of whom one was a woman, and eleven were soldiers; of these, fourteen were publicly burned, eleven of them being burned alive.

'That year there were race riots large and small in twenty-six American cities, including thirty-eight killed in a Chicago riot of August; from twenty-five to fifty in Philipps County, Arkansas; and six killed in Washington. For a day, the city of Washington in July 1919 was actually in the hands of a black mob fighting against the aggression of whites with hand grenades . . . in Arkansas, despite the slaughter of Negroes, ninety-four other victims were arrested; twelve were con-demned to death, and eighty sentenced to imprisonment. On top of that, not only did the agitation for residential segrega-tion increase, but there was an open revival of the Ku-Klux-Klan. In North Georgia a reign of terror began.' Later investigation revealed that 'in some counties the Negro is being driven out as though he was a wild animal; in others he is being held as a slave; in others no Negroes remain.'[10]

This was the position confronting coloured Americans at the time DuBois returned home from Paris. He immediately threw himself into the struggle. He was then fifty-one, at the height of his intellectual powers. His book *The Negro*, pub-lished in the Home University Library five years before this outbreak of mob violence had definitely established his repu-tation as one of the foremost sociologists in America. Dr DuBois's name was a household one among Negro intellec-tuals. For he was the first scholar of his race to have scien-tifically exposed the myth of 'white supremacy' and the economic facts behind European imperialism in Africa. Fur-thermore, his militant leadership during the war years in agitating for the training of black officers in the U.S. Army had enhanced his prestige.

As soon as the post-war racial tension subsided, DuBois gathered around him a small group of internationally minded

[10] W. E. B. DuBois: *Dusk of Dawn*, pp. 264-65.

Negro men and women and planned for a more representative Pan-African Congress.

He corresponded with Negroes in all parts of Africa and in other parts of the world and finally arranged for a Congress to meet in London, Brussels, and Paris in August and September, 1921.

But again he got little support from his white liberal and socialist friends and coloured colleagues. Explaining the reasons for this, DuBois writes: 'I found the board of directors of the N.A.A.C.P. not particularly interested. The older liberalism among the white people did not envisage Africa and coloured peoples of the world. They were interested in America and securing American citizens of all and any colour, their rights. They had no schemes for internationalism in race problems and to many of them it seemed quixotic to undertake anything of the sort. Then too there were coloured members who had inherited the fierce repugnance toward anything African, which was the natural result of the older colonization schemes, where efforts at assisted and even forcible expatriation of American Negroes had always included Africa. Negroes were bitterly opposed because such schemes were at bottom an effort to make slavery in the United States more secure and to get rid of the free Negroes. Beyond this they felt themselves Americans, not Africans. They resented and feared any coupling with Africa.'[11]

Determined not to allow the enthusiasm aroused among colonial peoples since the first Congress in Paris to dissipate, he decided to bear the financial expense of preparing for a second Congress. This was done at great personal sacrifice, for although a prolific writer, DuBois has never been a rich man.

While preparations were being made, Marcus Garvey burst upon the American scene by launching his Back to Africa Movement with fanfare and trumpets at a spectacular convention in New York City. The American Negro was caught between two irreconcilable programmes: that of the N.A.A.C.P., which stood for 'equal rights for blacks in America', and that of the U.N.I.A., which advocated mass migration

[11] Ibid., p. 275.

back to Africa on the ground that Negroes would never get racial equality in the United States.

Pan-Africanism stood midway between these two main conflicting currents. As one of the leaders of the N.A.A.C.P., DuBois naturally opposed Garvey's utopianism. He, like most American Negroes, considered America to be their true native land. But unlike his N.A.A.C.P. colleagues, he was equally interested in helping forward the emancipation of Africa. Where DuBois differed from Garvey was in his conception of the Pan-African movement as an aid *to the promotion of national self-determination among Africans under African leadership, for the benefit of Africans themselves.* Marcus Garvey, on the other hand, looked upon Africa as a place for colonizing Western Negroes under his personal domination. As a result, there was never any basis for collaboration between Garvey and DuBois, who, in their respective spheres, were then the two outstanding Negro leaders in the Western Hemisphere.

Marcus Garvey always had one great advantage over Dr DuBois, which DuBois himself admits. Garvey's 'was a people's movement rather than a movement of intellectuals . . . Its weakness lay in its demagogic leadership, poor finance, intemperate propaganda, and the natural apprehension it aroused among the colonial powers'.[12] The European Powers had good reason to be worried. For during the war, and after the end of hostilities in Europe, a number of spontaneous revolts had occurred in the French West African colonies and the Belgian Congo. About the same time, a Gold Coast barrister, Mr Joseph Casely Hayford, formed the West African National Congress to voice the united political aspirations of the Negro middle-class intellectuals in the four British colonies of Gambia, Sierra Leone, Gold Coast and Nigeria. The W.A.N.C. sent a delegation to England in 1920 to present the demands of the educated Africans for constitutional and other reforms to Lord Milner, the Secretary of State for Colonies.

Although Pan-Africanism adopted more Fabian-like methods than those employed by Garveyism, as it began to

[12] W. E. B. DuBois: *The World and Africa*, p. 236.

shows that 'of the hundred and thirteen delegates to this Congress, forty-one were from Africa, thirty-five from the United States, twenty-four represented Negroes living in Europe, and seven were from the West Indies. They came for the most part, but not in all cases, as individuals, and seldom as the representatives of organizations or groups.

The Congress was addressed by a number of distinguished British colonial experts of socialist persuasion, among them Sir Sydney Olivier, later Lord Olivier, a former Governor of Jamaica; and Dr Norman Leys, a leading authority on Kenya.

Dr DuBois delivered the presidential address, in which he reviewed the problems confronting the Africans, and the solutions that should be applied by the governing Powers. At the closing session, the delegates endorsed a *Declaration To The World*, drafted by the president. It stated that: 'The absolute equality of races, physical, political, and social, is the founding stone of world and human advancement. No one denies great differences of gift, capacity, and attainment among individuals of all races, but the voice of science, religion, and practical politics is one in denying the God-appointed existence of super-races or of races naturally and inevitably and eternally inferior. That in the vast range of time, one group should in its industrial technique, or social organization, or spiritual vision, lag a few hundred years behind another, or forge fitfully ahead, or come to differ decidedly in thought, deed, and ideal, is proof of the essential richness and variety of human nature, rather than proof of the co-existence of demi-gods and apes in human form. The doctrine of racial equality does not interfere with individual liberty; rather it fulfils it. And of all the various criteria of which masses of men have in the past been prejudiced and classified, that of colour of skin and the texture of the hair is surely the most adventitious and idiotic . . .

'The beginning of wisdom in inter-racial contact is the establishment of political institutions among suppressed peoples. The habit of democracy must be made to encircle the earth. Despite the attempts to prove that its practice is the secret and divine gift of a few, no habit is more natural or more widespread among primitive people, or more easily capable of development among masses. Local self-government with a minimum of help and oversight can be established tomorrow in Asia, in Africa, America, and the isles of the sea. It will in many instances need general control and guidance, but it will fail only when that guidance seeks ignorantly and consciously its own selfish ends and not the people's liberty and good.

'Surely in the twentieth century of the Prince of Peace, in the millennium of Mohammed, and in the mightiest Age of Human Reason, there can be found in the civilized world enough of altruism, learning, and benevolence to develop native institutions, whose one aim is not profit and power for the few . . . What then do those demand who see these evils of the colour line and racial discrimination, and who believe in the divine right of suppressed and backward people to learn and aspire and be free?

'The Negro race through their thinking intelligentsia demand:

(1) The recognition of civilized men as civilized, despite their race or colour.

(2) Local self-government for backward groups, deliberately rising as experience and knowledge grow to complete self-government under the limitation of self-governed world.

(3) Education in self-knowledge, in scientific truth, and in industrial technique, undivorced from the art of beauty.

(4) Freedom in their own religion and social customs and with the right to be different and non-conformist.

(5) Co-operation with the rest of the world in government, industry, and art on the basis of justice, freedom and peace.

(6) The return of Negroes to their land and its natural fruits and defence against the unrestricted greed of invested capital.

(7) The establishment under the League of Nations of an international institution for study of the Negro problems.

(8) The establishment of an international section of the Labour Bureau of the League of Nations, charged with the protection of native labour.

'In some such words and thoughts as these we seek to express our will and ideal, and the end of our untiring effort. To our aid we call all men of the earth who love justice and mercy. Out of the depths we have cried unto the deaf and dumb masters of the world. Out of the depths we cry to our sleeping souls. The answer is written in the stars'.[14]

Just imagine how things might have been if this appeal and others made over a quarter of a century ago, had been heard and responded to by Britain and other Colonial Powers. There would not today be the bloodshed, the racial hatred, and bitterness and frustration sweeping over Africa. Instead, there could have been genuine friendship and co-operation between white and black for the common benefit of both races. But it is not too late to save Africa from complete disaster, providing the cries of the blacks 'unto the deaf and dumb masters of the world' are heeded while there is yet time. The writing is on the wall for all to read. The future of Africa is in the lap of the gods!

When the Congress transferred itself to Brussels for its second session, it ran into trouble. Belgian Governments, quite regardless of their political complexion—Conservative, Liberal or Socialist—have always been less tolerant than the British Colonial Office of the political aspirations of subject peoples. Therefore, it did not require much prompting from the press to incite the Belgian Government against African nationalism which then, as now, was ascribed to Moscow's inspiration. Although in 1921 the Bolsheviks, as is well known, were still fighting bitterly for their own existence. Russian Communists had little thought to spare for Negroes.

It must be remembered that although Belgium is a small country it is rich, thanks to colonial exploitation. Many of Belgium's economic and material interests centre in Africa, in the Belgian Congo. Any political consciousness among the natives might result in interference with the sources from which so many Belgian capitalists draw their prosperity.

Voicing these fears, the *Neptune*, one of the leading Brussels papers, denounced the Pan-African Congress as 'an agency of Moscow and the cause of native unrest in the

[14] W. E. B. DuBois, *The World and Africa*, pp. 238-39.

Congo'. It called upon the Government to forbid the conference to meet in Brussels. In a leading article on June 14, 1921, it stated *inter alia* 'announcement has been made . . . of a Pan-African Congress organized at the instigation of the National Association for the Advancement of Coloured People of New York. It is interesting to note that this association is directed by personages who it is said in the United States have received remuneration from Moscow (Bolsheviks). The association has already organized its propaganda in the lower Congo, and we must not be astonished if some day it causes grave difficulties in the Negro village of Kinshasa, composed of all the ne'er-do-wells of the various tribes of the colony aside from some hundreds of labourers.'

That is the kind of ill-informed, anti-Negro propaganda still common in European and American imperialist circles even today. These reactionaries ascribe to the Communists the inspiration for everything Africans and other colonial peoples ever try to do to improve their status. And such intolerance has done more than all the Communist propaganda in the world to create in the minds of Africans and other Colonials the idea that the Communists are the only white people in the world who are sympathetic to their legitimate aspirations. For, as we have shown above, the Pan-African movement, like the N.A.A.C.P. and Garvey's U.N.I.A.— whatever people may think about them—have absolutely no connection officially or otherwise with Moscow. In fact, the Communists, as we shall describe later, looked upon all these Negro organizations as manifestations of *petit-bourgeois nationalism*, to be fought and destroyed before Communism could ever hope to make inroads in Africa or win the allegiance of the Negro masses in America to the cause of the 'Proletarian Revolution' and the victory of 'World Communism'.

To return to Brussels. Despite the hostility of the Belgian Press and certain imperialists with interests in the Congo, the police allowed the Congress to assemble. The declaration and resolutions adopted at the London session were endorsed and the Congress moved on to Paris for its third and closing session. It was presided over by Monsieur Blaise Diagne and attracted a large and representative gathering from the French Colonial Empire.

Apart from reiterating its demands for colonial reforms, the Congress elected a delegation under the chairmanship of Dr DuBois to present a petition to the Mandates Commission of the League of Nations. The delegation was introduced by the distinguished Negro writer and diplomatist, Dr Dantes Bellegarde, who was then the Haitian Ambassador to France and his country's permanent representative at the League of Nations Assembly.

The petition stated that: 'The Second Pan-African Congress wishes to suggest that the spirit of the world moves towards self-government as the ultimate aim of all men and nations and that consequently the mandated areas, being peopled as they are so largely by black folk, have a right to ask that men of Negro descent, properly fitted in character and training, be appointed a member of the Mandates Commission as soon as a vacancy occurs.[15]

'The Second Pan-African Congress desires most earnestly and emphatically to ask the good offices and careful attention of the League of Nations to the condition of civilized persons of Negro descent throughout the world. Consciously and subconsciously there is in the world today a widespread and growing feeling that it is permissible to treat civilized men as uncivilized if they are coloured and more especially of Negro descent. The result of this attitude and many consequent laws, customs and conventions, is that a bitter feeling of resentment, personal insult and despair, is widespread in the world among those very persons whose rise is the hope of the Negro race. We are fully aware that the League of Nations has little, if any, direct power to adjust these matters, but it has the vast moral power of public world opinion and of a body conceived to promote peace and justice among men. For this reason we ask and urge that the League of Nations take a firm stand on the absolute equality of races and that it suggest to the colonial powers connected with the League of Nations to form an international institute for the study of

---

[15] The Mandates Commission consisted of ten Europeans, appointed by the Council of the League, five of whom belonged to non-mandatory countries. G.P.

the Negro problem, and for the evolution and protection of the Negro race.'

MASSACRE OF THE HOTTENTOTS

Even before this petition could be considered by the Mandates Commission, the South African Government made it clear that blacks must not expect to get justice from the whites in the Union. In 1922, General Smuts, one of the very founders of the League of Nations and the main architect of the Mandates system, approved the bombing of the Bondelswarts, a defenceless tribe in South-West Africa, the former German colony which the League of Nations had entrusted to the Government of South Africa as a mandated territory.

The history of this massacre may be summed up as follows: 'The Bondel Hottentots were a poverty-stricken tribe living in a reserve in the southern part of the territory. They saw no advantage in working for local white farmers, who being ill-off themselves could neither feed, clothe nor pay them. A law, passed according to the Administrator's statement, in order to force the natives to work, imposed a prohibitive tax on the hunting dogs upon whose quarry the Hottentots managed to live. They were already on the worst possible terms with the local police, and open friction occurred when a native notable, one Abraham Morris, returned in good faith but without authorization from the Cape Colony, and was summoned to be arrested. The Hottentots refused to surrender Morris and apparently believing that the threats of the police meant that the white men intended to destroy them went into laager on a rock-covered hill at a place called Guruchas. By this time, the "Native war" scare was running hard through the country; the white population was terrified. The local police and magistrate made some efforts to communicate with the Bondels, who declared that they did not mean to fight, but refused to surrender Morris and the leaders unless amnesty was promised. Mr Hofmeyer, the Administrator of the territory, arrived, collected volunteers from the whites, and sent for aeroplanes from the nearest aerodrome. His forces surrounded the hill where the Bondels were encamped with their women and children. The hill was bombed by aeroplanes from three o'clock till dark. In the night a party of the Hottentots who were completely demoralised by this, to them, new and appalling form of attack, escaped from the camp. They were afterwards caught and completely defeated. The surviving women and children were taken away from Guruchas and fed from the captured stock of their tribe. After some time when the fighting was over they were allowed to return to their reserve. Abraham Morris was killed. Those of the leaders left alive were charged with high treason, and imprisoned, though the chief of them, Jacobus Christian, was released in 1924'.[16]

What General Smuts started in 1922 under the League of Nations, the British Colonial Secretary, Mr Oliver Lyttelton (now Lord Chandos), was still carrying on in 1954 against the Kikuyu adherents of Mau Mau in Kenya. It is this sort of legalized terrorism perpetrated in Africa in the name of 'law and order' that the Pan-African Congress was established to expose and combat.

[16] Freda White: *Mandates*, pp. 136-37.

VIII

GROWTH OF PAN-AFRICANISM

After the second Pan-African Congress, Dr DuBois conceived the idea of establishing a permanent secretariat in order to maintain regular contact between the representatives who had attended the various conferences. He hoped that in so doing the Pan-African idea would be kept alive until such time as political parties emerged and nationalism took deeper roots in African soil.

For though two Congresses had stimulated a feeling of brotherhood between Africans at home and abroad, the idea of Pan-Africanism was still largely confined to a small circle of colonial intellectuals and politically-minded Negroes on both sides of the Atlantic. Ideologically, DuBois was always ahead of his contemporaries. We saw how he had taken the initiative in spear-heading the 'Niagara' revolt of Negro radicals against the conservatives who supported Booker T. Washington's 'Atlanta Compromise' programme on Negro rights in America. Out of this revolt came the N.A.A.C.P., the largest and most influential Afro-American civil rights organization in the United States. Similarly, he was the first American Negro leader to realize the significance of the colonial liberation movements as part of the struggle of the darker races of Asia and Africa and the importance of fostering closer co-operation between native-born Africans and peoples of African descent in the Western Hemisphere.

Unfortunately, Dr DuBois was unable to carry out his organizational plans until the Fifth Pan-African Congress, which took place in Manchester, England, in 1945, immediately after the end of the Second World War. Meanwhile, he continued to assume full responsibility for keeping the movement alive. In the intervening years, two more Pan-African Congresses were held. The third one took place in London and Lisbon, and the fourth in New York. They corresponded with the meteoric rise and decline of Garvey's Back to Africa Movement.

COLLAPSE OF BLACK ZIONISM

Until the dramatic collapse of Black Zionism, Pan-Africanism was on the defensive. Garvey appealed to the Negro's emotions; DuBois to his intellect. Garvey's bombastic broadsides against the white man, coupled with his garish showmanship, had an hypnotic effect upon the unlettered, unsophisticated West Indian immigrants and Southern Negroes. Thousands of these blacks had flocked into the northern and eastern cities of America during the First World War as workers in the industries engaged in war production. DuBois could not compete with Garvey's appeal to these under-privileged people. He was too intelligent, too honest to play on their ignorance of the real situation in Africa. From his sociological and historical studies he knew so well that 'American Negroes have always feared with perfect fear their eventual expulsion from America. They have been willing to submit to caste rather than face this. The reasons have been varied, but today they are clear. Negroes have no Zion. There is no place where they could go today and not be subject to worse caste and greater disabilities at the hands of the dominant white imperialistic world than they suffer here today.'[1]

On the other hand, Garvey was especially contemptuous of DuBois and other leaders of the N.A.A.C.P. On one occasion the leader of Black Zionism declared that: 'The N.A.A.C.P. wants us all to become white by amalgamation, but they are not honest enough to come out with the truth. To be a Negro is no disgrace, but an honour, and we of the

[1] W. E. B. DuBois: *Dusk of Dawn*, pp. 305-6.

U.N.I.A. do not want to become white . . . We are proud
and honourable. We love our race and respect and adore our
mothers.' That was the kind of demagogic racialism Garvey
fed his disciples upon. However, it required more than dema-
gogy to drive the imperialists out of Africa. That is what
Garvey never seemed to have understood, so that, in spite of
the tremendous prestige and mass support he enjoyed during
the early period of his career and the millions of dollars he
collected from the Negro masses, nothing was left to Black
Zionism when he came up against the stern realities of the
African situation. Although less spectacular, and without the
popular mass backing and financial resources of Garveyism,
Pan-Africanism has survived the Back to Africa Movement.
But the survival has not been easy.

THIRD PAN-AFRICAN CONGRESS

The Pan-African Congress has had to face, not only the
opposition of Garveyism and the hostility of the imperialists,
but the vilification and machinations of the Communists. In
a later chapter we shall deal more fully with the opportunism
of the American Communists in relation to the U.N.I.A., the
N.A.A.C.P. and the Pan-African Congress—all of which they
tried to discredit as '*petit-bourgeois* black Nationalism' block-
ing the dissemination of Communist influence among the
Negroes. The attitude of most white Communists towards
Negro organizations has been one of contempt. If they cannot control them, they seek their destruction by infiltration.

Convinced of the need for Africans to control their own
affairs and mould their destiny in accordance with their legitimate needs and aspirations, while at the same time welcom-
ing the co-operation of all men of goodwill, the Third Pan-
African Congress met in London in the summer of 1923.
Attendance was even smaller than on the previous occasions.
But it enjoyed enough sympathy among British Socialists to
secure the attendance of Lord Olivier, Professor Harold Laski
and Mr H. G. Wells, who addressed the sessions. They all
assured the delegates of the fellowship and goodwill of the

British Labour Movement to the aspirations of the Negro peoples.

Mr J. Ramsay MacDonald, the Chairman of the Labour Party, sent greetings to the Congress and wrote a letter to Dr DuBois saying: 'Anything I can do to advance the cause of your people on your recommendation, I shall always do gladly'. Unfortunately, Mr MacDonald did not do as much as the Africans had expected of him when he became Prime Minister in the following year. Nevertheless, the Congress welcomed his gesture of goodwill for it marked official recognition of the justice of the black man's cause. The Congress resolutions reiterated its earlier demands and asked for Africans:

(1) A voice in their own governments.

(2) The right of access to land and its resources.

(3) Trial by juries of their peers under established process of law.

(4) Free elementary education for all; broad training in modern industrial technique; and higher training for selected talent.

(5) The development of Africa for the benefit of Africans, and not merely for the profit of Europeans.

(6) The abolition of the slave trade and the liquor traffic.

(7) World disarmament and the abolition of war; but failing this, and as long as white folk bear arms against black folk, the right of blacks to bear arms in their own defence.

(8) The organization of commerce and industry so as to make the main objects of capital and labour the welfare of the many rather than the enriching of the few.

The Manifesto concluded: 'In fine, we ask in all the world, that black folk be treated as men. We can see no other road to peace and progress. What more paradoxical figure today confronts the world than the official head of a great South African State striving blindly to build peace and goodwill in Europe by standing on the necks and hearts of millions of black Africans?'[2]

[2] This was General Jan Christian Smuts, who the British Press held up to their readers as one of the greatest liberal and democratic statesmen of the twentieth century.

Recalling the exposure of forced labour and slavery in Portuguese colonies made by the well-known English Quaker humanitarians, Joseph Burtt and William Cadbury, the liberal journalist and author, Mr Henry W. Nevinson, and the missionary, Rev John, afterwards, Sir John Harris, Secretary of the Anti-Slavery Society, Dr DuBois decided to hold the second session of the Congress in Lisbon. He hoped that this gesture would strengthen the agitation of a small group of Portuguese African intellectuals then living in Lisbon to achieve some measures of reform in the Portuguese colonies, especially Angola and the cocoa islands of Sao Thomé and Principe.

The Lisbon session was attended by representatives of eleven countries. The arrangements were carried out very effectively by the *Liga Africana*, described in the Congress report as 'an actual federation of all the indigenous associations scattered throughout the five provinces of Portuguese Africa and representing several million individuals . . . This *Liga Africana* which functions in Lisbon in the very heart of Portugal, so to speak, has a commission from all the other native organizations and knows how to express to the Government in no ambiguous terms but in a highly dignified manner all that should be said to avoid injustice or bring about the repeal of harsh laws. That is why the *Liga Africana* of Lisbon is the director of the Portuguese African movement, but not only in the good sense of the word, but without making any appeal to violence and without leaving constitutional limits.'[3]

Two former Colonial Ministers of Portugal addressed the Congress and promised to use their influence in getting their Government to abolish conscript labour and other much overdue reforms in the African colonies. Unfortunately, despite

[3] Consult: A *Modern Slavery* by H. W. Nevinson and *Labour in Portuguese West Africa* by William Cadbury. In her book *Slavery*, Lady Kathleen Simon says that 'The late Lord Cromer, who watched the development of Portuguese Africa more closely than most British administrators, came to the definite conclusion that the system of so-called "contract labour" in Portuguese Africa was indistinguishable from slavery, and he frequently described the condition of the contract labourers as that of slaves, and the system under which these contract labourers were obtained and held to the plantations as one of slavery', pp. 142-43.

many new decrees issued in Lisbon since then, forced labour
conditions in Angola, Mozambique and Sao Thomé are still
most deplorable.

FOURTH PAN-AFRICAN CONGRESS

Before the Fourth Pan-African Congress took place in 1927,
several events occurred which were destined to have far-
reaching effect both upon the future development of the
Pan-African movement and Anglo-African relations in West
Africa.

First, Garvey's Black Zionism collapsed even before the
Negro Moses set foot in the Promised Land of Africa. Second,
the British Government permitted Prempeh I, the Asan-
tehene, or over-lord of the Ashanti tribes, to return to the
Gold Coast in 1924. He had been exiled to the Seychelles
Island since 1900. Four years before Prempeh's homecoming,
Mr J. E. Casely Hayford and other members of the West
African National Congress delegation to London had sup-
ported the petition of the Ashanti people to allow their king
to return home, a sentiment also endorsed by the Pan-African
Congress.

Having broken the power of the Ashantis, the decision of
the British Government to allow Prempeh's return in 1924
served to heal a deep national wound in the hearts of the
people and provided a favourable psychological climate for
closer co-operation between them and their British rulers.
Furthermore, in the following year, the Colonial Office made
a significant political gesture to the West African politically-
minded middle classes by agreeing to reform the constitutions
by the 'recognition for the first time in the history of British
tropical Africa of the elective principle as far as Africans are
concerned'.[4]

While the immediate consequence was not of great importance in its effect upon political relationship between Europeans and Africans in the governments of West Africa, the

[4] R. L. Buell: *The Native Problem in Africa*, Vol. I, p. 741.

introduction of the elective principle opened a new perspective and brought the educated African commoners into the legislatures as spokesmen of the rising urban middle class of professionals, business men and traders.

The right of Africans everywhere to have a voice in their government had always been one of the basic demands of the Pan-African Congress. Now it was being recognized by the British in a modest way, a fact commented upon by Chief Amoah II of the Gold Coast and other representatives from West Africa who attended the Fourth Pan-African Congress in New York in 1927. There were 208 delegates from 22 States and 10 foreign countries at that Congress. The majority of the American delegates were the representatives of various women's organizations.

While these Negro women had no intention of voluntarily going back to Africa, they, like so many of their menfolk, took a lively interest in the land of their ancestors. Their sympathies found expression in generous contributions and social welfare work on behalf of various American Negro Methodist and Baptist denominations and churches carrying out medical, educational and evangelical work among native tribes in Africa. In the hope of securing their financial support, Dr DuBois planned to convene a conference on African soil for the first time, but disappointment soon awaited him. Tunis in North Africa was selected as the proposed meeting place because of its favourable position along the lines of communication between the United States and Europe, as well as East, West and South Africa. But as soon as the French authorities of the Protectorate of Tunisia got news of the conference, Dr DuBois was 'very politely but firmly informed that the Congress could take place at Marseilles or any French city, but not in Africa'.

Thus vetoed by the French authorities in North Africa, alternative plans had hurriedly to be made to hold the Congress outside Africa. But before these new plans got under way, the United States was suddenly plunged into the greatest financial crisis and economic depression the country has ever faced. Overnight, the middle-class Negroes, to whom Dr DuBois was looking for financial contributions to meet the expenses of the proposed fifth Congress stood in ruin. The life

savings of thousands of upper class Negroes completely dis-
appeared. Many others found themselves out of jobs. For the
Negro is always the first to be fired in times of depression
while the last to be hired in periods of prosperity. Such is
their precarious position in American society. The thirties will
always be remembered by them as a period of tragedy.

For the Pan-African Congress, the mass unemployment
meant a complete falling away of income, and Dr DuBois had
to abandon all hope of holding another conference until
better times returned.

The economic crisis in America also had its repercussions
in West Africa. The price of cocoa and other primary products fell to rock bottom. And throughout the world, men's
minds were turning to the danger of war which seemed to be
gathering over Europe. With the rise of Nazism to power in
Germany, Hitler's rape of Austria and Czechoslovakia,
Franco's civil war in Spain and, most important as far as
Africans were concerned, Mussolini's invasion of Ethiopia, Negroes were being forced to take an increasing interest in international affairs. The world had become one.

INTERNATIONAL AFRICAN FRIENDS OF
ABYSSINIA

Coinciding with Mussolini's preparations for war in Ethi-
opia, two political missions from the Gold Coast arrived in
England. One of them represented the tribal chiefs and unofficial members of the Legislative Council headed by Nana
Sir Ofori-Atta, a leading Paramount Chief. The other consisted of two officers of the Aborigines' Rights Protection
Society (A.R.P.S.), Mr George E. Moore and Mr Samuel R.
Wood. They came to protest to the Secretary of State for
Colonies against certain 'obnoxious laws' enacted by the Governor, Sir Shenton Thomas, and to demand a reform of the
constitution. This was in 1934.

The presence of the missions aroused considerable interest
in West African affairs among politically-minded Negroes in

Britain, and an *ad hoc* committee was formed under my chairmanship to assist the delegates of the Aborigines' Rights Protection Society to organize public meetings in order to enable the delegates to put their case before the British people. When Mussolini declared war against Abyssinia, the Gold Coast *ad hoc* Committee was reconstituted to become The International African Friends of Abyssinia (I.A.F.A.). The main purpose of this organization was to arouse the sympathy and support of the British public for the victim of Fascist aggression and 'to assist by all means in their power in the maintenance of the territorial integrity and political independence of Abyssinia'.

Among the sponsors of this I.A.F.A. were the two representatives of the A.R.P.S. Messrs Moore and Wood and Dr J. B. Danquah who was secretary of the Ofori-Atta led delegation from the Gold Coast. The officers of the I.A.F.A. were Mr C. L. R. James of Trinidad as chairman; Dr Peter Milliard of British Guiana and the Hon. T. Albert Marryshaw of Grenada as vice-chairmen; Mr Jomo Kenyatta of Kenya as honorary secretary; Mrs Amy Ashwood Garvey, former wife of the famous Negro leader, as honorary treasurer. They, together with Mr Sam Manning of Trinidad, Mr Mohammed Said of Somaliland, and the author formed the executive committee. The society organized a reception for the Emperor and other members of the Ethiopian Royal Family when they arrived at Waterloo Station in London in 1936, to spend years of exile in Britain. The society disbanded its activities when a number of influential English friends and admirers of Haile Selassie decided to carry on the propaganda work under the auspices of the Abyssinian Association (now replaced by the Anglo-Ethiopian Society) founded by Professor Stanley Jevons, Professor Norman Bentwich, Sir George Paish, Miss Rose Vernon, and Miss Muriel Blundell, as secretary. Also active in the defence of Ethiopia was Miss Sylvia Pankhurst, the well-known suffragist, who later founded a newspaper, the *New Times and Ethiopian News* to give publicity to the Emperor's cause.

The brutal rape of Ethiopia combined with the cynical attitude of the Great Powers convinced Africans and peoples of African descent everywhere that black men had no rights which white men felt bound to respect if they stood in the way of their imperialist interests. Not only did the Western Powers turn a deaf ear to the Emperor's appeal to the League of Nations for help, but actually connived at Mussolini's gassing of defenceless Ethiopians by selling oil to the dictator.

With the realization of their utter defencelessness against the new aggression from Europeans in Africa, the blacks felt it necessary to look to themselves.

INTERNATIONAL AFRICAN SERVICE BUREAU

It was twenty years since the last Pan-African Congress had met. Now the time was ripe for the Negroes of the world to close their ranks and revive the movement. The betrayal of Ethiopia and the hopes of hundreds of millions of coloured peoples in Asia, Africa and the islands of the seas, who had been led to place their faith in the League of Nations and collective security had forced upon Africans and peoples of African descent the resolve that they must not again be caught in a state of unpreparedness.

In this mood, some of the members of the erstwhile International African Friends of Abyssinia Society, together with a few newcomers, chief among them Mr T. R. Makonnen, who was later to become the general secretary of the Pan-African Federation in Britain, met in London in the early part of 1937 to form the International African Service Bureau, the forerunner of the Pan-African Federation.

The principal officers of the International African Service Bureau were Mr Wallace Johnson, the well-known West African trade unionist, general secretary; Mr Chris Jones of Barbados, organizing secretary; Mr C. L. R. James, author and journalist, editorial director; Mr Jomo Kenyatta, then the official representative in Britain of the Kikuyu Central Association, assistant secretary; and myself as chairman.

Mr Makonnen was elected honorary treasurer. It was largely through his exertions that the International African Service Bureau and later the Pan-African Federation were able to establish themselves successfully and launch the *Inter-*

national African Opinion. As financial officer, Makonnen was responsible for raising most of the funds to defray the expenses of the Fifth Pan-African Congress. He afterwards took the initiative in establishing *Pan-Africa,* a journal of African life and letters, which became the principal medium through which the ideology of Pan-Africanism was expounded throughout the Black World.

AIMS AND OBJECTS OF THE INTERNATIONAL AFRICAN SERVICE BUREAU

A non-party organization, the International African Service Bureau owed no affiliation or allegiance to any political party, organization or group in Europe. It represented progressive and enlightened public opinion among Africans and peoples of African descent. It supported the demands of Africans, Asians and other colonial people for democratic rights, civil liberties and self-determination. Although active membership of the Bureau was confined to Africans and people of African descent regardless of nationality, political creed or religious faith who accepted its aims and abided by its constitution, Europeans and others who desired to demonstrate in a practical way their interest in African welfare were permitted to become associate members.

While the officers of the I.A.S.B. realized that a subject people must assume the major responsibility in their struggle for self-government, they were definitely opposed to racial exclusiveness. Because of this, the constitution clearly stated that 'one of the chief functions of the Bureau was to help enlighten public opinion, particularly in Great Britain (and other democratic countries possessing colonies inhabited by Africans and people of African descent) as to the true conditions in the various colonies, protectorates and mandated territories in Africa and the West Indies'.

In this way, it hoped that the people of England and Europe would be in a better position to raise their voices in protest against abuses and injustices which obtain in the colonies and semi-coloured countries.

By lectures and discussions, the Bureau soon attracted a group of brilliant young Negro intellectuals in Britain. Many of them held Marxist views on economic and political problems, although they were never members of the British Communist Party, which until its present activities among West African and West Indian students in the United Kingdom, has never succeeded in attracting colonials. Politically-minded Negroes despised the opportunism of the British Communists, who during the 'Popular Front' period of the thirties, simply looked upon the Africans as 'backward, unsophisticated tribesmen'. Their legitimate grievances against Colonialism could be easily exploited in the interest of Soviet foreign policy, which at that time was seeking anti-fascist allies against the menace of Hitler's Germany. So in order not to alarm and frighten away those sections of the British ruling class that considered Hitler a greater danger to the British Empire than Stalin, the British Communists soft-pedalled the demand of Africans for immediate self-government, while paying lip-service to Indian independence. The blacks at that time were to be bribed with pettifogging reforms borrowed from the programmes of the Fabian Society and the Liberal Party, who after all never made any pretentions of being revolutionists. Turning away in disgust from the Communist hypocrites, the leftish members of the International African Service Bureau, many of whom are now holding prominent positions in the colonial nationalist and labour movements, orientated themselves to Pan-Africanism as an independent political expression of Negro aspirations for complete national independence from white domination—Capitalist or Communist.

Since the Pan-African Congress, from its very inception in 1919, had never been affiliated, or owed allegiance to any foreign government or political organization such as the Socialist or Communist Internationals, it was free to determine its own policies without having to take orders from any cabal or caucus over which Negroes have no control.

The association between Dr DuBois's Pan-African Congress and the International African Service Bureau was destined to have the most far-reaching consequences in Africa in the years following the Second World War. The link established during the war years stimulated the present revival of Pan-Africanism. By 1945, interest in the future status of Africans and peoples of African descent was sufficiently widespread to bring together for the first time representatives of the newly-formed colonial trade union and labour movements and the emerging nationalist forces in the African territories. It was the largest and most representative Pan-African Congress yet convened.

BIRTH OF PAN-AFRICAN FEDERATION

By this time, the International African Service Bureau had merged into the Pan-African Federation, which became the British section of the Pan-African Congress Movement. The merger was brought about in 1944, when the representatives of coloured and colonial organizations in Great Britain assembled in Manchester to form a Pan-African united front movement.[5]

The objects of the Pan-African Federation were in conformity with the broad principles proclaimed at all the earlier Pan-African Congresses, namely:

(1) To promote the well-being and unity of African peoples and peoples of African descent throughout the world.

(2) To demand self-determination and independence of African peoples, and other subject races from the domination of powers claiming sovereignty and trusteeship over them.

[5] Among the organizations represented were: The International African Service Bureau; the Negro Welfare Centre; the Negro Association (Manchester); the Coloured Workers' Association (London); the Coloured People's Association (Edinburgh); the United Committee of Coloured and Colonial People's Association (Cardiff); the African Union (Glasgow); the Association of Students of African Descent (Dublin); the West African Students' Union (Gt Britain & Ireland); the Kikuyu Central Association (Kenya); the African Progressive Association (London); Sierra Leone Section, African Youth League; The Friends of African Freedom Society (Gold Coast).

(3) To secure equality of civil rights for African peoples
     and the total abolition of all forms of racial discrimi-
     nation.

(4) To strive to co-operate between African peoples and
     others who share our aspirations.

By pooling resources and liberating themselves from the
eroding influence of doctrinaire Marxism which British Communists operating through certain Negro fellow travellers
were trying to impose upon the African national liberation
movements as a means of exercising Stalinist control over
them, the Pan-African Federation was able to take an independent ideological position on the colonial question.

Theoretical problems such as the methods and forms of
organization to be adopted by colonial peoples; the tactics
and strategy of the national freedom struggle; the applicability
of Gandhian non-violent, non-co-operative techniques to the
African situation were all openly discussed and debated in the
columns of the Federation's journal, *International African
Opinion*, edited by the distinguished West Indian historian,
C. L. R. James and assisted by William Harrison, an erudite
Afro-American Harvard scholar then doing post-graduate
studies under professor Harold Laski at the London School
of Economics.

The Pan-African Federation also published a number of
pamphlets dealing with specific colonial problems, written by
its members. Among them are: *The West Indies Today*;
Hands off the Protectorates (Bechuanaland, Basutoland,
Swaziland); *Kenya, Land of Conflict*; *African Empires and
Civilizations*; *The Negro in the Caribbean*; *White Man's
Duty*; *The Voice of the New Negro*; *The American Negro
Problem*; *The Native Problem in South Africa*; *The Voice
of Coloured Labour*.

Some of the leaders of the Federation published during the
pre-war years specialized studies of the Negro and Colonial
struggle, such as *The Black Jacobins* (an account of the
Haitian Revolution) and *A History of Negro Revolts*, by
C. L. R. James; *Facing Mount Kenya* (an anthropological
study of the Kikuyu tribe) by Jomo Kenyatta; *How Britain
Rules Africa* (a study in colonial administration) and *Africa*

and World Peace (an essay on international politics) by George Padmore.

Since then, these and other supporters of Pan-Africanism have made further contributions to the literature on Africa and the colonial question. The years immediately before the outbreak of the Second World War coincided with what is known in left-wing political circles as the 'Anti-Fascist Popular Front Period'. This period was one of the most stimulating and constructive in the history of Pan-Africanism. It was then that Congress had to meet the ideological challenge from the Communist opportunists on the one hand and the racist doctrines of the Fascists on the other, and to defend the programme of Pan-Africanism—namely, the fundamental right of black men to be free and independent and not be humbugged by those who preached acceptance of the *status quo* in the interest of power politics. It was also at this period that many of the Negro intellectuals who were later to emerge as prominent personalities in the colonial nationalist movements began to make a detailed and systematic study of European political theories and systems (Liberalism, Socialism, Communism, Anarchism, Imperialism, Fascism), and to evaluate these doctrines objectively—accepting what might be useful to the cause of Pan-Africanism and rejecting the harmful. In this way the younger leaders of the Congress were able to build upon the pioneering work of Dr DuBois and formulate a programme of dynamic nationalism, which combined African traditional forms of organization with Western political party methods.

A programme of *Positive Action*, based on the Gandhist technique of non-violent non-co-operation, was endorsed by the Fifth Pan-African Congress in 1945, and first applied in the Gold Coast in 1950 by Kwame Nkrumah, who had served as one of the joint international secretaries of the Congress.

IX

PAN-AFRICANISM COMES OF AGE

If the war years can be described as the coming-of-age period of Pan-Africanism, 1945 and after represents the beginning of its triumph and achievement. The ideas of Pan-Africanism had been claiming the attention of the younger generation of politically-minded Negroes seeking a way of achieving national independence and economic emancipation without allying themselves with the Communists, who are trying to seize control and exploit the Negro political movements. Immediately after the close of the Second World War, these ideas found endorsement in the programme hammered out at the Fifth Pan-African Congress. Here at long last was a philosophy evolved by Negro thinkers which Africans and peoples of African descent could claim and use as their own. The days of dependence upon the thinking and direction of their so-called left-wing European friends who had so often betrayed them, were over. From henceforth Africans and peoples of African descent would take their destiny into their own hands and march forward under their own banner of Pan-Africanism in co-operation with their own selected allies.

Even before the Congress convened in Manchester in October 1945, the Africans had demonstrated their political awakening and self-assertion. A group of West African newspaper editors, at the initiative of Dr Nnamdi Azikiwe, the leader of the National Council of Nigeria and the Cameroons, who has since become Prime Minister of Eastern Nigeria, had published a memorandum entitled *The Atlantic Charter and*

British West Africa, in which they endorsed the principle of self-determination which had been advocated by the Pan-African Congress since its foundation. The memorandum was issued in 1943, and based its demands upon clause 3 of the Atlantic Charter, signed by President Roosevelt and Prime Minister Churchill in 1941, affirming 'the right of all people to choose the form of government under which they may live'. The significance of the document lay in the fact that it was the first wartime expression of West African aspirations to be addressed to the British Government.

It asked for the immediate abrogation of the undemocratic Crown Colony system of government and the substitution of representative institutions for a period of ten years, to be followed by responsible self-government for a period of five years. It was presumed that these two terms of transitional government would provide the necessary grounding for the promotion of the British West African territories to 'self-determination within the British Commonwealth'.

Not unmindful of the urgent need to raise the economic, educational and social standards of the inhabitants of these territories, the Memorandum set forth a series of reforms for education, public health, agriculture, social welfare, mining, finance, trade and commerce. In fact, every single branch of modern democratic national life was covered. The proposals envisaged in large measure the taking over of the direction and administration of the West African colonies by Africans in the interests of Africans.

Though the West African Press Delegation was courteously received in British Colonial Office circles, no assurances were given to them as regards their aspirations. But the visit of the West African mission in the midst of war enabled Negro colonial leaders already in Britain to establish connections with the emerging nationalist forces in the West African colonies, and to discuss problems of common interest. It also served to stimulate nationalist feeling among the African university students in the United Kingdom to such an extent, that at the annual conference of the West African Students' Union, the delegates passed a resolution demanding 'internal responsible government now for each of the four West African colonies and the corollary from this demanded the democ-

ratization, now, of all West African native (or local) administrations, all municipal councils, all provincial and district
councils, all town and village councils'.[1]

While supporting the common cause in the war against
Nazism and Fascism, Negroes everywhere were equally determined to advance the frontiers of freedom and democracy for
themselves. The situation demanded colonial unity and concerted action. The Pan-African Federation was organized to
bring about the needed united front of Africans and people
of African descent working in the United Kingdom during the
war or serving in the British forces. It also tried to establish
links with Negro organizations of all kinds—political, trade
union, co-operative, nationalist, fraternal, religious, educational, sports, etc.—which existed in different colonial territories, and to bring them into direct fraternal touch with each
other. The purpose was to enable them to speak with one
voice on all matters affecting the economic, political, educational and moral well-being of the black peoples throughout
the world.

FIFTH PAN-AFRICAN CONGRESS

The preparation of the Fifth Pan-African Congress was
assigned by Dr DuBois, the International President, to the
executive of the British section of the Pan-African Federation.
It coincided with the establishment of the World Federation
of Trade Unions (W.F.T.U.), held at County Hall, London,
in February 1945. To this conference came representatives of
black labour from Nigeria, Gold Coast, Sierra Leone, Gambia,
Jamaica, Trinidad, Barbados, British Guiana, and other colonial lands. Most of the colonial trade unions represented at
the conference had only been formed shortly before or during
the war, when trade unionism was legally recognized for the
first time by many British colonial governments as a means of
helping the war effort. They had managed to build up sub-

[1] Proceedings of 'Conference on West African Problems,' in
W.A.S.U. Magazine, May 1943.

stantial memberships, and were working in close association
and friendly relationship with the progressive nationalist
movements struggling for self-government and independence.

It was not difficult, therefore, for the secretariat of the
Pan-African Federation to get together with them to issue a
joint appeal to all colonial political, trade union, farmers' and
co-operative movements to send representatives to the Fifth
Pan-African Congress, which was planned to coincide with
the second conference of the W.F.T.U., scheduled to take
place in Paris from September 25 to October 9, 1945.

A delegate conference representing all coloured organizations in the British Isles and colonial trade unions affiliated to
the W.F.T.U. was held at Manchester in March 1945, at
which a provisional programme and agenda for the forth-
coming Fifth Pan-African Congress was approved, and *rap-
porteurs* appointed. The preparatory work was assigned to a
special international conference secretariat consisting of Dr
Peter Milliard of British Guiana, chairman; Mr T. R. Makonnen of British Guiana, Treasurer; Messrs George Padmore of
the West Indies and Kwame Nkrumah of West Africa as
joint political secretaries; Mr Peter Abrahams of South Africa,
publicity secretary; Mr Jomo Kenyatta of East Africa, assistant secretary.

By August, the international secretariat was able to report
to a second delegates' conference that a number of replies
had been received from labour, trade union, co-operative and
other progressive organizations in the West Indies, West
Africa, South, Central and East Africa, in acknowledgment of
the formal invitation to attend the Congress. Most of these
bodies not only approved and endorsed the agenda, making
minor modifications and suggestions here and there, but
pledged themselves to send delegates. In cases where either
the time was too short or the difficulties of transport too
great to be overcome at such short notice, the organizations
gave mandates to the natives of the territories concerned who
were travelling to Paris to attend the World Federation of
Trade Unions Conference. Where territories did not send
delegates to the Trade Unions Conference, organizations
mandated individuals already in Great Britain to represent
them.

In this way the widest representation was assured, either through people travelling directly from the colonial areas to Britain, or individuals from those territories who were already in the British Isles. Apart from these overseas delegates, more than fourteen organizations of Africans and peoples of African descent in Great Britain and Ireland also expressed their willingness to participate.

While preparations were in progress, an event occurred in Britain which brought universal rejoicing to colonial peoples and added further encouragement to our efforts to make the Congress the grandest in the history of Pan-Africanism. This was the sweeping victory of the British Labour Party in the first post-war general election of July 1945.

OPEN LETTER TO LABOUR PRIME MINISTER

Inspired by this 'bloodless revolution', many colonial organizations sent telegrams of congratulations to the Labour Party. And the Pan-African Federation, acting on behalf of its African and other colonial affiliated bodies addressed an Open Letter to Prime Minister Attlee laying before his Government certain constructive suggestions on the colonies and the problems of colonial peoples generally.

'We wish to welcome Labour's great victory, for which we, as colonials, have hoped and worked alongside Britain's workers', the document stated. 'It makes possible the inauguration of the century of the common man. Courage, vision, planning and fearless work can turn this possibility into reality. The dark-skinned workers, no less than the pale-skinned, want freedom from war, want and fear. The victory of the common man here is the victory of the common man in Africa, Asia and other colonial lands.

'To consolidate this great victory, however, courage is needed. The courage to face squarely the fact that imperialism is one of the major causes of war. The courage to admit that any high-sounding blue prints that beg the question of man's territorial and political domination by other men, whether their skins are white, yellow or black, is only staving off the day when the evils of war with their ghastly new scientific twists will again be unleashed on humanity. It is the challenge of our time that you, Mr Attlee, and your Government should give the Socialist answer to the Tory imperialism of Mr Churchill's "What we have we hold". What will your answer be?

'To condemn the imperialism of Germany, Japan and Italy while condoning that of Britain would be more than dishonest, it would be a betrayal of the sacrifice and sufferings and the toil and sweat of the common people of this country. All imperialism is evil.'

The statement concluded by asking the Labour Government to take immediate steps to bring about the following reforms as an expression of Socialist goodwill towards the long-suffering Africans:

(1) That the Kenya Land Ordinance and the Sierra Leone Municipal Ordinance be held over, as the people request, that they might have the opportunity to state their viewpoint.

(2) That the flogging of African troops, as punishment, be ended immediately.

(3) That the various educational reforms embodied in the West Indian and West African reports on higher education be put into operation and speeded up.

(4) That the Royal Commission Report on the West Indies, suppressed since 1940, be published immediately.

(5) That the Sedition Deportation and Undesirable Literature Ordinances be repealed, as well as the Assessors' Ordinance, and that the colonial criminal code be brought into line with the criminal code of Great Britain.

(6) That discrimination because of race, colour or creed in Britain be made a punishable offence.

(7) That the principle of equal pay for equal work regardless of colour, race or creed, be made an established practice in the Colonial Civil Service.

(8) That Labour reaffirm its determination to keep race-ridden South Africa out of the Protectorates (Bechuanaland, Basutoland, Swaziland), and that Labour

pursues a vigorous policy to end the colour bar in the colonies.

The appeal also suggested that the Labour Government should call a conference of representatives of African and other colonial leaders elected by the people of the various colonies and discuss with them the problems of the common people in their lands and the solutions to those problems. 'That would indeed be heralding in the period of co-operation, of partnership, as against domination. It would be a great stride towards the Century of the Common Man.'

Unfortunately, the Labour Government failed to respond to this gesture of friendship and an opportunity was lost to establish a working partnership between the Socialist and trade union movements in Britain and colonial nationalist and labour leaders, who alone can build the bridge of friendship between the progressive and anti-colonialist forces in Britain and the awakening masses of Africa. Instead, the post-war Labour Governments, like the Tories, continued to rely upon the conservative chiefs and other tribalist elements in colonial society as their allies in a period of revolutionary change. Consequently, the politically-educated and nationally-conscious leaders emerging from the ranks of the common people all over Africa have come to look upon all British Governments—Socialist and Conservative—as opponents of social progress and political advance for colonial peoples, who will only make concessions under popular pressure. They see no difference between Mr Churchill's 'What we have we hold' attitude and Mr Morrison's 'Jolly old empire' outlook.

However, despite the feelings of disappointment and frustration which both Tory and Labour official policies have often created among colonial leaders, they have the most friendly feeling and admiration for the British people for the way they stood up against the onslaught of their new-found German 'friends'. As an expression of their admiration, the Fifth Pan-African Congress invited the Lord Mayor of Manchester, Alderman W. P. Jackson, to open its deliberations.

In thanking the Lord Mayor, Dr Milliard, the Chairman of the Congress Standing Orders Committee, said that although he had been born in British Guiana, he had lived and practised as a physician in Manchester for over twenty-five years, and felt that it was the most liberal city in England. He recalled how in the Civil War between the Northern and Southern States of America, the South was blockaded by the North. The cotton mills of Lancashire were largely dependent upon the South for their raw cotton and the mill owners decided that the British Government should send warships to break the blockade of the Southern ports. The Lancashire workers stood up as a man against this decision and thus helped to destroy slavery. This assistance to the Negro race has never been forgotten. The incident illustrated the hospitality and human understanding of the Lancashire people.

Dr Milliard concluded with the expression of the hope that Manchester would continue to merit the high opinion which is held of it by the descendants of the slaves. It was, therefore, no surprise that the Lord Mayor had come to address the Congress; he was simply expressing the high liberalism which Manchester had always maintained. Mr Wallace Johnson of Sierra Leone, speaking on behalf of the Negroes who were settled in that part of West Africa in the eighteenth century, and who, since then, have had close association with Lancashire, endorsed Dr Milliard's sentiments, and affirmed that the Pan-African Congress had established another link of friendship with Manchester now that Africans had come of age to demand equal status and equal rights with other peoples of the Commonwealth. For this reason, he, too, extended thanks to the Lord Mayor as the official representative of a great English city of liberal traditions.

TRIBUTE TO A NEGRO LEADER

The success of the Fifth Pan-African Congress was due in large measure to the wise guidance and selfless labours of Dr Milliard, upon whose shoulders fell much of the responsibility for its preparation.

Dr Milliard was a man of considerable charm and striking presence. He was widely read; a raconteur of no mean order and a great lover of the good things of life. He typified the finest traditions of the Edwardians—the period spanning his early manhood.

Peter McDonald Milliard was born in British Guiana in 1882, and received a classical education at Queen's College, the leading secondary school in the colony. He later went to the United States where he read Medicine at Howard University, graduating M.D. in 1910. His first appointment was at Freedman's Hospital in Washington, D.C. Dr Milliard left the United States for Panama, where he practised for many years among the West Indian emigrants brought into the Canal Zone by the Americans to help construct the Panama Canal. His professional ambition, however, was to obtain British registration, and with that object in view he came to the United Kingdom shortly after the First World War. During his sojourn in Panama, the doctor had assisted the Negro workers in forming the first trade union to demand higher wage rates from the American employers. At that time two currencies existed: gold for white Americans and silver for blacks. Because of his trade union activities, the United States authorities in Britain refused to grant him visa facilities to enable him to return to the Canal Zone after completing his post-graduate studies in Scotland.

Forced to become an exile from his adopted country— Panama—then completely under the control of the United States Government, Dr Milliard, who was a man happily endowed, as most Negroes are, with the facility to adapt himself to circumstances, went to Manchester in the year of his graduation from Edinburgh in 1923. By dint of hard work and professional skill, the doctor soon established a successful practice in Manchester and Salford.

Dr Milliard was a great favourite among the working-class people, for whom he had a deep sympathy and liking. This was in keeping with the man's whole political outlook as a life-long democrat and socialist. Although a great champion of his race, he was no narrow-minded racist. He was a passionate internationalist and served human beings regardless of race and colour as best he could. During more than twenty-five years residence in Manchester, Dr Milliard took an active interest in all matters pertaining to the Negro communities throughout the British Isles. No worthy appeal from Africans and people of African descent ever failed to enlist his support. A generous giver and loyal friend, his services and vast experience were always in demand as patron and supporter of worthy causes affecting African peoples. For many years before his death, Dr Milliard served as president of the Negro Welfare Association in Manchester and was the first chairman of the Pan-African Federation in Great Britain. His death, which occurred shortly after the Fifth Pan-African Congress, has been a great loss to the Negro race.

FIFTH PAN-AFRICAN CONGRESS DECISIONS

The most significant thing about the Fifth Pan-African Congress as compared with the earlier ones, was its plebeian character. Representation was drawn from the ranks of political, trade union and farmers' movements, as well as the nationalistically minded student elements. There were over two hundred direct delegates and observers. A new militant leadership was reflected, closely linked with the popular movements in the home lands. Earlier Congresses had centred around a small intellectual *élite*. Now there was expression of a mass movement intimately identified with the underprivileged sections of the coloured colonial populations. Alliance between the progressive middle-class intellectuals and the ordinary people was cemented in a series of resolutions resulting from detailed discussions of the many aspects of the African problem.

These discussions were conducted under the direction of Dr DuBois who, at the age of seventy-three, had flown across the Atlantic from New York to preside over the coming of age of his political child. This 'Grand Old Man', ever youthful, vigorous of mind and politically ahead of many much younger in years, was given an enthusiastic welcome by the delegates. For he had done more than any other to inspire and influence by his writings and political philosophy all the young men who had foregathered from far distant corners of the earth. Even among the older delegates there were many who were meeting the 'Father' of Pan-Africanism in the flesh for the first time.

The occasion was a remarkable personal triumph for Dr DuBois. Although by that time he had devoted half a century of selfless labour to the advancement of his race, he was by no means what can be called a popular leader, a fact which he himself admits. In his autobiography he says: 'My leadership was a leadership solely of ideas. I never was, nor ever will be, personally popular. This was not simply because of my idiosyncrasies but because I despise the essential demagoguery of personal leadership; of that hypnotic ascendancy over men which carries out objectives regardless of their value or validity, simply by personal loyalty and admiration. In my case I withdrew sometimes ostentatiously from the personal nexus, but I sought all the more determinedly to force home essential ideas.'[2]

Dr DuBois was by no means a silent spectator at the Fifth Pan-African Congress. He entered into all the discussions and brought to the deliberations a freshness of outlook that greatly influenced the final decisions; the implementation of which are already shaping the future of the African continent.

The first and second sessions of the Congress were devoted to discussion of the colour-bar problem in Britain. The main reporters were Messrs Edwin J. DuPlan and E. A. Akiwumi of the Gold Coast. Supporting statements were made by Dr J. C. de Graft Johnson and Dr Kurankyi Taylor of the Gold Coast, Mr Peter Abrahams of South Africa, and Mr A. E. Mussell of the United Committee of Coloured Peoples of Cardiff, after which the following resolution was adopted:

'To secure equal opportunities for all colonial and coloured people in Great Britain, this Congress demands that discrimination on account of race, creed, or colour be made a criminal offence by law.

'That all employments and occupations shall be opened to all qualified Africans, and that to bar such applicants because of race, colour or creed shall be deemed an offence against the law.

'That the Negro Welfare Centre, the League of Coloured

2 W. E. B. DuBois: *Dusk of Dawn*, p. 303.

Peoples, African Churches' Mission of Liverpool and other African organizations (social and religious) which have been doing legitimate welfare work among coloured children, students, seamen and others, shall be given every encouragement and assistance by the responsible authorities to continue the vital social work in which they are engaged.'

The problems of British, French and other West African colonies were fully discussed at the third and fourth sessions. The principal *rapporteur* was Mr Kwame Nkrumah, the joint political secretary of the Congress. His report was supplemented by statements from Mr G. Ashie Nikoi, representing the Gold Coast Farmers; Mr J. S. Annan, secretary of the Gold Coast Railway Civil Servants' & Technical Workers' Union[3]; Chief A. Soyemi Coker of the Trade Union Congress of Nigeria; Mr Wallace Johnson, secretary of the Sierra Leone Youth League; Mr J. Downes Thomas of the Bathurst Citizens' Committee of Gambia; Mr Joe Appiah, Mr Kankam Boadu,[4] Mr F. O. B. Blaize, delegates of the West African Students' Union; Mr Magnus Williams of the National Council of Nigeria and the Cameroons; Mr H. O. Davies of the Nigeria Youth Movement; Dr Raphael Armattoe of Togoland.

In light of the political events now taking place in West Africa, especially in the Gold Coast and Nigeria, it is well to recall the resolutions presented by Mr Nkrumah and unanimously adopted by the Congress on constitutional, economic and social problems for the guidance of the nationalist movements in these territories.

'In connection with the political situation, the Congress observed:

(a) That since the advent of British, French, Belgian and other European nations in West Africa, there has been regression instead of progress as a result of systematic exploitation by these alien imperialist powers. The claims of 'partnership', 'trusteeship', 'guardianship', and the 'mandate system', do not

[3] Mr Annan is now the Permanent Secretary in the Gold Coast Ministry of Defence.

[4] Mr Boadu is now the Chairman of the Gold Coast Cocoa Marketing Board.

serve the political wishes of the people of West Africa.

(b) That the democratic nature of the indigenous institutions of the peoples of West Africa have been crushed by obnoxious and oppressive laws and regulations, and replaced by autocratic systems of government which are inimical to the wishes of the peoples of West Africa.

(c) That the introduction of pretentious constitutional reforms in the West African territories are nothing but spurious attempts on the part of alien imperialist powers to continue the political enslavement of the peoples.

(d) That the introduction of Indirect Rule is not only an instrument of oppression but also an encroachment on the right of the West African natural rulers.

(e) That the artificial divisions and territorial boundaries created by the imperialist powers are deliberate steps to obstruct the political unity of the West African peoples.

Economic. As regards West African economic set-up, the resolution asserted:

'(a) That there has been a systematic exploitation of the economic resources of the West African territories by imperialist powers to the detriment of the inhabitants.

(b) That the industrialization of West Africa by the indigenes has been discouraged and obstructed by the imperialist rulers, with the result that the standard of living has fallen below subsistence level.

(c) That the land, the rightful property of West Africans is gradually passing into the hands of foreign governments and other agencies through various devices and ordinances.

(d) That the workers and farmers of West Africa have not been allowed independent trade unions and co-operative movements without official interference.

(e) That the mining industries are in the hands of foreign monopolies of finance capital, with the result that wherever a mining industry has developed there has been a tendency to deprive the people of their land holdings (e.g., mineral rights in Nigeria and Sierra Leone now the property of the British Government).

(f) That the British Government in West Africa is virtually controlled by a merchants' united front, whose main objective is the exploitation of the people, thus rendering the indigenous population economically helpless.

(g) That when a country is compelled to rely on one crop (e.g. cocoa) for a single monopolistic market, and is obliged to cultivate only for export while at the same time its farmers and workers find themselves in the grip of finance capital, then it is evident that the government of that country is incompetent to assume responsibility for it.

Commenting on the social needs of the area, the resolution said:

'(a) That the democratic organizations and institutions of the West African peoples had been interfered with, that alien rule has not improved education, health or the nutrition of the West African peoples, but on the contrary tolerates mass illiteracy, ill-health, malnutrition, prostitution, and many other social evils.

(b) That organized Christianity in West Africa is identified with the political and economic exploitation of the West African peoples by alien powers.'

In view of these conditions, the Congress unanimously supported the members of the West African delegation in declaring that complete and absolute independence for the peoples of West Africa is the only solution to the existing problem.

The Congress devoted special attention to the status of the non-Europeans in South Africa and warned against imposing federation of Central Africa without the consent and support of the African population in the Rhodesias and Nyasaland. It also criticized the *Herrenvolk* policy of the white settlers in East Africa, especially Kenya. Mr Peter Abrahams, a coloured South African novelist from Johannesburg, and Mr Marko

Hlubi, a full-blooded Zulu representative of the African National Congress, the largest non-European organization in the Union, delivered the main report on the economic, political and racial problems in Southern and Central Africa. Mr Jomo Kenyatta acted as the official *rapporteur* on East African affairs. He was supported by Mr Marko Hlubi (South Africa), Mr Bankole Renner and Mr C. D. Hyde (Gold Coast), Mr Garba Jahumpa (Gambia),[5] Mr Wallace Johnson (Sierra Leone),[6] and George Padmore, who emphasized the need for immediate constitutional and other reforms in Kenya and Uganda if a crisis in race relations between Africans and Europeans was to be avoided.

WARNING OF RACE CONFLICTS IN AFRICA

Warning of the danger of increasing racial conflict in East Africa, especially Kenya, the Congress issued a special appeal to the Labour Government then in office to implement the following immediate demands in order to ease the growing racial tension and frustration among politically-minded Africans.

'(1) The principles of the Four Freedoms and the Atlantic Charter be put into practice at once.

(2) The abolition of land laws which allow Europeans to take land from the Africans. Immediate cessation of any further settlement by Europeans in Kenya or in any other territory in East Africa. All available land to be distributed to the landless Africans.

(3) The right of Africans to develop the economic resources of their country without hindrance.

(4) The immediate abolition of all racial and other discriminatory laws at once (the Kipande system in particular), and the system of equal citizenship to be introduced forthwith.

[5] Mr Garba Jahumpa is now the Minister of Agriculture and Natural Resources in the Government of the Gambia.

[6] Mr Wallace Johnson is one of the leaders of the Opposition in the Sierra Leone Legislative Council.

(5)   Freedom of speech, press, association and assembly.
(6)   Revision of the system of taxation and of the civil
      and criminal codes.
(7)   Compulsory free and uniform education for all chil-
      dren up to the age of 16, with free meals, free books
      and school equipment.
(8)   Granting of the franchise, i.e., the right of every
      man and woman over the age of twenty-one to elect
      and be elected to the Legislative Council, Provincial
      Council and all other Divisional and Municipal
      Councils.
(9)   A state medical, health and welfare service to be
      made available to all.
(10) Abolition of forced labour, and the introduction of
      the principle of equal pay for equal work.'

The fifth session of the Congress also endorsed the demand
for democratic rights and self-government for the people of
Uganda, Tanganyika, Kenya, Somaliland and Zanzibar. It
condemned the *Apartheid* policy towards Africans and other
non-Europeans (Coloured and Indians) carried out by the
Government of the Union of South Africa which, while representing itself abroad as a democracy with a parliamentary
system of government, gave voting rights to whites only.
South Africa, therefore, manifested essentially the same racial
characteristics as those found in Fascist countries where the
Herrenvolk ideology has transformed itself into a mania, the
ruthless trampling underfoot of all human rights and the
erection of one system of law and morality for the white
'master race' and another quite different one for the non-
white 'inferior' races.

Recognizing the agitation of the non-European races in
South Africa for fundamental democratic rights as an integral
part of the national liberation struggle throughout Africa,
the Congress appealed to all the progressive forces in Britain,
especially the Labour Party and Trade Union Movement, to
extend the maximum support to the Africans and their white
and non-white allies against their *Herrenvolk* oppressors. It
also pledged support to the natives of Bechuanaland, Basutoland and Swaziland in resisting the annexation of these Protectorates by the fascist South African Government; and

appealed to the Labour Government to devote more attention
to the economic and social development of these territories for
the benefit of the Africans, and to provide them with democratic self-governing institutions as the best means of safeguarding their national identity. Mr Patrick Gordon-Walker
certainly did interest himself in the affairs of the Protectorates, but in the wrong direction. He banished Seretse Khama,
Chief Designate of the Bamangwata tribe of Bechuanaland,
after the young ruler had committed the unforgivable crime
of marrying a white woman.

As regards the people of Mediterranean Africa and the
Sudan, the Congress endorsed the demands of the indigenous
natives of Tunisia, Algeria, Morocco and Libya for democratic self-government and independence from French and all
foreign rule. It demanded the abolition of the Anglo-Egyptian
Condominium over the Sudan and the right of the Sudanese
to complete independence from British and Egyptian interference.

In keeping with the fundamental principle and objective
of Pan-Africanism not to be neutral in anything affecting the
destiny of Africans and peoples of African descent throughout
the world, the Congress sent greetings to the governments and
peoples of Ethiopia, Liberia and Haiti and pledged its support in mobilizing opinion among Africans and their descendants everywhere in the world in defence of their sovereignty
and national independence against all forms of external aggression—political or economic.

'We assure the Government and peoples of these States
that we shall ever be vigilant against any manifestation of
imperialist encroachment which may threaten their independence', declared a special Congress resolution. 'We take this
opportunity to inform the imperialist powers that we look
with jealous pride upon these nations and regard them as
symbols of the realization of the political hopes and aspirations of African people still under imperialist domination.'

Meeting at a time when the peoples of India, Indonesia,
and Viet-minh under President Ho Chi-minh, were struggling
to complete their independence, the Congress sent them
greetings, assuring them of the best wishes and solidarity of
the Africans. Congress also expressed the hope that before

long the peoples of Asia and Africa would have broken their centuries-old chains of colonialism. Then, as free nations, they would stand united to consolidate and safeguard their liberties and independence from the restoration of Western imperialism, as well as the danger of Communism.

Although the emphasis of the Congress was upon African affairs, the problems facing peoples of African descent in the Western Hemisphere were also considered. The main reports on the Caribbean territories were delivered by George Padmore and Mr Ken Hill of Jamaica, the representative of the People's National Party led by Mr Norman Manley, Q.C. Supplementary reports were made by Mr E. de Lisle Yearwood of the Barbados Labour Party; Mr Claude Lushington and Mr John Rojas of the West Indian Nationalist Party; Mr D. M. Harper of the British Guiana Trade Union Congress; Dr Peter Milliard and Mr J. A. Linton of the Negro Association; Mrs Amy Ashwood Garvey and Miss Alma LaBardie of the Jamaica Women's Movement; and Mr Wallace Johnson, President of the Sierra Leone Youth League and Civil Liberties Committee.

Dr W. E. B. DuBois reported on the Race Problem in the United States, reviewing the achievements of the Negroes in their struggle to obtain first-class citizenship. Like the delegates from West Africa, the Caribbean representatives supported the motion of George Padmore emphasizing the demand for federation of British Guiana and all the British West Indian islands on a voluntary and equal basis founded upon complete self-government and self-determination within the Commonwealth.

In support of this claim, the Congress passed a resolution unanimously approving the urgent need to reform the constitutions of the various Caribbean islands and mainland colonies of British Guiana and British Honduras, along the lines of internal self-government based on universal adult suffrage as a condition precedent to the establishment of West Indian Federation. It also pointed out that, hand in hand with constitutional advance in each of the territorial units to be federated, there must go a radical transformation of the present agrarian structure of West Indian economy, linked with educational, scientific and technical and social reforms at all levels.

DECLARATION TO COLONIAL POWERS

The Congress brought its deliberations to a close by issuing a challenge to the Colonial Powers to honour the principles of the Atlantic Charter. It declared that: 'The delegates believe in peace. How could it be otherwise, when for centuries the African peoples have been the victims of violence and slavery? Yet if the Western world is still determined to rule mankind by force, then Africans, as a last resort, may have to appeal to force in the effort to achieve freedom, even if force destroys them and the world.

'We are determined to be free. We want education. We want the right to earn a decent living; the right to express our thoughts and emotions, to adopt and create forms of beauty. We demand for Black Africa autonomy and independence, so far and no further than it is possible in this One World for groups and peoples to rule themselves subject to inevitable world unity and federation.

'We are not ashamed to have been an age-long patient people. We continue willingly to sacrifice and strive. But we are unwilling to starve any longer while doing the world's drudgery, in order to support by our poverty and ignorance a false aristocracy and a discarded imperialism.

'We condemn the monopoly of capital and the rule of private wealth and industry for private profit alone. We welcome economic democracy as the only real democracy.

'Therefore, we shall complain, appeal and arraign. We will make the world listen to the facts of our condition. We will fight in every way we can for freedom, democracy and social betterment.'

At long last the die had been cast and the issue joined. From Manchester the African and other colonial delegates returned home to put their hands to freedom's plough and furrow the ground for the seeds of liberty to grow.

X

PAN-AFRICANISM IN ACTION

The Fifth Pan-African Congress, having formulated concrete programmes for each of the principal geographical regions of black Africa—East, West, South and Central, around which popular support could be rallied, it was now up to the nationalists to give positive leadership to the emergent political movements for self-government.

Pan-Africanism had entered upon a new phase—that of Positive Action. The effectiveness of this depended upon the degree to which the African peoples were organized. Organization is the key to freedom. Without the active support of the common people, the intellectuals remain isolated and ineffectual. That is why the Fifth Congress, in its 'Declaration to the Colonial People', stressed the importance of forming a united front between the intellectuals, workers and farmers in the struggle against Colonialism. The Congress declared its belief in the right of all people to govern themselves. 'We affirm the right of all colonial peoples to control their own destiny. All colonies must be free from foreign imperialist control, whether political or economic.

'The peoples of the colonies must have the right to elect their own governments, without restrictions from foreign powers. We say to the peoples of the colonies that they must fight for these ends by all means at their disposal.

'The object of imperialist powers is to exploit. By granting the right to colonial peoples to govern themselves that object is defeated. Therefore, the struggle for political power by colonial and subject peoples is the first step towards, and the necessary prerequisite to, complete social, economic and political emancipation. The Fifth Pan-African Congress therefore calls on the workers and farmers of the Colonies to organize effectively. Colonial workers must be in the front of the battle against imperialism. Your weapons—the strike and the boycott—are invincible.

'We also call upon the intellectuals and professional classes of the colonies to awaken to their responsibilities. By fighting for trade union rights, the right to form co-operatives, freedom of the press, assembly, demonstration and strike, freedom to print and read the literature which is necessary for the education of the masses, you will be using the only means by which your liberties will be won and maintained. Today there is only one road to effective action—the organization of the masses. And in that organization the educated colonials must join. Colonial and subject peoples of the world, Unite!'

To give effect to this declaration, the Congress charged the executive of the Pan-African Federation to take appropriate steps to publicize the resolutions and other directives adopted by the delegates, and to establish suitable machinery through which advice and assistance could be extended to the organizations represented at the Congress.

WEST AFRICAN NATIONAL SECRETARIAT

Apart from the work directly undertaken by the executive of the Pan-African Federation, Mr Kwame Nkrumah took the initiative of organizing the West African delegates into a regional committee called the West African National Secretariat. The purpose of this body was to work out ways and means of implementing the basic policy resolution endorsed by the Pan-African Congress on West Africa, and to harmonize the relationship between the intellectuals and working class elements in Britain along the lines laid down in the Congress Declaration to the Colonial Peoples, quoted above. After a year of preliminary work among the West African community in the United Kingdom, the West African National Secretariat, with the support of the West African Students Union, convened a conference in London from August 30 to September 1, 1946, at which representatives from the British and French West African colonies endorsed the programme hammered out at the Pan-African Congress and pledged themselves to work not only for territorial self-government, but to promote the concept of a West African Federation as an indispensable lever for carrying forward the Pan-African vision of an ultimate United States of Africa.

The West African united front conference rejected the British Tory doctrine of 'trusteeship' and the Fabian thesis of 'gradualism'. It demanded immediate self-government. For in the words of the Pan-African Congress resolution, 'complete and absolute independence for the peoples of West Africa is the only solution to the existing problem'. The conference also endorsed the idea of reviving the West African National Congress. This body, as we have said elsewhere, was founded by the Gold Coast lawyer and elder statesman, the Hon. Joseph Casely Hayford in 1920, but became inactive after the founder's death in 1930. Not having deep roots among the common people, the West African National Congress gradually died, as the middle-class professional elements who had supported it during Mr Casely Hayford's lifetime started scrambling for membership of the new Legislative Councils set up in the various West African colonies.

While the West African nationalists in Britain were gathering their forces and preparing to carry the struggle back to their homelands, the Pan-African Federation was sustaining the efforts of the East Africans to secure a few modest reforms through the Kenya African Union. The natives of East and Central Africa have not yet reached the same level of political maturity as those in West Africa. In those parts of the continent, the problems of agitation and organization were more difficult because of the absence of constitutional channels of expression, and the hostility of the white settlers and the repressive colour-bar laws enacted at their instance. Furthermore, West Africans had access to land, thanks to the mosquito, which kept white settlers away. In Kenya, the majority of Africans are landless serfs, at the mercy of the

by Dr P. M. Milliard, Mr T. R. Makonnen and George Padmore, who served as Press Secretary to the N.C.N.C. delegation. By the time the Nigerian mission returned to West Africa, a working alliance had been established between the N.C.N.C. and the representatives of other African colonial movements in Britain. In fact, relations were so close that Dr Azikiwe endorsed the decision of the Fifth Pan-African Congress and the West African National Secretariat to work for immediate self-government and the realization of a United West African Federation.

There was not only an identity of political views, but close personal relationship had been established between the younger West African nationalists, all of which made for *esprit de corps* and helped to cement bonds of friendship in a common cause.

At the time when negotiations were taking place in London between West African nationalists, many of whom were later to emerge as the popular leaders and Ministers of their respective territories, a group of middle-class intellectuals in the Gold Coast decided to emulate the N.C.N.C. and form a nationalist movement. The new organization, called the United Gold Coast Convention, was launched in August 1947. Among the leaders were several well-known personalities who had at one time or another been associated with coloured organizations in Britain. For example, Dr J. B. Danquah the doyen of Gold Coast politicians, and Mr Samuel R. Wood, one-time secretary of the Aborigines' Rights Protection Society, had both served on the International African Friends of Abyssinia during the Italian invasion of Ethiopia in 1935; Mr William Ofori-Atta, the Cambridge-educated son of the late Nana Sir Ofori-Atta, had been a prominent member of the West African Students Union; and Mr Ako Adjei,[1] a young Accra barrister and member of the Executive Committee of the U.G.C.C. was a former president of the Students Union in London.

[1] Mr Ako Adjei is now the Minister of Trade and Labour in the all-African Gold Coast Government, headed by Dr Nkrumah.

BIRTH OF C.P.P.

A few months after the return of the N.C.N.C. delegation to Nigeria, Mr Kwame Nkrumah, who was directing the activities of the West African National Secretariat, of which Mr Kojo Botsio[2] was treasurer, was invited by the executive of the U.G.C.C. to return home and become the Convention's general secretary. Mr Nkrumah had been away from the Gold Coast for twelve years, during which time he had completed his academic studies in America and London and had served his political apprenticeship as a joint secretary with George Padmore of the Fifth Pan-African Congress.

Within a year of Nkrumah assuming the secretaryship of the United Gold Coast Convention, widespread labour disturbances and riots broke out in the Gold Coast. He and five other leading members of the organization were arrested in February 1948, on the orders of the British Governor, Sir Gerald Creasy, and deported to the Northern Territories of the Gold Coast.

A Parliamentary Commission was appointed to inquire into the causes of the unrest. After the arrival of the Commission in the Gold Coast, the six U.G.C.C. leaders were released in order to allow them to give evidence. Mr Nkrumah then resumed his political activities as secretary of the U.G.C.C. while the Commission completed their report. The members were three distinguished non-party politicians, Mr Aiken Watson, K.C., chairman; Professor Keith Murray of Oxford; and Mr Andrew Dalgeish, authority on trade unionism. They recommended the scrapping of the existing Burns Constitution as being 'out-moded', although it had been introduced only two years previously by the then Governor, Sir Alan Burns, and been endorsed by Labour Colonial Secretary, Mr A. Creech Jones, as the most progressive constitution in colonial Africa.

[2] Mr Kojo Botsio is now the Minister of State in the all-African Gold Coast Government. His first Cabinet appointment in 1951 was that of Minister of Education and Social Welfare.

The Commissioners also advised the Labour Government to appoint an all-African committee to draft a new constitution for the Gold Coast. The Colonial Office hesitantly agreed to this revolutionary proposal and instructed the Governor to set up the constitutional committee. The Governor proceeded to pack the committee with all manner of reactionary middle-class lawyers, business and professional men, as well as conservative chiefs, under the chairmanship of an African High Court judge, Sir J. Henley Coussey. Not one representative of the trade unions, farmers' societies or other sections of the under-privileged groups was included. This omission of the Governor's gave rise to much dissatisfaction among the ordinary people. Their criticisms found expression through the youth of the country, whose nationalist feelings had been stimulated by the propaganda activities of Nkrumah and a group of younger men called the Committee of Youth Organizations, which was associated with the U.G.C.C. Even the older leaders of the U.G.C.C. like Dr Danquah did not escape the attacks of these 'Young Turks', who were urging the moderate nationalist members of the Coussey Committee to demand 'Self-Government Now'. When this demand was resisted, Mr Nkrumah broke with the conservative leadership in control of the U.G.C.C. and formed the radical Convention People's Party (C.P.P.), in June 1949. Two months later, the Coussey Committee issued its report and after it was vetted by Mr Creech Jones's principal adviser in the Colonial Office, Mr (now Sir Andrew) Cohen, Governor of Uganda, the new constitution was debated in the 'outmoded' Burns Legislative Council and promulgated by Sir Charles Arden-Clarke, who succeeded Sir Gerald Creasy as Governor in 1949.

As the new constitution fell short of the aspirations of the radicals for immediate self-government, Mr Nkrumah called upon the supporters of the C.P.P. to register their protest in the form of a non-violent, non-co-operation campaign backed by Positive Action. The satyagraha methods introduced into Indian politics by Mahatma Gandhi had been discussed at the Fifth Pan-African Congress and endorsed as the only effective means of making alien rulers respect the wishes of an unarmed subject people.

'Your weapons—the strike and the boycott—are invincible,'
enjoined the Congress's Declaration to the Colonial Workers,
Farmers and Intellectuals. As in India, so in the Gold Coast,
the British Government met non-violence with violent police
measures. The leaders of the Trade Union Congress and the
C.P.P. were arrested, given a trial of sorts and sentenced to
long terms of imprisonment for daring to demand 'Self-
Government Now' which was then the main political issue
in the Gold Coast.

FIRST VICTORY FOR PAN-AFRICANISM

With Nkrumah and other radical leaders behind prison
bars, the Governor and his officials proceeded to prepare for
the first general election under the 1950 constitution. Although Nkrumah had described the Coussey Constitution as
'bogus and fraudulent', from his prison he advised his supporters to intensify the organization of the C.P.P. and contest
the election. His motive for not boycotting the legislature
was to get the C.P.P. to win as many seats as possible so as to
prevent the reactionary U.G.C.C. leaders and other conservatives who had helped to frame the new instrument, from
dominating the Assembly and working the constitution in the
way the Colonial Office intended. The election took place in
February 1951, while Nkrumah and many of his colleagues
were still in jail. It resulted in a sweeping victory for the
C.P.P. candidates, including Nkrumah, who was immediately
released by the Governor and invited to form the Executive
Council or Cabinet, the main instrument of government.

This was the first victory for the ideology of Pan-
Africanism. It proved definitely the effectiveness of organization and Positive Action based on non-violent methods.
'Organization decides everything' emphasized Nkrumah. Ever
since that initial victory, the continued strength of the C.P.P.
has rested on its superb organization. In the words of the
Declaration of the Fifth Pan-African Congress, 'today there
is only one road to effective action—the organization of the
masses'.

The Coussey Constitution which the C.P.P. was called upon to operate was so framed as to establish a mixed-bag legislature. The Legislative Assembly consisted of eighty-four members of whom seventy-five were elected, three ex-officio, and six represented foreign commercial and mining interests. The *ex-officio* members—the Chief Secretary, Financial Secretary and Attorney-General—and the foreign capitalist representatives were all nominated by the Governor. The others were selected in the following manner. Five municipal members were elected in a single stage election by universal adult suffrage; thirty-three rural members were elected in two-stage election by adult suffrage exercised through electoral colleges; nineteen members from the Northern Territories were elected by a special electoral college composed of chiefs and tribal officials; eighteen members were elected by the Territorial Councils of Chiefs representing the colony area, Ashanti and Southern Togoland under United Nations trusteeship, exercised by the United Kingdom Government.

The Speaker was elected by all members of the Assembly from among themselves or from outside the Assembly. The first Speaker, Sir Charles Emmanuel Quist who was elected by unanimous vote, was not a member of the Assembly.

The Executive Council, now called the Cabinet, consisted of eleven members. Eight of them were Africans, holding portfolios of Commerce and Industry; Labour and Cooperative; Agriculture and Natural Resources; Education and Social Welfare; Local Government and Housing; Communications and Works; Health and Economic Development. The three British Ministers held the portfolios of Defence and External Affairs; Finance and Justice.

The Constitution as originally devised made no provisions for the office of Prime Minister. The Colonial Office constitutional draughtsmen never anticipated the emergence of party politics in the Gold Coast. They expected a continuation of 'personality' politics—that is to say, so-called leaders without organized parties or programmes, who could be played off one against the other. Individuals not responsible to parties, would have made it easy for the Governor, with his three official advisers, to hand-pick the African members of the Executive Council and appoint from among them one to lead the team

of 'yes-men'. The leader of the pack was to be officially described as 'Leader of Government Business'.

Mr Nkrumah spoilt the imperialist game. Loyally adhering
to the decisions of the Pan-African Congress, that organization was the key to power, the first thing he set about doing
after breaking with the moderate U.G.C.C., was to form a
country-wide party on a non-tribal, non-religious basis. This
so alarmed the African conservative tribalists who saw their
political careers threatened, that they appealed to the Chiefs
and the British officials to suppress the C.P.P. as 'a dangerous
Communist conspiracy'. But it was too late to invoke the
'red bogy'. Party politics had caught on. The common people,
who, before the coming of Nkrumah, had been used as pawns
by the careerist politicians to further their own political ambitions, welcomed the new idea of parliamentary democracy
based on party lines. Consequently, when the C.P.P. emerged
from the election as the party with a majority over all others,
the Labour Colonial Secretary, Mr James Griffiths, had to
amend the constitution to recognize Dr Nkrumah, Prime
Minister *de jure*, in order to give legality to a *de facto* situation.

This change of status was instituted early in 1952, before
Labour fell from office. Events had confirmed Dr Nkrumah's
injunctions to his supporters: 'Seek ye first the political kingdom and everything else will be added unto you'.

PLANNING FOR SELF-GOVERNMENT

With the initiative firmly in his hands, and backed by an
overwhelming majority in both Legislative Assembly and
Cabinet, the Prime Minister immediately set out to introduce
long overdue economic and social reforms outlined in an
official Development Plan. Within an experimental period of
three years, the predominantly African Government was able
to bring about remarkable changes in the country. In a fitting
tribute to the Government at the last session held under the
Coussey Constitution on March 12, 1954, the Speaker said:
'We have obtained in the Assembly, a Prime Minister in the

person of Dr Kwame Nkrumah, a capable, energetic, sincere
and genuine statesman, who with his Cabinet containing a
majority of Africans, has been mainly responsible for the
progress to which I have alluded. Laws have been passed
establishing local government on a firm basis. Social legislation has been introduced in many forms to safeguard the well-
being and prosperity of the country and education has been
expanded widely. Economically, we are solvent and our last
Budget showed a surplus of £16 million. These are achievements of which we can rightly feel proud and which should
encourage us to approach and face the future with confidence.'

How did all this come about? Again we must return to
the ideological principles enunciated by Pan-Africanism. The
Fifth Congress asserted that, 'the object of imperialist powers
is to exploit', and the Congress declaration proceeded to say
that, 'by granting the right of colonial peoples to govern
themselves that object is defeated. Therefore, the struggle for
political power by colonial and subject peoples is the first step
towards, and the necessary prerequisite to, complete social,
economic and political emancipation.'

Using this fundamental analysis made by the Fifth Pan-
African Congress as a guide to *Positive Action*, Dr Nkrumah
has always enjoined upon his lieutenants to avoid violence and
maintain the closest contact with the masses, upon whom the
C.P.P. relies for support at every stage of the struggle for self-
government. He himself never makes a move before consulting public opinion, which the C.P.P. is constantly educating
in the three fundamental principles of Pan-Africanism—nationalism, political democracy and socialism—as the only effective forces against tribalism and regional separatism which
threaten the unity of all young nations like the Gold Coast.

Having demonstrated for three years that Africans are not
afraid of responsibility and that, given a fair chance, they are
capable of administering a modern state, the Prime Minister
announced in the Legislative Assembly in October 1953, that,
as a result of an exchange of views on constitutional matters
with the Tory Colonial Secretary, Mr Oliver Lyttelton, he
proposed to present to the British Imperial Government a
demand for complete self-government. Before presenting his
proposals to the United Kingdom Government, the Prime

Minister invited all members of territorial, municipal and local government councils, political parties, trade unions, co-operative societies, and other public bodies and prominent citizens to submit their views in writing on questions of constitutional reforms.

The response to this democratic procedure was tremendous. Supported by the majority of the local press, the entire country reacted enthusiastically. After the views and suggestions of all sections of the population had been received and collated in the Prime Minister's office, the African representative members of the Cabinet drafted concrete proposals which were published as an official White Paper, setting out in detail the demands of the people for the establishment of a more democratic constitution.[3]

The draft constitutional reforms were then presented to the Legislative Assembly and debated upon by the elected representatives of the people. The Assembly endorsed a formal motion moved by the Prime Minister to 'authorize the Government to request that Her Majesty's Government, as soon as the necessary constitutional and administrative arrangements for independence are made, should introduce an Act of Independence into the United Kingdom Parliament declaring the Gold Coast a sovereign and independent State within the Commonwealth; and, further, that the Assembly do authorize the Government, without prejudice to the above request, to amend as a matter of urgency the Gold Coast (Constitution) Order in Council, 1950, in such a way as to provide *inter alia* that the Legislative Assembly shall be composed of members directly elected by secret ballot and that all members of the Cabinet shall be members of the Assembly and directly responsible to it.'

While negotiations between the Prime Minister and the Secretary of State for Colonies were being carried on through the Governor, the Assembly approved plans for dividing the entire country into 104 constituencies and enacted legislation to deal with other electoral arrangements, so that by the last session of the Assembly in March 1954, the Speaker was able

[3] See Appendix III for full text of the Prime Minister's speech on the White Paper.

to adjourn Parliament *sine die* and announce the general election for the new Nkrumah Constitution.

The election took place on June 10th to 15th, 1954, and resulted in a sweeping victory for the C.P.P. which captured seventy-two seats as against the combined opposition parties and independent candidates, who won thirty-two seats.

THE NKRUMAH CONSTITUTION

Under the present transitional constitution from complete internal self-government to self-determination, all members of parliament have been elected by secret ballot. Chiefs, special foreign commercial and mining representatives as well as nominated British officials, have been excluded from membership of the Assembly. The composition of the Cabinet has also been changed from a multi-racial body to an all-African one of eleven members appointed by the Prime Minister, who will preside over Cabinet meetings instead of the Governor.

The Governor, however, retains in his own hands defence and external affairs. He will be advised in the exercise of these functions by a consultative committee on which three Africans —the Prime Minister, the Minister of State and Minister of the Interior—will serve. To assist the Governor in the discharge of his additional duties, formerly carried out by the Minister of Defence and External Affairs, a Deputy Governor has been appointed. This arrangement will continue during the transitional period, after which responsibility for defence and foreign affairs and other reserved matters affecting British Togoland will pass into the hands of a sovereign independent Gold Coast Government.

Apart from selecting his own Cabinet colleagues, the Prime Minister also has the right to appoint Ministerial Secretaries to assist the Cabinet Members in the discharge of their duties. They, unlike the permanent secretaries, who will continue to be civil servants, will be drawn from the C.P.P. assemblymen. These, in brief outline, are the essential features of the re-

formed constitution which came into operation on July 27,
1954.

APPEAL FOR NATIONAL UNITY AGAINST
TRIBALISM

Upon assuming office and appointing his new Cabinet the
Prime Minister, in a broadcast to the nation on June 23, 1954,
said *inter alia*: 'Freedom brings its responsibilities, and it is
my earnest hope that the hurdle we have just cleared will not
give rise within us to any complacency for what we have
achieved, or any false illusions about the hard work that lies
ahead. We all wish for rapid development, for the extension
of our social and productive services, and for the early achievement of a standard of living comparable with that of any
other country in the world. This result cannot be achieved
merely by words or plans, or even by the expenditure of vast
sums of money. There are three ingredients to this progress
without which all such plans must fail.

'The first of these is co-operation, and I ask you all, of
whatever tribe, race, colour, creed or political party, to work
together for the future of the Gold Coast. We are catching
up with the rest of the world, and I know that if we work
together in friendly co-operation, nothing is impossible. The
second basic ingredient of all true development must be hard
work, careful and efficient work; and the third ingredient
must be a high sense of duty. In these I cannot help you,
except by devoting all my energies and time to your welfare
and to making available to all who seek it, the opportunity for
constructive work. For the rest, you must help yourselves and
must strain every nerve to ensure that only your very best
is good enough. If you all help we will see our plans mature,
and the Gold Coast will rapidly rise above its past, and
take its rightful place among the respected nations of the
world . . .

'The self-government which we demand is the means by
which we shall create the climate in which our people can

develop their attributes and express their potentialities to the full. With this in mind, we are now ready to claim the right to our independence, and I shall open intensified negotiations with the British Government with a view to the transfer of ultimate responsibility to the people of the Gold Coast. Full self-government is only one step away; we must be very sure that we do not stumble at this final step in our journey to reach the end of the road.

'With all these thoughts in mind, we must now be deeply grateful for the blessings that we have received; for the opportunity to work towards the attainment of our ideals; for the freedom which permits us to abide by our principles, so that we need not compromise on our principle of preferring self-government with danger to servitude in tranquillity.

'We need, too, to be grateful for the goodwill and friendship of the other peoples of the world; for we are happy because we have more friends than enemies. Our friends believe in us, and we are sure that we can fulfil the hopes reposed in us. We must not fail them. We must succeed.'

In his hour of triumph and re-dedication, Dr Nkrumah let it be known that he intended to work for the promotion of the principles of Pan-Africanism with West African Federation as the first step. Towards this objective, he has announced his intention to convene a Sixth Pan-African Congress in the Gold Coast—which will be the first conclave of its kind to meet on African soil. Such a convention will serve to inspire and encourage Africans in other parts of the Continent to follow in the footsteps of the Gold Coast along the road of non-violent revolution instead of Mau Mauism.

PART FOUR

XI

BRITISH AND FRENCH COLONIAL
SYSTEMS COMPARED

Of all the imperial systems of colonial administration in Africa that of the British provides the greatest possibility for dependent peoples to attain self-determination along constitutional lines.

All political parties in Britain—Socialist, Conservative, Liberal—are in fundamental agreement upon the main political objective of imperial policy, which is 'to guide the colonial territories to responsible self-government within the Commonwealth in conditions which ensure to the people concerned both a fair standard of living and freedom from oppression from any quarter'.[1]

Enunciated by the Labour Government, this objective has been endorsed by Mr Oliver Lyttelton, the Conservative Secretary of State for the Colonies. Speaking in the House of Commons on November 14, 1951, he said: 'I should like to make it plain at the outset that His Majesty's Government intend no change in these aims. We desire to see successful constitutional development both in those territories which are less developed towards self-government and in those with more advanced constitutions. His Majesty's Government will do their utmost to help Colonial Governments and legisla-

[1] The Colonial Empire, 1947-48, Cmd. No. 7433.

tures to foster health, wealth and happiness of the colonial peoples.'[2]

While Her Majesty's Government and loyal Opposition are agreed as to the goal, their methods of attaining the agreed objective may differ. Similarly, while colonial nationalists accept the broad avowed aim of British imperial policy, they frequently take issue with all parties over the date of 'self-government within the Commonwealth'. The refusal of British Governments to agree to set a time limit to colonial tutelage, even at the demand of their wards, has served to cast doubts and suspicion on Britain's intent to honour her profession of ultimate self-rule for dependent peoples. The Labour Party in its 1954 policy statement has promised to fix a time limit for the transfer of power, but has limited the promise by saving clauses. The Tories on the other hand, have rejected the idea of a time limit as unpractical.[3]

As a colonial observer it is amusing to read the fantastic claims which Tory and Labour politicians make in seeking kudos for their respective parties. But as *The Times* remarks: 'Happily for the colonies, there is little basis in fact to support the thesis . . . that the policies of the Conservative and Labour Parties in colonial affairs are widely divergent. The only significant breach in recent years of the bipartisan colonial approach has been over the imposition by the Conservative Government in 1953 of Central African Federation. Even so, it was a Labour Government which initiated the policy and nobody knows what they would have done if they had been in power when it came to implementing it. In the event, they were in opposition, voted against it, *but agreed to help make it work* [italics mine. G.P.] . . . Nationalist politicians do not show any steady preference for one party or the other. They are disappointed that Labour conceded less than they expected; and surprised that Conservatism conceded so much . . . For instance, Mr Creech Jones set his face against Central African Federation, Mr Griffiths initiated it: Mr Lyttelton deposed the Kabaka, Mr Lennox-Boyd is trying to get

---

[2] House of Commons Debates, Vol. 493, Col. 985-86.
[3] For the latest Labour Party proposals on colonies, see *Facing Facts in the Colonies*, infra p. 202.

him back. Labour exiled both Seretse and Tshekedi Khama; the Conservatives brought about the return at least of Tshekedi. If we are to try and pinpoint the major formative influences in colonial policy in the decade after the war, we would not necessarily find them among political parties at all. Some professors and writers have exercised a strong influence, but probably the strongest of all has been exerted by a few Colonial and Civil Servants whose names are never heard of by the British public, except when they become involved in some imbroglio.'[4]

While Tweedledum and Tweedledee continue their debate, it might be useful to review the origins of present-day British colonial policy. Historically speaking, it had its beginnings in the struggle between the white colonists of Upper and Lower Canada and the British Crown during the early nineteenth century. Taking a warning from the revolt of the American colonies in 1776, the British Government adopted the recommendations of Lord Durham, who was sent to Canada to investigate the causes of the 1837 rebellion. His famous report on constitutional government for dependencies of the British Crown marked the starting point in the evolution of self-governing institutions throughout the Empire.

It having been accepted that the Canadian provinces were entitled to self-determination under the North American Act of 1867, it was only a matter of time before the same privilege would be extended to other overseas territories colonized by people of British stock.

Following the Canadian precedent, Australia acquired its independence from Britain in 1900, New Zealand in 1907, and South Africa in 1909. The constitutional relationship between these white self-governing units, then called Dominions, and the 'mother' country was regularized at the Imperial Conference of 1926, which defined them as 'autonomous communities within the British Empire, equal in status, in no way subordinate one to another in any aspect of their domestic or external affairs, but united by a common allegiance to the Crown and freely associated as members of the British Commonwealth of Nations'.

[4] *The Times*, May 12, 1955.

Five years later, the Imperial Government enacted the Statute of Westminster, to give legality to the sovereignty of the Dominions by repealing the Colonial Laws Validity Act of 1865. This Statute gave the Dominion legislatures the power to repeal or amend United Kingdom legislation applying to them.

With the example of these white nations of the Empire before them, the dark-skinned subject peoples of Asia, Africa and the islands of the seas gradually began to press their claims to be raised to equal independent status. Theirs was a more difficult task. For they were then considered 'the lesser breed without the law'. Despite many obstacles, and at great sacrifice, the nationalist movements in Asian countries grew from strength to strength, until India, Pakistan, Ceylon and Burma achieved their freedom in 1947.

The first three countries elected to remain in the Commonwealth, which by that time had dropped the designation 'British'. Burma seceded and declared herself a Republic outside the Commonwealth.

Although the claim is frequently made by the Socialists that they 'gave' these Asian nations their independence, the fact is that the Labour Government had no alternative. The spirit of nationalism following the war reached such a degree of revolutionary explosiveness that any attempt on the part of any British Government—Tory or Labour—to maintain the *status quo* would only have led to open revolt, especially in India and Burma. That would have left behind a bitter legacy of hatred. Instead, the wise policy of the Labour Government has contributed to a new relationship between the British and their erstwhile subjects. The British and Asians have never been friendlier throughout the centuries of their association.

BRITISH ATTITUDE TO COLONIAL NATIONALISM

Since it is the declared aim of British colonial policy to prepare dependent peoples for ultimate independence, they introduce the framework of parliamentary institutions in their colonies. But these institutions are only broadened under pressure of popular agitation when the level of political consciousness in a colony is advanced enough to demand the introduction of a more democratic form of government. It is out of the agitation for constitutional reform that the nationalist movements and political parties emerge. And once having emerged they are tolerated, provided they function within the constitutional limits as interpreted by the British.

For the British themselves realize that parliamentary democracy, as interpreted by them, can only function properly through the free expression of the popular will exercised through the party system. Africans do not object to this process of political evolution. What they do strenuously jib at is the slow pace of progress in advanced territories like Uganda and West Africa and their exclusion from participation on a basis of absolute equality with Europeans in Kenya and Central Africa—a principle upon which African leaders can never compromise without forfeiting the confidence of their people.

It is the disparity between the professions of British theory and its practice in parts of the African empire settled by white immigrants that is so largely responsible for the unhappy state of affairs in places like Kenya and Central Africa. Racial segregation breeds communalism. It poisons human relationships and gives rise to frustrations and hatred between the exclusive communities. It also destroys the possibility of Africans achieving self-government by constitutional means.

An examination of the structure and operation of the British administrative system shows that the African territories fall within two constitutional extremes. For example, British Somaliland is at the very bottom, while the Gold Coast stands before the top rung of the ladder of complete internal self-government. The next step upwards will remove the West African colony from the category of a dependent territory into that of 'a sovereign independent State within the Commonwealth'.

The process of constitutional evolution starts with the Governor as absolute ruler, responsible to no one within the territory over which he governs. The second stage is reached when the colony is given a Legislative Council to assist the Governor in an advisory capacity. This kind of legislature is at first composed largely of British Civil Service officials and a few local representatives of the commercial and communal interests. All the members of the Council are nominated by the Governor and serve at his discretion. At a later stage, the number of official members is reduced and the unofficial members increased, some still being appointed by the Governor. Others are elected on a communal roll or limited franchise based upon property, income or educational qualifications.

The Executive Council, the Governor's inner circle of advisers, changes its composition more slowly. This body usually consists of the Governor as chairman, and the senior European officers—Colonial Secretary, Financial Secretary, Attorney-General—and certain other heads of departments, with one or two pro-British natives thrown in. In the West African territories, such people are usually selected from among the tribal rulers, such as paramount chiefs, or educated 'yes-men'. They are usually described as 'men of substance', with 'a sense of responsibility'.

As political awareness grows and agitation for more popular representation increases, the official members of the Legislative Council are replaced by an unofficial majority, partly nominated, partly elected. About the same time the unofficial side of the Executive Council is also increased by adding a few more moderate upper-class natives, but the British ex-officio membership still retains its majority.

Internal responsible government is only reached when both the Legislature and Executive pass under the control of an elected unofficial majority. Even at this stage the Governor still holds certain special powers of veto and certification. Under the power of veto, the Governor may refuse to give his consent to any Bill passed by the Legislature which in his view is inimical to good government or British economic interests. Similarly, under the power of certification, he may give the force of law to a Bill which he considers necessary but which the Legislature has refused to pass.

However, when a Governor resorts to the use of these powers, he is supposed to report the matter to the Secretary of State for Colonies for his approval.

The final transition only begins when the party system has firmly established itself. At this stage, the Ministerial System is introduced. The Executive Council is transformed into a Cabinet with collective responsibility to the elected Legislature and not to the Governor. The Ministers are made the political heads of the various civil service departments and hold office only so long as the party to which they belong enjoys the confidence of the Legislative Assembly.

With the disappearance of the British ex-officio members from the Legislature and Cabinet, a colony is ready to move from dependent status into independence and full membership of the Commonwealth. This is consummated by an Act of Independence in the United Kingdom Parliament, giving legal recognition to the new sovereign state.

The British, it is said, are not a logical people. But they have empirically evolved a more workable system of imperial governance than any other Colonial Power, especially the French.

Underlying their colonial policy is the fundamental principle of decentralization of power, and the avoidance of rigid legalistic concepts. Britain, unlike France, has never favoured the idea of the representation of dependencies in the imperial Parliament, not even for the nineteenth-century white colonies. Just the opposite. Each colony was to be endowed with its own parliamentary institutions and encouraged to develop its own individuality. When of age, the colony would become independent, and still remain within the imperial family, held together not by legal ties, but by the bond of allegiance to a Common Crown or to the Sovereign as Head of the Commonwealth. As the British never laid down a time limit for the working out of this process, the realization of independence depends upon the colonial peoples themselves. If they accept their inferior status quietly, they get nothing. But if they organize and agitate, along constitutional lines, they are gradually granted concessions, until they reach the ultimate objective of complete self-government.

The British Commonwealth, unlike the French Union—which we shall describe presently—is neither a *Union* nor a

Federation, nor yet a *Confederation* or an *Alliance*. It is without any form of central authority, common defence force or judiciary. It does not have a written constitution. It is so unique that while the majority of its members recognize the Queen as their sovereign, India, which is a Republic, only recognizes her as Head of the Commonwealth. The Queen, therefore, is Queen of the United Kingdom, Canada, Australia, New Zealand, South Africa, Pakistan and Ceylon, all of whom owe common allegiance to her. In the case of India, the President of the Republic is the official Head of State. Nevertheless, as a member of the Commonwealth, India accepts the Queen as the *symbol* of the free association of the member nations. Not even the Romans could equal the British genius for political accommodation!

More important than these constitutional conventions is the common political pattern through which all the member nations of the Commonwealth have graduated. Despite their differences of race, religion and culture, it is the background of parliamentary democracy, based upon English political institutions, independent judiciary and non-political public service, which has given to all of them certain salient features in common.

In each country of the Commonwealth, government is carried on through a freely elected parliament (except in South Africa, where, for all practical purposes, the African majority is disfranchised); with an Executive of Cabinet Ministers, collectively responsible to the Legislature.

Except in India, government in each Commonwealth country is carried out in the name of the Queen, as the Sovereign. She is officially represented by a Governor-General, whom she personally appoints on the recommendation of the Prime Minister of the country to which he is assigned. The Governor-General carries out his duties on the advice of the local Cabinet, and is in no way responsible to the United Kingdom Government or Parliament.

Thus has the British genius for political adaptability enabled the 'mother' country to free, first her white and later her coloured Asian colonies, and yet retain their association as free and equal partners—separate as the fingers of the hand in all matters concerning their respective countries, but united as the fist in all matters affecting the common welfare of the Commonwealth.

STRUCTURE OF FRENCH EMPIRE

Since the Second World War, France has made drastic reforms in the constitutional arrangements of her overseas empire. Still she has not been able to evolve a *modus operandi* to satisfy the nationalist aspirations of her colonial subjects. The French Empire remains a highly centralized structure, dominated politically and economically by the metropolitan parliament or National Assembly, which exercises sovereign authority over all the territorial units comprising what is euphemistically called the French Union. Only Federation can save this Union from ultimate disintegration.

France's present empire was acquired largely in the latter part of the nineteenth century and, except for Indo-China, is located mainly in Africa. These territories, excluding the island of Madagascar, which lies off the east coast of Africa, cover over four million square miles, and have a population of nearly 38 million, mostly Negroid Africans. There are, in addition, some 14 to 15 million Arabs and Berbers in Algeria, Tunisia and Morocco. There are also a few ancient colonies in the Western Hemisphere—Martinique and Guadeloupe in the West Indies and French Guiana along the coast of the South American mainland, as well as Réunion in the Indian Ocean, New Caledonia, New Hebrides and Oceanic Islands in the Pacific. In addition to these territories, France exercises trusteeship over parts of Togoland and Cameroons, situated along the West African coast.

Before the Second World War, all these territories were administered in accordance with the French imperial doctrine of 'assimilation' and 'association', which meant that the metropolitan government in Paris exercised absolute control over every aspect of the political, economic and cultural affairs of the overseas empire. The French never had the British vision of a dependency evolving into a self-governing country, freely associating with others in a free commonwealth.

The French attitude towards the colonies is unabashedly mercantilist. The colonies supply the mother country with raw materials and certain tropical foodstuffs, as well as troops in time of war, and provide her with a guaranteed market for her manufactured goods and capital investments. In return, the native *élite* of the colonies is encouraged to 'assimilate French culture'. Those who became French are allowed to enjoy certain rights of citizenship, which open to them careers and opportunities denied to the unassimilated natives, who are only 'subjects'. Thanks to this device, the educated African *élite*, who, in British colonies, become the vanguard of the nationalist movements, are in French colonies associated with the white Frenchmen as junior partners in governing the mass of unassimilated natives still adhering to tribal customs and primitive institutions.

Commenting sharply on his country's colonial policy, General Georges Catroux, a former Governor-General of Indo-China, says: 'This so-called colonial or semi-colonial system was the logical outcome of the belief that the rights acquired by France overseas, either by conquest or by treaty of protectorate, conferred on France all the prerogatives of full sovereignty. It was also based on the conviction that the low level of political, economic and social development of the indigenous population when they came under French control made them incapable of managing their own affairs without a long period of political apprenticeship and experience in the technique and principles of good administration. It was assumed that Western administrative methods, because of their excellence should serve as the model. It was also assumed that the indigenous leaders, who would later provide the nucleus of a government, should be shaped by the mould of French culture because of its indisputable superiority and universality.

'Furthermore, the social evolution of these territories required, as a prerequisite, the development of productive capacity, involving the installation and operation of modern equipment and the rational exploitation of natural resources. Finally, colonial enterprises should not be a financial burden, on the contrary, should be revenue-producing; investments should be productive, should guarantee to France a monopoly

of raw materials market and should secure for its imports preferential treatment. In short, the interests both of the overseas territories and of France demand unremitting direct
French intervention in the management and fulfilment of a
long-term task designed ultimately to bring to backward
peoples the methods and advantages of modern life.

'These were the principles upon which French colonial
policy was based prior to the creation of the French Union—
a sovereign metropolitan country and subject peoples deprived
of any independent political and economic life, under the control of a distant and highly centralized administration which
strove for their cultural assimilation. Some degree of fiscal
autonomy was allowed with the understanding that the territories themselves paid the costs of administration. Elected
advisory assemblies were permitted to review the budgets,
but the representatives of the metropolitan country reserved
the right to prepare the budgets and to promulgate them.
Thus the colonies and protectorates were treated administratively as French provinces and were subject to the political
decisions of the metropolitan government. Their peoples
were dependent aliens with no voice. Without any political
rights, they were no more than subjects or French protégés.'[5]

The defeat of France in Viet Nam or Indo-China by the
Japanese, and the occupation of the metropolis by the Germans, delivered a shattering blow to the 'what we have we
hold' colonial policy of the Third Republic. At this period of
imperial crisis, it was a Negro Governor-General of Equatorial
Africa, Monsieur Félix Éboué,[6] who was the first French proconsul to rally to the defence of the prostrated motherland.
Immediately after the collapse of France in 1940, he declared his allegiance to the Free French exiled government
under General de Gaulle, and by his example inspired other
Colonial governors to break with the Vichy régime.

Ironically enough, the Negroes, who are the most despised

[5] General Georges Catroux: *The French Union*, International Conciliation No. 495, pp. 203-4.

[6] Governor-General Éboué was born in French Guiana in 1884
and educated at Bordeaux University and the School of Colonial
Studies in Paris, from which he passed into the French Colonial
Service as a political officer.

of the exploited races, seem to be always the ones destined to come to the aid of France in her hour of need. For twenty-five years before, when the Germans stood on the Marne, another black saviour came out of Africa. He was Monsieur Blaise Diagne, the Negro deputy of Senegal, who, in response to the appeal of Prime Minister Clemenceau, recruited thousands of black troops from West and Equatorial Africa to help stem the German advance on Paris during the most critical period of the First World War.

In the Second World War, Governor-General Éboué's adherence to the Free French not only provided military and economic aid to the stricken mother country, but gave white Frenchmen in exile a territorial base from which they could rally the forces of resistance.

Recognizing that the pre-war colonial system was completely discredited by France's inability to defend her white citizens at home, much less to assure the protection of her coloured colonial subjects, General de Gaulle as head of the Committee of National Liberation convened a conference in 1944 to review the future of France in relation to her overseas territories.

CONSTITUTION OF FRENCH REPUBLIC

The conference took place at Brazzaville, from January 30 to February 8, 1944, the headquarters of Governor-General Éboué, and was attended by all the Governors-General of the disrupted empire, and other high-ranking officials, among them M. Pleven, the wartime Commissioner for the Colonies in the French Government in exile. The conference decided to abandon the pre-war colonial doctrine of 'assimilation' in favour of 'closer association' between France and her colonies —a relationship which 'can no longer be contested, in view of the services which they have rendered the nation during the present war'.[7] However, the right of dependencies to complete self-government or independence was rejected.

[7] Daniel Boisdon: *Les Institutions de l'Union Française,* p. 15 (Berger-Levrault, Paris).

This was explicitly stated in the preamble to the Conference decisions, which declared that 'the objectives of the task of civilization accomplished by France in her colonies rule out any idea of autonomy, any possibility of an evolution outside the French bloc of the Empire; the eventual creation, even in the distant future, of autonomy for the colonies must be ruled out'.[8]

This intransigent attitude to the autonomous aspirations of French colonials, especially those of the Asian inhabitants of Indo-China, who were carrying on the resistance movement under Ho Chi-minh against the Japanese invaders, stands out in striking contrast to that of the British declaration to India two years before the Brazzaville Conference took place. It will be recalled that in March 1942, Sir Stafford Cripps visited India, where, on behalf of the wartime British Coalition Government, he promised the Congress leaders 'complete and absolute self-determination and self-government for India' after the cessation of hostilities in the Far East. Yet France, who was then in a much more precarious position than Britain, refused even to pay lip service to self-rule for her South-East Asian colony. Instead, all the political parties in the Resistance Movement, from the Communists on the extreme left to the Gaullists on the extreme right, including the middle-of-the-road Socialists and M.R.P.'[9] endorsed what they proclaimed was a new policy of the 'one and indivisible French Union'. This now stands exposed for what it always was, 'a bogus and fradulent' device to maintain French domination over her overseas dependencies behind the façade of a complicated bureaucratic structure called the 'French Union'.

Even the parties to this political manoeuvre are still unable to define what exactly the French Union is—a federal system or a free association with the right of secession? Nor are they even able to delineate the rights and status of the inhabitants of the different parts of the so-called Union. This conflict was reflected in the attitude towards the projected Assembly of the Union. All parties were agreed on the futility of

[8] *Encyclopédie Politique de la France et du Monde*, Vol. II, p. 12.
[9] *Mouvement Républicain Populaire* (Catholic Party).

an Assembly which would concentrate its attention on the problems of the overseas territories. However, the Communists and most of the Socialists wanted this Assembly of the Union to be the germ of a future free collaboration between France and her overseas territories. The M.R.P. and the Conservatives, on the other hand, stressed the function of the Assembly as a means of associating the peoples of the overseas territories more closely with the political life of the mother country than was provided for by their limited representation in the National Assembly. Both because of the necessity for compromise and because it was impossible to create overnight the structure of so vast a system as the French Union, it was decided to establish a fairly flexible skeleton framework which could be filled in later and modified in the light of experience.'[10]

The French, though usually a very intelligent and logical people, seem to have got themselves completely entangled in their 'L'Union Française', the new-fangled designation for their pre-war empire. Defining the new imperial structure, the Constitution of the Fourth Republic states that 'The French Union is formed on the one hand by the French Republic, which includes metropolitan France, the overseas departments and territories, and on the other hand by the Associate States and Territories.

'The members of the French Union combine their forces for the defence of the French Union. The Government of the Republic co-ordinates these forces and directs the defence policy.

'The Government's representative in each overseas territory or group of territories holds in his person the powers of the French Republic. He is the hand of the administration of the territory, and is responsible to the French Government.'

Let us examine the political realities behind this constitutional façade, and the methods which post-war Governments have adopted to keep control over the empire firmly in the grip of white Frenchmen.

[10] General Catroux: *The French Union*, p. 197.

UNION NEW NAME FOR OLD EMPIRE

To create the impression that the old empire has been voluntarily liquidated, and that the Europeans, Asians and Africans are one big happy family enjoying equal rights without distinction of race or religion, the term 'colony' has been expunged from the French political dictionary. More euphemistic labels are now applied to the colonies and other possessions. They fall into four main categories: *Overseas Departments, Overseas Territories, Associated Territories,* and *Associated States.* These in turn are administered through different Ministers under the metropolitan Government.

The Overseas Departments consist of the pre-Napoleonic colonies settled by French colonists or inhabited by people of African descent who have become completely 'assimilated' to French culture—for example, Réunion in the Indian Ocean; Algeria in North Africa; Martinique and Guadeloupe in the West Indies, and French Guiana on the South American mainland. Although separated by the seas, these territories are considered integral parts of metropolitan France, and the populations have been granted full-fledged French citizenship. For administrative purposes they come under the French Ministry of the Interior. In other words, they enjoy less autonomy than British Crown Colonies.

The colonies designated Overseas Territories are located mostly in West and Equatorial Africa, and include in addition Madagascar, French Somaliland and the Pacific islands. These are administered by the Ministry for France-Overseas. This Ministry is also responsible for the affairs of French Togoland and French Cameroons, held under United Nations trusteeship. These two former German colonies have been rechristened 'Associated Territories', since they are administered as integral parts of adjoining French territories under special agreement signed between France and the United Nations General Assembly.

The designation Associated States is applied to the Protectorates of Morocco and Tunis, and the Kingdoms of Viet Nam, Laos and Cambodia in Indo-China. The North African protectorates are controlled through the French Ministry of Foreign Affairs,[11] while the South-East Asian territories are under the Ministry of Associated States.

If the French had the same imperial arrangement as the British, the corresponding Ministry for Dependencies would be the Colonial Office instead of the Ministry for Overseas Territories, in which control over all dependencies is concentrated. The exceptions to the normal British pattern are Anglo-Egyptian Sudan which, as a Condominium is under the Foreign Office; and the internal self-governing dependency of Southern Rhodesia, and the Protectorates of Bechuanaland, Basutoland and Swaziland. These territories are administered through the Commonwealth Relations Office, which also acts as the liaison department between the United Kingdom Government and the self-governing member states or dominions of the Commonwealth.

Another distinction between the French Union and the British Empire and Commonwealth is reflected in the machinery of government. Although the Secretary of State for the Colonies is answerable to Parliament for the affairs of the colonial territories comprising the non-self-governing empire, all the colonies enjoy administrative and fiscal autonomy in varying degrees. On the other hand, the British Parliament and Government have absolutely no authority to legislate for the self-governing members of the Commonwealth, each of whom enjoys complete jurisdiction over its internal and external affairs.

Under the French system, this is not the case. *All* power over the French Union derives from one source—the metropolitan Parliament or National Assembly—which has supreme authority over fundamental legislation affecting all Overseas Territories, Departments and Protectorates.

With the pressure of the coloured races of West Africa, the West Indies and Malaya for independence from British

[11] When faced with revolt in Tunis and Morocco in the summer of 1954, Prime Minister Mendès-France established a special Ministry for North African Affairs to deal with the problems in the two protectorates.

control, the Labour Party has come up with a bogus imperial scheme borrowed from the French, aimed at reversing the historical process of constitutional evolution. In a pamphlet entitled, *Facing Facts in the Colonies,* the colonial experts of Transport House toy with the idea of a 'Union Britannique' in the form of a 'Grand Council of the Commonwealth and Empire with a membership representing the peoples of the U.K., Dominions and Colonies'.

The proposals are so fantastic as hardly to be worth the price of sixpence! It is only necessary to pose the question: Will representation in the proposed Commonwealth Parliament be based on population, regardless of race or colour? Or, like the Central African Federal Parliament, one white man will equal ten thousand coloured 'citizens'? The colonial problem is sufficiently complicated without being made more difficult by getting colonial nationalist leaders involved in the squabbles of the British and Commonwealth political parties and Governments. The task of the nationalist leaders is to get on with the job of laying the economic and social foundations of their emergent nations and not to play 'Irish politics' at Westminster. They must reject Labour's 'gift horse' out of hand.

COLONIAL DEPUTIES IN FRENCH
PARLIAMENT

The French Parliament consists of two chambers: first, the *National Assembly* (the former Chamber of Deputies) has 544 members elected by constituencies in metropolitan France and 83 from constituencies in *Overseas Departments* and *Territories,* a total of 627. Of these latter seats, 30 represent three departments in Algeria (15 elected for 1 million French settlers and 15 for 8 million Moslems); and 12 for the departments of Réunion, French Guiana and the ancient West Indian colonies of Guadeloupe and Martinique. The rest are distributed among some 21 other *Overseas Territories* and *Associated Territories.*

The second parliamentary chamber is called the *Council of the Republic*.[12] It is the successor of the Senate under the Third Republic. This body comprises 320 members, 249 elected to represent metropolitan France and 71 from overseas. By reserving the overwhelming majority of places in both the National Assembly and the Council of the Republic for Europeans, Frenchmen at home and abroad guarantee to themselves the final decision in all matters affecting the French Union.

In addition to Parliament, the constitution of the Fourth Republic provides for three other centralized organs to assist the Paris Government in conducting the internal and external affairs of the Union. These are the *Presidency*, the *High Council* and the *Assembly of the French Union* at Versailles.

As has been stated, the National Assembly is the true repository of political power. All other bodies are merely consultative and advisory. The office of the Presidency is exercised by the President of the French Republic, which designation applies only to metropolitan France and the Overseas Department and Overseas Territories. The countries called Associated States and Associated Territories are excluded. The President is elected by the National Assembly and, apart from being the Head of the Republic, is also Head of the French Union. In the latter capacity, he alone can convene the High Council and preside over its discussions. The High Council is a purely consultative body. It has no legislative or executive authority of its own and can only make recommendations to the French Cabinet. The membership is confined to four French representatives, appointed by the French Metropolitan Government, and one representative from each of the Associated States, such as Morocco, Tunisia, Cambodia, Laos and Viet Nam (Indo-China). These are appointed by the native rulers of the Associated States. It has never met.

Finally, we have a larger body called the Assembly of the Union. Again, this is a purely advisory council, which the

[12] The President of the Council of the Republic is Monsieur Gaston Monnerville, a Negro lawyer from French Guiana. He was formerly Under-Secretary of State in pre-war Radical-Socialist Governments.

French Government may or may not consult on matters relating to colonial affairs. The Assembly of the Union may also draw the attention of the French Cabinet to matters strictly relating to overseas problems. It consists of 204 members, divided equally between metropolitan France and all the Overseas Departments, Overseas Territories, Associated Territories and Associated States; and as such, symbolizes the 'one and indivisible' unity between European France and her overseas empire.

The metropolitan members of the Assembly of the Union are elected by both chambers of the French Parliament (National Assembly and Council of the Republic), but the overseas members are selected by local councils and assemblies, or hand-picked by the native heads of the Associated States.

Since the colonial councils and assemblies in the French overseas possessions have less powers than Legislative and Executive Councils in the British colonies, the tendency is for French colonial politicians to turn their attention to the National Assembly in Paris, where all power lies. But even if the coloured overseas representatives elected to the National Assembly were to combine into a colonial or overseas parliamentary bloc, they would still be a minority. For there are only 83 overseas deputies, including the representatives of the white colonists, as compared with 544 metropolitan members. Nevertheless, such a coloured bloc might be an important factor in situations of stalemate among the major French metropolitan parties. In recent years an attempt has been made by the Negro deputies from West and Equatorial Africa to form a parliamentary bloc under the title of *Indépendants d'Outre Mer*. Until 1950 the coloured parliamentarians were mostly attached to the metropolitan political parties and subject to the direction and control of the French party leaders. For example, the West Indian deputies, Léopold Bissol and Aimé Césaire of Martinique and Rosan Girard of Guadeloupe, were elected on the Communist party ticket, while their countrymen, Paul Valentine, E. H. Very and Madame Eugene Éboué, widow of Governor-General Félix Éboué were returned as Socialist candidates.

Some of the other prominent Negro deputies who have been elected to the National Assembly on the Socialist ticket are Professor Léopold Senghor, son-in-law of Governor-General Éboué and Monsieur Lamine Gueye, Mayor of Dakar in Senegal, West Africa. The majority of the other colonial deputies are attached to the *Mouvement Républicain Populaire* (M.R.P.); *Union Démocratique et Socialiste de la Résistance* (U.D.S.R.); *Groupe du Rassemblement du Peuple Français* (R.P.F.); *Républicain Indépendents* (R.I.); *Groupe Radical Socialistes* (R.S.); and *Section Française de l'Internationale Ouvrière* (S.F.I.O.).

The colonial representatives serving in the Council of the Republic and the Assembly of the French Union are also tied up with metropolitan political parties and groups such as the *Communist, Socialist, M.R.P., Rassemblement des Gauches Républicaines, Rassemblement du Peuple Français, Rassemblement d'Outre-Mer, Républicain Indépendents*. The R.D.A. (*Rassemblement Démocratique Africaine*)—which I shall discuss later—is the largest group of African members in the Assembly of the French Union independent of metropolitan party control. It has about a dozen members out of 204.

French political parties, regardless of their ideology, do not encourage African self-assertion outside their control. They have no objection to the blacks participating in metropolitan politics, provided they do not advocate self-government and autonomy outside the definition of the French Union. Nationalist demands like 'self-rule', 'self-determination' and 'independence' are not tolerated by the French. Such aspirations are abhorrent to Frenchmen, be they Communist, Socialist or Conservative. For it means the rejection of French culture by so-called backward races. Just as most Englishmen still believe in the 'White Man's Burden', so the majority of Frenchmen subscribe to the doctrine of *la mission civilisatrice*, which finds political expression in their colonial doctrine of 'assimilation' and 'association', the ideological foundations of the French Union.

THE DOCTRINE OF ASSIMILATION

Conscious of the contributions which the Colonial peoples made to the liberation of France, the radical Negro *élite* is gradually challenging the whole assumption of the French doctrine of assimilation and is demanding the liquidation of Colonialism. The first step in this direction occurred when the African representatives who took part in the deliberations of the Constituent Assembly which drafted the Constitution of the Fourth Republic were able to secure a larger measure of representation for the overseas territories to the National Assembly and other metropolitan councils. This right gave a fillip to the political consciousness which had been awakened in West and Equatorial Africa during the war, and stimulated the growth of political organizations.

By the time the Constitution was ratified and the National Assembly brought into being in Paris, a federal movement of existing parties and tendencies, known as the *Rassemblement Démocratique Africaine* (R.D.A.), had taken root throughout the French territories. The main objective of the R.D.A. was to rally the natives to fight for political, economic and social demands. In the first post-war elections, the majority of African representatives in the National Assembly and the Council of the Republic were adherents of the R.D.A., which at that time enjoyed great prestige.

In Paris, during the post-liberation period of exuberant leftism, some of these African deputies, headed by M. Gabriel D'Arboussier, the mulatto son of a former colonial governor came under the patronage of the Communists, who were then represented in the Government. In his capacity as secretary-general of the R.D.A., M. D'Arboussier served as the channel through which Communist ideology filtered back into the organization in Africa. When his patrons, the Communists, were thrown out of the Cabinet, the right-wing parties which took over the Government instituted a policy of repression in the colonies against the R.D.A. This led to a split between the adherents of M. D'Arboussier and those of the president of the organization, Dr Houphouet-Boigny in 1950. Dr Houphouet-Boigny maintained that the R.D.A.'s close association with the Communists was an embarrassment, since it gave the French colonial officials and police an excuse to brand the organization as subversive and victimize its leaders. D'Arboussier, on the other hand, favoured the continuation of the link with the Communists. Interpreting the situation to his supporters, Dr Houphouet-Boigny explained that the 'African parliamentary representatives cannot, by systematic opposition to the parties constituting the Government, achieve any results for their country. Of course, our break with the Communist Party will not by itself solve all our problems. But what is essential is not to give reactionaries the pretext for which they are looking, and to make possible a re-grouping of Africans.' Dr Houphouet-Boigny and his supporters then made a temporary *rapprochement* with M. Pleven's *Union Démocratique et Sociale de la Résistance*, in order to secure the greatest possible protection against the repression of the French Colonial officials, which was pursuing the members of the R.D.A. at the time. The only R.D.A. section still under pro-Communist influence is the *Union des Populations du Cameroun*.

While the struggle between the adherents of M. D'Arboussier and Dr Houphouet-Boigny was taking place within the R.D.A., a rupture occurred within the African Section of the Socialist Party in Senegal, which was headed by M. Lamine Gueye. This organization was as much an appendage of the Socialist Party of France as the R.D.A. had been to the Communists before the break. In 1951, the young Senegalese professor, Léopold Senghor, led a revolt against the French domination of the Senegal Socialist Party, and formed the *Bloc Démocratique Sénégalais*. Exploiting the nationalist sentiments of the Africans, the *Bloc* won the next elections on the slogan that a vote for Lamine Gueye's supporters meant to vote that Senegal would be run by Guy Mollet, who is the secretary of the French Socialist Party in Paris.[13]

[13] A serious clash occurred between the supporters of the two factions during the elections in January 1955, resulting in the death of three African Socialists.

Having freed themselves from the patronage of the French political parties, some of the overseas parliamentary representatives such as the *Bloc Démocratique Sénégalais*, the *Parti Républicain Dahoméen, Union progressiste Mauritanienne, Union du Niger, Parti Togolais du Progrès*, and other smaller groupings were able to form themselves into an alliance called the *Indépendents d'outre-mer* (I.O.M.). This detachment of African colonial deputies from the patronage of French political parties is a new development in French colonial politics. It is a sign of growing national consciousness, stimulated by the political agitation in the British West African colonies for complete self-government. The I.O.M. has some twelve adherents in the National Assembly and six in the Council of the Republic. If it succeeds in winning more adherents in the Assembly, it might become the most important parliamentary pressure *groupe* in advancing the political aspirations of the Africans seeking a greater measure of autonomy and self-government.[14]

The new current should facilitate closer identification with the ideas of Pan-Africanism, thus bringing the French colonial organizations in the various territories into closer association with those in the neighbouring British colonies working for complete self-determination and the federation of all West African territories.

[14] The main groups outside the I.O.M. are the *Parti Progressiste Soudanaise* allied with the S.F.I.O.; the *Parti Progressiste Congolaise* with the R.D.A., and the *Union Démocratique Tchadienne* with the R.P.F.

XII

BELGIAN, PORTUGUESE, SPANISH AND SOUTH AFRICAN NATIVE POLICIES

The British colonial system, as we have seen, provides the most flexible constitutional machinery for political evolution from dependent status to complete sovereign independence. Yet the racial relationship between French Europeans and the coloured colonial peoples living in France and her overseas territories is easier and more tolerant than that of Britain and her colonies. The French judge a man by his culture, the British by the colour of his skin. To the French, moreover, their own culture is the best in the world, and having assimilated it, the educated colonial finds a recognition and acceptance in French national life which is not extended to the coloured *élite* in any British community. In fact, British officials in the colonies place a premium on ignorance; the French on intellect. Politics apart, the French colonial officials are able to establish closer ties of personal friendship with the native *élite* than with the tribal Africans. There are no cultural links to bring them together with the illiterates. In the British colonies, it is the opposite. The Englishman is psychologically incapable of acting naturally towards an educated African. He either tends to bully the cultured Negro or patronize him. This kind of behaviour does not evoke the same resentment in an illiterate tribesman as it does in the educated Negro. Thus, the Englishman gets on better with the more backward and primitive African. In fact, the English colonial official is forever extolling the illiterate African—the 'noble savage'—over the educated African. It helps to flatter his middle-class ego and bolster his racial pride of 'superiority' over the native.

The educated man of colour is the unhappiest person under the Union Jack. This is not so under the French Tricolour. Collectively, the natives in the French colonies are more repressed than those under British rule, but individually, educated Africans enjoy greater human dignity and suffer far less from colour bars and racial segregation under French rule. This French attitude is due in large measure to the fact that Latin races are less emotionally upset by colour and race than the Anglo-Saxon peoples. There is also less racial tolerance in Protestant Christianity than in Catholicism, the predominant religion in France, Italy, Spain, Portugal and Latin American countries. This observation holds good even where the political régimes may formally be even less democratic than in the Anglo-Saxon Protestant countries like Great Britain and the United States of America.

For example, the Italian people, despite a quarter of a century of fascist indoctrination in racial mumbo-jumbo, manifest less prejudice towards coloured people than the English, who have enjoyed a much longer uninterrupted period of parliamentary democracy and freedom from racist propaganda sponsored by the State.

Although the subject of race prejudice is outside the scope of this book, we mention these facts because, while we are prepared to concede the British genius for constitutional accommodation as regards the national aspirations of subject peoples, we are convinced that the English can learn much from the Latins and Slavs in the sphere of race relations. In Soviet Russia, the propagation of race hatred is considered a serious crime and is severely punished. Communists recognize absolute racial equality between coloured and white peoples. This gives the Russian rulers a head-on lead over Britain and America in the 'cold war' in Asia and Africa.

The deep wounds which intolerable colour bars inflict upon Africans, especially educated and politically conscious ones, is largely responsible for the social conflict and racial tension in East and Central Africa. The psychological problem in Africa is as important as the political and economic ones. And until this is solved, there will be no lasting peace between white and black on the continent of Africa.

THE BELGIAN CONGO SYSTEM

The Belgian colonial policy can best be described as *imperial paternalism*. It operates on the principle of residential and social segregation between the races, but of economic co-operation in matters of industrial development of the Congo. Consequently, while the Belgians do not encourage African participation in political affairs, they have in recent years instituted a number of progressive economic and social welfare reforms in the interest of the indigenous population. The emphasis of Belgian colonial policy is 'jobs' instead of 'votes' for Africans. Thus, there is an absence of the industrial colour bar, alongside strict surveillance against any open manifestation of political awareness for African nationalism.

'The Belgians have never thought in terms of native self-government as the ultimate aim for the population of the Belgian Congo, nor have they thought in terms of assimilation either. It would appear that a policy of assimilation as a theory of colonial rule is only possible in countries where racial considerations are, at least theoretically, of no concern. That is not true for the Belgian Congo. Although individual Belgians are inclined to disregard racial lines, there exists a marked social cleavage between black and white. Belgian racial policy may be said to stand halfway between that of the British and the French, although officially, that is to say, legally and administratively, there is no outspoken or open discrimination'.[1]

The Congo is not only the brightest jewel in the Belgian Crown, but the treasure house of the industrial barons of Brussels and Antwerp. This vast Central African colony, cov-

[1] H. A. Wieschoff. *Colonial Policies in Africa*, p. 106. (University of Pennsylvania Press.)

ering an area twice the size of Britain and eighty times that of Belgium, is undoubtedly one of the richest dependencies in the world. It was originally the private property of one man, Leopold II, King of the Belgians. He acquired it at the time of the Berlin Conference in 1885, when Africa was being shared up among the European Powers.

As absolute monarch of the Congo Free State, Leopold granted vast concessions to 'carpet-baggers' to exploit the extensive natural resources of the country. Thousands of Negroes were rounded up in their villages and driven into the dense forests to collect elephant tusks and raw rubber under conditions amounting to slavery. Men, women and children were flogged, tortured and killed for failing to bring in the amounts levied upon them by the agents and overseers of the King and his collaborators.

Following the exposures by British humanitarians like Mr H. R. Fox-Bourne of the Aborigines Protection Society and E. D. Morel, founder of the Congo Reform Association and later the Union of Democratic Control, one of the earliest anti-colonialist organizations in Britain, world public indignation was so aroused that King Leopold was forced to institute a searching inquiry into the unspeakable crimes carried out on the defenceless blacks by his agents in the Congo Free State.

The story of these atrocities as told by Morel in his book *Red Rubber* is still fresh in the memories of educated Negroes. But we must not allow the past to prejudice our attitude to the constructive work which has been done in the Congo since the territory passed from the personal responsibility of the King to the Belgian State in 1908. Since the reorganization of the Congo administration, the colony has been granted a sort of constitution called the Colonial Charter. The Congo is no longer under royal patronage, but the direct control of a special Colonial Ministry in Brussels.

As a member of the Cabinet, the Colonial Minister is ultimately responsible to the Belgian Parliament, but he enjoys much wider powers than a British Secretary of State for Colonies. Apart from approving the annual Budget of the Congo, he presides over the Colonial Council of the Belgian Parliament, which acts as an advisory body to the Minister on all matters affecting the Congo.

The Council consists of fourteen members—six appointed by Parliament, three by the House of Representatives, and three by the Senate. The other eight are appointed by the King. The Chairman of the Council is always the Colonial Minister. Legislation for the Congo is carried out by decree, signed by the King on the advice of the Colonial Council. As head of the Congo, the King appoints a Governor-General to exercise authority in his Central African empire.

For administrative purposes, the Congo is divided into six Provinces, which are sub-divided into Districts and Territories. At the head of each Province is a Governor, under whom are District Commissioners, assisted by Assistant District Commissioners responsible for the governance of each administrative region.

All instructions and orders emanate from the office of the Governor-General, who enjoys much wider powers than any British or French proconsul. These directives filter downwards through the Provincial Governors to the District Commissioners and their Assistants until they reach the level of the native chiefs, who are used as paid agents of the Congo Administration in supervising village affairs, such as the collecting of taxes from the rural population and recruiting labour for road building and other essential public works.

Africans are completely excluded from all governmental functions above village and native urban townships level. The rights guaranteed them under the so-called Congo Colonial Charter are watched over by a Special Commission for the Protection of the Natives. The eighteen members of the Commission are appointed by the King on the advice of the Governor-General and the Colonial Minister. They usually consist of representatives of the Roman Catholic and Protestant missions, the former always being in the majority, and a few other Belgian citizens such as retired officials residing in the Congo. The Commission is a purely advisory body, which can make observations on matters affecting native interests and present recommendations to the Governor-General through the Attorney-General, who is the permanent chairman.

The nearest equivalent to a Legislative Council in a British

colony is the Governor-General's Advisory Council, which is
appointed by him. As the name implies, it acts in a purely
advisory capacity. Similar advisory bodies are provided for in
each of the six Provinces, under their respective Governors.
Apart from a few 'assimilated' Africans, the majority of members of the Advisory Council are the representatives of the
Roman Catholic Church and commercial and mining interests, who all work in close co-operation with the Belgian
officials in promoting the fundamental objective of the Congo
régime—Economic Imperialism. In conformity with this policy,
the Belgian Parliament is resolutely opposed to the transfer
of political control to the Belgian settlers who, like the white
settlers in British Central Africa, are demanding autonomy.

Rejecting the British conception of preparing their African
colonials for ultimate self-government on the one hand, and
the French policy of cultural 'assimilation' and political 'association' on the other, Belgium is chiefly concerned with the
efficient and scientific development of the great mineral resources of the Congo. In pursuance of this policy, the Congo
authorities have given liberal encouragement to the African
in his training for industry, by providing for his social betterment. In justification of their colonial system of economic
exploitation, the Belgians maintain that by drawing the rural
African into industry as a skilled worker, he will improve his
standards of living and general way of life, and by this process
become adjusted to modern urbanized conditions. As a result
of this policy of proletarianization, tribalism and traditional
customs are breaking down rapidly and the Congolese social
structure is undergoing a fundamental change. The Belgians
have devoted great attention to the improvement of native
health, the establishment of housing and hospitals; and have
in general shown a great awareness of native welfare. It cannot be denied that in all these things the Belgian Congo administration has made much better progress than any other
colonial government in Africa.

Though it may be asserted that such improvements are
made in the sole interest of the natives, it is more correct to
say that the Belgians, as wise industrialists, realized that well-
fed, well-housed, well-trained, and economically contented
Africans make much better and more efficient labourers than

ill-cared-for ones. Since the Belgian State, as distinct from private capitalist companies, has a considerable financial interest as a shareholder in various mining and other enterprises, the government officials work hand-in-glove with the managements of private concerns in combating nationalist propaganda and maintaining discipline among the native population.

In this connection, the Catholic missionaries, who, until the end of the last war, were the only religious bodies entitled to receive financial aid from the Congo Government, enjoyed a monopoly over native education, subject to official supervision. Protestant missions are now receiving Government subsidies, providing they conform to official policy. The emphasis in the education of the blacks is on what is officially described as 'spiritual guidance' and 'civic discipline'. Until recently, Africans were not encouraged to advance beyond purely technical training. Consequently, while in the British and French colonies there have appeared large numbers of university graduates and professional men—lawyers, doctors, journalists, senior civil servants, university and college teachers—a black *élite* of equal intellectual status is not to be found in the Congo. In fact, not one Congolese African has ever been allowed to graduate from a Belgian University.

Explaining why the Belgian Government had not given Congolese students an opportunity to study at Belgian universities, M. André Dequae, Minister for the Colonies, said that 'Civilization cannot be limited to a few individuals, or even to 1,000, for its purpose is to raise a whole people to a higher level. Moreover, I do not think that the method which some countries have applied has had very favourable results. We have seen that those natives who have been shown Europe and given a very advanced education did not always return to their homelands in a spirit favourable to civilization and to the mother country in particular. They have gone back as *blasés*, estranged from their own people, or turned against those who had opened the door to civilization for them. In our view a civilization founded on a solid basis in their own environment offers greater guarantees.' The Minister emphasized that 'in the Belgian Congo more than one-third of the population had been converted to Christianity. For us', he added, 'civilization is still synonymous with Christianity. We trust that our colony will become the future great Christian state of Central Africa.'

The Colonial Secretary boasted that 'Africans in the Congo had shown neither political consciousness nor interest'. He felt certain that 'if Europeans succeeded in making Africans understand that equal training and skill would give them equal opportunities, every cause for friction should disappear. Evidence of good-will and common sense, and the maintenance of the attitude of missionaries and the majority of the Belgian colonials, should guarantee the future of the Congo and the continuance of its ties with the mother country.'[2]

To save the Congolese from 'dangerous thoughts' which they are likely to pick up in Europe, the Minister of Colonies, in July 1954, approved the establishment in the Congo of the *Centre Universitaire Lovanium* in association with the University of Louvain in Belgium. This institution will be administered by a special board appointed by the Minister and will have authority to select the students, arrange the curriculum and award diplomas. The *Centre Universitaire* will be a sort of *lycée* or post-secondary school, where the African *élite* will be educated up to the equivalent of matriculation or general certificate standard obtaining in the British colonies. It is hoped in the next four years to provide accommodation for a maximum of 600 out of a population of 15 millions.

Because of the non-existence of a politically articulate *élite* capable of expressing the nationalistic feelings of the masses, M. Pierre Otis, the Belgian representative on the United Nations Trusteeship Council, was able to assert that 'the natives of Ruanda-Urundi, like those of the Congo and other colonies, had no political aspirations, and that if Colonial powers withdrew the result would be a return to savagery'. Significantly enough, Dr Malan, another defender of the *Herrenvolk* doctrine of 'white supremacy', has said exactly the same thing about Gold Coast Africans. Englishmen need not feel too smug. Many of them used to say the same about the Indians before the British were forced to quit India.

[2] André Dequae: 'Belgian Policy in the Congo', reported in *East Africa & Rhodesia*, London, April 22, 1954.

Consistent with the economic aims of Belgian imperialism, the skilled Africans employed in industry have all been trained locally. The Belgians contend that a humanistic and liberal arts education 'spoils' the native for the kind of mission to which their economic policy assigns him. As long as the black man is prepared to 'remain in his place', he is afforded opportunities of acquiring skills denied to him in the neighbouring British Central African territories and the Union of South Africa. Social equality, however, is strictly forbidden. Even the non-tribal Africans must carry passes to prove the status granted them under what is called the 'Immatriculation Law'. But they are not permitted in white areas after 9 p.m., and must use separate entrances at railway stations, just like the blacks in South Africa. They are however allowed to buy drinks in shops and to consume alcoholic beverages in cafés owned by Europeans. Previously all alcohol except beer was forbidden to Africans.[3]

From a purely imperialistic point of view, Belgian colonial policy has been most profitable. According to M. Robert Godding, who was Colonial Minister in the exiled wartime Belgian Government, 'during the war, the Congo was able to finance all the expenditure of the Belgian Government in London, including the diplomatic service as well as the cost of our armed forces in Europe and Africa, a total of some £40 million. In fact, thanks to the resources of the Congo, the Belgian Government in London had not to borrow a shilling or a dollar, and the Belgian gold reserve could be left intact.'[4]

Today, every Belgian citizen, regardless of class or party political affiliation, has a vested interest in the Congo, which the Minister for the Colonies in 1946 described as 'a kind of combination of private and public ownership. Of Capitalism, it has retained the main advantages: capital itself, the virtue of private enterprise and initiative, a greater efficiency in business methods. But', he added, 'it has very largely associated the State in the profits of private enterprise, without any risk to the public partner. According to our legislation,

[3] *The Times*, May 12, 1955.
[4] *Colonial Administration by European Powers*, by Royal Institute of International Affairs, p. 63 (Oxford).

mining companies pay to the State royalties varying from 10 per cent to 50 per cent, according to the proportion of profits to paid-up capital. The State has at the general meetings a voting power equal to that of all the private shareholders; it has the right to subscribe up to 20 per cent of new issues. Finally, it has on every board one or two delegates who supervise all undertakings and take part in board meetings. In addition, the State receives a large number of shares on the constitution of companies. Altogether, the State retains from 50 per cent to 53 per cent of the net profits of the mining companies. Needless to say, income tax, amounting normally to 17 per cent, and at present to 32 per cent, is paid to the State on profits distributed to shareholders.'[5]

Five giant corporations control and operate between them more than 90 per cent of the country's capital investment. Each of them is a state within a state, so vast are their resources and scope of operations. The *Société Générale de Belgique* controls a 60 per cent interest in the Congo's minerals, railways, cement and textile factories and, through its mining subsidiary, the world-famous *Union Minière du Haut-Katanga* (U.M.H.K.), controls 13,000 square miles of the richest mineral-bearing lands. In this area, larger than Belgium, U.M.H.K. produces uranium at Shinkolobue—the most heavily guarded mine in Africa—copper, radium, cobalt, gold, diamonds, silver and zinc. The output of copper alone contributes about half the colony's export trade, out of which the Belgian Government get some 50 million U.S. dollars in the form of export duty.

The second largest corporation is the *Société Commerciale et Minière du Congo*, popularly called the *Cominière*. This company is controlled by Nagelmackers, one of the biggest Brussels banks. In conjunction with its subsidiary, *Agricor*, *Cominière* controls not only electric power, rail, river and road transport, but is the biggest timber producer in Central Africa.

Huilever, another major concern, is engaged in wholesale trade and agriculture. It is the Belgian branch of the world's largest monopoly, the Anglo-Dutch firm of Unilever, which

[5] *Colonial Administration by European Powers—Belgian Congo*, pp. 49-50, Royal Institute of International Affairs (Oxford University Press).

owns the United Africa Company in Nigeria, Gold Coast and other British West African territories. In the Congo, *Huilever* is largely engaged in the production of palm oil, cotton and the distribution of manufactured commodities and consumer goods.

Next there is the famous *Brufina*, the popular name of the *Société de Bruxelles pour la Finance et l'Industrie*. Like its great rival, *Cominière*, *Brufina* is controlled by a powerful group of Belgian bankers and financiers connected with the Bank of Brussels. Like most Congo corporations, *Brufina* operates through subsidiary companies, the two largest of which are *Credit Foncier Africain*, specializing in the erection and running of hotels, commercial building and real estate; and *Symetain*, largely engaged in the exploitation of rich tin ore concessions.

Not the least important of the Belgian corporations operating in the Congo is the group of companies associated with Baron Empain's 'transport empire'—officially designated the *Compagnie des Chemins de Fer du Congo-Supérieur aux Grands Lacs Africains*—but popularly called C.F.L. This concern exercises major control over the Lake Tanganyika-Congo River railway and steamer transport systems which connect Central Africa with the Lobito Bay and Dar-es-Salaam railways—the Congo's main outlets on the Atlantic and Indian Oceans. Throughout the vast territories allotted to Baron Empain's syndicate, the Company has the right to grant agriculture and mining concessions.

As a result of the economic partnership between the Belgian State and these corporations, Belgium is able to maintain its population at one of the highest standards of living in the world. And this, after a devastating war during which the country was occupied for years and ravished by the Germans. Who says colonies don't pay?

PORTUGUESE COLONIALISM

At one time Portugal was the greatest colonial Power in the world. Today her empire is reduced to the sad relics of a few ancient settlements in Asia, Macao on the China coast; Goa, Damão and Diu in India and the Islands of Madeira, the Azores and Cape Verde. Her main colonies are, however, in Africa. They are the islands of Sao Thomé and Principe, and the mainland territories of Angola (acquired in 1491); Mozambique (acquired in 1505) and Portuguese Guinea (acquired in 1879).

The African colonies were originally exploited as labour reservoirs for the recruitment of slaves for Brazil, then the richest Portuguese colony. It was not until Brazil achieved independence in 1822 that Portugal began to take an interest in settling Portuguese colonists in Africa. Even this policy, sporadic at most, had to be abandoned during the period of constitutional strife and political upheavals in Portugal during the latter nineteenth century. And since the abolition of the monarchy in 1910 and the establishment of the Republic, the Salazar dictatorship has not had the financial and technical means to develop the resources of these virgin African territories, which cover a total area of nearly 800,000 square miles and contain a native population of nearly nine millions.

Before the First World War, Sir Edward Grey, the Liberal Foreign Secretary, feeling that it was beyond the capacity of Portugal to develop her colonies, pledged Britain's diplomatic support to Kaiser Wilhelm's Germany in acquiring Angola, in return for financial assistance to the newly set-up Republic. After this attempt by Portugal's oldest ally to dispose of her colonies, when he assumed dictatorial powers in 1932, Dr Salazar introduced a number of so-called reforms embodied in the Colonial Act of 1933. The Act defines the relationship between Portugal and her colonies and regulates the methods of administration as well as the status and obligations of the natives.

As in the French Empire, Portugal's colonies, although separated by thousands of miles from Portugal, are considered 'integral parts of the metropolitan country', and as such are indissolubly bound to Portugal. This illogical claim is being invoked by Portugal today to deny the Goans the right to unite with India.

The Portuguese colonies, like the French and Belgian, but unlike the British, are administered under a highly centralized

system of government, directed and controlled from the metropolitan country. All policy is vested in a Minister for the
Overseas Territories in Lisbon, who is advised by a Colonial
Council. Directives are implemented by the Governor-General
in each colony, who is not entitled to introduce legislation
without the approval of the Colonial Minister. Stripped of all
legislative powers, the Portuguese Governors are, however,
allowed to appoint the members of the local Colonial Councils, which serve as advisory bodies and make recommendations on matters affecting the Portuguese colonies for the decision of the Minister for Overseas Territories.

Every three years, a Colonial Governors' Conference is
held in Lisbon, under the chairmanship of the Minister, at
which colonial affairs are reviewed. Portuguese policy is one
of exclusive European control of political and economic affairs. African nationalism in Portuguese colonies is sternly
suppressed. The few educated Africans who have emerged
from the mass are encouraged to become 'assimilated' Portuguese. This status is acquired by adopting the Catholic religion
and the Portuguese language and culture, after which application may be made for full citizenship rights and racial
equality with white Portuguese. Those enjoying full citizenship in 1950 numbered 4,400 out of 5,640,000 in Mozambique
and 30,000 out of 4,000,700 in Angola. The overwhelming
majority of the so-called citizens are mulattos, who compete
with the Portuguese for white collar jobs. There are more
poor whites in Angola than in any other African colony. The
Portuguese population is over 100,000, with an annual increase of 2,000 immigrants since the end of the war.

The latest decree on the status of Africans issued by the
Portuguese Government in June 1954 defines the new conditions which natives must fulfil to become citizens. 'The applicant must be over eighteen years of age, must speak
Portuguese with fluency, have completed his military service,
possess either sufficient means or employment of trade to
maintain himself and his dependents, be law-abiding, and
have some realization of the obligations of citizenship.

'Baptized natives may marry in conformity with canon and
civil law, and polygamy in such cases is no longer permitted.
Selection of a mate is free and widows and children must not

be made over to the kin of the deceased as is the tribal custom.

'The term "native" as used in the new law has a technical meaning implying one still under tribal law and ineligible for citizenship.'[6]

Africans unable to meet these qualifications are ruthlessly exploited. If colour bar does not exist for the mulatto *assimilados* or native *élite*, forced labour certainly does for the unassimilated *indigènes*. 'The motto of Portuguese colonial policy seems to be to make the African work. Upon this the colonial administration has insisted, whether the African wants it or not, and in so forcing the natives a great many abuses have occurred which cannot be harmonized with the high ideals of the Colonial Act.'[7]

Labour conditions in the Portuguese colonies, especially Angola and the cocoa islands of Sao Thomé and Principe, constitute a shocking scandal in the twentieth century. This is in spite of the existence in each colony of a Commission for the 'Protection of Native Rights', consisting of the Director of Native Affairs and Roman Catholic missionaries appointed by the Governor.

Every Portuguese district officer (*Chefe de Posto* or *Chefe de Cantão*), is expected to supply a certain number of able-bodied men for the labour market. These are called 'contract labourers'. They are distributed among employers, who pay the Government a commission for each man supplied. The amount varies according to the law of demand and supply. When the demand is greater than the normal supply, the civil officials, aided by the military, make raids on the villages at nights and the captives are taken away by force. The average wage paid *contradados* in 1954 was about ten shillings per month. The money is paid to the Government Labour Bureau, which deducts a native poll tax of about £2 10. 0. per annum. The balance of the accumulated wage is handed over to the worker at the end of his term of contract, which may extend from one to five years.

Employers are responsible for providing shelter and food

[6] *The Times*, London, June 8, 1954.
[7] H. A. Wieschoff: *Colonial Problems in Africa*, p. 104.

for their workers, especially those working in the islands of Sao Thomé and Principe, and in places far away from their villages on the mainland. Under the forced labour system, over 300,000 Africans were recruited in 1954 in Angola. Mozambique also supplied about 100,000 for the gold mines of South Africa. Under the terms of the convention signed between the Portuguese and South African Governments, the mining companies pay the Mozambique Government a fee of ten shillings for each African supplied. The Portuguese claim that the Negroes are lazy and forced labour is the best method of teaching Africans the dignity of labour!

All Africans, even the *assimilados*, are denied any form of organized expression. Freedom of assembly and movement is forbidden without official permission. Africans are not allowed to leave their villages without first obtaining the consent of the *Chefe de Posto* or *Chefe de Cantão*.

Since the Portuguese colonies are the most backward in Africa, the economic opportunities and educational facilities necessary to the stimulation and nurturing of a native *élite* are more limited than in the Belgian Congo, which is the most highly industrialized colony in tropical Africa. For this reason, the policy of 'assimilation', once vigorously advocated by supporters of 'racial partnership', has not had the same success in the Portuguese Empire as in the French Union. And since Britain is under treaty obligation to protect the Portuguese Empire, the Salazar dictatorship feels that it can always invoke Britain's support to maintain the *status quo*.

SPANISH COLONIALISM

The Spanish American War of 1898 brought an end to the once great and glorious Spanish empire in the Western Hemisphere. Since then, this Iberian nation, formerly a great maritime nation, Portugal's contemporary in the age of discovery, has been left with only 133,780 square miles of territory along the north and north-western coast of Africa. This remnant of empire, consisting of the Protectorate of Spanish Morocco

and the colonies of Rio de Oro and Ifni, Spanish Guinea and
the island Fernando Po, symbolize the rise and fall of great
empires. It is a far cry from the fifteenth century, when the
Spanish Borgia Pope, Alexander VI, divided the world outside Europe between the crowned heads of Spain and Portugal, 'the faithful children of the Church'! Then, one could
write about a Spanish policy. Today, these relics of empire
are almost barren lands, scant reminder of a once great and
prosperous past. They merely serve to salve the national ego
of General Franco who, like all imperialist-minded dictators,
can only conceive of national 'greatness' in terms of dominion
over subject races.

His colonial policy is primarily militaristic. Spanish Morocco provided him with the initial contingent of troops to
overthrow the Republic and make himself the 'Sawdust
Caesar' of Spain.

As to the status of the Africans in Spanish Guinea, they
are thought of in terms of labour for the cocoa plantations of
Fernando Po, which are operated by Spanish landlords in a
semi-feudal conquistador style. The Moors, on the other hand,
have their religious and traditional Islamic customs respected
in return for their loyalty to the Franco régime.

Administrative authority in the Spanish colonies is exercised by Governors in the name of the Generalissimo, who,
as the Caudillo, is absolute ruler of Spain and her empire.
In the Spanish zone of Morocco, the traditional Sherifian authority of the Khalifa is upheld in matters relating to Islamic
affairs and the application of Koranic law. Over and above
the traditional administration is the Spanish authority, exercised through a High Commissioner with headquarters at
Tetuan.

The International Zone of Morocco, an area of 225 square
miles, is administered by a Commission in Tangier, consisting of representatives of Britain, America, Russia, France and
Spain.

SOUTH AFRICAN APARTHEID POLICY

The only other white Government exercising dominion over Africans and other non-European peoples on the continent is the Union of South Africa. The political, economic and social degradation of the non-Europeans is well known. As far as the status of the Africans and other non-whites is concerned, South Africa is as much a fascist state as Hitler's Germany. The Africans constitute the great majority of the population, being about 75 per cent. Yet they are denied all fundamental human rights, and are practically disfranchised because of their colour. The so-called South African Parliament consists entirely of Europeans and only represents the white minority population of 2,600,000. The other 8 to 10 million non-Europeans are, for all practical purposes, unrepresented.

For example, the House of Assembly has 159 members, of which number 150 are elected by white voters in the four provinces comprising the Union. The white population in South-West Africa, the former trusteeship territory forcibly incorporated into the Union by Dr Malan, also elect six European members. The other members, who must also be white, are elected by African voters in the Cape Province. In addition, blacks are also allowed the 'privilege' to elect four European members to the Senate, out of a total membership of 48. Africans living outside the Cape have no direct representation in the Assembly. Until 1936, the Africans in the Cape exercised the franchise on a common roll, but since then, they have been placed on a special voters' register. Similar steps are being taken at the time of writing by Dr Malan's Government to remove the Cape coloured or mixed race voters from voting along with Europeans. They, like the Bantu Africans, will be placed on a separate roll and allowed to elect four Europeans to 'represent' the million odd coloured people living in the Cape Province. Another disability is that while all Europeans, male and female, over the age of 21 are entitled to vote, only literate male Africans with an income of £75 a year and owning fixed property to the value of £50 will be allowed to register.

In 1936, when the franchise was taken away from the Africans, the Government of the late General Hertzog set up a Native Representative Council. This puppet body consisted of twelve African members, six officials and four nominated by the Governor-General, and had neither legislative nor executive powers. It was a purely consultative body, where Africans were allowed to let off steam. The Council is now inactive. For under pressure from the African National Congress, the members decided to boycott the Council in 1951 as a protest against the new series of Anti-African fascist laws and repressive policy of the Malan Government.

South Africa's native policy, officially known as *Apartheid*, not only denies Africans and other non-Europeans equality of participation with whites in the government, but opposes any form of political 'partnership', cultural 'assimilation' or human 'association' between the races as favoured by the French. It also rejects the British policy of self-rule and independence. Even the Belgian system of enlightened self-interest, aiming at the development of Africans as skilled labourers only, is not tolerated.

In short, *Apartheid* is a negation of all existing colonial policies. Its only positive feature is the absolute and complete oppression of the Africans in all spheres of life—political, economic, social, religious. Dr Malan's suicidal policy is summed up in the endorsement given it by the Dutch Reformed Church that *'there can be no equality between black and white in State and Church'*.

PART FIVE

XIII

BRITISH MULTI-RACIAL POLICY IN PRACTICE—KENYA

Having compared in broad outline the constitutional systems
of the Colonial Powers in Africa in so far as they relate to
self-government for the indigenous peoples, we can now examine in some detail the practical application of British policy
in two territories—Kenya and Nigeria—where constitutional
reforms are being experimented with. Such a comparison will
enable us to see the degree to which the racial factor in colonial politics has influenced the theoretical principles of British administration as they affect constitutional arrangements.
The fundamental ethnological difference between these two
colonies can be stated briefly.

Nigeria, the largest British dependency in Africa, is racially
homogeneous. That is to say, the indigenous population although composed of many tribes at varying degrees of cultural
development, are all so-called Negroes. The question of race
and colour, is, therefore, a negligible factor in the body politic.
On the other hand, tribal and religious differences do constitute a potential danger to the national unity of Nigeria.

In Kenya, the situation is radically different. Here all the
elements making for disunity in a plural society—race, colour,
tribe and religion—are in open conflict.

While the African population is composed of many tribal
groups, such as the Kikuyu, Luo, Masai, Kavirondo, Baluhya,
Wakamba and Meru, they together form the overwhelming

majority. But there are other racial communities which have established permanent homes in the colony. The largest of these alien groups is the Asian. They number 90,525. The next largest ethnic community is the European, mostly English settlers numbering 30,000. In addition there are 24,174 Arabs living mostly in the coastal region as well as 3,325 Goans[1]—Portuguese Christian Indians. Although the Europeans are the smallest of the three main communities, they are the most powerfully entrenched, both economically and politically, with strong social ties with influential political and business circles in Great Britain.

It is they who have obstructed and wrecked every attempt at peaceful development for Africans. They bitterly opposed the *African Magna Carta* enunciated by a former Conservative Secretary of State, the Duke of Devonshire, in 1923. This declaration stated that: 'Primarily, Kenya is an African territory and His Majesty's Government think it necessary definitely to record their considered opinion that the interests of the African natives must be paramount and that if, and when, those interests and the interests of the immigrant races should conflict, the former should prevail.

'Obviously the interests of the other communities, European, Indian or Arab, must severally be safeguarded. Whatever the circumstances in which members of these communities have entered Kenya, there will be no drastic action or reversal of measures already introduced, such as may have been contemplated in some quarters, the result of which might be to destroy or impair the existing interests of those who have already settled in Kenya. But in the administration of Kenya, His Majesty's Government regard themselves as exercising a trust on behalf of the African population, and they are unable to delegate or share this trust, the object of which may be defined as the protection and advancement of the native races. It is not necessary to attempt to elaborate this position, the lines of development are yet in certain directions undermined, and many difficult problems arise which require time for their solution. But there can be no doubt that it is the mission of Great Britain to work continuously for the training

[1] The figures given are taken from the 1948 census.

and education of the African towards a higher intellectual, moral and economic level when the Crown assumed the responsibility for the administration of this territory.

'At present, special consideration is being given to economic development in the native reserves, and within the limits imposed by the finances of the Colony all that is possible for the advancement and development of the Africans both inside and outside the native reserves will be done.'

This assurance of paramountcy was repeated by the Joint Select Committee of Parliament, which stated in its 1931 report that: 'The doctrine of paramountcy means no more than that the interests of the overwhelming majority of the indigenous population should not be subordinated to those of a minority belonging to another race, however important in itself.'

The Government White Paper (Cmd. 3573) issued about the same time warned the white settlers of the consequences of any betrayal of this pledge. It stated that: 'Any derogation from this solemn pledge would, in the view of His Majesty's Government, be not only a flagrant breach of trust, but also, in view of its inevitable effect upon the natives, a serious calamity from which the whole Colony would not fail to suffer.'

Today, this sacred promise of paramountcy, made to the trusting Africans in the name of the Imperial Parliament and British people, is a dead letter, murdered by the settlers and buried by another Conservative Colonial Secretary, the Rt. Hon. Oliver Lyttelton, now Lord Chandos.

This shameful betrayal of native interests, however, has not been a sudden affair. Even the last Labour Government bears a share of responsibility. For what is now happening in Kenya is the culmination of a gradual retreat of the Colonial Office under pressure of the European settlers, especially since the end of the Second World War. Here are a few examples of surrender of power to the European community at the expense of Africans which the leaders of the Kenya African Union pointed out to Mr Lyttelton in a memorandum presented to the Colonial Secretary during his visit to the Colony in November 1952.

(1) The adoption of the recommendations contained in the Carter Commission report.

(2) Sessional Paper No. 3 of 1945 which enables leaders of the European Settler community to assume control of important portfolios in the Government which at the moment include Finance and Agriculture.[2]

(3) Official surrender to local European opinion by the withdrawal of the White Paper No. 191 of 1946, which provided for equal representation of the major racial groups in the Central Legislative Assembly, and the substitution in its place of White Paper No. 210 which gives them a majority over any one of the other races. (It was imposed upon the Africans by Mr A. Creech Jones, the Labour Colonial Secretary. This one act destroyed all confidence in the Socialist Government. From then, Africans gave up hope of achieving political equality by peaceful means.)

(4) The retention of parity of European unofficial representation with that of all the other races combined, in spite of the meagre representation allowed to the Africans both in relation to their number and to the representation afforded to the other non-African communities in the Colony.

(5) The enactment of the County Council Ordinance, introduced by a former leader of the European Unofficials, which conferred upon the European community powers to dominate institutions of local government, in the teeth of strong non-European opposition.

These, and other similar measures, asserts the memorandum, 'have given rise to a fear in the minds of the Africans that the Government of the country is being steadily transferred to local Europeans, thereby creating a *fait accompli*, as in some other parts of the African Continent. This has brought about a deep sense of frustration and bitterness in the mind of the African who finds his efforts at constitutional progress thwarted and of no avail.'

The Mau Mau revolt which has captured the attention of

[2] See the Lyttelton Constitution (*infra*, p. 260), where the number of portfolios controlled by white settlers has been increased to 5, plus 2 Asians and 1 African.

the world, is merely a violent protest against the failure of
both the British Imperial and Kenya Governments to redress
the legitimate land grievances of the Kikuyu and the granting
of elementary human rights and social justice to Africans
generally.

The story that follows is a sad one of omission and commission. For everything that has happened, the violence and
bloodshed that has come over Kenya in the past four years
could have been avoided had the Government listened to
moderation and reason voiced by popularly supported African
leaders for over a quarter of a century.

HOW THE WHITES CAME TO KENYA

While Britain and France were annexing territories in West
Africa, in East Africa, the Germans stole a march over their
rivals, and by 1886 had taken over the vast area now known
as Tanganyika. The Kaiser proclaimed it a German Protectorate. The German missionaries Rebmann and Krapf—the
advanced guard of European imperialism—were the first white
men to penetrate into the interior of Kenya. There they found
the Kikuyu and Masai tribes occupying the fertile highland
regions, now the centre of the Mau Mau war. The Germans,
having secured Tanganyika, a territory covering 362,688
square miles of some of the best country in Africa, allowed
Britain a free hand to occupy the whole of Kenya and the
more westerly territory known as the Protectorate of Uganda.
The rival claims of the great European Imperialist Powers
having been adjusted by diplomatic means, the fate of the
African peoples inhabiting Kenya and Uganda was sealed.

By 1888 the British were firmly established along the coast
of East Africa. First came the missionaries, then the traders,
and finally the Union Jack. The missionaries, while motivated
by humanitarian and Christian sentiments, were fully supported by the imperialist and commercial classes in Britain,
who made generous financial contributions to the London
Missionary Society under whose auspices the religious pioneers
went out to Uganda. Following in the wake of the explorer,

Henry M. Stanley, the Protestant missions started proselytizing in 1877. They were soon joined by the French Roman Catholics of the White Fathers Order organized by the famous missionary leader, Cardinal Lavigerie. The Protestant converts were known in the language of the Africans as the *Wa-Inglesa* (party of the English) and the Catholics as the *Wa-Fransa* (party of the French), while those Africans who were converted to Mohammedanism by the Arab slave traders were called *Wa-Islamu* (party of Islam). The foreigners soon started inciting religious wars among the Africans, each hoping to secure control over Equatorial Africa with the aid of adherents to their respective faiths.

During the course of the civil war, the Protestant missionary, Bishop Hannington, was murdered by the supporters of the then King Mwanga of Uganda. The Christians united and drove the King away, but after victory over the Moslems, the Christian alliance broke down and fighting started between the Protestants and Catholics for control. When the French party was getting the better of the contest, the English missionaries appealed for assistance to the British East African Charter Company, then in occupation of the coastal area of Kenya. Indian and Sudanese soldiers, employed as mercenaries by the British Chartered Company, were dispatched to Uganda under the command of Captain Lugard, the famous soldier of fortune who later became the first Governor-General of Nigeria. On his retirement in 1919, Lugard was created a peer and became the leading colonial authority in the House of Lords.

After routing the *Wa-Fransa* and *Wa-Islamu* forces, the British arrested Kabaka Mwanga and banished him to the island of Seychelles in the Indian Ocean. Lugard returned to England in 1892 and persuaded the Foreign Minister, Lord Rosebery, to annex the country. The British Charter Company, which was responsible for carrying out the conquest, was substantially compensated for adding the rich and extensive East African territories of Kenya and Uganda to the British Empire. To consolidate the conquest, the British Parliament voted the sum of five million pounds to construct a railway from the Indian Ocean through Kenya to Uganda

which was started in 1892. Three years later, Kenya was officially declared a Colony and Protectorate. The construction
of the railway opened a new chapter in British colonization
in East Africa. It also marked the beginning of the present
trouble between the Kikuyu tribe and the European settlers
in the Highlands of Kenya.

THE EUROPEAN HIGHLANDS

The railway, which covers a distance of 879 miles from
Mombasa, the chief port of Kenya, via Nairobi (the capital)
up to Lake Victoria and later to Kampala in Uganda, was
constructed for military and economic purposes. It enabled
the British to transport troops from the coast to the interior
of Equatorial Africa to put down rebellion among the Africans on the one hand, and to facilitate the importation of
British manufactures and the exportation of the natural resources of the territories through which it ran, on the other.

Unfortunately for the Kikuyu, the railway cut right through
the heart of the Kenya Highlands, which they and their neighbours, the Masai and Wakamba, considered their tribal reserves. To protect the railway tracks from possible destruction
by hostile tribesmen, the Governor of Kenya, a retired soldier,
General Sir Charles Eliot, appealed to Englishmen of the
gentry class to come out to Kenya and settle as gentlemen
farmers. In addition to the temporarily unoccupied land
which the Europeans immediately seized as 'no man's land',
the Governor cleared the tribes occupying certain lands along
the railway track and granted them to his countrymen. Many
of those who benefited were well connected with the English
landed aristocracy. They received extensive plantations of the
most fertile parts of the Highlands, where the climate is
best suited to sustain good health for Europeans.

'The Protectorate is a White Man's Country', declared the
Governor. 'This being so, it is mere hypocrisy not to admit
that white interests must be paramount and that the main

object of our policy and legislation should be to found a white colony.'[3]

There were only thirteen British settlers in Kenya in 1901. Between May 1903, and December 1904, 222,000 acres of land were alienated from the Africans and distributed to 342 Europeans.[4] By 1911, the number of settlers had increased to 3,175. It reached 9,661 in 1921, 16,812 in 1931 and totalled 28,997 ten years later. Today the entire white population in Kenya numbers about 30,000, of whom not more than 3,000 are actually engaged in agriculture. The others are government, civil and military personnel, missionaries, merchants, traders, and employees in commercial, banking and other forms of private enterprise.

Among the farming community are people closely related to leading British landed gentry and aristocratic families. Kenya is not only a white man's paradise (at least until the present unrest) but a land of *pukka sahibs*. According to the American writer Negley Farson, 'it has the greatest proportion among its inhabitants of ex-soldiers, generals, colonels, majors, of any country in the world. It contains a goodly number of names in Burke's *Peerage*—and some terrible specimens in the flesh.'[5] When the Foreign Office offered 3,200,-000 acres free to the Zionists, the Christian settlers shouted: 'Down with the Jews' and the Government retracted.

The first leader of these colonialists was the well-known imperialist, Lord Delamere. Of him, Salvadori writes: 'Lord Delamere did not feel at ease in England; imbued with the feudal spirit, he preferred life in the colonies, where natives could be treated as they were in the former days in Europe, serfs attached to the land. Not being rich enough to live like a great lord in England, he knew that he could do so more easily in Kenya.'[6] Being among the first arrivals, Lord Delamere had the first pick of the best land. He acquired over 100,000 acres of the most fertile country between the Aberdare and Lake Naivasha. Other aristocrats like Lord Francis Scott, uncle of the Duchess of Gloucester, a relative of the

[3] Sir Charles Eliot: *The East Africa Protectorate* (Arnold, 1905).
[4] M. Salvadori: *La Colonisation européenne au Kenya*, p. 71.
[5] Negley Farson: *Behind God's Back*, p. 234 (Gollancz).
[6] M. Salvadori: *La Colonisation européenne au Kenya*, p. 25.

British royal family, and the Earl of Plymouth, secured about 350,000 acres between them. The son of the Duke of Abercorn acquired an estate of 30,000 acres, while other aristocrats and land speculators formed joint stock companies through which they control vast plantations, such as the East Africa Estates, which owns over 350,000 acres. The chairman of the Company is Viscount Cobham. His uncle, the Honourable R. G. Lyttelton, holds 14,108 shares in the company. Viscount Cobham is a cousin of Mr Oliver Lyttelton, the former Tory Secretary of State for the Colonies. Other big land-owning companies are the East Africa Syndicate, with 320,000 acres, the Grogan Forest Concessions with 200,000 acres, and the Dwa Plantations, controlling over 20,000 acres, for which they received not one penny compensation.

The Masai and the Kamba tribes lost hundreds of thousands of acres of fertile agricultural and pasture lands. They, too, got no financial compensation. To give the stamp of legality to this wholesale land grab, the Governor set up a Lands' Board to register title deeds, for which the settlers agreed to pay the British Government roughly a penny an acre. The Chairman of the Board was none other than Lord Delamere. By 1914, the Lands' Board had dispossessed the Africans of 3,412,728 acres and since the end of the Second World War, 16,000 square miles—the most fertile parts of Kenya—have passed into the hands of 2,000 European settlers and 52,009 square miles of inferior waterless country have been reserved for the accommodation of 5½ million Africans.

And even so, the Africans have no tenure of security, for under the Crown Lands Ordinance, power is vested in the Kenya Government 'to control land, to extinguish African rights of ownership, to lease or sell or alienate lands to non-Africans. The word "alienate", much favoured, means to dispossess Africans of the land of their birth and to give it to Europeans.'[7]

Having lost vast areas of their ancestral lands, the dispossessed Kikuyu and other tribes were removed to other parts outside the White Highlands, officially designated 'na-

[7] Mbiyu Koinange and Achieng Oneko, *Land Hunger in Kenya* (London), p. 5.

tive reserves'. Those who were unable to find accommodation in these over-populated areas became squatters on the plantations of the white expropriators. The squatter system is a form of forced labour for, unlike the *métier* system in French North Africa or share-cropping in the southern states of the U.S.A., African squatters are serfs tied to the landlord's property and forced to work for little or no wages while denied the right to cultivate commercial crops such as coffee and tea, which fetch high prices in the world markets.

There are over a quarter of a million squatters on white farms. Many of them are Africans who 'stayed put' when the Europeans moved in. Forced by the imposition of tax, they 'elected' to work for the invaders in return for permission to work a small plot and raise their own food and a cow or two.

Under the law, squatters are not allowed to rent lands from Europeans. They must work for the use of it. The Africans enter into a service contract running from one to five years, and they and their families must labour 180 days of the year on the European's land on such days as the master chooses, whether it interferes with the cultivation of their own small plot or not. Furthermore, they may grow on their own plot only such crops as the European permits. If the land is sold, a squatter passes into the service of the new owner until he finishes the contract entered into with the former owner. If he runs away, he can be caught and put in prison! No minimum wages are laid down and the Kenya Native Affairs Department reports that natives sometimes work for nothing but their food.

TAXATION AND FORCED LABOUR

Another method adopted by the Kenya Government in providing the European settlers with an abundant supply of cheap labour is the system of direct taxation. Every able-bodied African over the age of eighteen has to pay the Government a poll tax of about twenty-four shillings a year. Those

who are unable to make a living in the Native Reserves are
'encouraged' by the British district officials through the
Government-appointed chiefs who act as agents of the administration to go to work on the European plantations. When
the tax was first introduced in 1913 the leading European
newspaper in the colony congratulated the Government. It
said:

'We consider that taxation is the only possible method of
compelling the native to leave his reserve for the purpose of
seeking work. Only in this way can the cost of living be increased for the native . . . it is on this that the supply of
labour and the price of labour depend. To raise the rate of
wages would not increase, but would diminish the supply of
labour. A rise in the rate of wages would enable the hut or
poll tax of a family, sub-tribe or tribe to be earned by fewer
external workers.'[8]

Five years later, Mr John Ainsworth, the Chief Native
Commissioner, introduced a Bill in the Legislative Council to
compel Africans to make better use of their holdings in the
Native Reserves and to encourage improved husbandry. But
the Bill was opposed by the settlers. Their objection was that
such a law might restrict the flow of labour to their farms. In
face of this opposition, the Government withdrew the Bill
and threw its authority behind the recruiting of cheap labour
in the countryside.

To enable the employers to keep control over their workers,
every African is compelled by law to carry a *Kipande*, which
is a labour pass. Failure to have a *Kipande* is a criminal
offence under the Native Registration Ordinance and such
an African is liable to heavy fine, imprisonment, or both. The
purpose of the *Kipande* is clear. It guarantees that employers
retain their labour supply.

At the time the emergency was declared, there were
480,000 persons gainfully employed in the colony, of whom
438,702 were Africans. Almost three-quarters of these Africans were labourers; the remaining quarter were approximately 28,000 domestic servants and 90,000 semi-skilled and
clerical workers.

[8] *East African Standard*, February 8, 1913.

The wages of agricultural workers in 1953 were as follows: 48 per cent earned less than 25 shillings a month and 26 per cent less than 20 shillings a month of thirty working days. Some squatters received less than fifteen shillings. Africans employed in government service as clerks and other white collar jobs got less than fifty pounds a year, while the lowest grade of European official received 600 pounds per annum.

According to the Carpenter report on wages published in 1954, thousands of Africans employed in Nairobi were receiving fifty-two shillings plus seven shillings house allowance per month. Out of this paltry stipend, all adult Africans must pay poll and hut tax and provide food for themselves and dependents, many of whom live in the native reserves.

The cost of living in Kenya in 1953 had increased some 200 per cent, while the staple food of the Africans, a maize flour known as *posho*, had increased over 600 per cent since 1938. Even if all the African's wage is spent on food, the Medical Officer of Health of the city of Nairobi estimates that sixty shillings or three pounds a month is the very minimum required to feed an able-bodied adult.

The majority of African families working in the capital live in shacks and tenements. Those out of work and unable to pay for such accommodation sleep under shop galleries, between doorways and under the stalls in the Native market.

According to the 1953 United Nations Report on Social Conditions in non-Self-Governing Territories, the average earnings of each race group was Europeans, £660 per year; Asians and other non-Europeans £280 per year; and Africans £27 per year. The *per capita* personal incomes of Africans was £5 18. 0. per year and non-Africans £205 14. 0. The Africans, representing 97.1 per cent of the population received 49.1 per cent of the total personal income, whilst non-Africans —only 2.9 per cent of the inhabitants received 50.9 per cent.[9]

[9] Figures taken from a Special Study on Social Conditions in non-Self-Governing Territories by the United Nations, New York, 1953.

POLITICAL DOMINATION BY COLOUR BAR

Political democracy as defined by politicians on the western side of the global Iron Curtain means the will of the majority freely expressed through the ballot box with respect for the rights of minorities. Not so in Kenya. There democracy is interpreted as the right of a small white minority to rule an overwhelming black majority who have been denied all right of free political expression. To ensure the implementation of this distorted form of democracy, the British Colonial Office, which is responsible for the administration of Kenya, has given 30,000 European settlers a decisive voice in the government. They call the tunes to which the officials dance. Constitutionally, the settlers have the right to elect fourteen members of the Legislative Council, or local Parliament, while 5½ million Africans have only six members, who are not elected but hand-picked by the Governor from a list of names submitted to him by the electoral colleges in the six native areas, that is to say, by the district officers. The Governor also has the right to dismiss the Africans at any time. Apart from these so-called representatives, the 100,000 Indians—mostly descendants of coolie labourers brought into the country by the British to provide workers at the time when the Kenya-Uganda railway was being constructed—have six members in the Council (four Hindus and two Muslims). The small community of 24,000 Arabs who live in the port of Mombasa and other coastal regions have two representatives, one elected and one nominated. The official members—British Colonial civil servants appointed from London number twenty-six, eight ex-officio and eighteen nominated. They, together with the fourteen European-elected members, guarantee the whites an absolute majority of forty members in a Council of fifty-four over which the Governor presides.

Owing to their majority representation, the European settlers have been able to enact laws to safeguard their economic and political domination over the non-European communities, especially the Africans. The pattern of government is based upon the *Herrenvolk* philosophy of 'white supremacy'. The colour bar operates in every sphere of public and social life. The Africans are discriminated against in the allocation of public funds for health services, housing, agriculture and education. Since the whites not only control the Legislative Council but the Executive Council, the main policy-making body, they use their privileged position to tax the Africans to the limit and at the same time disburse the revenue in such a way as to starve them of essential funds for economic and social betterment.

For example, education, like all other Government departments, is conducted along strictly racial lines. The Kenya Government maintains three separate and distinct systems of education—European, Asian and African. Only white children enjoy free compulsory education. The majority of the African children of school-going age receive no education for, apart from a few Government schools, the majority of the state-aided schools are operated by missionaries. The head of the Kenya educational system is the British Director of Education. His decision on curriculum, the opening and closing of schools and the allocation of funds is final. Out of the annual budget for 1952, £512,581 was allocated to 7,115 European children and £1,089,742 to 337,000 Africans. In other words, each white child got seventy-two pounds and the black child three pounds. In the same period the Government spent out of the special Ten-year Development Fund, £999,207 on educational projects for white children and £350,196 for African.

KIKUYU INDEPENDENT SCHOOLS

In order to supplement the meagre educational facilities provided for native children by the Government, African political leaders established their own independently run schools in 1925. These schools were financed and maintained by voluntary contributions under the auspices of the Kikuyu Independent Schools Association and the Kikuyu Karinga Education Association. On November 14, 1952, six weeks after the present state of emergency in the colony was declared, the Governor ordered the closing of all African independent schools on the ground that these institutions were 'dangerous to good government of the colony'. The African Teachers' Training College, which prepared native teachers to staff these schools, has also been closed. This college, the first of its kind in East Africa, was founded by an American-trained Kikuyu, Mr Mbiyu Koinange, the son of ex-senior Chief Koinange.[10] Mr Mbiyu Koinange studied at Lincoln and Columbia Universities in the United States, where he obtained the Master of Science and Master of Arts degrees in sociology and education, respectively. As a result of the closing down of the independent schools, over 60,000 African children enrolled in these schools are being denied education. Apart from those fortunate enough to find accommodation in the missionary and government schools, it is estimated that 469,500 African children of school-going age were out of school in 1952. And even those who found places did not receive more than three years schooling.

Facilities for secondary and post-secondary education for Africans is even more meagre. Out of a population of 5½ million Africans, only 3,891 were enrolled in secondary schools in 1952 and 115 in post-secondary colleges. Despite the absence of facilities for professional and technical training in Kenya, very few scholarships have been awarded to Africans for study abroad. During the period under review, only thirty-four African students from Kenya were studying at Makerere, the East African university college in Uganda, and thirteen were in attendance at British universities and colleges, most of them studying education and linguistics. Since the annexation of Kenya and the imposition of British rule, not one African doctor, engineer, chemist, scientific agriculturalist has been trained at a British university.

The urgent need of educational provisions for Africans has continually been urged upon the British Government by African political and educational leaders. In a petition presented to the Secretary of State for the Colonies during the visit of

[10] The old Koinange and several members of his family have been arrested and held in prison without trial for the past four years as Mau Mau suspects.

Mr Oliver Lyttelton to Kenya in November 1952, the Kenya African Union asked for the extension of educational facilities, including technical training. Instead of meeting these demands with sympathy and understanding, ten days after they were presented to the Queen's Minister, the Independent African school was closed and the teachers arrested and thrown into detention camps as Mau Mau 'agitators'.

FORERUNNER OF MAU MAU

There is no doubt that the die-hard European settlers, aided and abetted by certain British officials and their influential friends in Britain, are the people really responsible for the present state of unrest in Kenya. The very term *Mau Mau* was invented by the settlers' Press to discredit the popular African leaders and justify the white man's legalized terror against a once peaceful and long-suffering people. Long before the world outside Kenya ever heard of Mau Mau, the Africans were begging and praying the British Government for help and deliverance from the white settlers' rule. They did so through what restricted constitutional means were open to them. The first attempt at peaceful agitation started as far back as 1922, when a group of Kikuyu young men, among them Jomo Kenyatta, and Harry Thuku who now co-operates with the officials, formed the East African Association. This society was soon suppressed for protesting against the eviction of Africans from the Highlands to make way for European ex-army officers who were encouraged by the British Government to settle in Kenya after the First World War. To placate the fears of the Africans, who were fast becoming a landless proletariat dependent upon the sale of their labour to the ever-increasing number of white immigrant farmers, the Duke of Devonshire, the then Secretary of State for Colonies, issued the *African Magna Carta* quoted above.

A few years later, the British Government appointed a Lands Commission under the Chairmanship of Sir Hilton Young to inquire into and report upon the claims of the Africans for lands to accommodate the rapidly increasing black population. To enable the Africans to present their case to the Commission of Inquiry, a new organization known as the Kikuyu Central Association was formed in 1928 and Mr Kenyatta was elected Secretary. In the next year he was dispatched to London to solicit parliamentary support from among members of the British Labour Party. On the strength of the Hilton Young Commission Report issued in 1930, the first Labour Government under the Premiership of Mr J. Ramsay MacDonald issued a memorandum on native policy, which solemnly pledged the British Government not to countenance any more confiscation of African lands for the benefit of European settlers.

Despite the solemn promise to the Africans to respect their land rights, the Kenya Government continued its policy of discrimination against them for the benefit of the European community. This gave rise to continued agitation by the Kikuyu Central Association and led to the appointment of another Lands Commission in 1932, under the chairmanship of Sir Morris Carter, but grievances still remained. The Commission recommended that 16,700 square miles of land in the Highlands should be reserved for European settlement, and that 2,629 square miles be added to the Native Reserves.

Commenting upon this arrangement some years later, Lord Hailey observed that 'At the time when the Commission reported, the actual area alienated to Europeans was 10,345 square miles, of which 11.8 per cent was cultivated, 40.7 per cent used for stock, 20 per cent occupied by native squatters, and 27.5 per cent not in use.'[11]

In other words, a further 6,355 square miles of fertile Highlands was allocated to Europeans who were not yet using the full amount of land already alienated, and only 2,629 square miles of inferior land were added to the vastly over-populated African reserves. At that time the African population was estimated at 3,004,141.[12] To silence the protest of the Africans against this unfair arrangement, as soon as Britain declared war against Hitler in 1939, the Kenya Government, on the advice of the C.I.D., suppressed the Kikuyu

[11] Lord Hailey: *An African Survey*, p. 751 (Oxford).
[12] Figures from the *Native Affairs Report* published by the Kenya Government.

Central Association as 'subversive'. According to Dr L. S. B. Leakey, the anthropologist, the African leaders were supposed to have been in contact with Italians in Somaliland. Dr Leakey, who is the son of an English missionary, was born in Kenya and grew up among the Kikuyus. During the war he served as an Intelligence Officer in the C.I.D., as he is one of the few white men in Kenya who speak Kikuyu and had known Kenyatta and other leaders of the Association intimately since his boyhood days in the Fort Hall district. The Africans, however, never trusted Leakey, whom the Government again employed in 1952 as the official interpreter at the trial of the leaders of the Kenya African Union charged with 'organizing and managing Mau Mau'.[13] It is significant to note that the line of the prosecution in this case was that Mau Mau was an offspring of the proscribed Kikuyu Central Association. Five years after the suppression of this organization at the end of the Second World War, the Africans set about forming another organization through which they could present their demands to the Government in a constitutional and law-abiding manner.

While the initiative was taken by the Kikuyu, the most politically advanced tribe in Kenya, the Kenya African Union set out to establish a 'united front' nationalist organization for all Africans, regardless of tribal affiliations, religion or caste. At the first Congress of the Kenya African Union held in Nairobi on June 1, 1947, delegates representing all the main tribes—Kikuyu, Luo, Masai, Kavirondo, Kamba, etc., adopted a constitution and programme of economic, political and social reforms which was submitted to the Kenya Government.

By 1950 the Union had built up a membership over one hundred thousand strong, with a network of branches throughout Kenya. Confining its activities to strictly constitutional methods, the leaders inaugurated a campaign for one million signatures to a petition to the British Parliament. The campaign proved such a success that within a few months after it was launched, the Union was able to dispatch two of its

[13] In October 1954, Mau Mau insurgents killed a brother of Dr Leakey who was a farmer in the Highlands.

executive members—Mr Mbiyu Koinange, a Kikuyu, and Mr Achieng Oneko, a Luo—to England to present their petition to the Secretary of State for the Colonies.

By the time the African mission arrived on November 6, 1951, the Labour Government had been defeated and the Tory Colonial Secretary, Mr Oliver Lyttelton, refused to receive the African leaders. Rebuffed in London, the Africans proceeded to Paris to lay their people's case before the Economic and Social Council of the United Nations then in session in the French capital. The mission was well received by the Secretary-General and other high-ranking officials like Dr Ralph Bunche, and the petition was distributed among the United Nations members of the Council.

On their return to England, the Kenya African Union spokesman, with the assistance of the Congress of Peoples Against Imperialism, under the chairmanship of Mr Fenner Brockway, MP, and a number of other sympathetic Socialist and Liberal Members of Parliament, addressed public meetings throughout Great Britain and secured additional signatures from progressive-minded British people (especially trade unionists and co-operators) to the petition which was to be presented to the House of Commons.

Having acquainted the British people with the urgent need of getting the Tory Government to redress the grave wrongs being inflicted upon the Africans in Kenya, Mr Oneko returned home to report back upon the mission carried out by himself and his colleague, Mr Koinange, who remained in London to carry on the work of public enlightenment on behalf of his people. When news of the widespread support the petition was getting among large sections of the British public became known to the white settlers, they immediately started to bring pressure to bear on the Governor, Sir Evelyn Baring, to suppress the activities of the Kenya African Union and to arrest the leaders. But since Jomo Kenyatta, the President of the Union, and other officers had publicly repudiated the use of violence and were conducting their campaign for economic, political and social reforms strictly along constitutional lines, the Governor found it difficult to justify the suppression of the Union. This made the representatives of the white settlers in the Legislative Council very angry and, aided by

XIV

WHAT AND WHO IS MAU MAU?

Although the name has never been satisfactorily defined, as no such word as 'Mau Mau' exists in the Kikuyu language, its socio-economic causes are easier to explain. Mau Mau is not an organized political movement with a regular membership, officers and constitution like the Kenya African Union. It is a spontaneous revolt of a declassed section of the African rural population, uprooted from its tribal lands and driven into urban slum life without any hope of gainful employment, due to the absence of an Industrial Revolution able to absorb them as proletarians. All the pseudoanthropological assertions about Mau Mau being a 'religion', is sheer nonsense. Mau Mau hymn singing and oath taking are merely psychological devices borrowed by desperate young men from freemasonry and missionary sources to bind their adherents to their cause. In trying to elevate Mau Mau into a 'religion' and ascribing obscene practices to them, the whites hope to shift all responsibility for what has happened upon the Africans and explain it all away as a sudden reversion to savagery, which demands their continued presence in Kenya to bring the Africans back on the path of civilization.

But for the grace of God and the wisdom and foresight of the Governor of the Gold Coast, Sir Charles Arden-Clarke, that colony, too, might have gone the way of Mau Mau. And Dr Nkrumah and his African Cabinet colleagues, who today are being lauded to the sky for their 'moderation' and 'statesmanship', would have been hunted down and denounced as black 'savages' and 'barbarians', just as Dr Malan even now describes them. Africans have not forgotten that during the last war then Germans, too, were described as 'butcher birds' by Englishmen like Lord Vansittart. Today the same kind of people who abuse the Africans, are courting the 'Huns', as 'defenders of Western Christian civilization'. Obviously, it all depends which side German 'butcher birds', like African 'savages', are prepared to support when Britain's imperial interest is at stake. No wonder educated Africans say: 'British hypocrisy stinks!'

Here are some of the socio-economic conditions which have created Mau Mau and which the settlers would like us to forget. It has been estimated that before the expulsion of Mau Mau gangs from Nairobi in 1954, there were over ten thousand young Africans permanently unemployed in the capital. Frustrated and embittered, many of the young men took to a life of crime. It is from among this *lumpen-proletariat* that 'delinquent' gang leaders have recruited adherents to avenge themselves upon the white man, whom they hold responsible for breaking up their tribal life and replacing it with nothing but serf labour on European farms. Like the slave revolts of Ancient Rome, the supporters of Mau Mau are fighting for land, without which they prefer death. For a piece of land is the only source of insurance against old age in African society.

Instead of applying social measures to redress the grievances of the Mau Mau, the settlers brought pressure to bear on the Attorney-General to apply the only remedy they know —'the big stick'.

On his return to Kenya after holding consultations with the Colonial Office officials in London, the Attorney-General introduced a number of emergency Bills at a special session of the Legislative Council on September 25th, 1952. The chief provisions were:

(1) Control of the African press and organization.
(2) Restriction of the movement of Africans suspected of belonging to the Mau Mau Society.
(3) Licensing of printing presses, unless specially exempted, and powers to seize and destroy newspapers printed on unlicensed presses.

(4) Registration of organizations with ten or more members, except co-operatives, trade unions and Freemasons. Societies not registered or exempted were automatically declared unlawful. Societies with international affiliations could be prosecuted.

(5) Confessions made to police officers may be used as evidence against Africans and evidence can be taken on affidavit.

(6) A British provincial commissioner who is satisfied that any African is a member of Mau Mau may order his arrest and deportation to a restricted area. Disobedience of such an order is punishable by a fine of a hundred pounds or twelve months imprisonment.

Since then, additional repressive laws have been enacted. Among these is collective punishment, which is imposed upon entire African communities accused of failing to disclose the identity of people accused of Mau Mau membership. Another gives the Minister of Internal Security power to order the complete evacuation of Africans in any specified area if required for public safety or the maintenance of order. The Minister also has the power to order the wholesale destruction of African livestock and movable property in any area scheduled for evacuation if he considers it is the best way to secure compliance with the order.

Having forced the Government to carry out the first part of their programme by enacting repressive legislation and adopting a strong-arm policy against Africans suspected of membership in the secret Mau Mau Society, the white settlers continued to press for direct action against the legal Kenya African Union. In this they also succeeded. For at dawn on October 21st, 1952, Jomo Kenyatta, the president, and twenty-five other officers were arrested. From then on, mass arrests of members of the Union have taken place daily during the past four years.

AN AFRICAN MANIFESTO

Replying to the new repressive policy of the Government, the acting Executive Committee of the Kenya African Union issued the following manifesto on October 28th, 1952:

In the name of the people of Kenya we demand:

(1) The abolition by law of all racial discrimination as being repugnant to morality and civilized standards and contrary to the principles of the United Nations.

(2) That the paramount need of the Africans for land be satisfied. Meanwhile, there must be no further immigration of Europeans or Asians, except on a temporary basis for the purpose of providing personnel for essential services and industries.

(3) The extension of educational facilities, including technical facilities by

    (a) establishing institutions of full university status in East Africa in the shortest possible time;

    (b) arranging for a greatly increased number of African students to proceed overseas for higher studies, and the provision of a Fund from which students wishing to go abroad can obtain loans;

    (c) multiplying the number of primary and secondary schools so that in the shortest possible time all African boys and girls shall have at least had the benefits of compulsory education.

(4) The immediate introduction of the system of election, not nomination, for all African unofficial members of the Legislative Council.

(5) A Common Roll for all three races.

(6) The reservation of an equal number of seats for Africans and non-Africans on the unofficial side of the Council.

(7) A franchise for Africans based initially on literacy and/or property qualifications and including women.

(8) The nomination of equal numbers of Africans and non-Africans on the official side of the Council.

(9) The direct election, not nomination, of all African members of the proposed Constitutional Committee for Kenya, and that the number of African, Asian, and European members of the Committee be equal— failing which, Her Majesty's Government in Britain should be requested to set up an impartial Committee of British constitutional experts.

(10) The election of Africans to all County, District, and Municipal Councils and Boards: and the establishment of County, District Locational and Municipal Councils and Boards on an electoral basis in the African Land Units. An immediate increase in the membership of African Councillors in the Nairobi Municipal Council representing not less than the membership enjoyed by the European community. The same to apply to the Municipal Boards of Mombasa, Nakuru, Eldoret and Kisumu.

(11) The trade unions be allowed to function freely, that registration be optional and not compulsory, and combination of trade unions be permitted.

(12) Full opportunity for Africans to demonstrate their loyalty to Kenya by serving in commissioned ranks in the Defence Forces and in the senior posts in the Civil Service.

(13) Assistance in the economic development of African farms, in the form of loans on easy terms and the provision of agricultural schools where appropriate courses can be administered to African farmers.

(14) The payment of uniform prices to all producers of primary produce of which the purchase and sale is controlled, and the abrogation of all restrictive practices in the growth of certain crops.

(15) Equal pay for equal qualifications and work.

(16) The immediate increase in the minimum wage by thirty-three and one third per cent to offset the high cost of living, and the provision of adequate housing accommodation for the thousands of homeless and bedless African workers in Nairobi and Mombasa.

(17) The right of freedom of assembly and speech, with-

out interference by the police or the administration; and the repeal of the relevant sections of the Police Ordinance; in accordance with the terms of the United Nations Charter.

(18) The terms of reference of the Royal Commission be widened to include a survey of lands in Kenya.

(19) The earliest possible repeal of all recent repressive legislation including the Bill for the Registration of Societies.

(20) The release or immediate trial of all persons arrested since October 20th.

(21) Facilities to enable the independent African press to start functioning again.

(22) The removal of all restrictions on the legitimate activities of the Kenya African Union.

(23) The immediate implementation of the Universal Declaration of Human Rights.

MILITARY OPERATIONS AGAINST MAU MAU

Redress of African grievances is the last thing the white settlers would ever dream of. Even to suggest the possibility of immediate small alleviations and reforms would, they declared, smack of 'appeasement'. On the contrary, they intensified their campaign against the Kenya African Union. Kenyatta and five of the Union's executive committee—Achieng Oneko, Secretary-General, Fred Kubai, chairman of the Nairobi branch, Bildad Kaggia, secretary of the Nairobi branch, Kungu Kurumba and Paul Ngei—were charged with 'assisting in the managing of Mau Mau contrary to the Penal Code'. After a trial of sorts lasting fifty-nine days—the longest and most sensational in British colonial history—the accused were all convicted and sentenced to seven years imprisonment with hard labour. All the prisoners appealed to the Judicial Committee of the Privy Council in 1954 which confirmed the sentence after hearing arguments of the leading defence lawyer, Mr D. N. Pritt, an English Queen's Counsel.[1] The day after the judgment of the trial was delivered on April 8th, 1953, the Kenya Government found it necessary to place the magistrate, Mr Thacker, under police protection and fly him out of the country for 'asylum' in England.

With Kenyatta and other leading nationalists safely behind prison walls, the white settlers renewed their compaign for the suppression of the hundred thousand strong Kenya African Union, which, despite the arrest of its officers, was still allowed to exist as the recognized political organization of the Africans. However, on June 8th, 1953, two months after the Kenyatta trial ended, the Governor announced the suppression of the Union. Sir Evelyn Baring had succumbed to the clamour of the settlers. In a broadcast statement to the people of Kenya, announcing the Governor's orders, the Chief Native Commissioner, Mr E. H. Windley, declared:

'There is no doubt that there are members of the Kenya African Union who have no connection with violent movements; but action has been taken because the Government has satisfied itself that there is ample evidence to show that the Kenya African Union has often been used as a cover by the Mau Mau terrorist organization, and that, both before and after the emergency was declared, there has been connection between many members of the Kenya African Union and Mau Mau terrorists.' The official spokesman hypocritically added:

'We would not have wished to stop political associations with sincere aspirations for the legitimate development of African interests and progress, but the Kenya Government can never again allow such an association as the Kenya African Union. Moreover, the Government cannot permit the formation of any African political societies on the same lines as the Union while there is still such trouble in the country. We will, however, give assistance and recognition to those local associations which have been reasonable and sincere in the interests of their own people.'

The Kenya African Union, as its title implied, sought to

[1] The other defence advocates were: Messrs. Chaman Lall, Jaswant Singh, A. R. Kapila from India; de Souza from Goa; Dudley Thompson from Jamaica and H. O. Davies from Nigeria.

unite all Kenya Africans into one united nationalist movement. The British, however, intended to pursue a policy of
'divide and rule' by encouraging the Government-appointed
chiefs and other stooges to form separatist tribalist organizations which the officials and settlers can play off against one
another and thereby prevent the Africans from presenting a
common all-African political front like the Convention People's Party in the Gold Coast for self-government. Even in
the Gold Coast, tribal politics is said to be backed by foreign
vested interests in the hope of disrupting that country before
it attains independence.

With the Mau Mau nationalists branded as 'terrorists', the
constitutionally based Kenya African Union suppressed and
its recognized leaders imprisoned, the European settlers, with
the active support of the Kenya Government, now hope to
consolidate their political and economic domination over the
Africans without fear of ever being challenged again. To
achieve the policy of making Kenya a 'white man's country',
like South Africa, the settler-dominated Government has let
loose a reign of counter-terrorism upon the Africans. What
started as an 'emergency' has already become a full-scale
military operation—the biggest colonial war in Africa since
the Boer War. Over thirty thousand British troops have been
assembled to assist the local police force, the Kenya Regiment
recruited exclusively from among the European male population, the Kikuyu Home Guards, and the King's African Rifles
are in open warfare against what the Africans call the Kikuyu
Land Liberation Army.

In an Order-of-the-Day issued on June 19th, 1953, General
Sir George Erskine, the Commander-in-Chief, East Africa,
announced his battle plan against the Mau Mau insurgents.
Three task forces will be formed, with the possibility of ad-
ditions later. The first will be mainly an infantry force of
brigade strength, whose deployment will be in the forest
areas, where infantry is most effective. The second task force
will consist of armoured car squadrons and mobile infantry
drawn mainly from the East African heavy anti-aircraft bat-
tery. And the third will be the Air Force, which will bomb
Africans out of their mountain strongholds by making pro-
hibited areas 'unwholesome' for Mau Mauists. The General

also said that when an area had been cleared it would then be taken over by the police and home guards recruited by the loyal chiefs.

In carrying out this operation under the military code name of 'Epsom', General Erskine, who was formerly Commander of the British Army stationed in the Suez Canal Zone in Egypt, is being assisted by Major-General W. R. N. Hinde as Director of Operations. This dirty colonial war against an unarmed people which was costing the British Government one million pounds a month in 1954, is expected to cost much more before it is ended. For the Government has refused to accept the services of responsible Africans like Kenyatta and other imprisoned leaders of the Kenya African Union to bring about peace. British political policy in Kenya is bankrupt. Under the guise of establishing the Queen's peace, the Kikuyu fighters for land and bread are being exterminated in order to provide *lebensraum* for a few thousand British colonists.

Reporting on the casualties up to April 14th, 1953, the Secretary of State told Parliament that two hundred and forty members of the security forces and civilians had been killed, and a hundred and sixty-six wounded. Since the emergency began, 82,840 persons had been arrested. Of these, 8,975 were released immediately, 38,947 were screened and released, 28,912 screened and tried, and there were 6,006 then awaiting trial. Of the persons awaiting trial 2,549 were in police custody, 2,116 in prison, and 1,291 in concentration camps. The number of Africans shot while resisting arrest or after being challenged to stop was four hundred and thirty. By the end of May 1953, the number reported shot 'while trying to escape' had reached one thousand, with more killings taking place every day since.

'We Europeans have to go on ruling this country and rule it with iron discipline tempered by our own hearts,' declared eighty-year-old Colonel Ewart Grogan, Member of the Legislative Council. The Colonel, who is the *doyen* of the settler community, was cheered by hundreds of Europeans when he addressed a meeting of the newly-formed Kenya British Empire Party in the Legislative Assembly hall in Nairobi. He told his audience that the east coast of Africa was in the front

line of any future strife and that a great battle was bound to
flare up sooner or later with hordes of coloured races of the
East rising up. The only answer to Mau Mau, declared this
Christian gentleman, 'was to teach the whole Kikuyu tribe
a lesson by providing a "psychic shock" '.

This most gallant octogenarian crusader for Western civilization recommended that the 'psychic shock' should take the
form of the Government arresting one hundred Mau Mau
suspects and hanging twenty-five of them upon a public
gallows before the eyes of the other seventy-five, who should
then be sent back to the Kikuyu reserve to spread the news
among their tribe. And should this fail to terrorize the Africans, those in possession of farms should be expelled from
them and their holdings handed over to Europeans until
they learn to respect the white man's rule. 'If the whole of the
Kikuyu land unit is reverted to the Crown,' maintains this
noble defender of white supremacy, 'then every Kikuyu
would know that our little queen was a great Bwana [white
ruler]'.

Significantly enough, this proposal of Colonel Grogan, one
of the most reactionary negrophobists among the colonists, is
precisely what the Governor decided to adopt. Addressing
the Budget Session of the Colony's Legislative Council on
October 20th, 1953, to mark the first anniversary of the declaration of emergency, Sir Evelyn Baring announced that:

'It is felt that some striking action should be taken against
the few villainous leaders of the Mau Mau movement. For
this reason a Bill will shortly be introduced providing for the
forfeiture of land held in the Kikuyu land unit by two classes
of persons. First, those convicted of certain serious offences
connecting the offenders with the direction of the Mau Mau
movement and, secondly, any still at large who might be
declared subject to the provisions of the Bill—that is in practice the best known gang leaders now opposing the forces of
law and order.'

On the same occasion, the Governor also announced other
security measures, including an expansion of the armed forces
and the intensification of the military campaign. Reviewing
the military situation on the day after the Governor disclosed
his new policies, General Sir George Erskine said that there

was no military answer to Kenya's troubles. The problem was 'purely political—how Europeans, Africans and Asians can live in harmony on a long-term basis. If the people of Kenya could address themselves to this problem and find a solution they would have achieved far more than I could do with security forces'.

Answering the white settlers who have criticized the Army for not having exterminated the Mau Mau patriots, the General said that there was no question of the Mau Mau having strong defences or being particularly gallant. 'It is just the opposite.' He went on:

'Mau Mau defences consist of sentries down every trail leading to hideouts. As soon as a sentry is engaged, the gang disperses and reassembles at prearranged places. Sitting in an armchair, it sounds very easy to catch these chaps. It is comparatively easy to get a sentry or two but much more difficult to get into or surround a gang. The gangs never wait to fight.'

Supplementing Mr Lyttelton's 1953 report on the casualties in this Colonial War, Mr Henry Hopkinson, Under-Secretary of State for Colonies, gave the House of Commons the following figures for the period up to July 3rd, 1954. Mau Mau insurgents killed numbered 5,567 and wounded, 622. The casualties suffered by the security forces amounted to 422 killed (including twenty-five Europeans, two Asians and 395 Africans), and 367 wounded, among them forty-four Europeans, ten Asians and 313 Africans.

During the same period, Mau Mau adherents killed 1,186 civilians (twenty-four Europeans, seventeen Asians and 1,145 Africans). The total number of Mau Mau suspects arrested and screened was 138,235, of whom only 82,000 have been released. 55,307 Africans were in concentration camps and 965 were awaiting trial. 756 have been executed since October 1952, mainly for being in unlawful possession of arms and ammunition, consorting with Mau Mau, and administering unlawful oaths. These facts were revealed in the House of Commons in November 1954 by the Colonial Secretary, Mr Lennox-Boyd, in reply to a question by Mr Fenner Brockway, the well-known Socialist champion of the colonial people.

A result of this indiscriminate mass rounding up of Afri-

cans has created a new social problem. Mr Tom Mboya, a
prominent African trade union leader in Kenya, returning
from a visit to England, told a press conference on September
1st, 1954, that there was 'no machinery for looking after the
families of the men held for "screening" in the anti-Mau Mau
drive. It is common practice to remove such families from
their homes and send them back to the reservations, where
they often had no way of supporting themselves.

'The children were found wandering into the markets, looking for food, and sleeping in empty houses. In one location
some children climbed the walls of a market and searched
the stalls for money.

'These children, whose father, and in some cases mothers,
have been detained under the Emergency Regulations, present a grave social problem.'

AFRICAN PEACE TERMS REJECTED

Despite the failure of the British military forces to impose
'unconditional surrender' upon the Mau Mau, influential
African political leaders who enjoy the confidence of their
people have expressed their readiness to try and bring the
fighting to an end.

Mr Joseph Murumbi, the Acting Secretary of the Kenya
African Union before it was proscribed in June 1953, arrived
in London in September the same year with the following
concrete peace proposals, which he presented to the Colonial
Office:

(1) Release on bail of the political leaders, on the basis of
    their co-operation in restoring peace and discussion
    with the Colonial Office regarding essential reforms.

(2) A Round Table Conference of Representatives of all
    races in Kenya with a view to acceptance of a pro-
    gramme of political, social and economic reforms.

(3) The development of land in the African Reserves to
    the fullest capacity.

(4) Making available to Africans land in the Highlands
    not yet sold to Europeans.

(5) Community Projects, Co-operative Farming and Rural Industries should be introduced in the Reserves and technical and financial help welcomed from the United Nations, British, American, Indian or other sources.

(6) The principle of parity should be adopted in representation in the Executive and Legislative Councils of Kenya.

(7) Political democracy should also be applied to local government.

(8) The progressive elimination of the colour bar.

(9) The encouragement of the co-operation of educated and politically minded Africans in all schemes of political, economic and social developments.

To prevent misuse of land, Mr Murumbi suggested that African farmers should be required to conform to strict farming practices under the direction of a Community and Co-operative organization, and that leases of such land should be on a temporary basis until the African farmer has proved himself efficient. During this period he should be subject to eviction if his farming failed to achieve the required standard.

Although the peace proposals had the endorsement of a number of well-known Labour Members of Parliament, British trade unionists and co-operators, they were rejected out of hand by the Colonial Office officials.

So the Mau Mau colonial war entered its third year with casualties increasing from day to day. 'Whatever form operations now take, they must last for some time,' writes *The Times* special correspondent from Nairobi.

'The authorities realize that military operations alone can never end the emergency. That can only come about when the bulk of the Kikuyu co-operate with the Security Forces and the Home Guards instead of with the Mau Mau, as they still do in too many places. In trying to win them over the authorities have to contend with many years of previous propaganda, intimidation, genuine grievances, and the popular belief that Mau Mau will win.'[2]

[2] *The Times*, October 19, 1953.

MULTI-RACIAL CONSTITUTION

In the hope of appeasing the settler community, which has been strongly critical of the British civil servants and the military in failing to stamp out the Mau Mau revolt, the Colonial Secretary announced in March 1954 certain constitutional reforms giving the European settler a greater voice in conducting the war. Under this transitional constitution, which will be reviewed in 1960, the Colonial Secretary has agreed to the setting up of a Council of Ministers which will be responsible for policy. In addition to the Governor and Deputy Governor, the Council of Ministers will consist of six British officials, six unofficials, of whom three will be local Europeans, two Asians (one Hindu, one Muslim), one African, and two nominated European members.

The African members of the Legislative Council asked that they be given two ministerial places, but their request was opposed by the European members. This led to the resignation of Mr Eluid Mathu, the senior African member of the Legislative Council and the only African on the Executive. Four of the unofficial members—two Europeans, one Asian and one African—have been allocated portfolios.

The Executive will continue in being and all members of the newly created Council of Ministers will be included in the Executive. In addition, there will be one Arab and two Africans nominated by the Governor, who will also have the right to appoint Under Secretaries to each of the Ministries, one of whom will be an Arab and two Africans.

This is the first time in the history of constitutional development in Kenya that an African has been included in the highest policy-making body even in a minority position. Mau Mau has certainly forced the European settlers along the road of multi-racial government.

But even this minor concession to African political aspirations has created a split among the Europeans. Those who have professed themselves as in favour of working the multi-racial constitution have formed the United Country Party, led by Mr Michael Blundell, who has for years been the leader of the European Electors Union and their official spokesman in the Legislative and Executive Councils. Those who are opposed to African participation in the Government, have aligned themselves in the Federal Independence Party. The latter party is unashamedly for 'white supremacy' and more honest than Mr Blundell and his followers. For the United Country Party, while it ostensibly supports multi-racial co-operation, limits its membership to Europeans only. 'The Party may open its membership to Africans and other non-Europeans when the multi-racial nation has been achieved,' declared Blundell. This astounding piece of political humbug is a testament to the paradox in which racial arrogance has caught up the white settlers of Kenya. Even their so-called liberal leader, Blundell, is unable to extricate himself from the *Herrenvolk* doctrine which he has himself helped to create.

Comparing the moderate demands of Mr Murumbi of the Kenya African Union with those presented to the Colonial Office by Mr Jomo Kenyatta and Mr Parmenas Mockerie, the delegates sent by the Kikuyu Central Association to England after the First World War, one is struck by their similarity. Exactly twenty-five years ago, the Kikuyu people presented a memorandum to the British Government embodying the following requests:

(1) That all land belonging to our tribe which has been alienated, including the land for Mission schools, be returned to us.

(2) That a sufficiently large area of fertile agriculture and grazing land be added to our present reserve with due regard to our present requirements and the future increase of our members.[3]

(3) That boundaries of present and future enlarged reserves should be marked in such an unmistakable manner that they should be easily known by sight to the present and future generations instead of being marked on plans and paper.

[3] The African population was then estimated at 2,404,000. It was 5,251,120 according to the 1948 census.

(4)   That no land should be alienated in the reserve for any purpose whatsoever to other than natives.

(5)   That within the reserve the system of Githaka should be maintained giving individual titles to clans and families with the safeguarding conditions of adding to or reducing the area according to the increase or decrease of the family.

(6)   That permission be granted to us to purchase land from Europeans or Indians if and when the members of our tribe are able to do so.

(7)   That sufficient area of forest be placed at the disposal of each clan to which they can have free access and cut fuel or timber according to their requirements which can be regulated by purely native councils.

(8)   That our livestock be allowed free access to all salt licks.[4]

These humble demands were rejected by the Colonial Office, and for sixteen years Mr Kenyatta, who was then the General Secretary of the Kikuyu Central Association, remained in Britain, appealing to Whitehall officials and sympathetic Members of Parliament to redress the grievances of the Africans. During that period, the writer was closely associated with Mr Kenyatta politically, and can testify that the Kikuyu leader availed himself of every constitutional channel to secure justice and fair play for his people.

As one of the leaders of the Pan-African Movement, Jomo Kenyatta eloquently pleaded the cause of his people before the Fifth Pan-African Congress at Manchester in 1945. The Congress pledged full support to the Kenya Africans in their struggle to attain the Four Freedoms by non-violent methods. A year after the Congress, Kenyatta returned to his country, where he joined the Kenya African Union and continued to agitate along strictly constitutional lines for the implementation of long promised reforms, until his arrest and imprisonment in 1953.

After the war, conditions for the Africans in Kenya went

[4] P. G. Mockerie: An African Speaks for his People, p. 95 (Hogarth Press).

a European, it is only natural that you should feel that we have something against Europeans. I feel that you should not have stressed so much that we have been entirely motivated by hatred for Europeans. Our activities have been against injustice to the African people and if you think that by asking for African rights we have turned out to be what you say is Mau Mau, we are very sorry you have been misled. What we have done and shall continue to do is to demand rights for the African people as human beings, that they shall enjoy the same facilities as other people. We look forward to the day when peace shall come to this land and that the truth shall be known that we, African leaders, have stood for peace.

'None of us would condone mutilation of human beings. We are human and have families of our own, and none of us would condone such activities as you think we are guilty of. I am asking for no mercy at all on behalf of my colleagues. We are asking that justice be done, and that injustices that exist may be righted.'

Now that the storm of violence has broken over the fair land of Kenya, leaving in its wake a trail of hatred and bitterness that will long be remembered by Africans of this and future generations, we must all work to restore peace. On the other hand, the tragic events in Kenya should serve as a lesson to the British that even under the most enlightened system of constitutional evolution to self-determination, theory breaks down in practice in multi-racial territories where a white minority, entrenched economically and politically, seeks to maintain permanent domination over a politically awakened and nationalistically-minded black indigenous majority.

Atrocities and unspeakable crimes have been inflicted on both sides, for it is a sort of Black and Tan war. And war is the greatest crime that can be inflicted upon any people. The task before us is to get rid of the underlying economic and psychological grievances which have given rise to Mau Mau. Until this is done there will be no lasting peace in Kenya, much less goodwill and co-operation between black and white.

Only when political and economic power is shared between all the racial communities on the basis of *absolute* equality in all spheres of public life, will national integration be achieved and a lasting solution found to the multi-racial problems of Kenya and other East and Central African territories. The time to act is now. Tomorrow will be too late. Jomo Kenyatta and the other leaders of the Kenya African Union should be set free. For they alone can help to bring sanity back to Kenya. After all, many Nazi leaders who have committed worse crimes against humanity than any ascribed to Mau Mau have been restored to liberty. Why should Kenyatta and other Africans suffer for the wrongs which white men have inflicted upon black folk in their own motherland?

These European settlers, like the French *colons* in North Africa, are the real opponents of inter-racial co-operation and partnership. They are the ones who deserve our condemnation, not the Arabs and Africans.[5]

[5] On January 27th, 1955, the Commander-in-Chief gave another report to the Press in which he disclosed that 260 Mau Mau had been killed for every European's life taken since the war began in October 1952. The civilian casualties were: thirty Europeans, nineteen Asians and 1,316 Africans—a total of 1,365 killed by Mau Mau. Security forces casualties were: thirty-eight Europeans, two Asians, 470 Africans killed; and sixty-two Europeans, twelve Asians and 392 Africans wounded.

The total Mau Mau losses were 7,811 killed, 844 captured wounded, and 349 captured unwounded, while 828 had surrendered. A total of 223 Mau Mau had been hanged for murder and 568 for other capital offences, such as carrying arms, and a further thirty Africans for what the General described as 'non-Mau Mau capital offences'.

These figures of Mau Mau losses do not include casualties inflicted by bombing in the forest by R.A.F. planes. There are over 7,000 Africans in concentration camps, and prisons; 600,000 Kikuyus have been removed from their homes and 150,000 huts destroyed. See *Hansard* (House of Commons), Column 921, April 27, 1955.

An official statement issued by the Kenya Government on October 19, 1955, disclosed that 'there are still 62,000 Mau Mau detainees and convicts, although 100 are being released each month . . . About 10,000 detainees are working on a big irrigation plan, known as the Mivea-Tebere scheme, which, if successful, may absorb 10,000 to 13,000 families'. A similar scheme is proposed for the Tana River.

XV

CONSTITUTIONAL DEVELOPMENT AND TRIBALISM IN NIGERIA

Turning our attention now to Nigeria, we find that the possibilities of achieving self-government there through purely constitutional means approximate those of the Gold Coast. As in the Gold Coast, there are in Nigeria no large white settler or other immigrant communities to obstruct the nationalist aspirations of the indigenous population. The Europeans in Nigeria, like those in Burma, India and Ceylon before the independence of these Asian countries, are mostly civil servants, military and police officers, agents of foreign commercial, trading, banking and mining companies, missionaries, and other birds of passage. They have no intention of making their homes in West Africa, and when the time comes for them to leave Nigeria, they will probably do so as gracefully as their fellow Britishers left South-East Asia.

While the mosquito has denied the Europeans permanent occupation of Nigeria, the problem of attaining self-government is, nevertheless, complicated by the conflicting claims of tribal and religious communalism. The inter-tribal conflict will become clearer to the reader as we review the evolution of constitutional development in Nigeria since the British occupation.

THE MAKING OF MODERN NIGERIA

Until 1914, the designation 'Nigeria' was merely a convenient geographical term applied to a number of regions which now make up that territory. The area comprising what are now called 'the Colony' and 'Protectorate' cover over 373,000 square miles—an area larger than France and Italy combined. Nigeria is the largest non-self-governing dependency in the British Empire, and has a population of over 31,000,000.

Prior to the slave trade in the seventeenth century, Europeans had no contact with this part of Africa. The Portuguese were the first to establish settlements along the Guinea coast, from where they exported slaves to the Western Hemisphere. The first British settlement was established at Lagos along the south-western coast. This was acquired by treaty from the Yoruba chiefs and declared a Crown Colony in 1861. After the Berlin Conference of 1885, the British also established a Protectorate over the Niger Delta and the entire Oil Rivers region along the south-eastern coast.

By the end of the century, British influence had been carried into the interior by the Royal Niger Charter Company, whose chief agent, Captain Frederick Lugard (afterwards Lord Lugard), acquired by treaty and conquest the vast territories which now comprise Northern Nigeria. Having brought this part of West Africa, with a population of over 17 millions, under the Union Jack, the Royal Niger Company surrendered its charter in 1899, and the Foreign Office proclaimed the Southern and Northern regions of Nigeria British Protectorates in 1900. Six years later, the Southern Protectorate was amalgamated with the Crown Colony of Lagos.

The Northern Protectorate remained under separate administration until 1914, when it was merged with the other two regions—Lagos and Southern Nigeria—to form what is officially designated 'the Colony' and 'Protectorate' of Nigeria. Ever since then, this artificially created country, comprising four main ethnic groups—the Fulani and Hausas in the North, the Ibos in the East, and the Yorubas in the West—Nigeria has had some form of unitary government operating from Lagos, as the capital. This unitary government has always been firmly in the hands of British administrative officials, who have kept the parts together.

CONSTITUTIONAL EVOLUTION

Nigeria started at the very bottom of the constitutional ladder. Long before the other regions comprising the Protectorate came into the political picture, Lagos was granted a constitution. That was in 1861, the same year that it passed out of the control of the Yoruba White Cap chiefs. The Lagos Legislative Council, as it was officially called, consisted entirely of British officials. The Council acted as an advisory body to the Governor, who, however, was under no obligation to accept its advice, as he was an absolute ruler.

This Council remained in being until 1922, by which time its composition had undergone certain changes. In 1922, it consisted of six officials and four nominated unofficials, of whom two were Africans. Its legislative function was confined to the Colony area only. It had no authority to make laws for the rest of Nigeria—the so-called Protectorate.

After the amalgamation between *the Colony* and *the Protectorate* had taken place in 1914, another legislative body, called the Nigerian Council, was established to act as an advisory body for both regions. But the Lagos Legislative Council remained in being. The Nigerian Council consisted of thirty-six members, including a majority of senior British officials, six unofficial European members representing foreign vested interests, and six Africans representing tribal communities in the southern coastal regions. All the members were appointed by the Governor and held office at his pleasure. The Nigerian Council and the Lagos Legislative Council functioned separately until 1922, when they were replaced by a single body known as the Legislative Council.

THE CLIFFORD CONSTITUTION

Under the 1922 Constitution (named after the then Governor, Sir Hugh Clifford), which came into operation in 1924, there were thirty-one official members and nineteen unofficial members in the reformed Legislative Council. Of these latter members, fifteen were nominated by the Governor and four elected. The elected members were Africans, representing the municipalities of Lagos and Calabar. The other members were partly Africans and partly Europeans representing British vested interests, such as trade and commerce, banking, mining and shipping. The electorate in Lagos and Calabar was confined to male British subjects with an annual income of not less than £100. The number of registered voters in the first election in 1924 was 1,055 out of a total adult African population of 126,108.

As the Northerners had no direct representation in the Legislative Council, it legislated only for the Colony area and the Southern Province of the Protectorate. Laws affecting Northern Nigerians were enacted by the Governor-in-Council. That is to say, the Governor exercised his authority through British political officers headed by a Lieutenant-Governor, who in turn utilized the services of traditional native rulers— the Sultans, Emirs and other chiefs—to maintain law and order, collect taxes and dispense 'justice' according to Islamic law. This system is known as Indirect Rule or Native Administration, and was introduced by Lord Lugard, the first Governor-General. He was not only responsible for conquering the North, but for amalgamating the various territories into one United Nigeria in 1914.

The second significant constitutional reform took place in 1942, when unofficial members were for the first time appointed to the Governor's Executive Council, the main instrument of government. This reform was instituted by the then Governor, Sir Bernard Bourdillon. He appointed three such unofficial members, of whom two were Africans. This number was later increased to four—all Africans—before the old Crown Colony Legislative Council was abolished.

The next constitutional reform was brought about largely through the agitation of the National Council of Nigeria and the Cameroons (N.C.N.C.), founded in 1944 by the late Hubert Macaulay, the Nigerian Elder Statesman, and Dr Azikiwe, its present president.

Sir Arthur Richards (now Lord Milverton) succeeded Sir Bernard Bourdillon in 1943. Three years later he promulgated a new constitution for the entire country.

THE RICHARDS CONSTITUTION

The Richards Constitution, however, did not satisfy the aspirations of the politically conscious sections of the population, and was vigorously opposed by the N.C.N.C., the most powerful political movement in Nigeria at the time. The constitution came into operation in January 1947. It was a hotch-potch affair, which attempted to combine the tribal autocracy operating in the North with the outward forms of parliamentary democracy and, naturally, failed miserably.

Under this form of dyarchic administration, the semi-feudal Islamic rulers of Northern Nigeria were given direct representation in the Central Government for the first time since the amalgamation of the Northern and Southern Provinces of the Protectorate. To implement the constitutional reforms, the Northern and Southern Protectorates were divided into three administrative regions—Northern Region, Western Region and Eastern Region—with separate regional Assemblies acting as electoral colleges for the Central Legislative Council.

There were two such bodies in the Northern Region—the House of Chiefs and the House of Assembly. The first consisted of first-class chiefs such as the Sultans and Emirs, and their second-class henchmen. The House of Assembly was composed of nineteen official members—British civil servants stationed in the Northern Region—and twenty-four unofficial members—six appointed by the Governor to represent special interests in the region and the others elected by the Northern Native Authorities. In the Western Region, the House of Assembly consisted of about fourteen British officials and nineteen unofficials. Five of the latter were appointed by the Governor and the others were selected by the Western Yoruba chiefs and the Native Authorities in that region.

The Eastern House of Assembly followed the same pattern, except that there is no traditional system of chieftainship among the Ibos, the largest ethnic group inhabiting this part of Nigeria. The Eastern Assembly consisted of about fourteen British officials and eighteen unofficials, five appointed by the Governor and the others nominated by the 'warrant chiefs'—men appointed by the British without any traditional status—and other Africans elected by the local Native Authorities.

Governor Richards endowed the regional assemblies with all the paraphernalia of parliamentary bodies but denied them all legislative authority. Their function, in addition to selecting representatives to sit in the Central Legislative Council in Lagos, was purely advisory. They were allowed to discuss proposed legislation affecting their respective regions, but that was all. Their views were then submitted to the Governor through the senior British officer of the region, known as the Chief Commissioner.

The real parliamentary functions of government were carried out by the Legislative Council, which consisted of the Governor as president, thirteen ex-officio members, three nominated official members, and twenty-four nominated or indirectly elected unofficial members, most of whom were Africans appointed by the regional assemblies acting as electoral colleges. They were divided as follows: four from the Northern House of Chiefs, five from the Northern House of Assembly, two chiefs appointed by the Governor from the Western House of Assembly and four appointed from the same body by the members, five members appointed by the Eastern House of Assembly and, finally, four members appointed by the Governor to represent foreign special interests, such as shipping, banking, commerce, mining.

The only 'democratically' elected members were four; three to represent the voters of the Colony area of Lagos, and one the eastern municipal area of Calabar. The suffrage was based on an income qualification of £50 per annum and confined to males over twenty-one years of age.

Although the composition of the Central Legislature changed, the Executive Council remained the same. Apart from the addition of four hand-picked Africans, the Executive was dominated by senior British officials, including an African Director of Medical Services. The Executive members decided policy and initiated all legislation. But they were not responsible to the Legislature or removable by it. The Legislative Council was just a glorified debating club. As soon as the fraudulent nature of the Richards Constitution became obvious to the people, a country-wide campaign was launched by the N.C.N.C. to demand a truly democratic constitution.

In 1947, soon after the Richards Constitution was put into operation, a delegation of the N.C.N.C. visited London to make representations to the Labour Government, then in power and submit amendments to the Constitution. The mission, headed by Dr Azikiwe, was received by the Secretary of State for the Colonies, Mr A. Creech Jones, who rejected their proposals and advised them to return home and give the Constitution a trial. Disappointed, the mission went back and intensified their agitation. Before long the whole country was seething against what the Africans considered an imperial *diktat*. Although the Constitution was supposed to last for nine years, it had to be reviewed within three.

Governor Richards, in putting forward his constitutional reforms, had assured the Africans that they were devised 'to promote the unity of Nigeria; to provide adequately within that unity for the diverse elements which make up the country; and to secure greater participation by Africans in the discussion of their own affairs'. Despite Governor Richards's first two claims, it was he who actually introduced the regional structure of government which laid the basis for tribalist politics to flourish and the disintegration of the country, upon which his successor, Sir John Macpherson, built.

THE MACPHERSON CONSTITUTION

Sir Arthur Richards, having served his full term of office
and more, retired in the latter part of 1947 and was created
a peer with the title of Lord Milverton of Lagos by the Labour Government, in appreciation of his proconsular services.
On his return to England he joined the Labour Party, but
within eighteen months he deserted Fabianism for Liberalism. But even Liberalism was too progressive for the erstwhile
Socialist lord, and he finally ended up in the Tory camp by
way of the National Liberals!

Lord Milverton was succeeded by Sir John Macpherson,
the former Comptroller of the West Indian Development
and Welfare Commission. He had had no previous experience
as a Governor, and his appointment to Nigeria, the largest
dependency in the Commonwealth, faced with complex political and multi-tribal problems, was certainly a bold experiment. Considering the mess Lord Milverton had left Nigerian
affairs in, the people figured Sir John would do no worse. But
they were soon to be disappointed.

Some time after assuming office, Sir John announced his
intention to review the Richards Constitution and hopes ran
high. By 1949, the Governor had appointed a committee
consisting of all the unofficial members of the Legislative
Council to do the re-drafting and as a result, a series of recommendations were presented to an All-Nigerian Constitutional
Conference at Ibadan in 1950. The Conference Report was
later debated and approved by the Regional Houses of Assembly and a Select Committee of the Legislative Council.
By the middle of 1951, the Macpherson Constitution came
into operation on the basis of direct and indirect elections
throughout the country.

The Constitution embodied many of the features of the
Richards Constitution, but went much further along the lines
of regional separatism. For example, the regional assemblies
were not only retained but were vested with legislative and
executive powers. Apart from the two houses which had al-

ready existed in the Northern Region—the House of Chiefs
and the House of Assembly—a second Upper House of Chiefs
was established in the Western Region. Each region was also
given an Executive Council with full powers in shaping the
policy of government for the region. And since the aim of the
Macpherson Constitution was supposed to be to promote
'regional autonomy within a centralized Nigeria,' a single
chamber Central Legislature, called the House of Representatives, was created to take the place of the Richards Legislative Council. As the all-Nigerian Parliament, the House of
Representatives consisted of 148 members selected by the
various regional Houses of Assembly acting as electoral colleges, with half the seats allotted to the Northern Region
because its population was equal to that of the Western and
Eastern Regions combined.

COALITION COUNCIL OF MINISTERS

The former Executive Council, which had been appointed
by the Governor, was transformed into a Council of Ministers, the principal instrument of policy on matters affecting
all the regions. It consisted of eighteen members—four Africans representing each of the three regional governments
and six Europeans—the three Lieutenant-Governors of the
Regions and three senior officials, the Chief Secretary, the
Financial Secretary and the Attorney-General. The Governor
was chairman, armed with reserved powers. This so-called
Cabinet was, in fact and reality, nothing else but a junta of
British officials in coalition with African politicians representing conflicting and irreconcilable tribal and religious interests and aspirations. The white members represented
British imperial interests, but the black members had no
common bond. In actual fact, their distrust and animosity
towards each other was greater than their dislike of their
white colleagues. The situation was further complicated by
the fact that the African Ministers were the *delegates* of
their respective regional governments. They had not been
elected by, nor were they responsible to, a majority party

in the House of Representatives. In like manner, the British civil service members were also *delegates* of the Colonial Office and directly responsible to the Governor.

THE POLITICAL PARTIES

The Northern Ministers belonged to the Fulani-dominated Northern Peoples' Congress (N.P.C.), a creation of the semi-feudal ruling caste of that region. It enjoys the active support of the British political officials, whose policy has always been to keep a division between the Muslims and non-Muslims. In this way they hope to 'protect' the Northerners from such 'dangerous' ideals as parliamentary democracy and national independence, preached by the anti-imperialist politicians in the south.

The leader of the N.P.C. is the Sardauna of Sokoto, one of the best educated members of the traditional ruling caste. He is Minister of Local Government in the Northern Regional administration. The opposition group in this region is the small but vigorous Northern Elements Progressive Union (N.E.P.U.), headed by an able and very intelligent young intellectual, Mallam Aminu Kano. The N.E.P.U. favours a reform of the system of Indirect Rule and the implementation of the U.N. Declaration of Human Rights, which guarantees freedom of movement, assembly, speech and press, at present denied by the autocratic Native Administrations in the Northern Region. N.E.P.U. also advocates the introduction of direct elections through secret ballot for the people of the Northern Province. All these reforms are strenuously opposed by the Sultan, Emirs, and other members of the black ruling caste, who are the favourites of the British officials and maintained in office by them.

The rival parties in the Southern Protectorate are the National Council of Nigeria and the Cameroons (N.C.N.C.), the Action Group and the United National Independence Party, a break-away group from the N.C.N.C. in the Eastern Region.

The N.C.N.C. is the majority party and heads the Eastern

Regional Government, under the leadership of Dr Azikiwe. The party also forms the official Opposition in the Western Regional Assembly. The majority party in the West is the Action Group, headed by Mr Obafemi Awolowo, Minister of Local Government. The N.C.N.C. is the older of the two Government parties. It was formed in 1944 and has always been the most militant and progressive nationalist organization in Nigeria. Until 1951, it was unchallenged, and Dr Azikiwe had every opportunity of becoming the accepted leader of the *whole* of Nigeria, as Dr Nkrumah is acclaimed in the Gold Coast. But since the emergence of the Action Group in 1951, tribalism has claimed the loyalties of the respective ethnic and religious groups. Hence the N.C.N.C., while it continues to enjoy popular support in all regions of the country, including sections of the Yorubas of the Western Region, it has more or less come to be identified with the Ibos, the largest tribe in the Eastern Region. In fairness, however, it must be said that although Dr Azikiwe is an Ibo, he has always vigorously opposed tribalism and racialism in politics. On the other hand, Mr Awolowo is definitely committed to tribal separatism. For him, '*Nigeria is not a nation. It is a mere geographical expression. There are no Nigerians*', he asserts.[1] Rejecting the concept of a unitary Nigeria, which Dr Azikiwe strongly supported throughout the years, Mr Awolowo advocates self-government and separatism not only for each of the existing regions, but claims autonomy for the dozen or more tribes which, he maintains, are 'nations', with nothing in common except their colour.

Mr Awolowo's organization began as a political off-shoot of the Egbe Omo Oduduwa, a Yoruba religious and cultural society whose patron is the Oni of Ife, a wealthy Ibadan chief. It came into being in 1951 under the auspices of Mr Awolowo and other Yoruba intellectuals who formerly belonged to the Nigeria Youth Movement, the pioneer nationalist organization in Lagos, as an opposition to 'Ibo domination in the West'. At the general election of 1951, the Action Group won the majority of seats in the predominantly Yoruba

[1] Obafemi Awolowo: *Path to Nigerian Freedom*, chap. 5 (Faber & Faber).

constituencies and since then has controlled the Assembly and Government in the Western Region. Its chief opponent, the N.C.N.C., won twenty-five seats in this region, four in the Northern House of Assembly, and thirty-eight in the Central House of Representatives. To this extent the N.C.N.C. can still claim to be the only political party enjoying support in all three Regional Assemblies as well as in the Central Legislature. But its main organizational strength is still centred chiefly in the Eastern Region, where it won 74 seats.

No one party has yet rooted itself firmly all over Nigeria to the same extent as the C.P.P. has in the Gold Coast. It is this over-all organizational weakness of the political parties which facilitates the growth of tribal chauvinism and regional exclusiveness in Nigeria, to the detriment of integration and national unity.[2] The remedy lies in a uniform electoral system.

1953 CONSTITUTIONAL CRISIS

The Anglo-African Coalition Government broke down in April 1953, when a motion was introduced into the House of Representatives by an Action Group back-bencher, calling upon the British Government to declare its willingness to grant Nigeria 'self-government by 1956'.

The motion was supported by the Action Group and N.C.N.C. members in the Central Legislature but opposed by representatives of the N.P.C. More significant, however, than the way the House reacted to this motion was the resignation of the Action Group *delegates* from the Council of Ministers. The other regional Ministers, including those from the Eastern Region who had recently broken away from the N.C.N.C., remained to keep the company of their white colleagues. They

[2] The N.C.N.C. won a majority in the Eastern and Western Regional general elections for the Federal House of Representatives in 1954 and has six out of ten African representatives in the Federal Council of Ministers.

and the N.P.C. representatives looked upon the Western Ministers as 'deserters'.

The resignation of the Western Regional Ministers precipitated a constitutional crisis at the Centre. Their withdrawal from the Cabinet brought to the fore the basic weakness of the so-called Federal Government. It could not function because the Ministers were not prepared to disregard their regional and tribal loyalties and adhere to the principle of 'collective responsibility'. The present party alignments preclude a common ideology and programme, the fundamentals necessary to bind the Ministers together. The parties had only to withdraw their *delegates* from the Council of Ministers over a matter of which they disapproved, and a Cabinet crisis was bound to follow.

The former Executive Council which had given place to the Council of Ministers had been able to function as a unitary body, superficially at least. All the members were the Governor's nominees and subject to his control. With the reformed Macpherson Constitution, the Governor's control over the Ministers was removed and the Council collapsed under the first strain put upon it.

A further weakness in the Constitution was revealed by the April crisis of 1953. This weakness was that elections to the House of Representatives were not based upon a uniform electoral system, which would have brought to the Centre a majority party independent of regional appeal and from which the Ministers would have been drawn. Such a constitutional provision would have created the climate in which a common Nigerian national outlook could grow. As matters stood at the time of the Cabinet crisis, the Ministers considered that they had a greater loyalty to their respective regions and parties than to the Governor, who himself was considered to be the leader of another faction, namely, the British ex-officio members of the Council of Ministers.

THE LONDON CONFERENCE

To resolve the April crisis, the Secretary of State for the Colonies invited the leaders of all the political parties in Nigeria to a constitutional conference in London in August 1953. The conference was attended by accredited representatives of the N.C.N.C., the Action Group, the Northern Peoples' Congress, the Northern Elements Progressive Union, and the United National Independence Party and cost £22,715.

Mr Oliver Lyttelton presided. At the end of a fortnight's deliberation, the conference reached a number of compromises which failed completely to resolve the crucial political problem: *To whom shall power be transferred?* Without a solution to this fundamental question, there will be no strong, stable, centralized all-African Government like that of the Gold Coast, capable of assuming full sovereign power from the British when they decide to quit Nigeria. At the moment, the British authority is the only stabilizing force in the country, holding the opposing regional and tribal factions together at a very weak centre.

For the decisions reached by the London Conference can only make the federal government, as reconstituted, less effective than the one it has displaced for coping with the centrifugal political pressures seeking to carve up the country into autonomous tribal states. Federal nations like Australia and U.S.A. have well entrenched Anglo-Saxon ruling strata, more or less homogeneous in religion and a culture derived from Europe; but Nigeria is still just a hotch-potch of tribes at all levels of social development and attached to different religions—Christianity, Islam, Animism. Such a country needs, above all things, a strong and stable unitary government, capable of knitting the differing tribal communities into a national whole. Such a centralized government, elected by and responsible to, Nigerians, can only be brought about by a nation-wide party able to speak with one voice on behalf of the whole of Nigeria in disregard of tribal allegiance and religious affiliation.

In the absence of a strong central authority based upon an all-Nigerian party, it is likely that the present artificial State will burst apart should the British decide to withdraw from Nigeria at an early date. For the so-called Regional Administrations are merely glorified local governments under African control, to which specific functions have been assigned. These parts are held together by the British imperial authority represented by the Governor-General, the regional Governors, and the British-controlled police and military forces at their disposal. The removal of this British authority will create a vacuum.

It was on this very question of the 'Pakistanization' of Nigeria that Mr A. C. Nwapa, a former Minister of Commerce and Trade, and other delegates of the United National Independence Party, walked out of the conference. Mr Nwape followed up this action with a statement to the British Press, in which he pointed out that 'in the present circumstances of Nigeria, with its multiplicity and diversity of cultural and ethnic groups, it is necessary to have a strong and independent Central Government', and that the transfer of residual powers to the Regions will result in 'a looser federation than the Nigerian public has been led to expect'.

For years past the N.C.N.C. had also been stressing the need for a strong Central Government, but under pressure of the Northern and Western delegates—both committed to regionalism upon the basis of tribal separatism—Dr Azikiwe perforce gave way in order to save the conference from breaking up. Had Dr Azikiwe not compromised, the Colonial Secretary would have had no other alternative but to impose a dictated constitution upon Nigeria in order to resolve the deadlock between the delegates. Such a constitution, however, could hardly have been worse than the one finally accepted by the conference, for it completely ignored the essential democratic element of a common electoral system based upon adult suffrage. The constitution also failed to provide for a Bill of Rights guaranteeing the Four Freedoms in all three regions of the federation.

The reality of the situation is contained in the fundamental question: *To whom shall the British Parliament transfer sovereignty?* To this question only the Nigerian political leaders can give the answer. And on this answer depends the whole future of their country. Dr Azikiwe could have supplied the answer some years earlier in 1947, after the N.C.N.C. mission returned home from London. At that time the all-Nigerian leadership was his for the taking. The N.C.N.C. had no serious opposition, as tribal and separatist organizations like the Action Group and Northern Peoples' Congress had not yet emerged to champion such chauvinism as West for the Westerners, North for the Northerners and East for the Easterners. Had Dr Azikiwe at that time taken stock of the N.C.N.C. and reorganized it on a more closely-knit basis, it is more than likely that Nigeria would have maintained its lead over the Gold Coast, which has now become the advanced guard of the African liberation movement. Thanks to the non-tribal structure of the C.P.P. which embraces members of all tribes, Gas, Fantis, Ashantis, Ewes and Northerners, Dr Nkrumah has been able to combat the kind of regional separatism and tribal exclusiveness advocated by the so-called National Liberation Movement led by certain Ashanti chiefs and lawyers hungry for political power.

Wherein did Dr Azikiwe fail? There are two main reasons. The N.C.N.C's chief weakness was in the very nature of its organizational structure. It was then also a federation of tribal unions which, while they gave the organization numbers, opened the way for the inevitable disintegration which set in when competing organizations of a purely tribal character arose to lure them away. With the emergence of political parties appealing to tribal and regional loyalties instead of political ideologies, the federated bodies defected one by one from the N.C.N.C., leaving it with a predominantly Ibo rump.

The second and equally important reason was the lack of a leadership selflessly dedicated to the arduous work of building up a nation-wide party on the basis of individual branch membership. They would have done for Nigeria what Dr Nkrumah and his fellow-leaders did for the Gold Coast through the C.P.P.—have given that tribe-riven country a majority party based upon popular support.

That is why we emphasize the urgent need for Nigerian leaders to build up strong all-Nigerian political parties on a non-tribal basis throughout all the regions. The N.C.N.C. is now attempting to carry out such a plan as shown by its victory in the 1954 Federal elections. The first party which achieves a majority in all three regions, and is returned to power at the Centre, will be able to control the Council of Ministers and negotiate on behalf of a united Nigeria the transfer of power, as the Convention Peoples' Party is now doing for the Gold Coast. To encourage the fragmentation of Nigeria is the greatest disservice which can be done to the people of that country and the African race in general. That is why the National Liberation Movement is fundamentally a reactionary form of opposition, for its policy would lead to the fragmentation of the Gold Coast, which is too small to maintain a federal form of government.

THE LYTTELTON CONSTITUTION

Having decided to give more powers to the Regional Governments, the London conference agreed to maintain the existing Regional Houses with slight modifications in their composition. For example, in the Eastern Region the ex-officio and special interests members are to be withdrawn and the total membership increased to eighty-four. The ex-officio members are likewise to be withdrawn from the Eastern Regional Assembly and Executive Council, but the Lieutenant-Governor, now designated Governor, will appoint a Speaker and Deputy Speaker after consultation with the leader of the majority party. The Governor will, however, continue to preside over the Executive Council, which will have no less than nine members—to be called Ministers— headed by a Prime Minister, who will be elected from the majority party in the House of Assembly. Similar arrangements will apply to the Western Regional House of Assembly, except that the special members will continue to serve in it. The ex-officio members, however, will no longer serve either in the Assembly or in the Executive Council. The Speaker and Deputy Speaker will be elected by the Assembly and the leader of the Government will be styled Prime Minister.

At the special request of the delegates of the semi-feudalistic Northern Peoples' Congress, the London Conference agreed to retain the present composition of the Northern Regional House of Chiefs and the House of Assembly. Membership in the latter will consist of four British officials, ten nominated members and ninety members indirectly elected. The Executive Council will be increased to sixteen—three British officials and thirteen Africans, headed by a Prime Minister. The Regional Governor will continue to be the president of the Executive Council. The Governor of Nigeria, who becomes the first West African Governor-General, will retain his powers of veto and certification over certain reserved matters affecting vital British imperial interests and the civil service. He will preside over the Central Council of Ministers and in this capacity he will be his own Prime Minister, as the Conference made no provisions for an African Prime Minister in the so-called federal set up due to the tribal cleavage between the three regional party leaders—Dr Azikiwe, Mr Awolowo and the Sardauna of Sokoto. Under pressure of the delegations from the Northern Peoples' Congress and the Action Group, the Conference decided to allocate certain subjects affecting the three regions of Nigeria to the Central Government and to transfer all residual subjects to the Regional governments. A list of concurrent subjects will be shared by the Central and Regional Governments, the federal law prevailing in the case of dispute. The Regional legislatures will now have the power to legislate without having to submit laws to the Central Council of Ministers.

Thus, the reduction of powers of the Central Government and the failure of the Conference to provide a uniform franchise for election from constituencies in the Regions to the Central House of Representatives is, in our opinion, one of the greatest weaknesses of the new constitution. As a result, the reformed Central Government may well prove as difficult to operate as the one it seeks to improve upon. Apart from providing for an increase in membership, each Region is to be allowed to frame its own electoral laws.[3] Furthermore, the Central Government Council of Ministers will still be under the influence of the Regional Prime Ministers. Unless, as it is unlikely to happen, one party has an absolute majority in the Central House of Representatives. As regards the Central Cabinet, instead of twelve African ministers (four from each of the three regions), it is now proposed to reduce the number to ten, three from each region and one from the Southern Cameroons. This part of the Trusteeship territory has been detached from Eastern Nigeria and given its own separate Legislative and Executive Councils on the same pattern as the Nigerian regional administrations.

The European official members of the Council of Ministers have been reduced from six to three. The Chief Secretary, the Financial Secretary and the Attorney-General will continue to control the principal portfolios in the Central Government. They will be appointed by the Governor-General, who will also have the right to appoint nine Africans from among the representative members of the House of Representatives, three from each of the regions and one from Southern Cameroons. In the absence of one party topping the poll in each of the three regional elections to the Centre, the present arrangements will only serve to perpetuate and foster tribal chauvinism and hold back the development of an all-Nigerian national outlook. The Central House of Representatives will consist of 184 elected members distributed among the three regions as follows: ninety-two from the North; forty-two from East and West respectively; six from the Trusteeship area of the Southern Cameroons, and two from the Colony area of Lagos, which will be the federal capital. In addition to the elected members, there will be three ex-officio members, namely, the Chief Secretary, the Attorney-General and the Financial Secretary of the Federation.[4]

[3] Eastern Nigeria is the only region in which universal adult suffrage obtains.

[4] The first federal election under the Lyttelton Constitution took place in the three regions, Southern Cameroons and Lagos at the end of 1954. The results were: N.C.N.C. 56, U.N.I.P. and Action Group Alliance 27, Independents 16, N.P.C. 79, and Kamerun National Congress 6.

The Speaker and Deputy Speaker will be appointed by the Governor in his discretion; the former from outside the House of Representatives and the latter from among its members. The reformed Constitution has strengthened the Regions at the expense of the Centre. It provides for the emergence of majority parties and Prime Ministers within each Region, but places the so-called Federal Government at the mercy of coalitions. This was precisely why the Constitution broke down in April 1953. Yet the same mistakes are being repeated in worse form. For the Regional Governments and the party leaders will now have more powers than they had before the London Conference met to control their supporters in the Federal House of Representatives and Council of Ministers.

By giving the Regional Governments the right to make their own electoral laws, minority parties such as the Northern Elements Progressive Union will have a difficult task to challenge the autocratic powers of the Sultans, Emirs, and their henchmen by constitutional means, unless the British bring pressure to bear upon them to democratize the electoral laws. The semi-feudal rulers of the North should, even in the interests of their own good government, be made to introduce, at the very least, universal suffrage for male taxpayers. It would be well, too, for them to guarantee freedom of movement, assembly, speech and press—guarantees which were not embodied in the Federal Constitution, since the Colonial Secretary, Mr Lyttelton, supported the Northern Peoples' Congress delegates in their contention that these were matters for each Region to decide. Such reforms which already exist in the Eastern Region are vitally necessary if the Muslim population of the North is to develop democratic institutions.

TRIBAL QUARREL OVER FEDERAL CAPITAL

The tribal structure of Nigerian Nationalism is best illustrated by the rift which occurred between the regional leaders over the future status of Lagos. This typically colonial port, while geographically located in the West and inhabited mostly by Yorubas, who also form the majority of the population in the Western hinterland, has always been the seat of government and as such has assumed the atmosphere of a cosmopolitan community. It is also the chief port and centre of trade and commerce in Nigeria.

Since the emergence of Yoruba tribalism as a virile force in Nigerian politics, the Action Group leaders have been demanding that Lagos be incorporated into the Western Region, for its exclusion would mean a loss of revenue to that Regional Government. This has been opposed by the other regional political leaders, especially the Northerners, as the bulk of their export commodities pass through Lagos for shipment abroad. Unable to agree among themselves over the administration of the town, all the delegates agreed to let Mr Lyttelton decide the issue. He decided that Lagos should remain the federal capital, with direct representation in the Central House of Representatives. Naturally, the decision pleased the Northerners and Easterners but so annoyed the Westerners that their leader, Mr Awolowo, walked out of the Conference and threatened secession of the Western Region from the rest of Nigeria.

The quarrel was, however, patched up when the London Conference re-convened in Lagos in January 1954, at which the allocation of the federal revenue and the reorganization of the Judiciary and public services were discussed. It was agreed that Lagos become Federal Territory with two Central Legislature representatives. This conference cost £14,475.

The Lyttelton Constitution leaves Nigeria fundamentally where it was before the 1953 London Conference took place. What it has done is to undermine further what little administrative unity existed before the constitutional crisis occurred, and open the door to the speedy disintegration of Nigeria into three or more so-called self-governing States. Already the Cameroons, formerly a part of Eastern Nigeria, has broken away from Nigeria as an autonomous region, while the inhabitants of part of Northern Nigeria are demanding separation from the North to form what they call a 'Middle Belt' region. To stop this mad fragmentation of the country, the regional structure should be scrapped and the country reorganized on an ethnic basis to provide direct representation in a second chamber on a basis of 'state' equality.

SELF-GOVERNMENT—1956?

The greatest failure of the London and Lagos Conferences was the inability of the Africans to work out between themselves a *modus operandi* whereby the three principal regions can draw closer together and weld into a strong, integrated all-African Nigerian Government, which alone will have the prestige and authority to negotiate the transfer of power when the Lyttelton Constitution comes up for review in 1956.

Already politicians who formerly paid lip-service to the slogan of 'Self-Government for Nigeria by 1956' are perforce pursuing separatist policies, which, if not quickly arrested, may well lead to an attitude of 'Each Region for itself, let the devil take care of Nigeria', well before 1956. The only two organizations represented at the London Conference which are committed in principle to 'one United Nigeria' are the United National Independence Party and the N.C.N.C. Unfortunately, Dr Azikiwe compromised the position of the N.C.N.C. in order to accommodate the Action Group and the Northern Peoples' Congress, both of which are in principle committed to separatism. Events since then have forced Dr Azikiwe to have a second thought. He has tried to retract his steps by emphasizing the need for a *modus vivendi* among the political parties to bring about a United Nigeria.

As matters stand now, the Governor-General has control over the Central Government, which is responsible for the really important departments of defence, foreign affairs, finance, currency, etc. What Governor Richards began and Governor Macpherson built upon, Mr Lyttelton rounded off, because the Nigerian leaders just fell for the Tory bait hook, line and sinker. All the Governor-General has to do is to sit comfortably back in his seat of real power and referee the fight between the political leaders to muscle in on each other's tribal preserves. In the first round of the Federal election, Mr Awolowo's Action Group suffered a big defeat by Dr

Azikiwe's N.C.N.C. in the latter's region, while the Sardauna routed both Southern leaders in the North.

Not without reason, Mr Lyttelton could magnanimously promise the Nigerian politicians that by 1956 'Her Majesty's Government would grant those regions which desire it full self-government in respect of all matters within the competence of the Regional Governments, with the proviso that *there should be safeguards to ensure that the Regional Governments did not act as to impede or prejudice the exercise by the Federal Government of the functions assigned to it now, or as amended by agreement in the future, or in any way make the continuance of federation impossible'.*

Nigerian politicians are simply deceiving themselves if they think that the British Government are just going to carve up Nigeria and hand out chunks to them on a silver platter in the name of 'self-government'. They should take to heart the warning given by the Gold Coast Prime Minister. Speaking on the dangers of sectarianism in colonial countries which are struggling to attain national independence, Dr Nkrumah told the Gold Coast Legislative Assembly that this was a time when the emphasis should be upon national unity. '*If in our struggle towards independence and nationhood, we tolerate the formation of political parties on regional, sectional, religious or racial basis, we shall be sowing the seeds of the destruction of our national existence.*'[5]

Even though the Gold Coast is the most constitutionally advanced colony in Africa, tribalism has not yet been completely eradicated. In fact, it is being fed by certain elements among the traditionalists and semi-feudal native aristocrats, who are opposed to political democracy based upon popular representation. With the approaching departure of the British, they seek to restore the autocratic powers and privileges which the chiefs once enjoyed, through a separatist organization calling itself the National Liberation Movement. This party was formed only a few months after Dr Nkrumah's warning in Parliament. Tribalism is, undoubtedly, the biggest obstacle in creating a modern democratic State and an inte-

[5] Report of Proceedings of Gold Coast Legislative Assembly, August 11, 1954.

grated nation out of small regional units inhabited by backward people still under the influence of traditional authority.

Many progressive Africans distrust the Tories. They suspect them of trying to exploit Tribalism in order to maintain Britain's traditional policy of 'divide and rule' and withhold the granting of independence as long as possible. To do so at the 'point of no return' would only drive the nationalists into the arms of the Communists and destroy for ever the hope of Africans attaining self-determination by non-violent means as advocated by the Gold Coast Premier. The Tories are certainly on the horns of a dilemma. To cheat the Africans on the threshold of independence would only prepare the psychological ground for the Russians when they turn their attention to Africa. Already, declared Mr Strydom, 'the South African Government took a serious view of the interest Russia is showing in Africa. Soviet arms deals in Egypt and the Middle East exposed the African continent to the danger of Russian influence spreading through adjacent territories . . . It is obvious that the territories of southern Africa and countries which have an interest here will have to keep in the closest touch with each other. We want to play our part in the defence of Africa.'[6]

But military defence against Communism will not be enough. White South Africa will have to put its own house in order by extending equality of citizenship to its non-European populations. For Africans and Indians will have no interest in defending the present regime. The solution, therefore, is entirely with the white colonizers if they fear Russian infiltration.

[6] *The Times,* Dec. 14, 1955.

XVI

COMMUNISM AND BLACK NATIONALISM

Economically depressed communities and racially oppressed peoples inevitably receive the attention of the Communists. Therefore, we are not surprised that they should have spent considerable effort to win the Negroes to their cause. Yet, sustained and energetic though this endeavour has been, the number of black converts to the cause of World Communism has been quite incommensurate with the time, money and effort expended to win them. To a large extent, the failure to make a greater impact upon popular Negro opinion has been due to the tactical mistakes and psychological blunders which the Communist Parties of the Western World—America, Britain, France and South Africa—have made in their approach to the darker peoples.

Negroes are keenly aware that they are the most racially oppressed and economically exploited people in the world. They also are very much alive to the fact, demonstrated by the opportunistic and cynical behaviour of the Communists, that the latter's interest in them is dictated by the ever-changing tactics of Soviet foreign policy rather than by altruistic motives. Their politically minded intellectuals know that the oppressed Negro workers and peasants are regarded by the Communists as 'revolutionary expendables' in the global struggle of Communism against Western Capitalism. They know that Africans and peoples of African descent are courted primarily to tag on to the white proletariat, and thus to swell the 'revolutionary' ranks against the imperialist enemies of the 'Soviet Fatherland'. This attitude towards the Negroes is fundamentally part and parcel of the Communist philosophy relating to racial minorities and dependent peoples, and it has been influenced by the experience of the Russian Bolsheviks in their struggle for power.

LENINIST ANTI-IMPERIALISM

Long before Russian Communism entered upon the stage of world history, Nikolai Lenin (Vladimir Ilyitch Ulyanov), the Father of Bolshevism and the guiding genius of the Russian Revolution, had formulated the broad outline of the strategy and tactics his party was to adopt in dealing with the racial minorities and subject peoples within the Russian Empire as a means of winning them to the side of Bolshevism in the struggle against Czarist autocracy and the capitalist and landlord classes.

The revolutionary blueprint drawn by Lenin was later amplified by Joseph Stalin (Joseph Vissarionovich Dzugashvili) in his book, *Marxism and the National and Colonial Question,* which has since become the official guide book for European and American Communist Parties in their dealings with the coloured races. Lenin claimed that the left-wing revolutionaries who described themselves as Bolsheviks, to mark themselves off from the Mensheviks or right-wing reformists, were the vanguard of the industrial proletariat. Both factions—Bolshevik means majority and Menshevik, minority—sprang from the same political womb—the Russian Social Democratic Party, which split over policy at the London Conference of 1903.

But the urban working class in Czarist Russia was quite small in relation to the total population of the empire, and Lenin considered it necessary for the Bolsheviks to find allies in order to guarantee the victory of his party in the revolution. The population of Russia was overwhelmingly peasant and illiterate, while at the same time the empire encompassed a sixth part of the earth's surface—extending in one continuous stretch from Central Europe to the Far East, from the Baltic Sea to the Pacific Ocean. This vast empire embraced multifarious peoples and tribes, with a culture partly European, partly Asiatic. Outside the Western borderlands, the Asiatic influence was much the stronger, so that if you scratched a Russian mujik you discovered a Tartar!

Alive to the social and ethnic heterogeneity of the empire, the Bolshevik Party addressed itself, from its beginning, to the task of evolving a programme and slogans which would win over both the Russian peasants and the non-Russian racial minorities. Claiming to speak for the three to four million industrial proletarians, the Bolsheviks promised to the peasants land and freedom from usury at the expense of the landed nobility, and to the subject races, national independence. All this and peace was offered in return for their support in overthrowing the Czar and the ruling classes. The alliance thus formed between the three groups—the Russian industrial workers (many of whom maintained close links with their villages), the peasants and the non-Russian nationalities—enabled the Bolshevik Party, under the direct guidance and leadership of Lenin, to achieve victory in October 1917. For Lenin's party alone among the anti-autocracy organizations which participated in the revolutionary upheaval, took a firm, uncompromising position on the question of national freedom and self-determination, which found response in the ambitions and aspirations of the subject nationalities and racial minorities living under Czarist rule.

The other parties—the Liberal Cadets, the Mensheviks, the Social Revolutionaries—were either lukewarm or quite opposed to granting complete independence to the non-Russians. Some were for the *status quo*; others for mere reforms. With his bold programme, Lenin was able to steal a march upon all of them. Even against the advice of some of his own colleagues, he insisted on offering the racial minorities and Colonial dependencies unconditional independence. As a result, the more politically advanced and culturally sophisticated peoples of the European part of the Russian Empire—the Finns, the Poles, the Letts, the Lithuanians—broke away and established independent bourgeois states which later became satellites of the Great Powers and formed Clemenceau's *cordon sanitaire* against the spread of Bolshevism into Western and Central Europe, a process reversed by Stalin at the Yalta Conference in 1945. The other remnants of the Empire in the Asiatic section, were reorganized into so-called independent federated and autonomous territories, to form part of the Union of Soviet Socialist Republics—the U.S.S.R.

Here we are only concerned with the political consequences of Lenin's National and Colonial policy. His grand gesture of offering self-determination to the non-Russian nationalities had a tremendous psychological effect upon the backward peoples not only in Asiatic Russia but throughout the Orient. It inspired confidence in the Bolsheviks at a time when the supporters of the former régime were conducting a bitter civil war in the hope of restoring the Czarist Empire. It rallied millions of the newly-emancipated coloured peoples of the Asiatic borderlands of 'Mother Russia' to the side of the Red Army and the young Soviet Government against the White Guard aristocrats, who were receiving financial and military support from the British and French Governments to carry on the counter-revolution.

The reactionaries failed largely because Lenin's bold anti-colonial strategy paid such rich dividends. Stalin, himself a colonial native born in Georgia, declared that but for the contributions made by the non-Russian national minorities, the Russian revolutionaries might not have been able to hold out against the overwhelming forces which were ringed around them. 'It need hardly be shown (wrote Stalin), that the Russian workers could not have gained the sympathies of their comrades of other nationalities in the West and the East if, having assumed power, they had not proclaimed the right of peoples to political secession, if they had not demonstrated in practice their readiness to give effect to this inalienable right of peoples, if they had not renounced their "rights", let us say, to Finland (1917), if they had not withdrawn the troops from Northern Persia (1917), if they had not renounced all claims to certain parts of Mongolia and China, and so on and so forth.'[1]

[1] J. Stalin: *Marxism and the National and Colonial Question*, p. 113 (Lawrence & Wishart).

The experiences of the civil war and foreign intervention left an indelible impression upon the Bolshevik leaders. It was during those years of crises that they discovered who were their real friends and allies. The expected revolution in Western European countries—Germany, Austria, Hungary, Poland—failed to materialize. This failure of the Western proletariat to come to the aid of the Soviet Republic caused the Communists to turn to the East, in the hope of undermining European capitalism through Asia. Here was a heretical departure from orthodox Marxism—a kind of Leninist 'Titoism'. For according to Karl Marx, the proletarian revolution which was to usher in Communism would occur first in the highly developed countries where there existed the economic and social prerequisites as well as an educated and cultured industrial working class to form the foundations of Socialism.

Lenin, faithful disciple of Marx though he was, unlike so many of his latter-day followers, disavowed dogmatism. He was a realist who refused to follow blindly his master's theories; he bent theory to the facts, not facts to the theory. Seeing that the Western European workers were in no hurry to perform the historic role which Marx had assigned to them in his *Communist Manifesto*, Lenin decided to forget about them and reach out to those who, still uncorrupted by capitalist reforms, yearned to break the fetters of imperialist domination. He sought allies among the coloured peoples of Asia, in particular, the hundreds of millions of China, in the attempt to undermine the colonial foundations upon which the great Western powers rested.

CHINA'S REVOLT AGAINST COLONIALISM

The revolutionary events in Russia and its Eurasian hinterland had demonstrated that the peasant masses of the industrially backward countries could, under militant leadership, play an important part in bringing about revolutionary change. In other words, what the illiterate workers and uncultured mujiks of Czarist Russia had begun, the even more backward workers and peasants of feudal China would complete. Then, with the united resources of the U.S.S.R. and emancipated China, backed by the active sympathies of the other darker races of Asia and Africa, the future of the Russian Revolution would be guaranteed. Revolutionary China and Communist Russia could together face the imperialist West with confidence.

This view was endorsed by Dr Sun Yat-sen, the Father of the Chinese Revolution, who welcomed Russian aid in helping his enslaved country to break loose from the grip of Western domination. In a letter to Stalin written from his death bed in March 1925, Dr Sun Yat-sen wrote: 'As I lie here stricken with an illness against which man can do nothing, my thoughts turn to you and the fate of my party and my country. You stand at the head of the Union of free republics, the heritage left by the immortal Lenin to the oppressed peoples of the world. With the help of that heritage the victims of imperialism will be able to escape from the international régime which is based upon servitude and injustice. I shall leave behind me a party (Kuomintang) which, as I have always hoped, will be allied with you in the historic task of freeing China and other exploited peoples once and for all from the yoke of imperialism. I must leave my task unfinished and must hand it on to those who will remain faithful to the party's principles and doctrines. I therefore charge the Kuomintang to carry on the work of the national revolutionary movement, so that China may be free. To that end I have commended my party to remain in constant touch with you. I have unwavering confidence that you will continue to help my country as you have done in the past. In taking leave of you, I desire to express the hope that the day may soon come when the Union of Soviet Socialist Republics will welcome a free and powerful China as a friend and ally, and that in the great struggle for the world's oppressed peoples, these two allies may advance side by side from victory to victory.'

These sentiments of Dr Sun Yat-sen found warm response from the Russians, who had already sent Michael Borodin (Grusenberg), a Bolshevik expert on party organization, Manabendra Nath Roy, head of the Comintern Far Eastern Bureau, and General Galen (Bluecher) to Canton, then the headquarters of the Kuomintang. Borodin's main job was to reorganize the bourgeois nationalist movement and create a political general staff to give guidance to the Kuomintang; while Galen's task was to plan the campaign for the Chinese revolutionary armies on their northward march to Peking against the war lords.

In this reorganization of the Kuomintang Government, my distinguished countryman, Eugene Chen (Chen Yujen) who was born in Trinidad, but had been invited to China by Dr Sun Yat-sen, was made Foreign Minister. 'Eugene Chen has been Foreign Minister in three Chinese Governments, but never in the national government since the Kuomintang turned right: first in Hankow, then in Canton during a short-lived Cantonese independent régime in 1931, then in 1934 in Fukien when the radical 19th Route Army set up a government there. Chen has one considerable achievement to his credit: he negotiated what is known as the Chen-O'Malley Agreement whereby the British voluntarily gave up their concession in Hankow—something it is not always easy to persuade the British to do.'[2] After Borodin had reformed the Kuomintang all went well until Chiang Kai-shek captured Nanking and slaughtered the Chinese Communists in a Shanghai blood-bath in 1927. The flower of the young, inexperienced Communist Party was annihilated. This brought about an open rupture between the right wing and the left wing of the Kuomintang; the later faction then in control of the government at Hankow. This marked the beginning of Chiang Kai-shek's anti-Red campaign which lasted for ten years and led to the Communists' 'Long March' into Kiangsi province under Mao Tse-tung and Chu Teh. 'The main cause of the split was a fundamental difference over whether the Nationalist revolution was to continue as a far-reaching social reform movement, which would affect not only the foreign powers and the war lords, but also the dominant Chinese economic groups. The left favoured this; the right desired a strong nationalist government, but feared rapid and drastic social change.'[3]

[2] John Gunther: *Inside Asia*, pp. 292-93 (Hamish Hamilton).
[3] Lawrence K. Rosinger & Associates: *The State of Asia*, p. 24 (Alfred Knopf, New York).

The rupture between the Communists and the Kuomintang actually started when Roy is alleged to have shown Wang Ching-wei, the leader of the Kuomintang left-wing government in Hankow a telegram sent to Borodin by Stalin calling upon the Communists to start the agrarian revolution and arm the peasantry. Wang Ching-wei, who is described as 'one of the most disloyal men in history' warned Chiang Kai-shek of the Communist plan. Chiang immediately staged a *coup d'état*. Following the suppression of the Communists, Wang Ching-wei ganged up with the right wing of the Kuomintang, but later deserted Chiang Kai-shek to become a Japanese quisling.

After the liquidation of the Hankow government and the dispersal of the Communist Soviets, Borodin and Roy returned to Moscow. At the post-mortem held by the Comintern, both men were denounced by the Russians who had to find a scapegoat to cover up Stalin's part in the fiasco. For Stalin was then under heavy fire by the Trotsky Opposition.

Borodin was disgraced and thrown to the party wolves. But some years later he was rehabilitated and installed as the editor of the *Moscow Daily News*, the leading English language newspaper in the Soviet Union. It was during this period that I got to know him quite well, as I often contributed articles to the paper on African affairs and the Negro Question.

Borodin was an able party organizer, but he was no expert on the Chinese peasant question like Mao Tse-tung. This not only applied to Borodin, who had studied at Indiana University in America and had only returned to Russia after the revolution, but to the Chinese Communist intellectuals, most of whom had studied in Paris and Berlin. For example, Li Li-san who, like Chou En-lai, had studied at the Sorbonne, and became a specialist on trade unionism, also underestimated the revolutionary potentialities of the rural poor. With all his intellectual brilliance as a labour organizer, he was too wedded to the orthodox Marxist doctrine that only the industrial proletariat could provide the driving force in the revolution. Whereas in China at the time, the party organizations in the industrial centres and commercial ports (Shanghai, Tientsin, Hankow, Nanking, and Canton) had been destroyed by Chiang Kai-shek, and the working class such as it was, had been beaten into submission.

Li Li-san, like Borodin, paid dearly for his mistakes. In 1931, he was removed from the Political Bureau of the Chinese Party which he dominated for years, and banished to Moscow to explain his 'ultra-left deviation'. As chairman of the Negro Bureau of the Profintern, I was appointed by its general-secretary, Lozovsky, to serve on a special committee to enquire into 'Li Li-sanism', which deviation had been strongly criticized by Mao Tse-tung. The commission endorsed Mao's policy; who, together with Chu Teh, had assumed control of the Party and Red Army. Despite his outstanding political abilities and his great personal charm, Li Li-san, was in my opinion, fundamentally a young romantic adventurer with an addiction to 'putchism'. He was then hardly more than thirty. Had Mao adopted his strategy of attacking the industrial centres before establishing firm rural soviets, the revolution would have failed completely.

After the Comintern inquest on the Borodin mission, Mr Roy, being an Indian and a non-Soviet citizen, was in a better position than his Russian colleague to assert his political views. He quarrelled with Stalin and went to live in Berlin. A few years later, he returned to India, where he was arrested and sentenced to six years' imprisonment in connection with the famous Meerut conspiracy case. Roy, a handsome Bengalese Brahmin, was self-educated and widely read in political science, history and philosophy. He was one of the most romantic of the early Asian revolutionaries. However, as representative of the Comintern in China, Roy came into conflict with Mao Tse-tung, whom he considered an 'undisciplined opportunist' for rejecting the advice Moscow offered the Chinese party before he and Borodin had to escape from Chiang Kai-shek. This was a blessing in disguise, for after their departure, Chairman Mao and his supporters were left free to implement Mao's agrarian policy which he called the 'New Democracy'. The Chinese are the first Communists to win State power by their own efforts without military aid from Russia. Unlike the Iron Curtain satellite leaders, Mao Tse-tung is no Moscow lackey.

M. N. Roy's career started in early boyhood, when he was

associated with the terrorist movement in Bengal. During the First World War he organized, with a group of Indian nationalists, the running of German guns into India, and fought many pitched battles with British patrols along the Bengal coast. After escaping the British net on many occasions, he went to Mexico, where he fought under Pancho Villa in the civil war there. From Mexico he turned up in Moscow in 1918, to be welcomed by Lenin, whom he assisted in drafting the Colonial Thesis for the Second Congress of the Third International. He also assisted in founding K.U.T.V.U.—the University for the Toilers of the East, where I once lectured on Colonial Affairs. This institution specialized in educating coloured students from Soviet Central Asia, South-East Asia and Africa. About the same time, the Russians established the Sun Yat-sen University under the rectorship of the famous publicist Karl Radek, where thousands of the first Chinese revolutionary leaders were trained. Among them Chiang Ching-kuo, the son of Chiang Kai-shek.

After leaving prison in India, Roy joined the Indian National Congress, but seceded to form a small splinter group called the Radical People's Democratic Party. When Gandhi and Nehru refused to co-operate with the Viceroy in the British war effort, Roy accepted subsidies from the Viceroy's Government to carry on war propaganda in the columns of a paper which he founded, called *Independent India*. After India achieved independence, Roy retired from active politics and founded the Radical Humanist Association to propagate the philosophy of Scientific Humanism.

However, in spite of his failures, Roy's name will always be coupled with that of Borodin as the initiators of Stalin's Sino-Russian policy. At the time they went to China, few Westerners realized the far-reaching historical significance of their mission. 'The thought that a great "white" nation should line up on the side of the Asiatic peoples to bring to its end the dominance of the white race in the world may shock us,' wrote Upton Close, then the leading American expert on the Far East. In his prophetic book, *The Revolt of Asia*, Mr Close warned American statesmen that 'a passionate prejudice against the Bolshevik Government may cause us to put its pro-Asiatic policy down as pure vindictiveness. But

when these hasty reactions have passed, and we set out to
study the great development from the standpoint of culture,
history, and the struggle of nations, we find it just as logical
and inevitable as all the great movements which have marked
turning points in the life of humanity.

'Russia's alignment with the Asiatic people has been
made easy by her cultural background. A large proportion of
her population is true Asiatic; notably the Mongol-Buriats
and Cossacks, the Tartars of Kazan on the Volga, the
Muslims of Turkestan, Zungaria and the Caspian region.
Since the period of Mongol rule, Tartar blood has been
strongly infused into the Slav and Germanic Russians of the
West . . . But even more significant, the cultural gap between the Russian people and their Asian neighbours is not
so wide as that which separates the European and American
workers from the downtrodden masses of Asia and Africa.

'The Russian peasant and even proletarian city dweller
exists on much the same standard as the Asiatic. The mujik
with his "shirt tails out" is a cultural kinsman to the Chinese
in the coolie coast. Both live on a dirt floor, break the ground
with a wooden plough, and eat cabbage and grain. The
Chinese keeps his fire under the raised portion of the floor,
the Russian puts his in the wall. The Chinese has much more
of civilization behind him and of the code of the gentleman
in him, but both have kindly humour, hospitality and the
cruelty that comes out of squalor when aroused . . . Thus
Russia followed her destiny towards Asia—not under the banner of the old imperialism but that of the new idealism. Or,
if that word in connection with the Soviet seems inadmissible,
one may call it "enlightened imperialism".'[4]

'Is Russia's benevolence going to prove sincere?' asked Mr
Close. 'I think so,' he replied, 'chiefly because it will have
small opportunity to be otherwise. Once she has assisted the
Asiatic peoples to nationhood, she will have to deal fairly lest
they turn upon her. Her leaders believe they will be able to
keep Asia's friendship, and even more—affection.'[5]

[4] Upton Close: *The Revolt of Asia*, Chapter vii: Russia in Revolt.
(First published in 1927 by G. P. Putnam's Sons, New York and
London.)
[5] Ibid., p. 145.

This was written some thirty years ago, when the Chinese were still the milch cow of the West and the Bolsheviks were licking their wounds from the civil war. Today, the situation has changed radically and Stalin's pro-Chinese policy is bearing fruit, as evidenced by Marshal Ivan Koniev's declaration to the Supreme Soviet on February 9th, 1955, that 'we are not alone. The great nation of China . . . and the Soviet Union form one camp and a powerful army for peace.'[6]

The significant thing to remember is that this alliance came about as a result of Lenin's departure from orthodox Marxism, which was a Western European doctrine to be applied to an industrialized society. Lenin saw clearly what Marx, having died before Imperialism attained its zenith, was unable to foresee, namely, the gradual corruption of the European Socialist movements through their 'bourgeoisification'. The capitalist system, which Marx had so brilliantly analysed, had, in Lenin's lifetime, reached out into the remotest corners of the earth—into decadent Asia and darkest Africa—drawing the great continents into its tentacles and squeezing super-profits from the toil of hundreds of millions of the 'lesser breed without the law'.

It was Lenin who described this later nineteenth-century phase of colonial expansion in his classic, *Imperialism—the Highest Stage of Capitalism*—the stage of history on which he played a supreme role. In arriving at his conclusions, Lenin drew much of his data from the distinguished Liberal, J. A. Hobson's famous study on *Imperialism*, which was first published in 1902[7]. Put briefly, Lenin's thesis was that Western capitalism had become international; monopolies had been established on a world scale, and whole continents and countries—Africa, China, India, Indonesia, Burma, Indo-China, etc.—had been reduced to colonies and economic dependencies of European nations. The financial and military strength of the Great Powers rested upon the continued exploitation of

[6] *The Times*, February 10, 1955.
[7] The three writers who have had the greatest influence upon the author's political views on Colonialism are J. A. Hobson, Nikolai Lenin and Prof. Parker Thomas Moon, whose *Imperialism and World Politics* still remains a constant source of reference. The first of these was an Englishman, the second a Russian and the third an American.

the coloured races, and the super profits derived from colonial spoliation enabled the ruling classes of the West to corrupt the white workers of the metropolis and blunt their revolutionary ardour. In support of his deductions, Lenin quoted the famous empire-builder, Cecil Rhodes, as saying: 'If you want to avoid civil war, you must become an imperialist!'[8] In short, the way to anticipate the proletarian revolution predicted by Marx was to bribe the workers—the 'grave-diggers of capitalism'—with reforms paid for out of colonial profits.

Hence, argued Lenin, the Western domination of the world can only be broken by stirring the coloured colonial and semi-colonial peoples of Asia and Africa to achieve their national independence. This neo-Marxism was allied with the National and Colonial Question as a tactical weapon of capital importance in the advancement of Communism in backward and undeveloped countries populated largely by coloured races. However, it was Stalin who initiated the Sino-Russian alliance after death removed the guiding hand of his master, Lenin. The Soviet dictator never forgot that he was no European, but one of the despised Asians. He never let an opportunity pass to castigate the European Socialists for ignoring the so-called inferior races. 'The tens of hundreds of millions of the Asiatic and African peoples suffering from racial oppression in its crudest and most brutal form did not as a rule enter the field of vision of the Socialists. The latter did not venture to place the white peoples and coloured peoples, the "uncultured" Negroes and the "civilized" Irish, the "backward" Indians and the "enlightened" Poles on one and the same footing. It was tacitly assumed that although it might be necessary to strive for the emancipation of the European non-sovereign nationalities, it was unbecoming for "decent Socialists" to speak seriously of the emancipation of the colonies, which were "necessary" for the "preservation" of "civilization". These apologists for Socialists did not even suspect that the abolition of national oppression in Europe is inconceivable without the emancipation of the colonial peoples of Asia and Africa from the oppression of imperialism and that the former is organically bound up with the latter.'[9]

[8] Nikolai Lenin: *Imperialism—the Highest Stage of Capitalism.*
[9] J. Stalin: *Nationalism and the Colonial Question*, pp. 111-12.

Lenin's Asiatic orientation first found response in Kemal Pasha, then leading the struggle for Turkey's independence. On February 29th, 1920, he sent the following telegram to Chicherin, the Soviet Commissar for Foreign Affairs: 'I am deeply convinced that on the day that the toilers of the West on the one side, and the oppressed people of Asia and Africa on the other, will understand that international capital uses them for mutual destruction and enslavement, solely for the benefit of their masters, on the day when the consciousness of the crimes of colonial policy will imbue the hearts of the toiling masses of the world—then the power of the bourgeoisie will be at an end.'

Today the Turkish rulers are among the most ferocious opponents of Communism, but in 1920 the Turkish Republic was fighting for its very existence, and Kemal Pasha was looking to Russia for help against the imperialist West, which was out to carve up Turkey. In politics there is no gratitude!

Having come to the conclusion that bourgeois nationalism constitutes a revolutionary reserve that could be turned to their advantage, the Bolsheviks went all out to arouse revolt among the coloured races of the Orient. When, therefore, the Third (Communist) International, popularly known as the Comintern, was established, it became incumbent upon all newly-formed Communist parties in the Western world which sought affiliation to it, to accept the Leninist programme on the National and Colonial Question.

COMMUNISM AND THE NEGRO QUESTION

Thus, a few years after the formation of the American party in 1920, an attempt was made to recruit Negro members. The two largest coloured organizations in the U.S. then were the Universal Negro Improvement Association (U.N.I.A.) or Garvey Movement, and the National Association for the Advancement of Coloured People (N.A.A.C.P.). The former had a proletarian membership composed largely of immigrants from the Southern States and the West Indies, who

were attracted to the industrial cities of the Northern and
Eastern States during and after the First World War. It was
about that time that the Jamaican Negro, Marcus Garvey,
emerged as the spokesman of the under-privileged blacks. The
other organization, the N.A.A.C.P., was more middle-class in
its composition and leadership and, therefore, more moderate than the U.N.I.A. But it, too, aimed at abolishing lynching and securing civil liberties for the Negro masses, especially in the Southern States, and at improving their political,
economic and social status by judicial, legislative and other
constitutional methods. For over thirty-five years, the activities of the N.A.A.C.P. were directed by the internationally-
known investigator of lynchings, Mr Walter White, who was
so white that he could mix with white mobs and ferret out
their plots against Negroes without being detected. In his
autobiography,[10] Mr White tells of his fight for justice and
equality for his people.

Applying their well-known tactics of 'boring from within',
the Communist Party encouraged certain Negro members and
fellow-travellers to infiltrate into the Garvey Movement. But
the Provisional President of Africa proved more than a match
for the Communists. Armed with an acid tongue and a sharp
pen, Garvey turned upon the infiltraters and ejected them
lock, stock and barrel. He then took the offensive right into
the Communist ranks by inciting his fanatical disciples to
break up Communist street-corner meetings in Harlem. Negro
members were denounced as 'Red Uncle Toms' and 'traitors
to the black race', for Garvey's racialism made him intolerant
of any kind of co-operation with white radicals. In one of his
broadsides, he asserted that 'The danger of Communism to
the Negro in countries where he forms the minority of the
population is seen in the selfish and vicious attempts of that
party or group to use the Negro's vote and physical numbers
in helping to smash and overthrow by revolution a system
that is injurious to them as the white under-dogs, the success
of which will put their majority group or race still in power,
not only as Communists but as white men. The Negro needs

[10] *A Man Called White* (Gollancz). Mr White died suddenly in
New York on March 21, 1955.

to be saved from his (?) "friends" and beware of "Greeks bearing gifts". The greatest enemies of the Negroes are among those who hypocritically profess love and fellowship for him, when, in truth and deep down in their heart, they despise and hate him.'[11]

Garvey's anti-Communist tirades had a demoralizing effect upon neophyte Negro party members, some of whom were expelled for 'black nationalist deviations'. 'With his emphasis on the proud tradition of the African past', upon 'race pride', and particularly upon the virtue of 'blackness', Garvey put steel into the spine of many Negroes who had previously been ashamed of their colour and of their identification with the Negro group. Before his time, such things as coloured dolls or calendars with coloured families and heroes were a rarity; today they are commonplace. Garvey didn't get many Negroes back to Africa, but he helped to destroy their inferiority complex, and made them conscious of their power.'[12]

The biggest mistake that the white Communists made was to attack Garvey openly and try to disrupt his movement before they had won confidence among the Negroes as a party different from the old-established Republicans and Democrats to which the Negroes gave their divided loyalty. By fighting the Communists with their own weapons of half-truths, vilification and thuggery, Marcus Garvey was the first black leader to force them to keep their hands off Negro organizations. It was not until his imprisonment and later deportation back to Jamaica that the Communists were able to make any sizeable headway among American Negroes from the South and immigrants from the West Indies settled in New York.

Learning from past failures, the Communists set about forming their own coloured front organization called the American Negro Labor Congress. It was unable, however, to attract any appreciable support even though its programme was moderate in character and emphasized 'the abolition of all discrimination, persecution and exploitation of the Negro race and the working people generally'. After a few years of

[11] Marcus Garvey: *Philosophy and Opinions*, Vol. II, pp. 69-70 (U.N.I.A., New York).

[12] St Clair Drake and Horace C. Cayton: *Black Metropolis*, p. 752 (Harcourt Brace & Co., New York).

precarious existence, the Communists folded up the American
Negro Labor Congress, which was being challenged by a num-
ber of other mushroom organizations. The African Blood
Brotherhood, the Equal Rights League, The Friends of Negro
Freedom, and other groups, were all competing with the
Communists for the support of the Negro masses, left lead-
erless by the downfall of Marcus Garvey.

After a period of intensive propaganda carried on directly
under party auspices, the Communists returned to the use of
party-front organizations to enlist Negro supporters on a
nation-wide basis. They now formed the League of Struggle
for Negro Rights, under the chairmanship of the well-known
coloured poet, Langston Hughes. But this proved as abortive
as its predecessor, and had to be wound up. All the well-tried
tactics, from 'infiltration' to 'united front', having failed to
capture the Negroes, the Comintern decided to intervene in
a spectacular way. Emphasizing the need for a drastic change
in tactics, the Sixth Congress of the Comintern scathingly
criticized the failures of the American Communists in the
sphere of Negro work. The previous Congress had also observed that 'By ignoring the question of racial antagonism our
Party has allowed the Negro liberation movement in America
to take a wrong path and to get into the hands of the Negro
bourgeoisie, which has launched the nationalist slogan
"Back to Africa".'

It was therefore decided that, since Marcus Garvey had
rallied popular support by promising to establish a 'National
Home' for blacks in Africa, the American Communists
should go one better and offer the American Negroes a state
of their own in the Black Belt. As popularly defined, the Black
Belt is that strip of territory in the heart of the southern part
of the U.S.A. extending south and south-west from the eastern
part of Virginia to the border of Texas, in which the Negro
population exceeds the white. It was hoped by this manœuvre
to satisfy the nationalist aspirations of those Negroes who still
hankered after 'Black Zionism' and turn them away from
Garveyism to Communism.

The blueprint of the 'Black Republic', a utopia as fantastic
as Garvey's mythical Negro Empire, was the brain child of
a former Finnish university professor of Marxist sociology,

Dr Otto Kussinin, now the President of the Karelo-Finn Soviet Republic. Dr Kussinin, a member of the Faculty of Red Professors, was at the time one of the secretaries of the Comintern. To make theory fit his plan, the professor rejected the findings of all the acknowledged sociological experts in America, that the Negroes suffered disabilities as 'a racial minority'. According to Kussinin, this was not so. The Negro problem, he asserted, was a 'national minority' one, and its solution called for the application of the Stalinist formula. The doctrine of self-determination, with the right of secession, and the establishing of an independent Negro nation, was declared applicable to Negroes in the Southern United States.

This was Marxist sociology turned upside down. With Stalin's blessing, this amazing piece of nonsense was imposed upon the American party. Those who rejected Kussinin's thesis were expelled as 'right-wing deviationists'. Among the victims of this purge were many of the most intelligent Negroes. Those outside the party contemptuously rejected Moscow's gift horse. The Negroes wanted to know how they, a poor down-trodden and unarmed racial minority group were to establish an autonomous self-governing 'Black Belt State' within the Republic of the United States. But even assuming that it was possible, a territory inhabited exclusively by Negroes would be no different from Dr Malan's *Apartheid*, which aims at segregating the Africans in the Union of South Africa into an all black 'Bantu State'—a sort of glorified Native Reserve.

Voicing the indignation of the Afro-Americans at this piece of Communist humbug, *The Crisis*, the official organ of the N.A.A.C.P., went for the white comrades hammer and tongs. 'They (the Communists) swear by all that's holy that such a plan of plain segregation is *not* segregation, but who can predict what they will say tomorrow or next week? Anyway, we maintain that the mere existence of the proposal proves that the idea of separateness is uppermost in the minds of the Red brain-trust and not the idea of oneness. And in advancing this theory of separation, the Communists are hand in hand with the southern ruling class which they so delight to lambast. But since the Moscow masters are opportunists in the matter of war profit (in Ethiopia),[13] who would dare to criticize the American followers for opportunism in a little thing like race segregation? Who, indeed, except the segregated American Negro?'[14]

In face of the implacable hostility of all sections of the Negro population, from middle-class to workers, from radicals to conservatives, the 'Black Belt State' proposal proved a heavy flop. It happened that just a few years before the 'Black Belt' slogan was dropped, the Soviet cinema industry had planned to make a film depicting lynchings and racial oppression in the Southern States, and a cast of coloured American actors had been engaged and taken to Moscow for the purpose. Before work on the film was started, the news leaked out and Colonel Hugh L. Cooper and other white Southern American engineers directing the construction of the Dnieperstroi hydroelectric project protested to Stalin, who ordered the film to be abandoned. To save face, the Negroes, headed by Langston Hughes, were flatteringly entertained by top-ranking Soviet leaders and then quietly shipped back to the United States. Shortly after their return in 1933, President Roosevelt extended diplomatic recognition to the Soviet Union. It was only then that the full story about the suppression of the Negro film was revealed in the press by Mr Henry Lee Moon and Mr Ted Poston, both distinguished coloured journalists who had been engaged as script writers.

These revelations of Communist cynicism and opportunism dealt the American party a terrific blow, and once again it suffered the loss of many of its ablest Negro intellectuals, this time by their withdrawal in disgust at discovering that

[13] This reference to Ethiopia concerned charges against the Soviet Government having sold oil to Mussolini when the fascist dictator was planning his invasion of Ethiopia. This aroused great indignation among American Negroes and led to the resignation of many of them from the Communist Party. These courageous comrades—for it required great courage to challenge the authority of the party at that time—were harried by the leaders, who used their influence wherever possible to get them dismissed from jobs. During the Roosevelt regime, the C.P. cells were well entrenched in all Government employment and social relief organizations set up under the New Deal programme. G.P.

[14] *The Crisis*, October 1935, New York.

they were being used as 'Red Uncle Toms'. Once more the Communists had to reorientate their tactics on the Negro Question. In the hope of retrieving lost prestige, the party nominated its leading Negro member, Mr James W. Ford, as Vice-Presidential candidate on the Communist ticket. But even this bait did not catch many black votes, and a further change of tactics was initiated. This coincided with the deepening of American economic crisis and the gathering war clouds over Europe, which led to the formation of the Popular Front. In line with this more moderate trend, the party toned down its revolutionary talk. This manœuvre was adopted in order not to frighten off its middle-class allies. Instead of talking about storming barricades, the party campaigned on practical and immediate bread-and-butter issues like work or relief, food, clothing for the unemployed and education for their children. Special emphasis was placed on social equality for Negroes.

The Popular Front net was cast so wide that it caught Negroes of all political and religious persuasions and in all walks of life. The Communists even called off their campaign of slander and vilification of the middle-class leaders of organizations like the N.A.A.C.P., which had consistently resisted Communist infiltration. The League of Struggle for Negro Rights, which the Communists had established to oppose the N.A.A.C.P., was closed down in 1936. To take its place, a united front body called the National Negro Congress was founded. The nationally known Negro Communist leaders took an active part in setting up the new party front organization, but later most of them kept discreetly in the background, directing affairs through fellow-travellers on the executive. Conveners of the Congress appealed 'to all Negroes, native and foreign born. To all Negro organizations, churches, labour unions, farm and share croppers' organizations. To all fraternal, civil, professional and political groups. To all organizations and persons of whatever race, who are willing to fight for economic and social justice for Negroes.'

Such a wide appeal brought many non-Communists under the Congress banner, and its outward appearance of bourgeois respectability enabled it, for a time at least, to escape being branded as just another Communist front organization.

The inaugural conference in Chicago was attended by 817 delegates representing 585 organizations of the most heterogeneous kind, from religious associations to Negro business groups. Things ran fairly smoothly until Hitler invaded Poland in 1939, when the Communist elements within the National Negro Congress came more and more into the open, using the organization as a forum in defence of the Stalin-Hitler Pact. The party line at that time was that the conflict was an 'imperialist war' on both sides, and coloured people should keep out of it. Accordingly, the party launched a propaganda campaign among the Negroes to oppose President Roosevelt's policy of aid to the countries resisting Nazism. The executive secretary of the National Negro Congress, Mr John P. Davis, an ex-university professor fellow-traveller, issued a public statement in which he asserted that 'the American Negro will refuse to join America or world imperialism in any war against the Soviet people'. As this was done without the approval of the non-Communist members of the executive, it provoked great resentment.

The chairman, Mr A. Philip Randolph, the most distinguished Afro-American socialist and founder and president of the Pullman Car Porters' Union, the largest organization of Negro railway workers in America, immediately resigned. Other non-Communists followed his example. Explaining the reason for his resignation, Mr Randolph declared that 'Negroes do not reject the Communist Party because it is revolutionary or radical or because of its alleged extremism. They reject the Communist Party because it is controlled and dominated by a foreign state whose policy may, or may not, be in the interests of the United States or the Negro people.

'American Negroes will not follow any organization which accepts dictation and control from the Communist Party. American Negroes will not follow any organization which accepts dictation and control from any white organizations.

'Whatever is the source of the money with which the Congress is run, that will also be the source of its ideas, policies and control . . . The Congress should be uncontrolled and responsible to no one but the Negro people . . . When the National Negro Congress loses its independence, it loses its soul and has no further reason for being. It also forfeits and

betrays the faith of the Negro masses. I am not only opposed to domination of the Congress by the Communists, but
I consider the Communists a definite menace and danger to
the Negro people and labour, because of their disruptive
tactics in the interest of the Soviet Union.'

The resignation of Randolph left the Communists in full
control of the executive of the National Negro Congress,
which, under the instructions of the party, embarked upon a
series of zigzag manœuvres. United Front activities were
gradually dropped and the Communist elements turned upon
their former middle-class allies and denounced them as being
'fake petty bourgeois liberals', 'capitalist stooges', and 'agents
of Wall Street imperialism.'

One of the principal anti-war propagandists among the
Negroes was Dr Max Yergan, a former Y.M.C.A. missionary
in South Africa, about whom we shall have more to say later.
Dr Yergan was installed as president of the National Negro
Congress in place of Philip Randolph. In commending him
to its Negro members and supporters, the Communist Party
declared, 'that the outlook for the Congress with Dr Yergan
at its helm is indeed bright. He is a man of sterling qualities,
unselfish and indefatigable. He is staunch in his championship of Negro rights and unbounded in his devotion to human
freedom.'[15] Despite Dr Yergan's vaunted qualities, Negroes
continued to support Roosevelt's 'Aid to Britain' and membership of the Congress dropped heavily. Then, suddenly, there
was another reversal of Communist policy when Hitler fell
upon his ally, Stalin, and attacked Russia in June 1941. Overnight, too, the Communists in the Congress dropped their
anti-war campaign and announced full support for Russia.
The 'imperialist war' had now become a 'war of liberation'.
An attempt was even made to revive the United Front, but
despite all blandishments, the coloured leaders, on whom the
Communists had heaped the most irresponsible denounce-
ments during the Hitler-Stalin honeymoon, refused absolutely
to have any further truck with the Congress double-dealers.
Rebuffed and discredited, the Communists had the effron-

[15] See report by T. R. Bassett on the Third National Negro Congress in *The Communist*, New York, June 1940.

tery to appeal to the Negroes to suspend their agitation for employment in war industries, the principle of equal pay for equal work, and abolition of racial segregation in the armed forces. Those who refused to abandon the *Pittsburgh Courier* 'Double V' campaign—'Victory over the Axis abroad; Victory over racial discrimination at home'—were denounced as 'sabotaging the war effort'; 'aiding the Axis enemy'; and of endangering the 'unity of the American people'.[16]

Chief among those castigated by the Communists turned 'super patriots' was Mr Philip Randolph, who, following his resignation as president of the National Negro Congress, initiated the March on Washington Movement (M.O.W.M.) as a counter force against the Communists. The M.O.W.M. was denounced for supporting President Roosevelt's Administration and 'betraying' the Negro masses in their struggle for equality of treatment.

What was the M.O.W.M.? And in what did it 'betray' the Negro people? Let one who was associated with both the National Negro Congress and the M.O.W.M. explain: the Rev Dr Adam Clayton Powell, head of the Abyssinian Baptist Church, the largest Negro congregation in America, and coloured Congressman from Harlem in the U.S. House of Representatives.

Dr Powell writes: 'Within six months after World War Two began the Negroes were called on to be tested. As the nation was waging the white man's war, war plants flatly and openly declared they would not hire Negroes. The challenge had to be met. Under the leadership of A. Philip Randolph, President of the International Brotherhood of Sleeping Car Porters, a national unity committee of nine was set up, some of whom were Walter White of the N.A.A.C.P., Channing Tobias of the National Y.M.C.A., and William Lloyd Innes[17] and myself of the Co-ordinating Committee. We immedi-

---

16 *The Pittsburgh Courier* which initiated the Double V Campaign is the largest Negro owned newspaper in the United States, founded by a coloured lawyer and politician, Robert L. Vann of Pittsburgh.

17 The Rev Dr Innes was a most distinguished Negro scholar and theologian in New York, Pastor of St James's Presbyterian Church. G.P.

ately decided to stage a march on Washington, D.C. Marching blacks were literally going to hit the Glory Road, to convene, from all over the nation, at the capital. Hundreds of
thousands in silence would march on the White House. The
plan caught on like fire. All over America the hosts stirred.
This was the showdown. A few 'Uncle Tom' Negroes scoffed
at the movement, but it grew ever faster until on June 18th
the President of the United States, the Secretary of War, the
Secretary of the Navy and other high Government officials
conferred with the leaders of the movement. We were asked
to call off the march. This we refused to do unless some
specific step was taken by the Government to start putting an
end to domestic fascism.

'One week later Franklin Delano Roosevelt issued Executive Order 8802 which banned discrimination on account of
race, creed or colour in any industry holding a Government
contract for war work or training workers for war jobs. This
was the most significant gain ever made by Negroes under
their own power. The world stood up and took notice. The
Negroes were no longer children but a mature minority. They
not only had unity and, therefore, mass power, but they
knew what to do with it.'[18]

This was the movement which the Communists tried to
stab in the back, and whose leader, Randolph, was branded
as a 'black traitor' and 'agent of Wall Street capitalists'. Character assassination has always been one of the most deadly
weapons employed by the Communists. But despite their
treacherous behaviour from time to time and attempts to
sabotage the struggle of the Negroes for civil rights whenever
this has conflicted with Russia's momentary needs, the
coloured people have never allowed themselves to be used by
American reactionaries like Senator McCarthy in Red-baiting
campaigns. The reason for this is quite simple. Most Negroes
outside the political sophisticated *élite*, tend to make a sharp
distinction between the American Communists, whom they
consider just another set of white radicals trying to use them,
and the Russian people, whom they admire because they hear

[18] A. Clayton Powell: *Marching Blacks*, pp. 149-50 (Dial Press,
New York).

that colour bar and racial discrimination is illegal and severely punished in the U.S.S.R. And that accounts for the reason why Negro leaders, regardless of their ideologies, show great sympathies with other coloured races, be they Asians or Africans, who are struggling to throw off Western foreign domination and take their place as equals in the white man's world; which until now has been based upon the philosophy of 'racial superiority'.

Because of their tolerance on race and colour, the Russians and the Chinese are going to get on marvellously. The West need have no illusions about that. Communist power politics apart, the Russian people are undoubtedly the least colour-conscious white folk in the world. The coloured Soviet citizens of Central Asia—Uzbekians, Tajiks, Kazans, Turkmans, Tartars, Kirghizans, Chuvashians, Kalmuks, Buriats, etc.—enjoy absolute racial equality with those of Slav descent. If they are sometimes persecuted, it is not for their race as are the non-Europeans—Africans, Indians and Coloureds—in South Africa, but for political 'deviations'. And even this did not affect the few Negroes working in Russia at the time of the first Five Year Plan, for they had the commonsense to keep out of Soviet internal politics. So purges did not affect them. No doubt, it is this absence of racial intolerance that influenced Mr Paul Robeson, the internationally-known singer and actor, to have his only son educated in the Soviet Union; for the great artist has himself been the victim of racial snobbery in his own country and Britain. In this respect, I can myself endorse Mr Robeson's admiration for the Soviet régime. For in 1930, while I served as a deputy on the Moscow Soviet, the authorities ordered the deportation of two white American engineers employed on the Five Year Plan who objected to eating in the same factory restaurant with an American Negro engineer named Robinson. The Soviet leaders, whatever may be said against them, treat any manifestation of racial chauvinism with great severity. After all, Pushkin, one of the greatest literary ornaments of Russia, was of African descent. His is the most magnificent statue in Moscow. Appreciative of what this descendant of Peter the Great's Negro General, Hannibal, has done for Russian literature, Soviet film and plays, unlike in the West, never treat the Negro race with ridicule and contempt. This sympathy for the blacks is reflected in all levels of Russian society. The writer once witnessed an entire Muscovite audience in tears when a play based on Harriet Beecher Stowe's *Uncle Tom's Cabin* was performed at the famous Meierhold Theatre.

It is a pity that white Communists in Britain and America are not entirely free from racial prejudices. According to Marxist philosophy, that no doubt can be explained by the bourgeois environment in which they live! However that may be, these Anglo-American Communists have done more harm to the Soviet cause than good. Their intolerance has destroyed much of the Negro's instinctive sympathy for Russia, which, with all its imperfections, has suppressed all forms of racial distinctions and colour bars within its borders.

At the end of the Hitler war, the American Communists tried to ingratiate themselves back into the favour of the Negro people, but they found themselves cold-shouldered by all coloured organizations except a small anti-Colonialist propaganda committee. This is the Council of African Affairs, headed by Mr Paul Robeson. This Council was formed in 1939 by the same Dr Max Yergan, the former missionary who worked in South Africa for over twenty years and to whom we have referred above. Under the guiding eye of Mr Robeson and the financial backing of a white millionaire sympathizer, Mr Frederick V. Field, the Council on African Affairs set up well-equipped offices in the heart of New York's commercial centre. It was never more than a sort of leftish welfare organization, whose main activity consisted in collecting food, clothing and money from American friends and sympathizers to help destitute Negroes in South Africa engaged in opposing Dr Malan's *Apartheid*. Apart from its charitable work, the Council on African Affairs issued a weekly cyclostyle news letter on current affairs in Africa as seen through Communist spectacles.

With the outbreak of the cold war, the organization was listed as 'subversive' by the U.S. Attorney-General Herbert Brownell. This brought about a split in the executive. Dr Yergan, who was then its director, issued a press statement denouncing his erstwhile Communist comrades and he was expelled by the chairman, Mr Robeson. The quarrel between the two Negro 'leaders' was dragged through the courts and by the time the legal battle was over—with victory going to the Robeson faction—the majority of members had resigned and the Council was without funds. It was a sorry business. Another example of Communist intolerance!

While the wrangling was going on in the left-wing camp, conflict also broke out among the Negro moderates. As a result of differences between himself and the board of directors of the N.A.A.C.P. over policies, Dr DuBois, who had given a lifetime of service to the organization, was dismissed from his post as Director of Special Research. He was then eighty, without a job or private means, but still very vigorous in body and mind. Desirous of continuing his African researches and writings, Dr DuBois accepted an invitation from Mr Robeson to join the Council on African Affairs as vice-chairman on a non-salary basis. He was merely provided with office accommodation and secretarial assistance. 'I accepted', he said, 'for two reasons: first, because of my belief in the work which the Council should do for Africa; and secondly, because of my belief that no man or organization should be denied the right to a legal career because of political or religious beliefs.'[19]

Being the only member with an international reputation as an authority and writer on African affairs and a life-long champion of colonial peoples, Dr DuBois's association with it lent considerable prestige to the Council. But he could not save it from the attacks of reactionaries in Washington, especially the Department of Justice. For after breaking with his erstwhile friends, Dr Yergan launched a vendetta against the Council. His successor, Dr W. A. Hunton, a former university lecturer, the son of another Negro Y.M.C.A. official, was subpoenaed to appear before a Washington Grand Jury on October 7, 1954, to submit all correspondence of the Council with the African and the Indian National Congresses of South Africa. This action followed evidence presented to the Grand Jury by Dr Yergan, who had made a tour through Africa in 1953 and on his return had reported on Communist activities in South Africa in the well-known Washington magazine, U.S.

[19] W. E. B. DuBois: *In Battle for Peace*, p. 17 (Masses & Mainstream Publication, New York).

News and World Report.[20] True to their fashion, the Communists denounced their former ally as a 'Wall Street stooge', conveniently forgetting that just a few years before they had described this apostate as 'a man of sterling qualities, unselfish in his championship of Negro rights and unbounded in his devotion to human freedom'.

For his part, Dr Yergan, doubtless embittered against the white American Communists at having been used by them to do their dirty work and then been thrown out of the African Council, distorted and exaggerated Communist influence among the non-Europeans in South Africa. And in order to rationalize his love turned to hatred against his former Communist comrades, Yergan had been forced into the position of having to whitewash Malan's racialism as the lesser evil to Communism. This naturally brought down upon his head the condemnation of even anti-Communist Africans and Afro-American leaders like the distinguished secretary of the N.A.A.C.P., Mr Walter White, who was an opponent of Communism long before Dr Yergan appeared on the political scene. Whatever his Communist or non-Communist critics may think about him, the ex-missionary is now accepted in American official and business circles as a 'leading expert on Communism' and 'the foremost authority on Africa in the United States',[21] although he has never published any book on the subject. When he tours Africa, Dr Yergan travels like a real American State official, staying as the guest of colonial governors. In fact, he is the only American Negro who has freedom of movement across African iron curtains. When a black man is allowed such privileges by European colonial governments, he is certainly *persona grata* on the highest level in Washington.

[20] See issue of May 1, 1953. The Council was wound up on June 17, 1955.

[21] Dr Yergan was so designated by the editor of *U.S. News & World Report* in the issue of May 1, 1953. See also his essay 'The Communist Threat in Africa' in *Africa Today* (Johns Hopkins Press, 1955).

COMMUNISM AND ANTI-IMPERIALISM

The inability of the American Communist Party to rally the Negro masses behind the slogan of a 'Black Belt State' in Dixie had serious consequences for certain international plans discussed at the sixth congress of the Comintern. The role which had been assigned to coloured Americans was not just that of 'revolutionary expendables'. It had been intended that under Communist guidance, they were to provide the leadership for the anti-imperialist struggle in Africa.

That is why, when Garvey advanced the slogan of 'Back to Africa', the Communist International countered his move by putting forward the conception of the 'Black Belt State' as an inducement to the Negro masses to fix their gaze upon the proletarian revolution in America and forget about returning to Africa.

Had the Communists succeeded in capturing the Garvey Movement and in gaining control of other black nationalist groups, specially selected Negro militants were to have been recruited and trained in Moscow as cadres for colonial work in Africa.

While on the subject of training revolutionaries, it might help to explain the difference between Party and State educational institutions as existed in the Soviet Union up to the time when Stalin closed down the Comintern in 1943.

Apart from the pre-Revolution universities directly under the Soviet Ministry of Education, the Russian Communist Party and the Comintern maintained special institutions for the training of Communist leaders in the U.S.S.R. and abroad. Among the most famous of these were the Lenin University, which catered for students from the advanced Western capitalist countries—Germany, France, Italy, Britain and the U.S.; and the Kutvu University, which drew its students from Soviet Asian Republics, South-East Asia, India and Africa.

Unlike the Chinese students who attended the Sun Yat-sen University in their thousands annually, there were never more than a dozen Africans at Kutvu. There were many more American Negroes at Lenin University. Over and beyond these two party universities was the Academy of Red Professors. The Academy students constituted the Communist intellectual *élite* and provided the teaching staff for the other party institutions. The course of study at the Academy covered a period of nine years. Many were admitted but few graduated. Those who got through its intensive course were immediately assigned by the Comintern and the Russian party to important theoretical work according to their specialization.

The main courses offered at Lenin and Kutvu universities were: history, foreign languages, economics, political science, philosophy, sociology, party and trade union organization, techniques of propaganda and agitation, public speaking and journalism. The period of study lasted about three years. As to be expected, all the social sciences were taught from a Marxist point of view.

Until Africa was able to provide her own Communist leaders, the foremost American Negro party theoretician, Mr James W. Ford, suggested that 'from among the American Negroes in industry must come the leadership of their race for the struggle for freedom in the colonial countries. In spite of the denial of opportunity to the Negro under American capitalism his advantages are so far superior to those of the subject colonial Negroes in the educational, political and industrial fields that he is alone able to furnish the agitational and organizational ability that the situation demands.'[22]

This suggestion was not without historical significance, for the two most dynamic black nationalist ideologies which the Communists have had to encounter in their efforts to win a foothold among Negroes had their origin in America: Garveyism and Pan-Africanism, both of which have influenced African leaders like Dr Azikiwe and Dr Nkrumah. In one important respect these militant Negro ideologies both resemble Marxism, which also originated outside the country where it was first successfully applied. The Marxist doctrine based on German philosophy, English political economy and French socialism, was transplanted from Western Europe

[22] James W. Ford: *The Negro and the Struggle Against Imperialism*, published in *The U.S. Communist*, Vol. ix, January, 1930.

into semi-Asiatic Russia by George Plekhanov. From Russia, Marxism was later exported to China, where it was transformed by the political genius of Mao Tse-tung to suit the national traditions and needs of the Chinese people, whose social philosophy is deeply rooted in Confucianism and Mandarin bureaucracy. Tito is the only other non-Russian Communist who has adapted Marxism to serve the peculiar conditions of his country. The others have blindly swallowed the zig-zag turns of the Kremlin.

Since the Communist parties operating in the homelands of empire—Britain, France, Holland, Belgium, Portugal—had sadly neglected anti-imperialist work since their formation, the Russians decided that the Comintern should assume direct responsibility for organizing and directing their anti-Colonialist activities. Thus the Sixth Congress, meeting in Moscow in 1928, devoted considerable attention to the Colonial Question. After reviewing the existing revolutionary movements in Asia and Africa in relation to the international situation at the time, the Congress asserted that the 'thesis on the National and Colonial Question drawn up by Lenin and adopted by the Second Congress are still valid, and should serve as a guiding line for the further work of the Communist parties.'

The attitude of the Third or Communist International towards colonies and semi-colonial countries differed radically from that of its rival, the Second or Socialist International. Most Western European Socialist parties belonged to the Second International, which was looked upon as an exclusively 'white man's club', in the same way as Dr Malan and other British Empire racialists regarded the Commonwealth. The national aspirations of Asians and Africans were never taken into serious account by European Socialists until quite recently. Apart from an occasional pious resolution against some flagrant outrage committed against native races in the colonies, such as King Leopold's régime in the Congo, the problem of the coloured peoples never figured prominently in their deliberations. In fact, most European Socialists looked upon colonies as being necessary economic appendages of the Western capitalist system. This doctrine of 'Socialist Imperialism' was openly expounded by Dr Eduard David, a leader of the German Social Democratic Party. Addressing the Stuttgart Conference of the Socialist International in 1907, Herr David declared that *'Europe needs colonies. She does not even have enough. Without colonies, from an economic point of view, we shall sink to the level of China.'* And what European wishes to live like the 'primitive' Chinese?

Introducing the resolution of the Colonial Commission of the Stuttgart Congress, the Dutch delegate, Van Kal, said that as a 'representative of one of the oldest colonizing peoples', he wanted to emphasize that 'the Congress . . . does not condemn in principle and for all time every kind of colonial policy, which—under a socialist régime—can be a work of civilization'. Socialism and Empire! What a contradiction in terms!

Forty years later, Mr Ernest Bevin, the British Socialist endorsed the thesis of his German fellow Socialist, Herr David. In a speech in the House of Commons emphasizing Western Europe's dependence on colonies for its economic rehabilitation and defence, the Foreign Secretary said: 'In the first place, we turn our eyes to Africa, where great responsibilities are to be shared by us with South Africa, France, Belgium and Portugal, and equally to all oversea territories, especially South-East Asia, with which the Dutch are closely concerned. That involves the closest possible collaboration with the Commonwealth and with the oversea territories, not only British, but French, Dutch, Belgian and Portuguese.' The Foreign Secretary then emphasized the economic importance of the colonies for the maintenance of European living standards.

'These oversea territories are large primary producers . . . They have raw materials, food and resources which can be turned to very great common advantage, both to the peoples of the territories themselves, to Europe, and to the whole world. The other two great world powers, the United States and Soviet Russia, have tremendous resources . . . If Western Europe is to achieve its balance of payments and to get a world equilibrium, it is essential that these resources should be developed and made available and the exchange between them carried out in a correct and proper manner . . . We shall thus bring together resources, manpower, organization and opportunity for millions of people.'[23]

The European Communists, on the other hand, have tried to mask their own opportunism by spreading the falsehood that *all* Socialists are imperialists. This is untrue, for there are many British and French left-wing Socialists who are definitely opposed to Colonialism and the colour bar and give their active support to the struggles of dependent peoples for self-government and human rights. But, unfortunately, they represent a minority point of view, which has little or no influence on the official politics of their parties. This has enabled their right-wing colleagues to pursue a bi-partisan colonial policy with the conservative parties and other pro-colonialist groups in the French and British Parliaments. And since the Communists have never had to shoulder the full responsibility of governing a colonial empire, they can pose as the 'only true champions of colonial freedom'. But it must not be forgotten that after the liberation of France in 1945, the Communist Ministers serving in the Government of Premier Paul Ramadier approved the despatch of an expeditionary force to China to fight the Viet-minh, headed by a coloured fellow-Communist, President Ho Chi-minh. I mention this to show that European Communists have no right to claim moral superiority over European Socialists in their attitude to coloured Colonial peoples. But the double-talk of the Western Communists has never embarrassed the Russians, who have been clever enough to let the European parties bear the odium for unpopular Soviet foreign policies while pretending to be against the 'White Man's Burden'. As a demonstration of Russia's anti-colonialism, the members of the Communist Party of the Soviet Union serving on the Colonial Presidium of the Comintern inspired the convocation of a world-wide Anti-Imperialist Conference in Brussels in 1927.

The idea behind this move was to revive the disbanded League for the Liberation of the East on a wider basis, to encompass not only Asians but Africans and other coloured races. This League had been inspired by Stalin, who was Commissar for Nationalities during the hectic days of the 1917

[23] *Hansard* (House of Commons), August 5, 1947.

Revolution. It had limited its appeal to the colonial and semi-colonial peoples of the Orient, to arouse them against the West. The Manifesto declared: 'It is the aim of the League for the Liberation of the East to unite all the separate movements striving for new life in the awakening East, in order so to create an anti-imperialist united front at the very source of imperialism in Asia.'

It went on to assert that: 'Those who undertake the great task of national self-determination and constitutional reconstruction now facing the whole vast territory of the Orient cannot belong to the class of large landlords and princes, who have for the most part no interest in the destruction of Western imperialism in the East; nor can they come from the intermediate grade of the intellectuals, who belong to no class; only the labouring masses of Asia can undertake this task . . .'

The Russians even went so far as to sketch the future United States of Asia which they envisaged after national liberation. 'The medley of nationalities in the East involves the danger that national dissensions already inflamed, may break out anew, and that a species of nationalism typical of the great powers may appear, for it is constantly springing up on this soil. In order to avert this danger, unification in the East must be based upon absolutely equal rights for all the peoples of Asia, and that in federal form. It may begin with a more limited federation—in India, for instance—and develop into the United States of Asia.'

Such was the early dream of the Bolsheviks for the liberation of Asia and its reconstruction under Communist direction. Events, however, did not work out as anticipated. But in 1927, the Soviet leaders figured that the awakening East required their renewed attention. Not wanting, however, to focus attention upon themselves, they assigned the responsibility of organizing the new anti-imperialist movement to the German Communists. Shorn of her African and other colonies following defeat in the First World War, Germany was no longer a colonial power; and it was thought that an anti-imperialist call coming from Berlin would arouse less suspicion among colonial and dependent peoples than one coming from Western European capitals—London or Paris—possessing overseas empires. The German Socialists who controlled the

Weimar Republic, however, refused permission for the conference to be held in Berlin, and Brussels was therefore selected as the most convenient meeting place.

The German Communists carefully disguised their part in
the affair, operating through an *ad hoc* committee of distinguished liberals and progressive politicians, writers, professors,
artists, scientists and internationally-known personalities,
many of whom had pro-Communist leanings. The Conference committee was discreetly guided and directed from behind the scene by the popular and genial German editor and
publicist, Willi Munzenberg, the 'Barnum' of the Comintern. The German had a flair for organization and showmanship. The Brussels Conference was a tremendous success. Herr
Munzenberg gathered Colonial representatives from moderate bourgeois to extremist nationalist movements from all over
South-East Asia, the Middle East, Africa, Latin America and
the West Indies. The people of Brussels had never seen such
an exotic gathering in their city before. There were Muslims,
Hindus, Chinese, Negroes, Arabs, Koreans, Vietnamese, Bur-
mese, Ceylonese, Egyptians, Senegalese, Indonesians, all prom-
enading the streets of the Belgian capital in their different
national attire. Among them was Jawaharlal Nehru, then the
rising star of the Indian National Congress. The South African
National Congress was represented by its president, J. T. Gumede, and J. A. La Guma, the secretary of the Non-European
Trade Union Federation. The coal black Senegalese delegation was headed by Lamine Senghor and Garan Kouyatte,
chairman and secretary-general respectively of the militant
Ligue pour la Défense de la Race Nègre. Kouyatte was shot
by the Nazis when the German Army occupied Paris in 1940.
In a memorable and prophetic speech, Senghor declared:
'The Negroes have slept too long. But beware, Europe! Those
who have slept long will not go back to sleep when they wake
up. Today, the blacks are waking up!'

Associated with Munzenberg in organizing the League
Against Imperialism was an Oxford-educated Indian, Viran-
dranath Chattopadhaya, the brother of Mrs Sarojini Naidu,
the celebrated poetess and one-time president of the Indian
National Congress. Mr Chattopadhaya (popularly called
Chatto) was assigned the role of 'friend, philosopher and

guide' to the colonial delegates, a part he played to perfection. For he was undoubtedly a most likeable person—suave, gracious and unusually well-informed on colonial and international affairs. Although a passionate anti-imperialist, Mr Chattopadhaya was never bitter, even when denouncing British rule in India! Hovering in the background was a fanatical Indian of a different type—a typical Communist intellectual—joyless and doctrinaire. He was Clements Dutt, brother of Mr R. Palme Dutt, the theoretician of the British Communist Party. Willi Munzenberg carried out the Comintern directives so skilfully that he persuaded the delegates to elect Mr Fenner Brockway, the well-known British left-wing Socialist M.P., the first International Chairman of the League Against Imperialism.

Mr Brockway was then the political secretary of the Independent Labour Party, the only British political party which has consistently opposed Colonialism. But even more important as far as the Communists were concerned, Brockway was highly respected among Indian political leaders. He had been active on behalf of Indian freedom as Joint Secretary of the British Committee of the National Congress and editor of *India*. A Socialist with pronounced anti-imperialist views (which is not always combined), Brockway was considered a godsend to the Communists. Such an ally had to be carefully courted. Even in those far-off days the Communists had evolved a technique of cultivating prominent people whose prestige could be used to support the party line. They seem to know just how to exploit human gullibility, especially among intellectuals. Mr Munzenberg once told the writer that it was the easiest thing to get signatures of famous Europeans, providing the right approach was used. He obviously spoke with authority, since he was for many years the chief collector of signatures for Soviet inspired causes.

Mr Brockway's titular leadership of the League enabled the German Communists to use his name to attack the German Social Democratic Party leaders who had forbidden their followers to join the German section of the League. And since they had no intention of allowing their Communist rivals to undermine their authority, the Social Democratic Party Executive protested to the Second International against Mr

Brockway's association with a Communist-sponsored organization. As Mr Brockway was at the same time the I.L.P. representative on the executive of the Socialist International, he was advised by his party to resign from the League. His place was taken by Mr James Maxton, who did not last long. The I.L.P. leaders having served their purpose, the Communists manœuvred to replace Mr Maxton and other non-Communists on the executive of the League Against Imperialism with their own party members and trusted fellow-travellers.

This is typical Communist behaviour. They do not believe in permanent co-operation. Their object is to use their allies to advance the party line at a given time. Alliances, therefore, are temporary; and if their allies prove unmalleable, the Communists find ways and means of disrupting the brief united front. Hence, anti-imperialism having served the momentary needs of Soviet foreign policy, the League Against Imperialism was gradually disbanded to make way for antifascist and anti-war organizations, following the rise to power of Adolf Hitler. Here again the role of organizer was played by Willi Munzenberg, who had managed to escape from Germany to Paris. The Comintern used his organizing abilities to convene a first International Congress Against War. A past-master in the technique of exploiting the services of internationally famous people, Munzenberg secured for his new enterprise the support of men of letters like Henri Barbusse, Romain Rolland, Heinrich Mann, Theodore Dreiser, John Dos Passos, Sherwood Anderson, Scott Nearing, as well as the Indian Congress leader, Sardar Vallabhbhai Patel; Sen Gupta, Mayor of Bombay; Madame Sun Yat-sen, and General Von Schoenaich, an anti-Hitler Prussian officer. In the face of the growing menace of war in Europe, the Russians no longer had time for the struggles of the colonial peoples, and even the Chinese Communists had to make their revolution against the Kuomintang without Russian aid. After all his years in the service of Communism, Munzenberg broke with the Russians when Stalin signed his pact with Hitler. For him, all his life's work had been destroyed. Munzenberg was left a broken and disappointed man, a little later to meet a violent death. He was strangled in a forest in the south of France while try-

ing to escape before the advancing Nazi forces. Some say he
was murdered by the Gestapo, others say G.P.U. agents. I
just don't know. One fact I do know: the colonial peoples
lost a sympathetic friend in this likeable German.

During their pre-Second World War anti-imperialist period, the Communist parties conducted campaigns in various
countries. After the inaugural conference of the League
Against Imperialism in Brussels in 1927, the Russians, who
by then completely bossed the Third International, ordered
its affiliated sections in the Western countries—Britain,
France, Belgium, Holland—to set up local Leagues Against
Imperialism. Until then, these metropolitan parties had done
very little in the way of establishing direct connections with
nationalist movements in Asian and African colonies. In fact,
so little had been done that when the Sixth Congress met in
Moscow the year after the Brussels Conference, it handed
down the following directives:

'The Congress makes it a duty of the Communist Parties
in the metropolitan countries to put an end to the indifference
which they have exhibited in regard to the mass movements
in these colonies, and instead to afford energetic support both
in the imperialist centres and in the colonies themselves to
these movements, at the same time attentively studying the
situation in these countries for the purpose of exposing the
bloody exploits of imperialism and of creating the possibility
of organizational connections with the developing proletarian
elements there which are so mercilessly exploited by imperialism . . .

'In the Central African colonies of imperialism, colonial
exploitation takes on the very worst forms, uniting slave-
owning, feudal and capitalist methods of exploitation. In the
post-war period, capital from the imperialist metropolitan
countries has flowed in an ever-increasing stream to the African colonies, compelling the concentration of considerable
masses of the expropriated, and proletarianized population in
plantations, mining and other enterprises.'

Unfortunately, the Western European Communist parties
were then too weak and lacked the practical experience of the
Russian party to enable them to translate into action the anti-
imperialist policies laid down by the Sixth Congress. For

example, the Portuguese Communist Party was underground. The Belgian and Dutch parties were small and impotent. The British Party—the Cinderella of the Comintern—while not quite as ineffective as those in the Low Countries, had no mass basis in the organized working-class movement. It did make attempts from time to time to stimulate interest in colonial work among its own members and fellow-travellers. To put these sporadic activities on a firm basis, the party organized a British section of the League Against Imperialism, under the secretaryship of Mr Reginald Bridgeman, C.M.G., M.V.O., a retired Foreign Office official. As a former diplomatist, Mr Bridgeman lent respectability to the British League, which was run from behind the scene by Communist party stalwarts like Mr Ben Bradley, who was involved in the famous Meerut conspiracy case in India. Thanks to Mr Bridgeman's patronage, the League succeeded for a time in attracting support from among a wide section of progressive middle-class people outside the narrow ranks of the Communist Party.

The Indian freedom struggle then dominated British imperial politics. It was, therefore, natural that the main activities of the League should centre around the Indian question, and this helped the Communists to spread their influence among the Indian communities—especially the students—in Great Britain. In this sphere of activity, the League's chief propagandist was Shapurji Saklatvala, a brilliant left-wing Labour Party M.P. Mr Saklatvala, who was related to the Tata family, the millionaire Parsee industrialists, was popularly known as Sak. He was a dynamic personality, who denounced British imperialism both in Parliament and from public platforms up and down Britain. He was one Indian who had no time for opportunistic trimmers and sycophants. The most independent-minded Communist ever. A Titoist before Tito!

Apart from carrying on propaganda on behalf of Indian freedom, the League issued a number of popular pamphlets on British rule in Africa and other colonies; published statements against injustices against coloured races in the Empire; organized public meetings, conferences and demonstrations, at a time when interest in colonial affairs was limited to a very small circle of British Empire experts. Yet despite the excellent work of enlightenment which the League performed within left-wing circles, it never succeeded in recruiting colonial membership. It was not for want of trying. But the objective conditions were even more unfavourable then than they are today. The majority of the coloured population of London and the provincial cities, apart from itinerant seamen living in the dock areas of London, Liverpool and Cardiff, was made up chiefly of students. These African and West Indian intellectuals came mostly from prosperous middle-class and religious families. They were, if anything, even more conservative than English university students, who had, to some degree, been radicalized by the economic depression of the thirties and the Marxist ideas disseminated through the Left Book Club, over which the Communists exercised considerable influence.

It is only since the end of the Second World War and the emergence of nationalist movements and trade unions in colonial territories that the Communists have been able to worm their way into the ranks of African and West Indian students, who are more politically conscious than the pre-war generations. Moreover, many of the present-day students come from artisan families and peasant communities, and are, therefore, more responsive to Communist propaganda than those connected with the chieftain caste and long-established professional and middle-class trading families. It would be unwise, however, to exaggerate the influence of Communism even among these young colonial students. It is just a part of youthful intellectual curiosity. It is the fashion among coloured students to be 'left'. But they are never so 'left' as to let themselves be left behind when the politicians in office offer them jobs! In fact, most of them shed their Marxist garments on returning home and revert to what they have always been at heart—bourgeois nationalists. Some even degenerate into out-and-out tribalists, preaching the most reactionary kind of political mumbo-jumbo as a means of getting themselves elected to legislatures. With these professional Africans, it is largely a case of being 'revolutionary' at twenty, moderate at thirty, conservative at forty, and reactionary at fifty. The British Communist Party will be sadly disappointed

if it is relying upon these opportunistic intellectuals to lead
the proletarian revolution in Africa!

Like a good many other Communist party front organizations everywhere, the League Against Imperialism went into
decline when Russia decided to enter the League of Nations
in 1934—the beginning of the Soviet *rapprochement* with
Britain and France in face of the growing menace of the
Axis powers. A hastener of its demise was the shock caused
to its non-Communist members by the revelation in the British press that Stalin had sold oil to Mussolini during the fascist invasion of Abyssinia in 1935. This Soviet stab in the
back made the League Against Imperialism exceedingly unpopular among non-Communist British anti-imperialists
whose sympathies were with Abyssinia. The few Africans in
London who were associated with the League through affiliated membership of the Negro Improvement Association,
headed by Arnold Ward, a West Indian, severed their association with the Communists and helped to form the International African Friends of Abyssinia, with the objective of
rallying support for Emperor Haile Selassie against Sawdust
Caesar Mussolini. About the same time, the International
Trade Union Committee of Negro Workers, with which I
was associated as secretary, was liquidated, in keeping with
the pro-League of Nations orientation in Soviet foreign policy.

After the League Against Imperialism had folded up, the
British Communist Party, acting under instructions from the
Comintern, threw all its resources into the Popular Front
movement, which dominated left-wing politics after the rise
of Hitler. The decision to drop the anti-imperialist line and
concentrate upon anti-fascism was endorsed by the Seventh
Congress of the Comintern in 1935. This Congress, dominated by Dimitrov, the Bulgarian Communist hero of the
Reichstag fire, also instructed all Communist parties to enter
into alliances with Socialists, Liberals, Catholics, Jews and
any other elements opposed to Nazism and Fascism.

In Britain, the Communist Party toned down its revolutionary talk and worked hand in hand with the I.L.P., the Socialist League and other left-wing elements of the Labour Party.
This led to the expulsion of Sir Stafford Cripps, the leader of
the Socialist League. To spread its anti-fascist propaganda,

the Communist Party made full use of the Left Book Club which was organized by the publisher, Victor Gollancz, and directed by himself, Prof. Laski and John Strachey. The Left Book Club was the most effective instrument of Communist policy during the period up to the Hitler-Stalin pact. Having used the British Lib-Labs, and other middle-class anti-fascists, the Russians, who, like the British ruling class, have 'no permanent friends nor permanent enemies but only permanent interest'—namely, the survival of the Soviet Union—threw their British anti-fascist allies to the wolves. The Communists were instructed to find other allies in defence of the Hitler-Stalin pact. To this end, the Communist Party revised the Leninist doctrine of 'revolutionary defeatism', and described the conflict which had broken out in 1939 as an 'imperialist war'. Mr Pollitt, who had favoured support for the war from the beginning, was denounced by his colleague, Mr Palme Dutt, as a 'right-wing deviationist', and removed from the secretaryship of the party. He was only reinstated after Hitler attacked Russia, for by then the 'imperialist war' had become an 'anti-fascist war', and the Communist Party went all out for capitalist support for Russia.

As we saw, the same metamorphosis took place in America. In Asia, the Chinese Communists did not have to make this change about as they were already fighting side by side with Chiang Kai-shek's Kuomintang against the Japanese. But in India, the Communists deserted the national liberation front, headed by the Congress Party under Gandhi and Nehru. All the party leaders then in prison were freed by the Viceroy in return for their support of the British war effort. It was during this period of collaboration with British imperialism that the Indian C.P. established a firm hold in Andhra State among the Kamma and Reddi castes of Indian kulaks, who until now have constituted the main supporters of Indian Communism. In South Africa, the only part of the Black Continent where a Communist Party existed, the Communists encouraged the Africans to join the forces, but General Smuts refused to arm the blacks. Non-Europeans were used exclusively in labour battalions and other forms of non-combat duties. On the home front, the Communists discouraged strikes and soft-pedalled their agitation for African rights after Hitler attacked Russia.

COMMUNISM IN NORTHERN AFRICA

In France, the Communists made a similar about-turn on the anti-imperialist question. There, the consequences were more disastrous for the colonials, since the French section of the League Against Imperialism was a larger and more effective organization than the one in Britain. Due to their revolutionary tradition and absence of colour bar, the French Communists were able to establish close contact with organized North African Arabs working in France. The Sixth Congress had directed that: 'In the French colonies of North Africa, the Communists must carry on work in all the already existing national-revolutionary organs in order to unite through them the genuine revolutionary elements on a consistent and clear platform of a fighting bloc of workers and peasants. As far as the organization *Etoile Nord Africain* (North African Star) is concerned, the Communists must secure that it develops, not in the form of a party, but in the form of a fighting bloc of various revolutionary organizations, collectively associating with it as a whole the trade unions of industrial and agricultural workers, peasants' unions, etc.

'The Communist organization in each individual country must attract into its ranks in the first place native workers fighting against any negligent attitude to them. The Communist parties, actively basing themselves on the native proletariat, must formally and in fact become independent sections of the Communist International.'

Things, however, did not work out exactly as the French Stalinists had planned. Despite all efforts to impose their ideology, the nationalist movements in Algeria, Tunisia and Morocco tended to develop along Pan-Arab lines and maintained an organizational independence which later brought them into open conflict with the Communists, who tried to bring them under the control of the French party. At that time, the outstanding North African nationalist was Messali Hadj, the founder of the North African Star, and later the Algerian People's Party. The year after the foundation of the former organization, the principal aim of which was to promote unity between the North African Arabs in the struggle for independence, Messali Hadj attended the Anti-Imperialist Congress at Brussels. There he established contact with Nehru, Ali Jinnah, Mohammed Hatta of Indonesia, and other Asian leaders. On his return to Paris, from where he carried on his activities, Messali Hadj set about broadening the basis of the North African Star by establishing branches among the Algerian immigrant workers in different parts of France. This proved so successful that the Government took alarm and suppressed the organization in 1929. Then followed a series of prosecutions against the leading Algerian nationalists. Messali Hadj was sentenced to a long term of imprisonment.

Although the North African Star was driven underground, anti-Colonialist sentiment continued to grow, and by the time the ban was lifted by the Popular Front Government of Léon Blum, the Algerian liberation movement was stronger than ever before. Taking advantage of the amnesty, Messali Hadj transferred his political activities from France to North Africa.

In the early days of his struggle to bring unity among the Algerian immigrants in France, Messali Hadj had cooperated with the Communists, Socialists, and other left-wing parties and groups which expressed sympathy with the cause of colonial liberation. The North Africans, therefore, placed great hopes in the Popular Front Government which came into being in 1936. But these hopes were soon dashed when the Algerian administration, under the pressure of the white settlers in Algeria, suppressed the North African Star in January 1937. 'Experience and time were to prove that French leaders, whether belonging to the extreme left or extreme right of the Government, have one and the same colonial policy,' declared Messali Hadj. The Socialist excuse for the repression was the opposition of the Arab leaders to certain reforms proposed by Governor-General Viollett, which aimed at gallicizing the Algerians.

To accommodate itself to the new situation, the North African Star became the Algerian People's Party. Seven months later, in August 1937, Messali Hadj, Hochine Lahouel, secretary-general of the party, and three other prominent Arabs were arrested on the orders of the Socialist Governor-General and imprisoned for 'having, against French sovereignty, refounded a league which had been dissolved'. After their release, Messali Hadj was again imprisoned in 1938, released once more in August 1939, and re-arrested in October of the same year. When metropolitan France was occupied by the Nazis, the French officials in Algeria, who supported the pro-Nazi Pétain Government, sentenced Messali Hadj to sixteen years hard labour and confiscated all of his property for appealing to the Arabs to resist fascism. Even after the occupation of Algeria by the Allied forces and the replacement of the Pétain administration by that of de Gaulle, Messali Hadj remained in exile, first at Ain-Salah in the southern Sahara, then at El Golea, and finally at Brazzaville in Equatorial Africa. He was only allowed to return to his home at Ben Zareah in Algeria in October 1946, after the Allied forces had liberated France.

When the Algerian People's Party was under violent attack by the French colonialists and other imperialists in 1937, the Algerians were deserted by the Communists, who were then the main allies of the Socialists in the Popular Front. But after the dissolution of the Popular Front, the Communists made a complete somersault and tried to ingratiate themselves once more into Arab favour. Messali Hadj would have nothing to do with these double-crossers. They got their revenge when the Algerian People's Party was driven underground in 1939 under a decree signed by the President of the French Republic, M. Albert Lebrun. The suppression was maintained by Marshal Pétain under the Vichy régime, and remained in force even when General de Gaulle's National Liberation Committee took over. General Catroux, the war-time Governor-General of Algeria, released Communists and Socialists who had been placed in concentration camps by Vichy officials, but the Algerian nationalists, among them Messali Hadj and deputies Ferhat Abbas and Salah Abdel-kader, were kept in concentration camps. Repression also fell on West African nationalists. One of their most prominent leaders, M. Emile Faure, the Senegal-born president of the Ligue pour la Défense de la Race Nègre and secretary of the Rassemblement Coloniale, the organization uniting the nationalist societies of Algeria, Tunisia, West Africa, Madagascar and Indo-China (Viet Nam), was arrested and banished to the Sahara for the duration of the war. Even the representatives of the left-wing parties in the French Liberation Committee raised no word of protest on behalf of these colonial fighters for freedom. Left to struggle alone, the North African nationalist leaders addressed themselves to the Algerian people to support a manifesto which declared that: 'At the end of hostilities, Algeria must be raised to the level of a sovereign state with a constitution to be drawn up by a sovereign Algerian Constituent Assembly elected by all inhabitants of Algeria on the basis of universal vote, without distinction of race or religion.'

This was denounced by the French settlers who brought down further repressions upon the heads of the Arab nationalists. To counter the support for the manifesto, the de Gaulle Government revived the rejected Popular Front policy of 'assimilation'. But this manœuvre was no more successful than that tried by Léon Blum's Government. Realizing the growing strength of the Movement for the Triumph of Democratic Liberties (the name under which the banned Algerian People's Party functioned), the French authorities in Algeria provoked a clash with the nationalists in May 1945. It is estimated that over 10,000 Africans were killed by bombing and machine gunning at Sétif. That was how the French settlers in Algeria celebrated the Allied victory over Hitlerism! Thousands of Arabs were also killed during uprisings in 1952 and 1954. But in spite of all forms of repression, imprisonment, torture and violence, the nationalist spirit survived, and in the first post-war elections to the French National Assembly, the candidates put forward by the Movement for the Triumph of Democratic Liberties (M.T.L.D.), won a sweeping victory. Using the French Parliament as a forum, the Arab representatives from Algeria continued to voice the aspirations of their people. In the hope of influencing the Movement for the Triumph of Democratic Liberties, and controlling the leadership, the French Communist deputies in the National Assembly pretended to be friendly. When the Arabs rejected their gesture, the Communist representatives in the Ramadier Government supported the repressions in Algeria on the ground that the Arabs were 'terrorists' who wanted to detach Algeria from the 'mother' country and set up an independent Algerian democratic and social republic.

In opposition to the M.T.L.D. is the Communist Party composed largely of Frenchmen and gallicized Arabs; the moderate U.D.M.A. which favours local 'home rule' for Arabs within the framework of the French Union; and the Arab quislings grouped around what is called the League of Franco-Arab Amity.

Although Communist influence is even more negligible in Tunisia and Morocco, the French *colons* use the 'red bogy' to smear the Neo-Destour and Istiqlal nationalist movements in these territories. Of all the North African liberation movements associated with the Committee for the Liberation of the Arab West, with headquarters in Cairo, the Neo-Destour is the best organized. It is under the able leadership of Habib Bourguiba and Salah Iben Yusuf, who were arrested and exiled in 1952 after the suppression of the Chanik Government.[24] This nationalist party also enjoys the active support of the U.G.T.T., the non-Communist trade union movement directed by Ferhat-Hached, who was killed by French terrorists called Commandos of the Red Hand in 1952.[25]

Outside French North African territories, Communism has gained most support among West Indians, who are so completely assimilated that they can truly be described as 'black Frenchmen'. There are branches of the French Communist Party in Martinique and Guadeloupe; but some of the Negro leaders are seeking to establish closer links with non-Communist West Indian progressive movements in the British West Indian colonies which are moving towards federation and self-government. In other words the French West

[24] M. Bourguiba was allowed to return to Tunisia in May 1955 where he received a royal welcome by over 300,000 Arabs.

[25] For a full account of the French policies in North Africa, consult Jean Rous, *Tunisie-Attention* (Deux Rives, Paris) and Daniel Guerin, *Au Service des Colonies* (les Editions de Minuit, Paris).

Indian Communists are showing dissatisfaction with the doctrine of 'assimilation' which binds them to the 'mother' country and isolates them from their Caribbean neighbours.

After the Liberation, the French Communists attempted to spread their influence to the Black African colonies through a united front movement called the Rassemblement Démocratique Africain, and the C.G.T.—the Communist-controlled trade unions affiliated to the W.F.T.U. But Communism is meeting with stubborn resistance from the adherents of Pan-Africanism, which places its emphasis on African political autonomy and opposes European economic monopoly and white colonization. For attempting to implement these demands, the Malagasy deputies Drs Ravoahangy, Raseta and Rabemananjara were condemned to death following the suppression of a revolt in Madagascar in 1947. The death sentences were later commuted by the President of France, who ordered the nationalist leaders to be exiled for life to Belle Ile off the south coast of Brittany.

In South-East Asia, the French Communists have played a two-face role. The party ministers in the post-Liberation Coalition Government approved the military credits on March 23, 1947, and the despatch of the French expeditionary forces to conquer Viet Nam after the breakdown of Fontainbleau Conference between President Ho Chi-minh and the French Government. The Communists only came out in support of the Viet-minh Republic after they had been expelled from the Ramadier Coalition Government in May 1947, following a breach between the Communists and their Socialist-M.R.P. colleagues over industrial disputes. These events coincided with the outbreak of the cold war between Russia and the West.

COMMUNISM IN BLACK AFRICA

Since the split between Soviet Russia and her wartime Western allies, the British Communist Party has revived its anti-imperialist activities in the colonies. The new party line was enunciated at the first post-war conference of British

Commonwealth Communist parties held in London in 1947. Linking up anti-Colonialism with Soviet propaganda for peace, the conference declared: 'We greet with enthusiasm the unprecedented upsurge of the colonial and subject peoples in the great struggle for liberation . . .' and went on to proclaim:

'The fight for the peace of the world, the advance of the subject peoples to independence, the struggle of socialism are all part of the common fight . . . The leading role in building the solidarity of the peoples of the Empire countries must be borne by the working class in Britain, the Dominions and the colonial countries. Foremost in this task will be the Communist parties with their socialist understanding and international spirit.'

It can be safely predicted that if the East and West settle their differences, the Russians will liquidate the Cominform and the British Communists will again desert their present 'Allies for Freedom', as the colonials are now flatteringly called. For then it will no longer be necessary to exploit the African liberation movement as a whip against the main spearhead of anti-Communism and defenders of the colonial *status quo*. Today the Communists conduct their colonial activities through the World Federation of Trade Unions (W.F.T.U.) instead of through exclusively anti-colonial organizations like the pre-war League Against Imperialism. They are trying to infiltrate the colonies through the affiliated sections of the W.F.T.U., hoping to strengthen the Soviet bloc in the cold war struggle by hitting at the soft underbelly of the West in South-East Asia, Africa and the Caribbean. There is no doubt that these areas constitute the most vulnerable sectors of the Western bloc, the Achilles heel of imperialism.

The only force capable of containing Communism in Asia and Africa is dynamic nationalism based upon a socialist programme of industrialization and co-operative methods of agricultural production. This means setting the colonies immediately on the road to self-government, since only popularly elected leaders can harness the emotions and loyalties of the common people of town and country, and marshal their enthusiasm along the path of peaceful economic and social reconstruction. No alien ruler, however benevolent, can perform this role. The Communists know this only too well.

The time is fast passing when coloured folk will continue to accept their colonial status, which in the modern world signifies racial and national inferiority. If the Western Powers are really afraid of Communism and want to defeat it, the remedy lies in their own hands. First, it is necessary to keep one step ahead of the Communists by removing the grievances of the so-called backward peoples, which the Communists everywhere seek to exploit for their own ends. Secondly, there must be a revolutionary change in the outlook of the colonizing Powers, who must be prepared to fix a date for the complete transfer of power—as America did in the Philippines—and to give every technical and administrative assistance to the emerging colonial nations during the period of transition from internal self-government to complete self-determination. Fortified with the knowledge that, regardless of their stage of development, full responsibility will be theirs on the agreed date, the colonial peoples will throw their full energies into making the experiment a success. Only responsibility can develop the latent potentialities of a subject people, as events in the Gold Coast have shown. None of the members of the present All-African Cabinet in the West African colony had any experience in governing prior to taking office in 1951.

Doctrinaire Marxism, especially as it is propagated by the British Communists, who have made not one single original contribution to the practical application of Leninism, has no particular appeal for colonial nationalists. No self-respecting African wishes to exchange his British masters for Russian ones. Africans only lend ear to Communist propaganda when they feel betrayed and frustrated; when they have lost hope in the professions and promises of Western so-called Christians, who, while paying lip service to 'the brotherhood of man', perpetuate the 'exploitation of man by man', especially coloured man. The Communists' strength lies in the knowledge that Western democracy is caught in its own dilemma when confronted with the fulfilment of its own professions to the darker peoples. And since Communists have nothing to lose, and everything to gain by fishing in the troubled waters of Asia and Africa, they can well afford to pay lip service unreservedly in support of colonial freedom. They also know that repression only adds grist to their mill by confirming their constant assertion that no imperial nation will under any circumstances peacefully surrender power to a subject people.

Despite the peaceful transfer of power in India, Pakistan, Ceylon and Burma, and the similar process now taking place in the Gold Coast and Sudan, British Communists still maintain their dogmatic assertion. To revise it would amount to a Marxist heresy, a privilege permitted only to independent leaders like Tito and Mao Tse-tung, who has evolved his own Asiatic doctrine of neo-Marxism. Lacking both the ability and audacity to tackle a new approach to the Colonial Question in its African context without Russian approval, British Communist Party colonial 'experts' are still spouting the old party clap-trap of the inter-war years that only 'the proletarian vanguard can liberate Africa'. Whereas in China, the peasantry did the liberating.

Well-groomed in parroting his masters, Mr Ademola Thomas, described as national organizer of the West African Students' Union and 'leader' of a small group of Nigerian so-called Communists in Britain, boasted to delegates of the Conference of Commonwealth Communist Parties held in London in April 1954 that: 'There can be no real advance in Nigeria's fight for national liberation until all genuine Marxist elements come together in a united party which will fulfil the role of Marxism and working-class leadership within the broadest national front, and so advance the struggle against imperialism and its reactionary puppets.'

While waiting for Mr Thomas to return to West Africa and consolidate the 'proletarian vanguard' in Nigeria, the British Communists seem to be more optimistic about their Sudanese colleagues capturing power in the Sudan, where the Communists control the so-called Movement for National Liberation. Reporting on behalf of the executive, the veteran English Communist colonial 'expert', Mr Ben Bradley, assured the conference that in the Sudan 'the imperialists have not been able up to now to form a Nkrumah régime to stem the movement as in the Gold Coast'.[26]

The conference was also informed that the revolution was advancing under the red banner of the Sudanese Democratic Liberation Movement, which was 'based on Marxist principles. Young, militant with deep roots mainly among the railway workers in Omdurman and Khartoum and more recently among a large section of Gezira scheme peasants.'[27]

All this is just bravado. The truth is that the Sudan Communists, even those disguised as 'independents', did not win a single seat in the December 1954 general election.

In the Gold Coast the crypto-Communists suffered a similar defeat. Even their most prominent ideologist, Mr Bankole Awoonor Renner, who, incidentally, is chairman of the fanatically religious Muslim Association Party, was defeated by a C.P.P. candidate[28] for a seat in Accra at the last general election in June 1954. To protect his party and Government from Communist infiltration, as well as to avoid a constitutional crisis, such as occurred in British Guiana in 1953, Dr Nkrumah was forced to take certain disciplinary action against two prominent members of the C.P.P., Mr Anthony Woode and Mr E. C. Turkson Ocran. These two fellow-travellers were found guilty of associating with the Communist-controlled W.F.T.U. According to a press statement issued by the secretariat of the C.P.P. at the time of their expulsion, both men, without obtaining the permission of their party or the Gold Coast T.U.C., of which they were executive members, secretly left the country in 1954 and attended a conference of the W.F.T.U. in the Soviet sector of Vienna. This was in flagrant violation of a decision of the Gold Coast T.U.C. not to become involved in the cold war controversy between the W.F.T.U. and its rival, the

[26] *Allies for Freedom*—Report on Second Conference of Communist Parties in the Commonwealth. Published by the C.P. of Great Britain, 1955, p. 109.

[27] See *New Commonwealth*, June 24, 1954—'British Communists and the Colonies.'

[28] Mr T. Hutton Mills, Deputy Gold Coast Commissioner in London.

I.C.F.T.U. (the International Confederation of Free Trade Unions).

For spiking their plans, the Gold Coast Prime Minister has been denounced by the Communists as an 'imperialist stooge'. At the same time, he is also regarded by capitalists and tribalist opponents as a 'Communist Dictator'. The life of independent minded Asian and African socialists like Nehru and Nkrumah is certainly a difficult one! One must be either a Communist or an anti-Communist. This is typical white man's thinking, whether of the left or right. And it is here that the European makes his greatest psychological mistake. He fails to realize that one of the first reactions of politically awakened self-respecting coloured leaders is the desire to be mentally free from the dictation of Europeans, regardless of their ideology. Naturally, this assertion of intellectual independence is resented by most whites and interpreted as anti-European, anti-British, anti-white. And brought forward as evidence of the black man's unwillingness to collaborate with the European settlers in East and Central Africa, in operating what is now fashionably called 'Partnership'. Few whites can envisage a world in which they are not pushing coloured folk around. A society in which all men are equal regardless of their colour or race is to such people utopian.

In South Africa the very idea of racial equality is treason. 'Racial segregation is the only way the white man can maintain his supremacy', said Prime Minister Johannes Strydom, addressing the Union Parliament on April 18, 1955. Mr Strydom was replying to a speech by the Indian Prime Minister in which Mr Nehru criticised South Africa's policy of *Apartheid*—racial segregation. 'The idea of partnership between Europeans and non-Europeans', added Mr Strydom, 'is a mirage.'

At the back of this policy is the fact that, 'South Africa is a fear ridden country. Fear of the black man and to a lesser extent of Communism is the explanation of our oppression and illiberal legislation. The fear is very general that the blacks if they are not kept strictly under control will in time drive the whites from Africa, and in any event will take their jobs and lower the standard of living . . . It is not surprising that there is growing rapidly a burning hatred of the whites. That this

will culminate in the immediate future in a violent outburst
is unlikely. But in these days of speedy changes who would
venture to assert that such a thing could not happen in the
next ten or even the next five years.'[29]

Outside the Sudan and West Africa, the only colonial territories inhabited largely by people of African descent in which
the British Communists have directed operations in recent
years are the West Indies and British Guiana. There the
field is more favourable than in West Africa. Apart from
Negroes, there are East Indians, among whom there is much
poverty, as well as land hunger in Guiana, Jamaica and
many of the smaller Caribbean islands. Infiltration of the
trade unions is being carried on under the direction of the
West Indian representative of the W.F.T.U., Mr Ferdinand
Smith, a Jamaican trade union boss who lived in the United
States for over thirty years, until he was expelled for Communist activities by the F.B.I. Exiled back to his native land,
Mr Smith has rediscovered the 'downtrodden proletarians',
whom it is his ambition to rescue from such 'bourgeois mis-
leaders' as Norman Manley, whom the Communists have
labelled as just another 'British imperialist stooge' like
Grantley Adams, Prime Minister of Barbados, and T. Albert
Marryshaw, 'Father' of West Indian Federation and Elder
Statesman of the Caribbean.

Unable to capture the Caribbean Labour Congress, an
organization established in 1945 to co-ordinate the activities of the regional trade unions and Socialist parties on an all-
West Indian basis, the Communists have succeeded in disrupting its activities. They made a similar attempt to capture
Mr Manley's People's National Party. This failed and the
Communist faction led by Mr Richard Hart, a young Kings-
ton lawyer, and Mr Ken Hill, a well-known local journalist,
both active workers in the trade union movement, were expelled from the P.N.P. Since then, splits have taken place
among the Communists. Mr Hill, once the bright hope of
King Street, the 'Kremlin' of the British party, has lost favour
with his English mentors. His place has been taken by Mr

[29] Mr Justice F. A. Lucas of the Transvaal Court and the chairman of the Wage Board of the Union of South Africa in a letter
to the New York Times—April 16, 1955.

Ferdinand Smith. Cold-shouldered by his erstwhile British comrades, Mr Hill tried to form an alliance with the former Chief Minister, Sir Alexander Bustamante, who made use of him against his political rival and cousin, Mr Norman Manley, but dropped Hill as a political liability on the approach of the 1955 general election. For Sir Alexander is as big a 'red-baiter' as Senator Joe McCarthy. Mr Hill, who was once an able P.N.P. member of the House of Representatives, is now in the political wilderness.

The only Caribbean colony in which the Communists have succeeded in establishing a bridgehead is in British Guiana, thanks to Dr and Mrs Jagan, supported by an active Communist faction within the People's Progressive Party (P.P.P.).

The vast majority of the members, however, are not Communists. They supported the party because it was the only militant organization fighting on behalf of the urban workers, the farmers and lower middle-class Negroes and Indians. Since the suppression of the constitution in 1953, divergences have developed within the leadership of the party. A socialist faction, while equally opposed to imperialism as the Communist element, favours a more constructive constitutional approach in achieving the party's political, economic and social objectives. These democratic socialists are led by a brilliant young Negro barrister, Mr Forbes Burnham, the chairman of the party and former Minister of Education and Social Welfare.[30]

While a split within an anti-imperialist movement is always regrettable before the attainment of self-government, Communists cannot be allowed to squander the peoples' sacrifices and jeopardize the limited opportunities grudgingly conceded them to plant their feet firmly on the constitutional road to independence, just to conform to some myopic pseudo-Marxist doctrinaire policy which bears little relation to the immediate needs of the masses at their level of political development. Even Lenin taught that Marxism is not a dogma to be mechanically applied, but a guide to action, according to local circumstances and the political development of a peo-

[30] For a detailed account of Communist activities in British Guiana, see Report of the Robinson Commission, 1955. H.M. Stationery Office, London.

ple. Had Lenin and Mao Tse-tung been doctrinaire Marxists, they could never have led successful revolutions. Dogmatism is the disease of parvenu-Communists. 'There are people who think that Marxism is a kind of magic truth with which one can cure any disease', declares Mao Tse-tung. 'We should tell them that dogmas are more useless than cow dung. Dung can be used as fertilizer.'

In contrast to the opportunity lost in British Guiana, the Gold Coast offers an encouraging and hopeful picture despite all the tribal back-wash which the application of democracy there has aroused. Thanks to the wise and constructive social-ist leadership of Dr Nkrumah, the West African colony which started on its journey of self-determination in 1951 under a constitution similar to that granted to British Guiana two years later, had arrived by 1954 at the very threshold of in-dependence. Instead of indulging in revolutionary romanti-cism, it would have been wiser if Dr Jagan had made the maximum use of the power that was in his hand to demon-strate to the people his party's ability to govern. Once the people had been convinced of the sincerity and honesty of the P.P.P., Jagan could then have mobilized the widest popu-lar support for a more advanced constitution. And by pursuing a policy of permanent agitation *pari passu* economic and social reforms, the P.P.P. would have achieved by non-violent means for British Guiana what the C.P.P. has won for the Gold Coast, complete internal self-government in less than three years. Instead of this, Dr Jagan and his amateur band of revolutionaries played right into the hands of the local reactionaries and foreign imperialists, who were only too glad to exploit the mistakes of the P.P.P. leaders to get the consti-tution, which, despite its limitations, they intensely disliked, suspended by the Tory Government. And where are his Brit-ish Communist friends to restore the constitution?

COMMUNISM AND BANTU NATIONALISM

With the exception of a few white liberals, who can be counted on the fingers of one hand, and the members of the

Anglican Community of the Resurrection headed by the Rev Father Trevor Huddleston and the Bishop of Johannesburg, the Rt Rev Dr Ambrose Reeves, the only Europeans in South Africa who have taken an uncompromising stand on behalf of racial equality for non-Europeans are the Communists. On the question of human rights for Africans, the Communists have never faltered. They have, in fact, been so staunch in this that many churchmen, like the Rev C. F. Andrews, the famous English missionary and co-worker of Mahatma Gandhi, have paid public tribute to them. They are, declared Mr Andrews, 'the only Europeans in South Africa who really and honestly were against what is called the "white labour policy" and were ready to admit Indians, Cape Coloured and Bantu on equal terms.'

Had the Russians, who, until the liquidation of the Communist International in 1943 dictated the policies of the foreign parties, allowed the South African party more freedom to assert its initiative and develop according to local conditions, it would have become a real force among the Bantus. But because South African Communist leaders were so completely tied by the Russian umbilical cord, they were forced to follow all the zigzag manœuvres of Soviet foreign policy. This completely discredited the party even before it finally degenerated into a miserable sect and was wound up in 1948. Without roots in the people it purported to serve, the party could offer no resistance to Dr Malan when he introduced the Suppression of Communism Act. The elimination of the Communist Party left the political field wide open to the *Herrenvolk*. For while the Communists carried on a disruptive policy in their dealings with Bantu nationalist organizations, in the repressive conditions which prevail in South Africa they could have provided a rallying force for progressive Europeans. The party's disappearance has enabled the Malanazis to poison the white workers with their Hitlerian philosophy of 'racial superiority' to the almost complete extinction of liberal democracy. Today, South Africa is almost a police state.

As to the Christian Church, most of the Anglican and Nonconformist missionaries are as reactionary as the Dutch Reformed Church Predikants on the race question. All Christian dignitaries, with few exceptions, capitulate before the *Apartheid* onslaught of Afrikander nationalism. Only the non-Europeans—Africans, Indians and Coloured (the mixed race population of Cape Province)—have made any attempt to offer organized resistance.

To understand why Communism failed to root itself among the Bantu—the most racially oppressed and economically exploited people in the Union—it is necessary to review the history and social composition of the party's European leadership. The party was formed in 1921 on the initiative of the International Socialist League, a small group of left-wing skilled workers and intellectuals who had broken away from the South African Labour Party. Like the American Communist Party, the majority of the original members were Eastern European Jewish immigrants, with a sprinkling of British trade unionists employed in the gold mining industry of the Transvaal. The first secretary of the party was the veteran English labour leader, W. H. (Bill) Andrews, with whom was associated David Jones, a Welsh miner and one-time secretary of the South African Labour Party, and Sydney Bunting. Mr Bunting was later to become the foremost European champion of the black man. He belonged to the upper middle class. His father was Sir Percy Bunting, the distinguished founder and editor of the *Contemporary Review* and great-grandson of the Rev Dr Jabez Bunting, the famous Wesleyan divine.

Mr Bunting's Communism was typically British, owing more to Nonconformist evangelism than Marxist philosophy. This led ultimately to his expulsion from the party as 'a right-wing deviationist'. Bunting went out to South Africa as a young man during the Boer War. The war over, he settled down to practise law at the Transvaal Bar. With the outbreak of the Russian Revolution in 1917, he immediately associated himself with the left-wing labour leaders, whom he often defended in the courts, to found the South African Communist Party, of which later he became the secretary-general. During the early years of the party, when the leadership was in the hands of Mr Bill Andrews, the overwhelming majority of the members were white. Bunting led a campaign within the party to give it a black coloration, in which course he gradually succeeded. This, however, brought about internal dissensions. As Africans came into the party, the middle-class European elements gradually dropped out, and after the resignation of Mr Andrews as secretary, Mr Bunting retired from legal practice and took over active leadership.

About ten years before the appearance of an official Communist Party in South Africa, the Bantu intellectuals, with the support of their chiefs, had established the African National Congress to unite the various tribes in Southern Africa in their fight to preserve their lands and other native rights guaranteed them by the British in the former Cape and Natal colonies, which were being threatened by the Botha Government under the newly established Act of Union. The African National Congress sent delegations to England to present the people's grievances to the British Imperial Government and acted as the mouthpiece of the Africans until the end of the First World War. It was then superseded by a more militant organization, known colloquially as the I.C.U. (Industrial and Commercial Union). While the African National Congress was purely political, the I.C.U. combined political agitation with industrial activities. It organized the African workers in town and country to fight for economic betterment by means of strikes, demonstrations and other forms of mass pressure.

Within a few years of its formation in 1919 by Clements Kadalie, a missionary-educated native of Nyasaland, the I.C.U. had achieved a membership of a quarter of a million. Mr Kadalie was a remarkable young Negro. Like Dr Nkrumah of the Gold Coast, he had many natural gifts, including a pleasant personality and remarkable brilliance as a platform speaker, who never lost the common touch. An able organizer, Kadalie, although he could not speak any of the South African Bantu languages and always spoke in fluent English which had to be translated, was able, within next to no time, to sweep aside all the moderate Bantu leaders of the African National Congress. He became the uncrowned king of the black masses. No other Negro in recent South African history has enjoyed the popularity which was Kadalie's at the height of his power. The whites feared him as they feared Dingaan, the last of the Zulu warrior kings.

This movement of Negro protest in South Africa started from modest beginnings like that of the Garvey movement in America which had a great influence on Kadalie. An insignificant incident gave birth to what became the greatest challenge the white man has yet faced in South Africa. Mr Kadalie tells the story himself in a speech delivered at the seventh congress of the I.C.U. in 1927:

'I was walking down Hanover Street, Cape Town, with two friends . . . We met a police constable who had something to say to my friends. I interfered and the constable pushed me off the pavement. We decided to report the constable, but while we were discussing the matter, a European passing by asked who was assaulted. We told him . . . He said that such behaviour on the part of the police was the reason why there was no friendship between black and white in this country. He handed me his card and we took the number of the policeman and reported him to his sergeant. That was the beginning of the I.C.U. The European gentleman was none other than Mr A. F. Batty. After talking things over with Mr Batty, we decided to start a non-European trade union, and the first meeting was held on January 7th, 1919, with Mr Batty in the chair . . . Mr Batty made it plain that he wished this to be a purely non-European trade union, and he would only identify himself with it in as far as he could give advice. That night twenty-four members joined and collected £1 4s. which was next day deposited in the Standard Bank. The second meeting was held on January 25th, and I was appointed first secretary of the I.C.U. Mr J. Paulsen, who was foreman at the Union Castle Docks, was appointed chairman. From that time Mr Batty never interfered with the internal affairs of the I.C.U.'

The new organization spread like a prairie fire. Kadalie and a group of lieutenants toured the length and breadth of South Africa enrolling members in town and countryside. Everywhere thousands of black workers and peasants flocked into the I.C.U., and by 1928 the organization boasted a membership almost a quarter of a million strong. By that time the I.C.U. had reached its zenith.

Such a formidable movement irresistibly drew the attention of the Communists. Certain Africans who had been enrolled into the party, then firmly in the hands of Mr Sydney Bunting, were assigned the task of boring into the I.C.U. and capturing its leadership. Although these Communist infiltrators failed in this attempt, they did manage to cause deep disruption within the movement before they were finally expelled in 1926. Weakened by internal factionism, the I.C.U. split into three groups. One faction remained under Kadalie in the Cape, another under a Zulu organizer, W. A. Champion, was based in Natal. The third faction passed into the hands of a Scot trade unionist, W. G. Ballinger. Mr Ballinger was sent out from England by a committee of British progressives calling themselves The Friends of Africa, which was organized by the novelist, Miss Winifred Holtby, and Mr A. Creech Jones, to advise Mr Kadalie how to run his organization. Resenting Mr Ballinger's intrusion into their affairs, the majority of Africans refused to co-operate with him, and the I.C.U. broke up completely. Taking advantage of the split, Mr Bunting seized the opportunity to set up a rival organization, which he called the League of African Rights. He appointed as leader Mr James T. Gumede, a former president of the moribund African National Congress, who had been among those members of the I.C.U. whom Kadalie had expelled as 'Communist intriguers'.

Mr Gumede had returned shortly before then from Europe, where he and Mr J. A. La Guma had attended the Brussels Conference of the League Against Imperialism. After the Conference, both men had visited Moscow, where they were feted by the Russians. By the time they got back to South Africa they were full of enthusiasm for the Soviet Union. To leaven the Communist elements in control of the League of African Rights, the party installed Mr Doyle Modiagotha as vice-president. This African was a fellow-traveller who had joined the Ballinger section of the I.C.U. The key posts of joint secretaries were reserved for two of the ablest young party leaders, Mr Albert Nzula, an African, and Dr Eddie Roux, a European.[31]

From the point of view of capable leadership, the League of African Rights was well equipped for the job Mr Bunting

[31] Mr Nzula died in Moscow in 1931, and Dr Roux resigned some years later.

had in mind for it. But no sooner had it embarked upon its mission of mobilizing support from the African masses, who had been left leaderless by the disintegration of the I.C.U., than instructions were received from the Comintern which laid down a new turn in colonial tactics. The South African Communist Party was instructed overnight to close down the League of African Rights and to apply the orthodox Stalinist policy on the National and Colonial Question. Instead of agitating for racial equality and equal citizenship for Africans, they were to be offered a 'Native Republic' along the lines of the 'Black Belt State' for Negroes in the Southern States of America.

Africans had never demanded any such nonsense. Consternation was therefore great when the new Comintern directive was received ordering that 'the party must determinedly and consistently put forward the slogan for the creation of an independent Native Republic, with simultaneous guarantees for the rights of the white minority, and struggle in deeds for its realization.'[32]

Most of the white members, including Mr Bunting, opposed the crazy Stalinist policy. Moscow then initiated a purge, which was carried out by an English Communist, Mr Douglas Wolton, who was installed as Bunting's successor. Among the other white victims of the purge were Mr Solly Sachs, the general secretary of the European Garment Workers Trade Union; Mr Benny Weinbrun, Mr Sam Malkinson and Mr Andrews. Ironically enough, Mr Sydney Bunting's son, Brian, who joined the party after his father was purged, has himself been purged by Malan from membership of the South African Parliament, to which body he was elected in 1954 by African voters in the Cape as one of the three European 'representatives' for the Bantus in the House of Assembly.

The expulsion of Mr Sydney Bunting and other prominent European trade unionists from the party did not save Stalin's policy from being rejected by the Africans. They, like the Negroes in America, while opposed to all forms of racial disability have never demanded separatism, either in the

[32] Sixth Congress Resolution on Revolutionary Movements in the Colonies—1928.

form of *Apartheid* or 'Native Republic'. Rather, the Africans
have always demanded full citizenship rights within a multi-
racial society. They, therefore, looked with deep suspicion
upon the new Communist slogan of a 'Native Republic', which
they interpreted as an attempt to segregate them into some
sort of Bantu state, for they knew that Europeans—even
those calling themselves Communists—would resent living
under an all-African Government. Rebuffed by the Africans,
the newly-installed party leaders had quietly to drop the 'Native Republic' slogan and revert to the policy of infiltrating
the African National Congress, which, since the disintegration
of the I.C.U., was gradually reviving with Communist encouragement.

Political tension among the Bantus reached a high pitch
when General Hertzog, who had formed an alliance with
General Smuts to establish the United Party and Fusion Government in 1933, presented a number of anti-African Bills
before Parliament in 1936. These, the Prime Minister
claimed, would 'settle the Native Question once and for all'.
Among the Bills was one designed to remove the Africans in
the Cape from the common voters' roll, a privilege which they
had enjoyed since 1853. Another deprived the Africans of
the right to buy land outside the already over-crowded Native
Reserves; and a third regulated the movement of Africans
from the rural areas into the urban locations or ghettoes. To
meet these threats to their already limited rights, the Africans rose spontaneously to demand united action, and leaders
of all shades of opinion, forgetting their differences for once,
convened a Conference at Bloemfontein on Dingaan's Day,
December 16th, 1935.

Denouncing the Hertzog Bills, the delegates agreed to set
up a new organization, the All-African Convention. This movement was founded upon a federal structure, with the following aims: (1) to act in unity in developing the political
and economic power of the African people; (2) to serve as a
medium of expression of the united voice of the African
people on all matters affecting their welfare; (3) to formulate
and give effect to a national programme for the advancement
and protection of the interests of the African people; and
(4) to assist in rehabilitating dormant and moribund African

organizations or bodies affiliated to the All-African Convention.

At the second conference of the All-African Convention from June 29th, to July 12th, 1936, a number of well-known Bantu intellectuals were elected officers of the new liberation movement, among them Professor D. D. Tengo Jabavu, a former president of the African National Congress, was elected to the presidency of the Convention. Dr A. B. Xuma was made vice-president; Dr J. S. Maroka, treasurer; Mr H. Selby Msimang, general secretary; Mr R. H. Godlo (a prominent Wesleyan of radical views), recording secretary; and Professor Z. K. Matthews, adviser. A year later, the third conference approved a constitution and agreed upon tactics.

This attempt to forge unity among Africans frightened the *Herrenvolk* and the Government immediately set about spiking the Convention. Having decided to remove the Africans from the common voters' roll, provisions were made for the setting up of a dummy Native Representation Council, consisting of twenty-two members, of whom six were European native commissioners, under the chairmanship of the Minister of Native Affairs. The remaining sixteen members comprised four appointed by the Governor-General on the advice of the Minister, and twelve elected by African voters. The Council was purely advisory, the Government being under no obligation to accept its recommendations unless endorsed by the Minister and the European members.

To the All-African Convention, this Council was an insult, and it called upon Africans to boycott it. Nevertheless, the South African Government succeeded by this manœuvre in disuniting the Convention. Though recognized as just a 'talking shop', certain Bantu intellectuals were attracted by the large salary provided for members to stand election to the Council.

These opportunists were backed by the Communist Party, who saw here an opportunity of getting some of its black members elected to a statutory Government Council. The party also had hopes of getting white members elected to Parliament as 'representatives' of the Africans. The scheme miscarried, as all the Communist candidates were defeated. Having lent support to an opportunistic plan which brought a split in the ranks of the All-African Convention, the Communists shamelessly turned around and denounced the successful African representatives and liberal European M.P.s elected by African constituencies in the Cape as 'misleaders' and 'collaborators with the imperialists'.

While the Communists were carrying on a campaign of abuse against the African National Congress 'collaborators', a violent quarrel broke out within their own ranks over Stalin's collaboration with Hitler following the pact between the two dictators in 1939. Mr H. M. Basner, the leading party lawyer, led a revolt against the Hitler-Stalin compact and broke away with a number of others. But since a dissident white Communist could not hope to find any mass support among the European population, Mr Basner, who had been among the party candidates who had failed to get elected to Parliament in 1937, set about forming his own organization among non-Europeans. He called it the African Democratic Party, but it quickly collapsed for lack of popular support. However, a few years later, Mr Basner achieved his political ambition by getting himself elected a senator to 'represent' one of the African constituencies in the Cape. In this role, Senator Basner and four other European ex-Communists organized a small propaganda group called the Socialist Party. That, too, soon collapsed.

Despite the confusion created by the disruptive activities of the Communists on the one side, and the defection of the African National Congress on the other, the All-African Convention continued to rally the Africans for united action. This was no easy task as many of the leaders of the African National Congress had become members of the African Representative Council, and resented the criticism of the All-African Convention as 'collaborators' of Hertzog. In retaliation, they withdrew the Congress from affiliation to the Convention. However, a reconciliation took place before the second election to the dummy Native Representative Council, by which time even the most conservative Africans serving on it had come to realize that it was just a waste of time. Even the handsome salary could no longer induce them to continue membership, as they were being completely discredited before their people.

To try and retrieve its declining prestige, the leadership of the African National Congress was changed. The Rev Z. R. Mahabane was replaced in 1940 by a prominent fellow-traveller, Dr A. B. Xuma of Johannesburg, for at that time the Stalinist faction in the Congress exercised considerable influence. At the request of Dr Xuma and the new Congress executive, an invitation was sent to the All-African Convention requesting the setting up of a joint three-man co-ordinating committee to re-establish unity between the two organizations. After several protracted meetings, the co-ordinating committee observed that: 'Whereas it would appear that there exists some overlapping of activities and misunderstanding as to the status and position of the two bodies, the All-African Convention and the African National Congress, in the organizational life and activities of the African race, both of which claim to be the co-ordinating body of the different organizations in the country.'

To resolve their differences, the joint committee recommended that:

(1) The two bodies be requested so to amend their constitutions that they will clearly define their respective spheres of labour.

(2) The definitions of their scope should as far as possible be on the following lines:

   (a) The African National Congress should confine itself to the political aspirations and constitutional rights of the Africans and to other cognate matters.

   (b) The All-African Convention shall be the co-ordinating and consultative committee of African organizations dealing with social, educational, economic, political and industrial matters.

   (c) Wherever possible the representation of affiliated national organizations on the consultative committee shall be president, chairman and secretary of such organizations.

(3) Except in special circumstances, organizations of a mainly local character shall not be eligible to the All-African Convention.

With their functions clearly defined, the way was now open

for unity among the Bantus on a nation-wide basis. Such
hope was, however, soon dashed by the intervention of the
Communists. While arrangements were going on to bring
about the final organizational merger between the All-African
Convention and the African National Congress, the Communist elements within the African National Congress succeeded in persuading Dr Xuma to get his organization to
join them in forming an Anti-Pass Committee. Dr Xuma was
made chairman of a working committee, set up in 1943,
which was packed with fellow-travellers under the guidance
of an Indian Communist, Dr Dadoo, who was put on as
deputy chairman. The purpose of this Anti-Pass Committee
was to win a mass African following for those who were opposed to the unity movement sponsored by the All-African
Convention. The Communists hoped to gain such adherence
by sponsoring a nation-wide campaign against the pass laws
which bore so heavily on the Africans.

The scheme proved a fiasco, although the campaign at
first showed signs of gaining popularity, 'for the carrying of
passes had always been a source of bitter resentment among
the Africans. Desperate with the desire to rid themselves of
this badge of slavery, they were ready to clutch at anything
if it held out such a promise. Conferences were held in the
various provinces, rallying them to the anti-pass slogans; dates
were fixed in advance for the great pass-burning day. Then,
as enthusiasm mounted, the day was postponed. A few people
in isolated locations burned their passes, and paid the penalty.
The movement as such, being deserted by the leadership,
had dwindled away'.[33]

As a result, the membership of the party decreased, many
Africans in it deserting, as they felt they had been let down.
The Anti-Pass Committee was wound up, and the All-African
Convention then took the initiative in forming the Non-
European Unity Movement, in conjunction with the Anti-
Coloured Advisory Department Movement. The latter organ-
ization was formed by some left-wing elements among the
Coloured (mixed blood) teachers and other intellectuals of
the Cape, in opposition to the Coloured Advisory Department

[33] I. B. Tabata: *The Awakening of a People*, pp. 125-26.

(later rechristened Coloured Affairs Council). This was a body sponsored by the Government to look after the welfare of the mixed-blood population, with much the same functions as the Native Representative Council for the Bantu Africans.

With the appearance of the Anti-Coloured Advisory Department Movement, a new element entered into non-European politics, giving rise to an ideological conflict. Until that time, non-European politics had been characterized largely by a conflict of personalities rather than of ideologies; but the composition of the Anti-Coloured Advisory Department Movement changed that. Its membership, composed largely of Cape Coloured radicals, adhered to the Trotskyite school of Communism, while the Transvaal Communists who supported the African National Congress belonged to the Stalinist school. To complicate matters further, the leaders of the Indian National Congress, representing the third largest non-European community, were also Stalinists.

The non-European Unity Movement launched under the auspices of the All-African Convention departed radically from the earlier campaigns of the Convention by making its appeal not only to Africans but also to the Coloured and Indians for common action against European domination. Such a united front had long been advocated by Professor N. G. Ranga, a prominent member of the Congress Party and disciple of Mahatma Gandhi and later expounded in his book: *The Colonial and Coloured Peoples' Front*. But conservative Hindu leaders of the Indian National Congress, who represented mercantile and business interests, rejected a united front with the Africans and Coloured on the grounds of class. The rich Indians were hoping that with the support of the New Delhi Government they would come to a compromise agreement with the South African Government to protect their properties and commercial interests under the Pegging Act, which circumscribed the rights of Indian traders in Natal. The attitude of the Indian capitalists provoked a conflict between them and the working-class Indian elements within the Congress led by two Stalinist Communists, Dr Yousef M. Dadoo and Dr G. M. Naiker. They used the Anti-Segregation Council, a party front organization, to oust the reactionaries from control of the Congress executive. However, no sooner had the Communist faction gained control, under the pretence of promoting unity with the Africans and Coloured nationalists, than the two Indian doctors broke off relations with the Non-European Unity Movement and the All-African Convention. That was in 1947, by which time the cold war between Russia and the West had crystallized and the Communist Party adjusted its line to conform with the new change in Soviet foreign policy.

Under instructions from their party executive, Dr Dadoo and Dr Naiker, now in full control of the Natal and Transvaal sections of the Indian Congress, formed a pact with Dr Xuma, who controlled the Transvaal section of the African National Congress, and established an *ad hoc* organization with the long-winded title of The Transvaal-Orange Free State Votes for All Assembly, which was to embrace 'all men and women of goodwill of all races—Europeans and non-Europeans'. This Communist manœuvre was immediately denounced by the left-wing youth section of the African National Congress, and Dr Xuma and his Indian Communist friends had to drop the project before it got under way.

This, however, was not the first time that the Indian Communists had made use of Dr Xuma to advance the sectional interests of the Indian community. For instance, when General Smuts enacted the Asiatic Land Tenure and Indian Representation Bill, designed to segregate the Indians in Natal in just the same way as General Hertzog had segregated and disenfranchised the Africans ten years before, the Indian capitalists appealed to the Government of India for support in opposing the ghetto laws. Socialist Congress leaders in India, especially Nehru, wisely advised the South African Indians to form an alliance with the Africans, since both communities suffered from similar racial disabilities. This advice was rejected by the wealthy Indians in Natal, who provided the main financial backing for the South African Indian Congress. They were hoping that with the Indian Government's support they would be able to force General Smuts to convene a round table conference to discuss matters with them. To facilitate such a compromise, the capitalist Indians, mostly

Moslems, formed a separate body called the South African Indian Organization to promote their vested interests.

When these attempts at compromise came to nothing the radicals in control of the South African Indian Congress launched a passive resistance campaign and at the same time sent a delegation to the United Nations. To secure support for their cause, Dr Xuma, who was then president of the African National Congress, was invited to join the Indian Congress delegation, headed by Dr Dadoo. That was how the first pact between the three doctors (Dadoo, Naiker and Xuma) came about. By keeping certain influential leaders of the African National Congress in tow, the Communists have been able to make use of these Africans when they needed to put over some policy in which they were specially interested. That is why the Stalinists have always opposed unity between the African National Congress and the All-African Convention under the ægis of the Non-European Unity Movement. The realization of such an alliance would upset their 'divide and control' tactics, a fact which has not escaped comment. As Mr Tabata, one of the leading personalities of the All-African Convention remarks: 'It has long been the Communist Party line either to control or to kill an organization. It cannot tolerate a movement or organization which is not dominated by itself. Every time there is political excitement over some oppressive measure, the Communist Party is the first to set up a hue and cry against it. They do not call upon the existing organization of the non-Europeans to fight the issue. They either organize the people around the Communist Party itself or set up an *ad hoc* body or committee in which their own men play a leading part; when the campaign comes to an end they dissolve the *ad hoc* body— but with a few new recruits to the credit of the Communist Party. It is true that disillusionment comes to these recruits in the course of time, but the point is that the people's organizations themselves are not allowed to develop because they are not allowed to fight the issue under their own banner and hence grow into a permanent independent force. In other words, the people are kept defenceless so that when the next onslaught takes place the Communist Party can always appear as their champion. At all times the Communist

Party gets hold of one or other of the leaders of the non-Europeans and uses him as a decoy.'[34]

The same manœuvre has been applied among Negroes in Britain since the end of the Second World War. By means of infiltration tactics, the Communists have captured and wrecked the League of Coloured Peoples, founded in 1931 by the late Dr Harold Moody, a distinguished Jamaican, as well as the London branch of the Caribbean Labour Congress founded in 1946 by West Indian residents in London.

Since 1948, the political situation in South Africa has changed radically for the worse. The Malan Government, committed to a policy of extreme racialism and anti-Communism, has forced the Communist Party into liquidation under the Suppression of Communism Act. This piece of vicious legislation gives the Minister of Justice the authority to define Communism as any form of opposition or criticism of the Government. Any person designated a Communist can be restricted in his activities and movement. There is no right of appeal to a court of law. The penalty for advocating 'Communism' as defined by the Minister is ten years imprisonment with hard labour.

Apart from anti-Communism, the Malanites have imposed tighter restrictions upon all sections of the non-European population by means of a series of legislative enactments. The Natives Representation Council was abolished. This ended the long drawn-out wrangle between the African National Congress and the All-African Convention over the question of boycotting this advisory council. Inter-marriage between Europeans and non-Europeans has been made illegal. The various racial communities have been zoned off under the Group Areas Act and Asiatic Pegging Act, which applied especially to the Indians of Natal.

The Government also proposes to victimize the Cape Coloured voters, until now the step-children of the Europeans, by removing them from the common voters' roll and giving them separate representation on the same principle as the Bantu Africans.

Although the Malan Government has outraged all three

[34] I. B. Tabata: *The Awakening of a People*, p. 37 (Cape Town).

non-European communities, who together constitute the overwhelming majority of the nation, the non-Europeans have
not been able to offer effective opposition, due to the fratri-
cidal conflicts between the non-European organizations and
leaders. Having rejected the conception of a united front
based upon the Ten Point Programme drawn up by the Non-
European Unity Movement, the African National Congress
and the Indian National Congress set up their own separate
ad hoc committee to campaign against Malan's fascist racial
laws. But since a number of the most influential leaders of
these organizations follow a Stalinist political line, while the
leftish Cape Coloured leaders of the Anti-C.A.D. organization, the main backer of the Non-European Unity Movement,
reflect Trotskyist tendencies, ideological barriers have come
between the political *élite* of the three races—Africans, Indians and Coloured. These intellectuals are the greatest hair-
splitters in Africa!

Instead of uniting before the common enemy—*Apartheid*
—the non-European political leaders spend their time and
energies debating the various ideological brands of Communism—Stalinism and Trotskyism—while the masses are left
leaderless. After the failure of the 1952 Anti-Pass campaign
(despite great sacrifices on the part of the African population) the differences between the two ideological camps became even greater. The Cape Coloured Trotskyites, mostly
teachers, accused the African and Indian Stalinists of 'betraying' the Non-European Unity Movement and its Ten
Point Programme. Despite the ever-increasing repressiveness
of Strydom, Malan's successor, towards all sections of the non-
Europeans, the leaders show no indication of resolving their
sectarianism and forging unity among themselves. The latest
Stalinist manœuvre is the setting up of another *ad hoc* organization in 1955 called the Congress of Peoples, to draw up
a 'Charter of Freedom' to present to the Strydom Government. This body has been sponsored by fellow-travellers in
control of sections of the African National Congress, the
Indian National Congress and the Coloured People's Organization, as well as the so-called Congress of Democrats, composed of a couple of dozen Europeans—liberals and former
members of the disbanded Communist Party. In the name of

unity, the Communist sponsors of the Congress of Peoples
are simply helping to maintain disunity among the non-
Europeans by creating the impression among these oppressed
people that salvation will come from outside their own ranks.
Amidst the confusion and organizational disunity, the South
African Government continues to oppress the Africans with
impunity. Even the little education hitherto provided by the
missionaries is being curtailed. In future, Africans are to be
trained under direct state control to become docile 'hewers
of wood and drawers of water' for the white 'master race'.

COLONIAL PRESSURE GROUPS

Apart from what they have done in South Africa, the
Communists have also tried to spread confusion among the
political parties and trade unions in Jamaica, British Guiana,
Barbados, Trinidad, Gold Coast, Nigeria, Sierra Leone,
Sudan, and other politically awakened territories. That is why
the British Communist Party, with all its revolutionary
phrase-mongering is not a constructive, but a disruptive, influence upon emerging colonial liberation movements. In
fact, even its sincerity may be questioned, for its general
secretary has, in his own words, repudiated the charges of
the Tories that the British Communists seek to destroy what
remains of the Empire. Reporting to the second conference
of Commonwealth Communist Parties meeting in London on
April 21st-23rd, 1954, Mr Harry Pollitt said that 'The
enemies of Communism declare that the Communist Party,
by underhand, subversive means, is aiming at the destruction
of Britain and the British Empire. This is a lie. On the contrary, it is precisely the Tories and the Labour leaders who
are doing this by their policy of armed repression and colonial exploitation.' Claiming that his party is more capable
than the Tories and the Labour leaders to maintain Britain
as a great power, Mr Pollitt went on to explain that only by
the application of the Communist colonial policy of handing
over sovereignty to governments freely chosen by the peoples,
'can Britain be assured of the normal supplies of the vital

food and raw materials necessary for her economic life, obtaining them in equal exchange for the products of British industry, needed by those countries for their economic development'.[35]

This kind of double-talk of watch-dogging for British capitalism on the one hand and liquidating the Empire on the other, does little to deceive the British Tories, who, in a recent pamphlet published by the Conservative Commonwealth Council, maintain that: 'The most thorough-going anti-colonialism here or anywhere else is naturally to be found in Communist doctrine and propaganda.'[36]

The Communists, however, are not the only British anti-colonialists whom the Tories consider to be 'enemies' of the Empire. For them, even more dangerous is the Socialist-inspired Movement for Colonial Freedom, which has the support of over sixty Labour Party M.P.s and other well-known non-Communists. The objects of this movement are to support:

(1) The rights of colonial peoples to independence (self-government and self-determination) and of all peoples to freedom from external economic or military domination.

(2) The application throughout the world of the principle of 'fair shares for all', by extending to under-developed territories economic aid free from exploitation or external ownership.

(3) The application of the Four Freedoms and the Declaration of Human Rights to all peoples, including contempt for the abolition of the colour bar.

(4) Technical assistance to educational and economic advance in the under-developed territories, particularly to the Trade Union and Co-operative Movements.

(5) The substitution of internationalism for imperialism in all economic and political relations, including action through the United Nations.

Unlike the Communist Party, the Movement for Colonial

---

[35] *Allies for Freedom*, pp. 127-28. Report on Second Conference of Communist Parties in the Commonwealth—1955.

[36] *Colonial Rule—Enemies and Obligations*—Conservative Commonwealth Council, 1955.

Freedom enjoys one great advantage. It does not have to trim its sails to every Soviet breeze, and can therefore be consistent in policy. The Communists on the other hand, are absolutely unreliable. They support the colonial struggle only when it fits into Soviet foreign policy.

The chairman of the Movement for Colonial Freedom is Mr Fenner Brockway, M.P., whom the Tories describe as a 'veteran agitator', with Mr Anthony Wedgwood Benn, M.P. (Lord Stansgate's son and heir), as treasurer, and Mr Douglas Rogers, former editor of the *Socialist Leader*, as secretary.

Africans have so many 'friends' today that it is well to recall those who championed their cause at a time when it was not considered so fashionable to denounce Colonialism and Racialism. We think of pioneers like J. A. Hobson, H. W. Nevinson, E. D. Morel, H. N. Brailsford, John Harris, Roger Casement, Lady Kathleen Simon, McGregor Ross, Norman Leys, Leonard Woolf, Emrys Hughes, Ethel Mannin, Sylvia Pankhurst, Jimmy Maxton, Rev Conrad Noel, Harold Laski, William Mellor, Canon John Collins, Charles Roden Buxton, Leonard Barnes, Stafford Cripps, Lord Olivier, H. G. Wells, Fenner Brockway, Leslie Hale, Michael Scott, Dorothy Woodman, Reginald Sorensen, A. Creech Jones, Arthur Carr, Reginald Reynolds, J. F. Horrabin, F. A. Ridley, Reginald Bridgeman, W. W. Greenidge, Richard Acland, Nancy Cunard, and others. One may not always have agreed with what they said and wrote, but no African could doubt their sincerity and goodwill. From what I know of colonial students in Britain and America, few university professors have had a greater influence on their political development than Professor Harold J. Laski of London School of Economics and Political Science and Professor Ralph J. Bunche[37] head of Howard University department of Political Science, although both of these teachers are too modest to claim such a distinction.

Since the Second World War, and the emergence of Black Nationalism as a force to be reckoned with, all kinds of groups have appeared in Britain to carry on the work of these early champions of the Africans. These organizations are vying hard to take direction of the politically-conscious leadership, while

[37] Dr Bunche who is the first Negro Nobel Prize Winner is now Assistant Secretary-General of the United Nations.

the Africans, appreciative though they may be of such gestures of goodwill, have passed the stage where they are willing to accept any form of European tutelage.

To the right of the Movement for Colonial Freedom are a number of British organizations and pressure groups specializing in colonial affairs. Among the best known are the Fabian Colonial Bureau, the Africa Bureau, the Anti-Slavery Society, Racial Unity, and Christian Action. Both main parties—Conservative and Labour—maintain Commonwealth departments, which operate, without any formal compact, a more or less bi-partisan colonial policy. The Liberals, on the other hand, are often out of step with the official policies of their opponents, even to the point of being accused by the Tories of rocking the imperial boat by projecting 'their old libertarian dogmas into the colonial sphere' and preaching 'immediate emancipation somewhat indiscriminately'.[38]

Operating outside the purely political sphere is Moral Re-Armament (M.R.A.). Since the outbreak of the cold war, this organization has emerged as the most formidable challenger to the Communists in the colonial field. Because of its financial resources and its distribution of lavish entertainment and seductive propaganda, M.R.A. is the only organization active among coloured colonials in Britain which has been able to make headway against Communist infiltration in Africa. Where these two rival movements get their money from is anybody's guess. The Communists assert that M.R.A. is financed by capitalists, while the Moral Re-Armers allege that the Communists get their funds from Moscow. Whoever is providing the money, there seems to be plenty available to both movements; and African fellow-travellers are having the time of their lives junketing on both sides of the Iron Curtain as guests of Communists and Moral Re-Armers.

Claiming to have the only ideology which can 'save Africa from Communism', an M.R.A. Task Force toured West Africa in 1953 to propagate the 'Four Absolutes' of its American founder, Dr Frank Buchman: 'Absolute honesty', 'absolute unselfishness', 'absolute purity', and 'absolute love'. These anti-Communist crusaders seem to have had a tremendous

[38] See *Colonial Rule—Enemies and Obligations*, p. 4, published by the Conservative Party—1955.

success in Nigeria, where they enticed into their net prominent personalities like Dr Nnamdi Azikiwe, the Prime Minister of Eastern Nigeria; Mr Mbonu Ojike, Minister of Works, Eastern Government; Mr Abubakar Tafawa Balewa, Muslim Minister of Transport in the Federal Government; Mr Kola Balogun, Minister without Portfolio; Mr T. Mbu, Minister of Labour; Mr Mohammadu Ribadu, Minister of Lands, Mines and Power; Mr Inuwa Wada, Minister without Portfolio. In addition to these top-ranking politicians, M.R.A. has captured the following influential Nigerian tribal rulers: the Oni of Ife; the Alake of Abeokuta; Chief Baba Isale Oba of Lagos; Chief Ona Ishokun of Oyo; Chief Obaseki of Benin; as well as Sir Kofo Abayomi; Mr Akimelu Obiesesan, president of the Co-operative Union in Yorubaland. In 1954, these chiefs joined with ten Ministers in the Eastern Government to form an All-Nigerian Moral Re-Armament Movement, whose main object is to combat Communism and save Africa for the West.

While M.R.A. has not been as successful among the politicians in the Gold Coast, its 'Task Force' succeeded in enrolling some prominent Ashanti chiefs and the influential Tolon Na, president of the Northern Territories Council of Chiefs.

'Moral Re-Armament is doing for Africa what Abraham Lincoln did for America', asserted Chief Tolon, who is one of the leaders of the Northern People's Party, the official Opposition which is threatening to split the unity of the Gold Coast in the name of 'federalism'. 'This ideology is pregnant with hope and promise that it deserves acceptance throughout the Negro World', declared a manifesto signed by coloured delegates to the World Assembly for M.R.A. meeting at Mackinoc in Lake Michigan in 1954.

Since M.R.A. set out to capture the blacks, dozens of 'converts' have been flown to Caux, its palatial headquarters in Switzerland overlooking Lake Geneva, to be 'inducted' by Dr Buchman and to undergo a course of indoctrination. Before returning to their countries to carry on propaganda, these Negro emissaries of Buchmanism are encouraged to confess their 'sins' and record a message of inspiration to the black world. Talking like a tired business man enjoying a quiet holiday, Dr Azikiwe described the million dollar mansion at

Caux 'as an island of peace in a sea of discord'. In his pamphlet, *Spiritual Rebirth for Africa*,[39] the Eastern Nigerian Prime Minister tells the full story of his 'conversion' to Buchmanism.

Striking a more bellicose note, Mr Nelson Uko, founder and first president of the Eastern Nigerian Ex-Servicemen's Association confessed that in 1949: 'We were ready for revolution, but our leader (Dr Azikiwe) went to Caux and found a better answer.' Another militant African nationalist, Dr William Nkomo, founder and first president of the African National Congress Youth League of South Africa, called Caux a place 'where every nation is welcomed to the family of nations. I saw something greater than nationalism at work. I saw an ideology which is superior because it is for everyone, everywhere.' He added his belief that 'this is the one road which will be best for my people and for South Africa. It is God's gift to a world confined and divided by hate.' How much more useful it would be if M.R.A. could use their influence to convert the European racialists in Africa!

Similar sentiments on the influence of M.R.A. on the lives of Africans have been recorded by Mr Goodwin Lewanika, founder and first president of the African National Congress of Northern Rhodesia; the Ashanti Paramount Chief Kwasi Afrani III of Ejisu, who promised Dr Buchman to abolish 'landlordism' in his state by distributing 4,000 acres of royal lands to his landless subjects for cultivation.[40] Striking a real spiritual pose, another Gold Coast African, Mr Isaac Kumah, vice-president of the Trades Union Congress of that colony, declared that 'God built the world on a moral plan and gave man the will to continue rebuilding. But because of selfish nations the world is today being destroyed. Together we are responsible to rebuild the world.'

The Communists have not been inactive in the face of this challenge by M.R.A. Unable to operate as openly as their rival, they have been carrying on in an underground way.

[39] Published by M.R.A., Hays Mews, London, W.1.
[40] See *Colour*, January 1955; also distributed by M.R.A. This chief was arrested and charged with the alleged murder by shooting of a C.P.P. political opponent at a party rally in Ashanti in May 1955. He was acquitted.

Their two media have been the African trade unions associated with the W.F.T.U. and the colonial students' organizations in contact with the Communist-controlled World Federation of Democratic Youth (W.F.D.Y.) in Budapest, and the International Union of Students (I.U.S.) with headquarters in Prague, where many West African youths have gone for indoctrination.

Following the disclosure of Communist infiltration to bring about a constitutional breakdown like that in British Guiana, the Federal Council of Ministers and Regional Governments of Nigeria announced that African Communists whose names had been handed over to the authorities by one of their number who had been won over to M.R.A., would be debarred from employment in certain sensitive branches of the public services. Among the departments listed are the police, political administration, railways, posts and telegraphs, civil aviation, labour, education and broadcasting.

Warned that unless certain Africans who had studied in Iron Curtain countries were purged from the trade unions and political parties, the British Government might have to take drastic constitutional action to combat Communism in Nigeria, the African Ministers agreed to issue the following statement on October 14, 1954:

'After careful examination of the situation in Nigeria and in other countries, particularly those in the British Commonwealth which are on the threshold of self-government or have recently become self-governing territories, the Council of Ministers has reached the conclusion that steps are necessary to prevent the infiltration of active Communists into posts in the service of the country in which divided loyalty might be dangerous to the interest of Nigeria.

'The first loyalty of a Communist lies not to Nigeria, but to a foreign Communist organization, the objective of which is the political, economic, and social subjugation of Nigeria. The Governments of Nigeria are therefore of the opinion that persons who are indoctrinated with Communism should not be permitted to occupy posts in the service of Government in which it is possible for them to further the ends of the organization to which they owe allegiance.

'In taking this step the sole desire of the federal and

regional Governments is to safeguard the country from insidious attack by outside organizations whose purposes are hostile to Nigerian aspirations, that is the attainment of free, self-governing nationhood within the British Commonwealth of Nations.

'The Federal and Regional Governments also take this opportunity of inviting the attention of trade unions, public corporations (particularly those engaged in public utilities and the maintenance of essential services), and other important bodies which have a vital part to play in the national life, to the danger in which they stand from Communist infiltration.'

Most Nigerians were surprised to learn that their Governments had unearthed sufficient information on underground Communist activities to make it necessary to take such drastic precautionary measures to protect the public services from being undermined. Until then, nothing seems to be known of the actual Communist strength but it is suggested that there is a small hard core within the labour movement. Recently the railway workers' union appointed a secretary who had been trained in Prague and Moscow, but he has since resigned. The unions themselves a few months later openly denounced Communism. Whatever Communist activities there are exist only behind the scenes or underground.[41]

Since then, many Nigerians, especially students in England who were flirting with the British Communist Party, are reported to have resigned their membership. Some have gone over to M.R.A.; others, whose names will not be mentioned, have taken up appointments in Government service in 'non-sensitive' departments. The defection has caused a crisis within the ranks of the Nigerian fellow-travellers. But this wholesale desertion should cause no surprise to the Russians. For the unreliability of the colonial petty bourgeoisie had been noted by the Sixth Congress of the Communist International as far back as 1928. The Congress resolution on the vacillation of colonial intellectuals stated that:

'Experience has shown that, in the majority of colonial and semi-colonial countries, an important if not predominant part

[41] *The Times*, October 15, 1954.

of the Party ranks in the first stage of the movement is recruited from the petty-bourgeoisie, very frequently students.
It not uncommonly happens that these elements enter the
Party because they see in it the most decisive enemy of imperialism, at the same time not sufficiently understanding that
the Communist Party is not only the Party of struggle against
imperialist exploitation . . . but struggle against all kinds of
exploitation and expropriation. Many of these adherents of
the Party, in the course of the revolutionary struggle will
reach a proletarian class point of view, another part will find
it more difficult to free themselves to the end, from moods,
waverings and half-hearted ideology of the petty bourgeoisie.'[42]

Whether or not the West African Governments acted
wisely in dealing with their native Communists, it is not for
me to say. As a socialist and democrat, I would say that I am
in principle opposed to any official interference with freedom
of expression, however much I may disagree with the view expressed, providing it does not incite to violence and conforms
to normal standards of public decency. Too often, however,
colonial Communists behave in such an irresponsible way as
to give their political opponents the impression that they are
more interested in promoting the foreign policies of the Soviet
Union than in advancing the national liberation of their own
dependent countries. This is the main psychological reason for
conflict between colonial Communists and colonial nationalists, even when they agree on fundamental programmes of
national reconstruction and economic development. And it is
precisely because these pseudo-revolutionaries are looked
upon by their compatriots as being unpatriotic that the African Ministers asserted: 'The first loyalty of a Communist lies
not to Nigeria, but to a foreign Communist organization, the
objective of which is the political, economic and social sub-
servience of Nigeria.'

This attitude of putting the interest of a foreign power first
and that of one's own country last is most unlike that of Russian Communists. They are the most patriotic and nationalist-
minded people, to the extent that the Soviet leaders dis-

[42] Report on the Sixth World Congress of the Communist International—Revolutionary Movements in the Colonies and Semi-
Colonies—1928.

carded Marx and Engels—both Germans—when Hitler invaded their country, and fought the Nazi invaders in the name of 'Holy Russia'. They even invoked the spirits of such Czarist patriots as Prince Alexander Nevsky, Prince Suvarov and Field Marshal Kutuzov, who were no more Communist than Sir Winston Churchill. For although these men were reactionaries according to Marxist standards, they were Russian patriots who placed the love of country foremost. That is why Stalin respected them. Until African Communists learn to love their country in the same way that their Russian comrades love Russia, they deserve to be treated with contempt by their fellow-countrymen.

Despite the precautionary measures of the West African Governments, Communism, in my opinion, is no immediate threat to African national unity. Tribalism, on the other hand, is a present menace. For it can be, and is being exploited by unscrupulous politicians to spread disunity and separatism among the more politically backward sections of the people, and undermine the forces working for national integration. The only force which can combat this danger effectively is Pan-Africanism which advocates the formation of democratically-based nation-wide political parties on a non-tribal, non-regional membership. The best example of such a non-regional, non-tribal organization in Africa today is the Convention People's Party in the Gold Coast.

While it is true that the colonizing European powers did not create Tribalism, they cannot escape the responsibility for keeping it alive. By holding back the industrialization of the colonies, which alone can liberate the Africans from their conservative traditions and prejudices and open up wider vistas, Africa is today facing tremendous difficulties of rapid transition from tribal and feudal society to modern nationhood based on parliamentary democracy.

In order to facilitate easy control of African territories, the early colonial administrators, like Lugard, Cameron and Guggisberg—and still represented by proconsuls like Governor Twining in Tanganyika—actually instituted measures to bolster up and strengthen the tribal structure. Lord Lugard was the first proconsul to elevate the system of chieftancy rule into a *rationale*, known as Indirect Rule or Native Administration. It is only now, when the common people have become politically conscious and demand a voice in their own affairs, that enlightened present-day administrators are becoming aware of the terrible legacy of tribalistic and feudalistic administrations which has been handed on to them. These administrators, like Sir Charles Arden-Clarke in the Gold Coast, are beginning to realize that the political democracy and economic development to which the nationally-awakened masses aspire cannot be carried out within the existing anachronistic tribal structure. Sir Andrew Cohen's failure to recognize this was the fundamental cause of the Buganda crisis which led to the deposition of Kabaka Mutesa II in 1953. Apart from the collectivistic land tenure system and communal forms of village labour, the tribal mores and customs of African societies are too static to generate of themselves the dynamism necessary to modernization and progress.

The traditional African way of life needs a cataclysm to free it from its own decay. It is the newly emancipated younger generation of Africans with a detribalized outlook, who, under the stimulus of Western political ideas and technocracy, alone can bring about the necessary regeneration. But these young reformers are up against the traditionalists who have a vested interest in maintaining their autocratic powers. Instead of trying to adjust themselves as constitutional rulers to the new democratic demands of their people, most of the older chiefs (this is less so among the progressive and younger educated ones like the Kabaka) are often encouraged and supported by Tory-minded expatriate officials, and disgruntled middle-class 'been-tos'.[43] Like the autocratic chiefs, they resent the passing of power to the common people, men without patronage, who have made their way to the top through their own exertions. This cleavage has assumed

[43] The term 'been-to' is applied to African intellectuals who have been to Britain for university or professional training, to distinguish them from those who have received their education locally. The older generation of 'been-tos' consider themselves the *élite*, since they once constituted the only ones educated abroad. It is only since the end of the Second World War that thousands of students from the poorer classes have been able to study abroad on Government scholarships or through other forms of public assistance.

a form of 'class conflict' between the self-made men and the so-called aristocrats and accounts for much of the present tension to be observed in many African territories which are passing through rapid political transition. This transition from internal self-government to independence has brought into the open many concealed antagonisms in African traditional society and is in many ways the most difficult period in the evolution to independence. It calls for confidence, tolerance and trust on all sides. Also involved are the expatriate officials as well as the colonial ministers, who are responsible for making policies which the official civil servants are expected to execute loyally. Friction and misunderstanding between them is bound to arise from time to time. For unless political power is used to liberate the African masses from their state of abject poverty, ignorance and disease, self-government is meaningless. And since African politicians are under constant pressure from those who elected them to fulfil the economic and social aspirations of their people, they are often impatient to get things done. The expatriate officials, on the other hand, are under no such pressures, since they are not elected, and therefore tend to move at a more leisurely pace than their ministers. Yet, however painful the birth-pangs of progress may be, once a colony has taken the plunge along the road to self-government and self-determination, there can be no turning back.

What then, can be done by the progressive forces in Britain to smooth over the transition? Africa needs today a new type of missionary. There are enough of the purely evangelical sort engaged on saving souls. What is badly wanted is the 'know-how' missionaries—men and women with technical knowledge and skills who are willing to go out and help the Africans to save their bodies and minds from the ravages of disease and superstition, and help to raise their standards of living.

In this new field of human endeavour, the British Co-operative and Trade Union movements, as well as humanitarians like the Society of Friends or Quakers, could make a most valuable contribution. But African political leaders will also have to play their part. They must teach their people to trust and respect those who come to their countries, not as *masters* but as friends and co-workers in a humanitarian cause.

The task of developing backward countries emerging from primitive colonial conditions to civilized standards involves a two-way traffic. Those who give their knowledge must be made to feel that their services are welcome and appreciated. On the other hand, white folk who want to help Africa must be prepared to work *with* Africans on the basis of complete racial equality. For racial arrogance and colour bars are greater obstacles to peace and co-operation in Africa than Communism.

In this connection of aid to Africa, if America, the 'foremost champion and defender of the free world' is really worried about Communism taking root in Africa and wants to prevent such a calamity from taking place, I can offer an insurance against it. This insurance will not only forestall Communism, but endear the people of the great North American Republic for ever to the Africans. Instead of underwriting the discredited system of Colonialism by bolstering up the European regimes, especially in North, Central and South Africa, with military and financial aid, let American statesmen make a bold gesture to the Africans in the spirit of the anti-Colonialist tradition of 1776.

This gesture should take the form of a Marshall Aid programme for Africa. Having regard, moreover, to the fact that millions of Africans were taken from the Guinea coast during the period of the Slave Trade and their labour used to lay the foundations of the fabulous wealth of the Republic, what could be a finer way of making restitution for past wrongs inflicted upon Africa than for the U.S. Congress to construct the Volta River project in the Gold Coast—the first African country to achieve independence in the twentieth century, the 'Century of the Common Man'? Such a free national gift without strings from America would achieve more than all the propaganda in the world to cement the bonds of eternal friendship between a grateful African people and a generous American nation. Already Russia is offering such aid to Egypt and Sudan; India and Burma.

Africans have lived so long on promises. What they want to see are a few concrete deeds. They are tired of listening to pious sermons about 'democracy' and 'freedom' while the chains of servitude still hang around their necks. Africans, too, want to live as human beings and enjoy with white folk some of the material benefits of modern civilization.

I shall not attempt to sketch any economic and social blue prints for bringing civilized amenities to Africans. Development plans cannot be drawn up *in vacuo*, but must reflect the concrete situation and needs in each territory—and Africa is a vast continent. Moreover, there are enough plans already in existence in the form of official reports and recommendations of commissions to make a start. The latest is the Royal Commission Report on East Africa. Yet plans are not enough. What is equally important is the removal of *fear* among Africans that plans, however attractive on paper, are not for their welfare, but for other people's benefit. Only with the removal of fear can *confidence* be established and the *goodwill* of Africans ensured. For without their goodwill and co-operation, as post-war events in the Gold Coast and Nigeria have demonstrated, even the best economic and social plans cannot work.

Once confidence, trust and mutual respect is established between African leaders and their European advisers, there is nothing to prevent the rapid economic and social advancement of Africa. It is a continent of great potentialities. In planning its welfare and development certain basic principles should be observed. For example, the main sector of the national economy should be State controlled, since there is not enough local capital available to undertake large scale enterprises. But the rest should be left to private initiative. The Africans must be encouraged to do things for themselves and not just sit back and expect Government to do everything for them. The emphasis must be upon *Self-Help*. In undertakings sponsored by the Government, they must not be managed by civil servants, but should be operated through statutory bodies which must enjoy the maximum amount of freedom from bureaucratic control. History is moving fast and Africa can no longer afford to remain what the French call *le musée vivant*. Land should be controlled and made available to the rural populations engaged in agriculture. Africans must never surrender their communal land tenure system in favour of landlordism—the great curse of Asia. The co-operative movement must be encouraged, strengthened and extended to embrace the greatest number of primary producers. Measures must also be taken to develop the consumers' co-operative movement among the wage-workers and lower paid salaried employees. Trade Unionism and the Four Freedoms—freedom of assembly, press, speech and worship—must be guaranteed by law. And last but not least, African leaders must encourage social discipline, civic responsibility and honesty among themselves and the people, who must be made to realize that democracy can only succeed to the extent that the voters elect honest and incorruptible rulers. Much of the Communists' strength in Asia lies in the fact that they have been able to offer the people honest government in China and Viet-minh—even if it is sometimes oppressive.

Old-fashioned paternalistic government planning will make no appeal to politically-awakened Africans. They must be able to take a part in the control of the plans by representation on the various committees and boards. To win the trust and confidence of Africans, the Colonial Office must push on with constitutional advance even at the risk of temporary set-backs. At present there is too much hesitation and double-talk in official quarters. For example, while the Colonial Office pays lip service to the principle that Uganda is to be regarded as 'primarily an African State', the Governor has proceeded to draft a constitution that will introduce the menace of communalism into the body politic by giving a few thousand Europeans and Indian immigrants who do not consider themselves citizens of Uganda, communal representation in the Legislative Assembly and Executive Council that no community of African immigrants in Britain or India would dare to demand. Is this how the confidence of Ugandans is to be won? If so, the Colonial Office is going to be faced with constitutional crises and political deadlocks for a long time to come. Africans are no longer asleep. They are becoming increasingly conscious of their rights to be rulers of their own countries. So Britain may as well face up to the problem and not wait until it has to be solved by violence. That is the great mistake that France is making throughout her empire, and losing the friendship of her subjects as a consequence. The French bourgeoisie, like the Bourbons, 'learn nothing and forget nothing'. They will only leave Africa when they suffer a series of disasters there like Dien-Bien-Phu.

Again I repeat, Communism is no immediate threat to Africa. If ever the Africans turn to Communism it will be due to the stupidity of the white settlers. What the majority of Africans know about Communism is what their imperialist rulers have told them of the red bogey. Even the handful of West African intellectuals claiming to be Communists are of a kind that orthodox Marxists would find it difficult to recognize as true disciples of Marx, Lenin and Stalin. The word 'Communist' is just a term of abuse, used loosely by Europeans and reactionary black politicians to smear militant nationalists whose views they dislike. There is hardly a colonial leader worth his salt who at some time or another has not been branded a 'dangerous Communist agitator'. For example, Dr Nkrumah was so designated by a former Labour Under-Secretary of State for Colonies in the House of Commons when the agitation for self-government in the Gold Coast started in 1948. Today, the Gold Coast Prime Minister is hailed as a democratic socialist and the foremost statesman in black Africa by other Labour politicians.

As long as the African leaders remain true to the people, they have nothing to fear but fear. Destiny is in their own hands. For already they have the powerful moral support of the Asian-African Conference, which declared that 'Colonialism in all its manifestation is an evil which should speedily be brought to an end . . . That the subjection of peoples to alien subjugation, domination and exploitation constitute a denial of fundamental human rights is contrary to the Charter of the United Nations and is an impediment to the promotion of world peace and co-operation.'[44]

In our struggle for national freedom, human dignity and social redemption, Pan-Africanism offers an ideological alternative to Communism on the one side and Tribalism on the other. It rejects both white racialism and black chauvinism. It stands for racial co-existence on the basis of absolute equality and respect for human personality.

[44] See Appendix V. Declaration of Problems of Dependent Peoples —Official Communiqué of Asian-African Conference—Bandung—April 24, 1955.

Pan-Africanism looks above the narrow confines of class, race, tribe and religion. In other words, it wants equal opportunity for all. Talent to be rewarded on the basis of merit. Its vision stretches beyond the limited frontiers of the nation-state. Its perspective embraces the federation of regional self-governing countries and their ultimate amalgamation into a *United States of Africa*.

In such a Commonwealth, all men, regardless of tribe, race, colour or creed, shall be free and equal. And all the national units comprising the regional federations shall be autonomous in all matters regional, yet united in all matters of common interest to the African Union. This is our vision of the Africa of Tomorrow—the goal of Pan-Africanism.

APPENDIX I

LIBERIAN DECLARATION OF INDEPENDENCE

PREAMBLE

We, the representatives of the people of the Commonwealth of Liberia, in convention assembled, invested with authority for forming a new government, relying upon the aid and protection of the Great Arbiter of human events, do hereby in the name and on behalf of the people of this commonwealth publish and declare the said commonwealth a FREE, SOVEREIGN AND INDEPENDENT STATE, by the name and style of the REPUBLIC OF LIBERIA.

CAUSES LEADING TO COLONIZATION AND INDEPENDENCE

While announcing to the nations of the world the new position which the people of this Republic have felt themselves called upon to assume, courtesy to their opinion seems to demand a brief accompanying statement of the causes which induced them, first to expatriate themselves from the land of their nativity and to form settlements on this barbarous coast, and now to organize their Government by the assumption of a sovereign and independent character. Therefore, we respectfully ask their attention to the following facts:

NATURAL RIGHTS AND GOVERNMENT TO PROTECT THEM

We recognize in all men certain natural and inalienable rights: among these are life, liberty and the right to acquire, possess, enjoy and defend property. By the practice and consent of men in all ages, some system or form of Government is proven to be necessary to exercise, enjoy and secure these rights; and every people has a right to institute a Government and to choose and adopt that system or form of it, which, in their opinion, will most effectually accomplish these objects, and secure their happiness, which does not interfere with the just rights of others. The right, therefore, to institute government and all the powers necessary to conduct it is an inalienable right, and cannot be resisted without the grossest injustice.

DENIAL OF NATURAL RIGHTS IN THE UNITED STATES

We, the people of the Republic of Liberia, were originally the inhabitants of the United States of North America. In some parts of that country, we were debarred by law from all rights and privileges of men; in other parts, public sentiment, more powerful than law, frowned us down. We were everywhere shut out from all civil office. We were excluded from all participation in the Government. We were taxed without our consent. We were compelled to contribute to the resources of a country, which gave us no protection. We were made a separate and distinct class, and against us every avenue to improvement was effectually closed. Strangers from all lands of a color different from ours were preferred before us. We uttered our complaints, but they were unattended to, or met only by alleging the peculiar institution of the country. All hope of a favorable change in our country was thus wholly extinguished in our bosom, and we looked with anxiety abroad for some asylum from the deep degradation.

WEST AFRICA AS A PLACE OF REFUGE

The Western Coast of Africa was the place selected by American benevolence and philanthropy for our future home. Removed beyond those influences which depressed us in our native land, it was hoped we would be enabled to enjoy those rights and privileges and exercise and improve those faculties which the God of nature has given us in common with the rest of mankind. Under the auspices of the American Colonization Society we established ourselves here on land acquired by purchase from the lords of the soil.

SUPERVISION OF THE COLONIZATION
SOCIETY NO LONGER NECESSARY

In an original compact with this Society, we, for important reasons delegated to it certain political powers; while this institution stipulated that whenever the people should become capable of conducting the Government, or whenever the people should desire it, this institution would resign the delegated power, peaceably withdraw its supervision, and leave the people to the government of themselves. Under the auspices and guidance of this institution, which has nobly and in perfect faith redeemed its pledges to the people, we have grown and prospered.

INCREASE OF POPULATION, TERRITORY AND
COMMERCE

From time to time our number has been increased by immigration from America and by accessions from native tribes; and from time to time, as circumstances required it, we have extended our borders by acquisition of land by honorable purchase from the natives of the country. As our territory has extended and our population increased, our commerce has also increased. The flags of most of the civilized nations of the earth float in our harbours, and their merchants are opening an honorable and profitable trade. Until recently these visits have been of a uniformly harmonious character, but as they have become more frequent, and to more numerous points of our extending coast, questions have arisen, which it is supposed can be adjusted only by agreement between sovereign powers.

ASSUMPTION OF GOVERNMENT BY PEOPLE

For years past, the American Colonization Society has virtually withdrawn from all direct and active part in the administration of the Government, except in the appointment of the Governor, who is also a colonist, for the apparent purpose of testing the ability of the people to conduct the affairs of government; and no complaint of crude legislation, nor of mismanagement, nor of maladministration has yet been heard. In view of these facts, this institution, the American Colonization Society, with that good faith which has uniformly marked all its dealings with us, did, by a set of resolutions in

January, in the year of our Lord, one thousand eight hundred and forty-six, dissolve all political connection with the people of this Republic, return the power with which it was delegated, and left the people to the government of themselves. The people of the Republic of Liberia, then, are of right, and in fact, a free, sovereign, and independent State; possessed of all the rights, and powers and functions of government.

RELIANCE ON CONSIDERATION OF THE CIVILIZED WORLD

In assuming the momentous responsibilities of the position they have taken, the people of this Republic feel justified by the necessities of the case, and with this conviction they throw themselves with confidence upon the candid consideration of the civilized world.

NO GREED OF TERRITORY

Liberia is not the offspring of grasping ambition, nor the tool of avaricious speculation. No desire for territorial aggrandisement brought us to these shores; nor do we believe so sordid a motive entered into the high consideration of those who aided us in providing this asylum. Liberia is an asylum from the most grinding oppression.

HOPES ENTERTAINED ON COMING HERE

In coming to the shores of Africa, we indulged the pleasing hope that we should be permitted to exercise and improve those faculties, which impart to man his dignity; to nourish in our hearts the flame of honorable ambition; to cherish and indulge those aspirations, which a beneficent Creator hath implanted in every human heart, and to evince to all who despise, ridicule and oppress our race, that we possess with them a common nature, are with them susceptible of equal refinement, and capable of equal advancement in all that adorns and dignifies man. We were animated with the hope, that here we should be at liberty to train up our children in the way they should go, to inspire them with the love of an honorable fame, to kindle within them the flame of a lofty philanthropy, and to form strong within them the principles of humanity, virtue and religion. Among the strongest motives to leave our native land, to abandon for ever the scene of our childhood, and to sever the most endeared connections, was the desire for a retreat where, free from the agitations of fear and molestation, we could in composure and security approach in worship the God of our fathers.

REALIZATION OF HOPES

Thus far our highest hopes have been realized. Liberia is already the happy home of thousands, who were once the doomed victims of oppression; and if left unmolested to go on with her natural and spontaneous growth; if her movements be left free from the paralyzing intrigues of jealous ambition and unscrupulous avarice, she will throw open a wider and a wider door for thousands, who are now looking with an anxious eye for some land of rest.

COURTS, SCHOOLS AND CHURCHES OPEN TO ALL

Our courts of justice are open equally to the stranger and the citizen for the redress of grievances, for the remedy of injuries, and for the punishment of crime. Our numerous and well-attended schools attest our efforts and our desire for the improvement of our children.

Our churches for the worship of our Creator, everywhere to be seen, bear testimony to our piety and to our acknowledgment of His providence. The Native African, bowing down with us before the altar of the living God, declare that from us, feeble as we are, the light of Christianity has gone forth; while upon that curse of curses, the slave trade, a deadly blight has fallen, as far as our influence extends.

APPEAL TO NATIONS

THEREFORE in the name of humanity, and virtue and religion; in the name of the Great God, our common Creator and our common Judge, we appeal to the nations of Christendom, and earnestly and respectfully ask them, that they will regard us with the sympathy and friendly consideration to which the peculiarities of our condition entitle us, and to extend to us that comity, which marks the friendly intercourse of civilized and independent communities.

APPENDIX II

TEXT OF ORIGINAL LIBERIAN CONSTITUTION WITH AMENDMENTS

PREAMBLE

The end of the institution, maintenance and administration of government is to secure the existence of the body politic, to protect it, and to furnish the individuals, who compose it, with the power of enjoying in safety and tranquillity their natural rights and the blessings of life; and whenever these great objects are not obtained the people have a right to alter the government and to take measures necessary for their safety, prosperity and happiness.

Therefore We, the People of the Commonwealth of Liberia, in Africa, acknowledging with devout gratitude the goodness of God in granting to us the blessings of the Christian Religion, and political, religious, and civil liberty, do in order to secure these blessings for ourselves and our posterity, and to establish justice, insure domestic peace, and promote the general welfare, hereby solemnly associate and constitute ourselves a Free, Sovereign, and Independent State, by the name of the REPUBLIC OF LIBERIA, and do ordain and establish this constitution for the Government of the same.

ARTICLE I

BILL OF RIGHTS

Section 1. All men are born equally free and independent, and have certain natural, inherent and inalienable rights, among which are the rights of enjoying and defending life and liberty, of acquiring, possessing, and protecting property, and of pursuing and obtaining safety and happiness.

Section 2. All power is inherent in the people; all free governments are instituted by their authority and for their benefit, and they have the right to alter and reform the same when their safety and happiness require it.

Section 3. All men have a natural and an inalienable right to worship God according to the dictates of their own consciences, without obstruction or molestation from others; all persons demeaning themselves peaceably, and not obstructing others in their religious worship, are entitled to the protection of law in the free exercise of their own religion, and no sect of Christians shall have exclusive privileges or preference over any other sect, but all shall be alike tolerated, and no religious test whatever shall be required as a qualification for civil office, or the exercise of any civil right.

NO SLAVERY OR DEALING IN SLAVES

Section 4. There shall be no slavery within this Republic; nor shall any citizen of this Republic, or any person resident therein, deal in slaves either within or without this Republic, directly or indirectly.

Section 5. The people have a right at all times, in an orderly and peaceable manner to assemble and consult upon the common good, to instruct their representatives and to petition the Government, or any public functionaries for the redress of grievances.

Section 6. Every person injured shall have remedy therefor by due course of law; justice shall be done without sale, denial or delay; and in all cases, not arising under martial law or upon impeachment, the parties shall have a right to a trial by jury, and to be heard in person, or by counsel, or both.

Section 7. No person shall be held to answer for a capital or infamous crime except in cases of impeachment, cases arising in the army, or navy, and petty offenses, unless upon presentment by a Grand Jury; and every person criminally charged shall have a right to be seasonably furnished with a copy of the charge, to be confronted with the witnesses against him, to have compulsory process for obtaining witnesses in his favor, and to have a speedy, public, and impartial trial by a jury of the vicinity. He shall not be compelled to furnish or give evidence against himself, and no person shall for the same offence be twice put in jeopardy of life or limb.

Section 8. No person shall be deprived of life, liberty, property or privilege, but by the judgment of his peers, or the law of the land.

Section 9. No place shall be searched nor person seized on a criminal charge or suspicion, unless by warrant, lawfully issued upon probable cause, supported by oath or solemn affirmation specially designating the place or person and the object of the search.

Section 10. Excessive bail shall not be required, nor excessive fines imposed, nor excessive punishments inflicted; nor shall the Legislature make any law impairing the obligation of contracts, nor any law rendering any act punishable in any manner in which it was not punishable when it was committed.

Section 11. All elections shall be by ballot, and every male citizen of twenty-one years of age possessing real estate shall have the right of suffrage.

Section 12. The people have a right to keep and to bear arms for the common defence. And as in time of peace armies are dangerous to liberty, they ought not to be maintained without the consent of the Legislature, and the military shall always be held in exact subordination to the civil authority and governed by it.

Section 13. Private property shall not be taken for public use without just compensation.

Section 14. The powers of Government shall be divided into three distinct departments: Legislature, Executive and Judicial, and no person belonging to one of these departments shall exercise any of the powers belonging to either of the others. This section is not to be construed to include Justices of the Peace.

Section 15. The Liberty of the Press is essential to the security of freedom in a State; it ought not, therefore, to be restrained in this Republic. The printing press shall be free to every person, who undertakes to examine the proceedings of the Legislature, or any branch of Government, and no law shall ever be made to restrain the rights thereof. The free communication of thoughts and opinions is one of the invaluable rights of man and every citizen may freely speak, write and print on any subject being responsible for the abuse of that liberty. In prosecutions for the publication of papers investigating the official conduct of officers, or men in a public capacity, or where the matter published is proper for public information, the truth thereof may be given in evidence. And in all indictments for libel, the jury shall have a right to determine the law and the facts under the direction of the court as in other cases.

Section 16. No subsidy, charge, impost, or duties ought to be established, fixed, laid or levied under any pretext whatsoever, without the consent of the people or their representatives in the Legislature.

Section 17. Suits may be brought against the Republic in such manner and in such cases as the Legislature may by law direct.

Section 18. No person can in any case be subject to martial law, or to any penalties or pains by virtue of that law, except those employed in the army or navy, and except the militia in actual service, but by the authority of the Legislature.

Section 19. In order to prevent those who are vested with authority from becoming oppressors, the people have a right at such periods and in such manner as they shall establish by their frame of government, to cause their public officers to return to private life, and to fill up vacant places by certain and regular elections and appointments.

Section 20. That all prisoners shall be bailable by sufficient sureties, unless for capital offences, when the proof is evident or presumption great; and the privilege and benefit of the writ of *habeas corpus* shall be enjoyed in this Republic, in the most free, easy, cheap, expeditious, and ample manner, and shall not be suspended by the Legislature except upon the most urgent and pressing occasions, and for a limited time not exceeding twelve months.

ARTICLE II

LEGISLATIVE POWERS

Section 1. The Legislative power shall be vested in a Legislature of Liberia, and shall consist of two separate branches: a House of Representatives, and a Senate, to be styled the Legislature of Liberia, each of which shall have a negative on the other; and the enacting style of their acts and laws shall be 'It is enacted by the Senate and House of Representatives of the Republic of Liberia in Legislature Assembled.'

Section 2. The representatives shall be elected by and for the inhabitants of the several counties of Liberia, and shall be apportioned among the several counties of Liberia as follows: The County of Montserrado shall have four representatives, the County of Grand Bassa shall have three, and the County of Sinoe shall have one,[1] and all counties hereafter which shall be admitted into the Republic shall have one representative, and for every ten thousand inhabitants one representative shall be added. No person shall be a representative,

[1] Amended, May, 1849, to read: 'three representatives'; and further amended, May, 1861, to read: 'and the County of Maryland shall have three representatives'.

who has not resided in the county for two whole years previous to his election, and who shall not when elected be an inhabitant of the county and does not own real estate of not less value than one hundred and fifty dollars in the county in which he resides, and who shall not have attained the age of twenty-three years. The Representatives shall be elected biennially and shall serve two years from the time of their election.[2]

Section 3. When a vacancy occurs in the representation of any county by death, resignation, or otherwise, it shall be filled by a new election.

Section 4. The House of Representatives shall elect its own Speaker and other officers; it shall also have the sole power of impeachment.

Section 5. The Senate shall consist of two members from Montserrado County, two from Bassa County, two from Sinoe County, and two from each county which may be hereafter incorporated into this Republic. No person shall be a Senator, who shall not have resided three whole years immediately previous to his election in the Republic of Liberia, and who shall not when elected be an inhabitant of the county which he represents, and who does not own real estate of not less than two hundred dollars in the county, which he represents, and who shall not have attained the age of twenty-five years. The Senator for each county who shall have the highest number of votes shall retain his seat four years and the one who shall have the next highest number of votes two years and all who are afterwards elected to fill their seats shall remain in office four years.[3]

Section 6. The Senate shall try all impeachments; the Senators being first sworn or solemnly affirmed to try the same impartially and according to law, and no person shall be convicted but by the concurrence of two-thirds of the Senators present. Judgment in such cases shall not extend beyond removal from office and disqualification to hold an office in the Republic; but the party may still be tried at law for the same offence. When either the President or Vice President is to be tried the Chief Justice shall preside.

Section 7. It shall be the duty of the Legislature as soon as conveniently may be after the adoption of this constitution, and once at

[2] Amended, May, 1907, to read: 'The representatives shall be elected quadrennially, and shall serve for four years from the time of their election.'

[3] Amended, May, 1907, to read: 'The Senators shall serve for six years and shall be elected quadrennially, and those elected in A.D. 1905 shall retain their SEATS for six years from the time of their election, and all who are otherwise elected shall serve for six years'.

least in every ten years afterwards to cause a true census to be taken
of each town and county of the Republic of Liberia; and a representative should be allowed every town having a population of ten
thousand inhabitants, and for every additional ten thousand in the
counties after the first census one representative shall be added to
that county until the number of representatives shall amount to
thirty, afterwards one representative shall be added for every thirty
thousand.

Section 8. Each branch of the Legislature shall be judge of the
election returns and qualifications of its own members. A majority
of each shall be necessary to transact business, but a less number may
adjourn from day to day and compel the attendance of absent members. Each House may adopt its own rules of proceedings, enforce
order, and with the concurrence of two-thirds may expel a member.

Section 9. Neither house shall adjourn for more than two days
without the consent of the other, and both houses shall always sit
in the same town.

Section 10. Every bill or resolution, which shall have passed both
branches of the Legislature, shall before it become a law be laid before the President for his approval; If he approves it, he shall sign it,
if not he shall return it to the Legislature with his objections; If the
Legislature shall afterwards pass the bill or resolution by a vote of
two-thirds in each branch it shall become law. If the President shall
neglect to return such bill or resolutions to the Legislature with his
objections for five days after the same shall have been so laid before
him, the Legislature remaining in session during that time, such
neglect shall be equivalent to his signature.

Section 11. The Senators and Representatives shall receive from
the Republic a compensation for their services to be ascertained by
law, and shall be privileged from arrest, except for treason, felony or
breach of the Peace while attending at, going to, or returning from
the session of the Legislature.

ARTICLE III

EXECUTIVE POWERS

Section 1. The Supreme Executive Power shall be vested in a
President, who shall be elected by the people and shall hold his office
for the term of two years.[4] He shall be Commander-in-Chief of the

[4] Amended, May, 1909, to read: 'Four years and be elected quadrennially'.

army and navy; he shall in the recess of the Legislature have power to call out the militia or any portion thereof into actual service in the defence of the Republic; he shall have power to make treaties, provided that the Senate concur therein by a vote of two-thirds of the Senators present; he shall nominate and with the advice and consent of the Senate appoint and commission all Ambassadors and other public Ministers and Consuls, Secretaries of State, of War, of the Navy, and of the Treasury; Attorney-General, all Judges of Courts, Sheriffs, Coroners, Marshals, Justices of the Peace, Clerks of Courts, Registrars, Notaries Public, and all other officers of State, civil and military, whose appointment may not be otherwise provided for by the constitution, or by standing law; and in the recess of the Senate he may fill any vacancies in those offices until the next session of the Senate. He shall receive all ambassadors and other public ministers; he shall take care that the laws be faithfully executed; he shall inform the Legislature from time to time of the condition of the Republic, and recommend any public measures for their adoption, which he may think expedient; he may after conviction remit any public forfeitures and penalties, and grant reprieves and pardons for public offences except in cases of impeachment; he may require information and advice from any public officer touching matters pertaining to his office; he may adjourn the two houses whenever they cannot agree as to the time of adjournment.

Section 2. There shall be a Vice President who shall be elected in the same manner and for the same term as that of the President, and whose qualifications shall be the same; he shall be President of the Senate, and give the casting vote when the house is equally divided on any subject; and in case of the removal of the President from office or his death, resignation or inability to discharge the powers and duties of the said office, the same shall devolve on the Vice President, and the Legislature may by law provide for the cases of removal, death, resignation, or inability both of the President and Vice President, declaring what officer shall then act as President, and such officer shall act accordingly until the disability be removed or a President shall be elected.[5]

Section 3. The Secretary of State shall keep the records of the State and all the records and papers of the Legislative body and all other public records and documents not belonging to any other de-

[5] Amended, May, 1907. The addendum reads: 'That when a vacancy occurs in the office of Vice President by his death, resignation or otherwise after any regular election of President or Vice President, the President shall immediately call a special election to fill said vacancy'.

partment and shall lay the same when required before the President or Legislature. He shall attend upon them when required and perform such other duties as may be enjoined by law.

Section 4. The Secretary of the Treasury or other persons who may by law be charged with the custody of the public moneys shall before he receive such moneys give bonds to the State with sufficient security for the acceptance of the Legislature for the faithful discharge of his trust. He shall exhibit a true account of such moneys when required by the President or Legislature and no moneys shall be drawn from the Treasury but by warrant of the President in consequence of appropriation made by law.

Section 5. All Ambassadors and other public Ministers and Consuls, the Secretary of State, of War, of the Treasury, of the Navy, the Attorney General and Postmaster General shall hold their office during the pleasure of the President. All Justices of the Peace, Sheriffs, Coroners, Marshals, Clerks of Courts, Registrars, and Notaries Public shall hold their offices for the term of two years from the date of their respective commissions, but may be removed from office within that time by the President at his pleasure; and all other officers whose term of office may not be otherwise limited by law shall hold their offices during the pleasure of the President.

Section 6. Every civil officer may be removed from office by impeachment for official misconduct. Every such officer may also be removed by the President upon the address of both branches of the Legislature stating the particular reason for his removal.

Section 7. No person shall be eligible to the office of President, who has not been a citizen of this Republic for at least five years; and who shall not have attained the age of thirty-five years, and who is not possessed of unencumbered real estate to the value of six hundred dollars.

Section 8. The President shall at stated times receive for his services a compensation which shall neither be increased nor diminished during the period for which he shall have been elected; and before he enters upon the execution of his office he shall take the following oath or affirmation:

'I do solemnly swear (or affirm) that I will faithfully execute the office of President of the Republic of Liberia, and will to the best of my ability preserve, protect, and defend the Constitution and enforce the laws of the Republic of Liberia.'

ARTICLE IV

JUDICIAL DEPARTMENT

Section 1. The judicial power of the Republic shall be invested in one Supreme Court and such subordinate courts as the Legislature may from time to time establish. The Judges of the Supreme Court and all other judges of courts shall hold their office during good behaviour, but may be removed by the President on the address of two-thirds of both houses for that purpose or by impeachment, or conviction thereon. The judges shall have salaries established by law, which may be increased but not diminished during their continuance in office. They shall not receive other perquisite or emoluments whatever from parties or others on account of any duty required of them.

Section 2. The Supreme Court shall have original jurisdiction in all cases affecting ambassadors or other public ministers and consuls, and those to which a county shall be a party. In all other cases the Supreme Court shall have appellate jurisdiction both as to law and fact with such exceptions and under such regulations as the Legislature shall from time to time make.[6]

ARTICLE V

MISCELLANEOUS PROVISIONS

Section 1. All laws now in force in the Commonwealth of Liberia and not repugnant to this Constitution, shall be in force as the laws of the Republic of Liberia until they shall be repealed by the Legislature.

Section 2. All judges, magistrates, and other officers now concerned in the administration of justice in the Commonwealth of Liberia, and all other existing civil and military officers therein shall continue to hold and discharge the duties of their respective offices in the name and by the authority of the Republic until others shall be appointed and commissioned in their stead pursuant to this Constitution.

Section 3. All towns and municipal corporations within the Re-

[6] Amended, May, 1907, to read: 'The judges of the Supreme Court shall be a Chief and two Associate Justices'.

public constituted under the laws of the Commonwealth of Liberia shall retain their existing organizations and privileges, and the respective officers thereof shall remain in office and act under the authority of this Republic in the same manner and with the like powers as they now possess under the laws of the said Commonwealth.

Section 4. The first election of President, Vice President, Senators and Representatives shall be held on the first Tuesday in October in the year of our Lord eighteen hundred and forty-seven in the same manner as the election of members of the Council are held in the Commonwealth of Liberia, and the votes shall be certified and returned to the Colonial Secretary and the result of the election shall be ascertained, posted and notified by him as is now by law provided in case of such members of council.

Section 5. All other elections of President, Vice President, Senators and Representatives shall be held in the Representative towns on the First Tuesday in May in every two years,[7] to be held and regulated in such manner as the Legislature may by law prescribe. The returns of votes shall be made by the Secretary of State, who shall open the same and forthwith issue notices of the election to the persons apparently so elected Senators and Representatives; and all such returns shall be by him laid before the Legislature at its next ensuing session, together with a list of the names of the persons who appear by such returns to have been duly elected Senators and Representatives; and the persons appearing by said returns to be duly elected shall proceed to organize themselves accordingly as the Senate and House of Representatives. The votes for President shall be sorted, counted, and declared by the House of Representatives. And if no person shall appear to have a majority of such votes the Senators and Representatives present shall in convention by joint ballot elect from among the persons having the three highest number of votes a person to act as President for the ensuing term.

Section 6. The Legislature shall assemble once at least every year, and such meeting shall be on the first Monday in January, unless a different day shall be appointed by law.[8]

Section 7. Every Legislator and other officer appointed under this

[7] The amendments, May, 1907, increasing the terms of President and members of the Legislature from two years to four years, and providing for the election quadrennially, necessarily operate as an amendment of this provision.

[8] The Legislature meets annually on the first Monday in December. But by Act passed and approved, February 12th, 1926, the time of meeting shall be 'on the second Monday in October, except the month of October succeeding each quadrennial election, when it shall meet on the second Monday in December'.

constitution shall before he enters upon the duties of his office take and subscribe a solemn oath or affirmation to support the Constitution of this Republic and impartially to discharge the duties of such office. The Presiding officer of the Senate shall administer such oath or affirmation to the President in convention of both houses; and the President shall administer the same to the Vice President, to the Senators and to the Representatives in like manner. When the President is unable to attend the Chief Justice of the Supreme Court may administer the oath or affirmation to him at any place, and also to the Vice President, Senators and Representatives in convention. Other officers may take such oath or affirmation before the President, Chief Justice, or any other person who may be designated by law.

Section 8.   All elections of public officers shall be made by a majority of the votes, except, in cases otherwise regulated by the Constitution or by law.

Section 9.   Offices created by this Constitution which the present circumstances of the Republic do not require that they shall be filled shall not be filled until the Legislature shall deem it necessary.

Section 10.   The property of which a woman may be possessed at the time of her marriage, and also that of which she may afterwards become possessed, otherwise than by her husband, shall not be held responsible for his debts; whether contracted before or after marriage. Nor shall the property thus intended to be secured to the woman be alienated otherwise than by her free and voluntary consent, and such alienation may be made by her either by sale, devise or otherwise.

Section 11.   In all cases in which estates are insolvent, the widow shall be entitled to one third of the real estate during her natural life, and to one third of the personal estate, which she shall hold in her own right subject to alienation by her by devise or otherwise.

Section 12.   No person shall be entitled to hold real estate in this Republic unless he be a citizen of the same. Nevertheless, this article shall not be construed to apply to colonization, missionary, education, or other benevolent institutions so long as the property or estate is applied to its legitimate purpose.

Section 13.   The great object of forming these colonies being to provide a home for the dispersed and oppressed children of Africa, and to regenerate and enlighten this benighted continent, none but persons of color shall be admitted to citizenship in this Republic.[9]

Section 14.   The purchase of any land by any citizen or citizens from the aborigines of this country for his or their own use or for the

[9] Amended, May, 1907, to read: 'None but negroes, or persons of negro descent, shall be eligible to citizenship in this Republic.'

benefit of others in estate or estates in fee simple shall be considered null and void to all intents and purposes.

Section 15. The improvement of the native tribes and their advancement in the arts of agriculture and husbandry being a cherished object of this Government, it shall be the duty of the President to appoint to each county some discreet person, whose duty it shall be to make regular and periodical tours through the country for the purpose of calling the attention of the natives to these wholesome branches of industry and of instructing them in the same; and the Legislature shall as soon as it can conveniently be done make provisions for these purposes by the appropriation of money.

Section 16. The existing regulations of the American Colonization Society in the Commonwealth relative to emigrants shall remain the same in the Republic until regulated by compact between the Society and the Republic; nevertheless, the Legislature shall make no law prohibiting immigration. And it shall be among the first duties of the Legislature to take measures to arrange the future relations between the American Colonization Society and this Republic.

Section 17. This Constitution may be altered whenever two-thirds of both branches of the Legislature shall deem it necessary; in which case the alterations or amendments shall first be considered and approved by the Legislature by the concurrence of two-thirds of the members of each branch and afterwards by them submitted to the people and adopted by two-thirds of all the electors at the next biennial[10] meeting for the election of Senators and Representatives.

Done in convention at Monrovia, in the county of Montserrado, by the unanimous consent of the people of the Commonwealth of Liberia this Twenty-sixth day of July in the year of Our Lord One Thousand Eight hundred and Forty-seven and of the Republic the First. In witness whereof we have hereunto set our names.
Montserrado County:

S. Benedict, President
J. N. Lewis
H. Teage
Beverley R. Wilson
Elijah Johnson
J. B. Gripon
Grand Bassa County:
John Day
A. W. Gardiner

[10] See note 7, p. 371.

Amos Herring
Ephraim Titler
Sinoe County:
R. E. Murry
Jacob W. Prout, Secretary to the Convention

APPENDIX III

DR NKRUMAH'S SPEECH ON THE MOTION FOR INDEPENDENCE[1]

Mr Speaker, I beg to move that this Assembly, in adopting the Government's White Paper on Constitutional Reform, do authorize the Government to request that Her Majesty's Government, as soon as the necessary constitutional and administrative arrangements for independence are made, should introduce an Act of Independence into the United Kingdom Parliament declaring the Gold Coast a sovereign and independent State within the Commonwealth (Hear! Hear! Hear!); and further, that this Assembly do authorize the Government to ask Her Majesty's Government, without prejudice to the above request, to amend as a matter of urgency the Gold Coast (Constitution) Order in Council, 1950, in such a way as to provide *inter alia* that the Legislative Assembly shall be composed of members elected by secret ballot, and that all Members of the Cabinet shall be Members of the Assembly and directly responsible to it. (Hear! Hear! Hear!)

Mr Speaker, it is with great humility that I stand before my countrymen and before the representatives of Britain, to ask this House to give assent to this Motion. In this solemn hour, I am deeply conscious of the grave implications of what we are about to consider and, as the great honour of proposing this Motion has fallen to my lot, I pray God to grant me the wisdom, strength and endurance to do my duty as it should be done. (Hear! Hear! Hear!)

We are called upon to exercise statesmanship of a high order, and I would repeat, if I may, my warning of October, that 'every idle and ill-considered word . . . will militate against the cause which we all

[1] Delivered by Dr Kwame Nkrumah to the Gold Coast Legislative Assembly, July 10, 1953.

have at heart'. It is, as Edmund Burke said some time ago, and I am quoting him here:

> 'Our business carefully to cultivate in our minds, to rear to the most perfect vigour and maturity, every sort of generous and honest feeling that belongs to our nature. To bring the dispositions that are lovely in private life into the service and conduct of the commonwealth, so to be patriots as not to forget we are gentlemen.'

At the outset, I would like to remind Honourable Members of a passage in the White Paper, that 'only after the Legislative Assembly debate will the proposals of this Government take their final shape and be communicated to the United Kingdom Government'. Therefore, let your arguments be cogent and constructive. The range of this debate must be national, not regional; patriotic, not partisan (Hear! Hear! Hear!); and I now ask that a spirit of co-operation and goodwill pervade this debate. It was Aristotle the master who knows who said:

> 'In practical matters the end is not mere speculative knowledge of what is to be done, but rather the doing of it. It is not enough to know about virtue, then, but we must endeavour to possess it, and to use it . . .'.

As with Virtue, so with Self-government; we must endeavour to possess it, and to use it. (Hear! Hear! Hear!) And the Motion which I have prepared is the means to possess it. (Cheers.)

In seeking your mandate, I am asking you to give my Government the power to bring to fruition the longing hopes, the ardent dreams, the fervent aspirations of the Chiefs and people of our country. Throughout a century of alien rule our people have, with ever increasing tendency, looked forward to that bright and glorious day when they shall regain their ancient heritage, and once more take their place rightly as free men in the world. (Hear!—)

Mr Speaker, we have frequent examples to show that there comes a time in the history of all colonial peoples when they must, because of their will to throw off the hampering shackles of Colonialism, boldly assert their God-given right to be free of a foreign ruler. Today, we are here to claim this right to our independence.

Mr Speaker, the Motion is in two parts. The first part not merely states our aim, but poses the question to Her Majesty's Government which is more fully set out in the White Paper. There is a general demand in the Gold Coast for self-government within the Commonwealth, and the United Kingdom Government should be informed of this demand, and be requested to make a declaration recognizing the existence of this demand and expressing Her Majesty's Government's readiness to introduce an Act of Independence. This is the question which we are asking Her Majesty's Government in terms which clearly require an answer. That is the first thing we want; a declaration. But even more important, we want to possess our self-government; we want an Act of Independence.

The second half of the Motion sets out in a straightforward manner to obtain the authority of the House for the presentation to Her Majesty's Government of the detailed proposals which we have made for immediate constitutional reform. We ask that these proposals may be considered on their merits and without prejudice to the request which has been made in the first half of the Motion. We request that the composition of our Assembly may be so amended that all its members shall be directly elected by *secret ballot*. Similarly, we have gone forward to request that the whole Cabinet may be composed of representative Ministers. We have also made other proposals of immediate and striking importance, and I am confident that this Assembly will give the Motion before it its unanimous endorsement and support. (Hear!—)

Last year, I brought this House changes in the Constitution which were, at the time, regarded as of minor importance. I was accused, indeed, of personal ambition in seeking the title of Prime Minister. We can now, Mr. Speaker, see the result for ourselves. (Hear!—) Certainly nobody outside the Gold Coast has regarded my position as anything but what the name implies. The prestige of the Gold Coast Government overseas has, in fact, been enhanced by this change. Even the co-ordination of the functions of my own colleagues has been made more successful by the increase in status. I believe that there is more decision in our activities as a Cabinet than there was before, and that we are better equipped to get things done. The freedom we demand is for our country as a whole—this freedom we are claiming is for our children, for the generations yet unborn, that they may see the light of day and live as men and women with the right to work out the destiny of their own country.

Mr Speaker, our demand for self-government is a just demand. It is a demand admitting of no compromise. The right of a people to govern themselves is a fundamental principle, and to compromise on this principle is to betray it. To quote you a great social and political scientist:

'To negotiate with forces that are hostile on matters of principle means to sacrifice principle itself. Principle is indivisible. It is either wholly kept or wholly sacrificed. The slightest concession on matters of principle infers the abandonment of principle.'

The right of a people to decide their own destiny, to make their way in freedom, is not to be measured by the yardstick of colour or degree of social development. It is an inalienable right of peoples which they are powerless to exercise when forces, stronger than they themselves, by whatever means, for whatever reasons, take this right away from them. If there is to be a criterion of a people's preparedness for self-government, then I say it is their readiness to assume the responsibilities of ruling themselves. (Hear!—) For who but a people themselves can say when they are prepared? How can others judge when that moment has arrived in the destiny of a subject people? What other gauge can there be?

Mr Speaker, never in the history of the world has an alien ruler granted self-rule to a people on a silver platter. Therefore, Mr Speaker, I say that a people's readiness and willingness to assume the responsibilities of self-rule is the single criterion of their preparedness to undertake those responsibilities.

I have described on a previous occasion in this House what were the considerations which led me to agree to the participation of my party in the General Election of 1951, and hence in the Government of the Gold Coast under the terms of the 1950 Constitution Order-in-Council. In making that decision, I took on the task of proving to the world that we were prepared to perform our duties with responsibility, to set in motion the many reforms which our people needed, and to work from within the Government and within the Assembly, that is, by constitutional means, for the immediate aim of self-government. We have only been in office, Mr. Speaker, for two and a half years, and we have kept these objectives constantly before us. Let there be no doubt that we are equally determined not to rest until we have gained them. We are encouraged in our efforts by the thought that in so acting we are showing that we are able to govern ourselves and thereby we are putting an end to the myth that Africans are unable to manage their own affairs, even when given the opportunity. We can never rest satisfied with what we have so far achieved. The Government certainly is not of that mind. Our country has proved that it is more than ready. For despite the legacies of a century of colonial rule, in the short space of time since your Representative Ministers assumed the responsibilities of office, we have addressed ourselves boldly to the task of laying sound economic and social foundations on which this beloved country of ours can raise a *solid democratic society*. This spirit of responsibility and enterprise which has animated our actions in the past two years will continue to guide us in the future, for we shall always act in the spirit of our party's motto: 'Forward ever, backward never.' For we know notwithstanding that the essence of politics is the realization of what is possible.

Mr Speaker, we have now come to the most important stage of our constitutional development; we can look back on the stages through which we have passed during these last few years; first, our discussions with the Secretary of State leading to the changes of last year; then the questions posed in the October statement, which were to be answered by all parties, groups and councils interested in this great issue; the consultations with the Territorial Councils, with the political parties, with the Trade Union Congress. We have proceeded logically and carefully, and as I view it, the country has responded fully to my call. Every representation which we received—and there were many—has received my careful consideration. The talks which I had with the political parties and the Trade Union Congress, and the committees of the Asanteman and Joint Provincial Councils, were frank and cordial.

I had also received a special invitation to attend a meeting in Tamale with the Territorial Council, the Traditional Rulers and the Members of the Legislative Assembly. Naturally, I accepted the invitation, because it was clear that if I had not held discussions with the Northern Territories, the unity of the Gold Coast might have been endangered and our progress towards self-government might have been delayed. The reverse has been the case. (Hear!—) We have adapted some of our proposals to meet Northern Territories wishes, and have been able to set their minds at rest on several issues of the greatest importance, to them, and to the Gold Coast as a whole. Mr Speaker, sir, the days of forgetting about our brothers in the North, and in the Trust Territory are over. (Hear!—)

Criticisms have been levelled against the Government for the secrecy with which these talks were surrounded, and I should like to tell the country why this was necessary. When we went to the talks, of course, the Government members had some idea of the way their collective view on the representations were being formulated. We carefully explained, however, that our views were not finally decided and they would not be until we had had an opportunity of hearing any further views which these bodies might care to express in addition to their memoranda submitted. Having heard these views, we also sought an expression of opinion on specific problems which had occurred to us. But in order that our discussions could be of true value, frank and unreserved, I stated at an early stage that I should be grateful if the conversations could be regarded as strictly confidential. I am glad to

place on record the value of the discussions which we held and the
extent to which the undertaking which I was given was honoured.
(Hear!—) I hope that the bodies which were consulted also feel that
the discussions were worth while.

Mr Speaker, knowing full well, therefore, the will of the Chiefs
and people whom we represent, I am confident that with the support
of this House, Her Majesty's Government will freely accede to our
legitimate and righteous demand to become a self-governing unit
within the Commonwealth.

I put my confidence in the willing acceptance of this demand by
Her Majesty's Government, because it is consistent with the declared
policy of successive United Kingdom Governments. Indeed, the final
transition from the stage of responsible government as a colony to
the independence of a sovereign state guiding its own policies is the
apotheosis of this same British policy in relation to its dependencies.

Mr Speaker, pray allow me to quote from Britain's own Ministers.
Mr Creech Jones, as Colonial Secretary in the first post-war Labour
Government, stated that 'The central purpose of British Colonial
policy is simple. It is to guide the Colonial Territories to responsible
self-government within the Commonwealth in conditions that ensure to the people concerned both a fair standard of living and freedom from oppression from any quarter'.

Again, on 12th July, 1950, in the House of Commons, Mr James
Griffiths, Mr Creech Jones's successor, reiterated this principle: 'The
aim and purpose,' he said, 'is to guide the Colonial Territories to
responsible self-government within the Commonwealth and, to that
end, to assist them to the utmost of our capacity and resources to
establish those economic and social conditions upon which alone
self-government can be soundly based.'

Last, I give you the words of Mr Oliver Lyttelton, Colonial Secretary in Her Majesty's Government of today: 'We all aim at helping
the Colonial Territories to attain self-government within the Commonwealth.'

Nor is this policy anything new in British Colonial history. The
right to self-government of Colonial Dependencies has its origin in
the British North American Act of 1867, which conceded to the
Provinces of Canada complete self-rule. The independence of the
other white Dominions of Australia and New Zealand were followed
by freedom for South Africa. And since the end of the Second World
War, our coloured brothers in Asia have achieved independence, and
we are now proud to be able to acknowledge the sovereign States of
India, Pakistan, Ceylon and Burma.

There is no conflict that I can see between our claim and the professed policy of all parties and governments of the United Kingdom. We have here in our country a stable society. Our economy is healthy, as good as any for a country of our size. In many respects, we are very much better off than many Sovereign States. And our potentialities are large. Our people are fundamentally homogeneous, nor are we plagued with religious and tribal problems. And, above all, we have hardly any colour bar. In fact, the whole democratic tradition of our society precludes the *Herrenvolk* doctrine. The remnants of this doctrine are now an anachronism in our midst and their days are numbered. (Hear!−)

Mr Speaker, we have travelled long distances from the days when our fathers came under alien subjugation to the present time. We stand now at the threshold of self-government and do not waver. The paths have been tortuous, and fraught with peril, but the positive and tactical action we have adopted is leading us to the New Jerusalem, the golden city of our hearts' desire. I am confident, therefore, that I express the wishes and feelings of the Chiefs and people of this country in hoping that the final transfer of power to your Representative Ministers may be done in a spirit of amity and friendship, so that, having peacefully achieved our freedom, the peoples of both countries—Britain, and the Gold Coast—may form a new relationship based on mutual respect, trust and friendship. Thus may the partnership implicit in the Statute of Westminster be clothed in a new meaning. For then shall we be one of the 'autonomous communities within the British Empire, equal in status, in no way subordinate one to another in any aspect of their domestic or external affairs, though united by a common allegiance to the Crown, freely associated as members of the British Commonwealth of Nations', in accordance with the Balfour Declaration of 1926, which was embodied in the Statute of Westminster in 1931.

Today, more than ever before, Britain needs more 'autonomous communities freely associated'. For freely associated communities make better friends than those associated by subjugation. We see today, Mr Speaker, how much easier and friendlier are the bonds between Great Britain and her former dependencies of India, Pakistan and Ceylon. So much of the bitterness that poisoned the relations between these former colonies and the United Kingdom has been absolved by the healing power of a better feeling so that a new friendship has been cemented in the free association of autonomous communities.

These, and other weighty reasons, allied with the avowed aim of British colonial policy will, I am confident, inspire Britain to make manifest once more to a sick and weary world her duty to stand by her professed aim. A free and independent Gold Coast, taking its rightful place in peace and amity by the side of the other Dominions, will provide a valid and effective sign that freedom can be achieved in a climate of goodwill and thereby accrue to the intrinsic strength of the Commonwealth.

The old concepts of Empire, of conquest, domination and exploitation are fast dying in an awakening world. Among the colonial peoples, there is a vast, untapped reservoir of peace and goodwill towards Britain, would she but divest herself of the outmoded, motheaten trappings of two centuries ago, and present herself to her colonial peoples in new and shining vestments and hand us the olive branch of peace and love, and give us a guiding hand in working out our own destinies.

In the very early days of the Christian era, long before England had assumed any importance, long even before her people had united into a nation, our ancestors had attained a great empire, which lasted until the eleventh century, when it fell before the attacks of the Moors of the North. At its height, that empire stretched from Timbuktu to Bamako, and even as far as to the Atlantic. It is said that lawyers and scholars were much respected in that empire, and that the inhabitants of Ghana wore garments of wool, cotton, silk and velvet. There was trade in copper, gold and textile fabrics, and jewels and weapons of gold and silver were carried.

Thus may we take pride in the name of Ghana, not out of romanticism, but as an inspiration for the future. It is right and proper that we should know about our past. For just as the future moves from present so the present has emerged from the past. Nor need we be ashamed of our past. There was much in it of glory. What our ancestors achieved in the context of their contemporary society, gives us confidence that we can create, out of that past, a glorious future, not in terms of war and military pomp, but in terms of social progress and of peace. *For we repudiate war and violence.* Our battle shall be against the old ideas that keep men trammelled in their own greed; against the crass stupidities that breed hatred, fear and inhumanity. The heroes of our future will be those who can lead our people out of the stifling fog of disintegration through serfdom, into the valley of light where purpose, endeavour and determination will create that brotherhood which Christ proclaimed two thousand years ago, and about which so much is said, but so little done.

Mr Speaker, in calling up our past, it is meet, on a historic occasion such as this, to pay tribute to those ancestors of ours who laid our national traditions, and those others who opened the path which made it possible to reach today the great moment at which we stand.

As with our enslaved brothers dragged from these shores to the United States and to the West Indies, throughout our tortuous history, we have not been docile under the heel of the conqueror. Having known by our own traditions and experience the essentiality of unity and of government, we constantly formed ourselves into cohesive blocs as a means of resistance against the alien force within our borders. And so today we recall the birth of the Ashanti nation through Okomfo Anokye and Nana Osei Tutu and the symbolism entrenched in the Golden Stool (Hear!—); the valiant wars against the British, the banishment of Nana Prempah the First to the Seychelles Islands; the temporary disintegration of the nation and its subsequent reunification. And so we come to the Bond of 1844. Following on trade with the early merchant adventurers who came to the Gold Coast, the first formal association of Britain with our country was effected by the famous Bond of 1844, which accorded Britain trading rights in the country. But from these humble beginnings of trade and friendship, Britain assumed political control of this country. But our inalienable right still remains, as my friend, George Padmore, puts in his recent book, *The Gold Coast Revolution*, and I quote, 'When the Gold Coast Africans demand self-government today they are, in consequence, merely asserting their birthright which they never really surrendered to the British who, disregarding their treaty obligations of 1844 gradually usurped full sovereignty over the country.' (Hear!—)

Then the Fanti Confederation. The earliest manifestation of Gold Coast nationalism occurred in 1868 when Fanti Chiefs attempted to form the Fanti Confederation in order to defend themselves against the might of Ashanti and the incipient political encroachments of British merchants. It was also a union of the coastal states for mutual economic and social development. This was declared a dangerous conspiracy with the consequent arrest of its leaders.

Then the Aborigines Right Protection Society was the next nationalist movement to be formed with its excellent aims and objects, and by putting up their titanic fight for which we cannot be sufficiently grateful, formed an unforgettable bastion for the defence of our God-given land and thus preserved our inherent right to freedom. Such men as Mensah-Sarbah, Atto-Ahuma, Sey and Wood have played their role in this great fight. (Hear!—)

Next came the National Congress of British West Africa. The end of the first Great War brought its strains and stresses and the echoes of the allied slogan, 'We fight for Freedom' did not pass unheeded in the ears of Casely Hayford, Hutton-Mills and other national stalwarts who were some of the moving spirits of the National

Congress of British West Africa. But the machinations of imperialism did not take long to smother the dreams of the people concerned, but today their aims and objects are being more than gratified with the appointment of African Judges and other improvements in our national life. (Hear!—)

As with the case of the National Congress of British West Africa, the United Gold Coast Convention was organized at the end of the Second World War to give expression to the people's desire for better conditions. The British Government, seeing the threat to its security here, arrested six members of the Convention, and detained them for several weeks until the Watson Commission came. The stand taken by the Trades Union Congress, the Farmers, Students and Women of the country provides one of the most epic stories in our national struggle.

In June 1949, the Convention People's Party (cheers) with its uncompromising principles led the awakened masses to effectively demand their long lost heritage. And today, the country moves steadily forward to its proud goal.

Going back over the years to the establishment of constitutional development, we find that the first Legislative Council to govern the country was established in 1850; thirty-eight years later the first African in the person of John Sarbah was admitted to that Council. It was not until 1916, that the Clifford Constitution increased the number of Africans which was four in 1910, to six. But these were mainly councils of officials.

The Guggisberg Constitution of 1925 increased the unofficial representation in the council almost at par with the officials. This position was reversed by the Burns Constitution of 1946 which created an unofficial majority. The abortive Colony-Ashanti Collaboration of 1944 was the prelude to this change.

The Coussey Constitution of 1951 further democratized the basis of representation; and now, for the first time in our history, this Government is proposing the establishment of a fully elected Assembly with Ministers directly responsible to it. (Hear!—)

We have experienced Indirect Rule, we have had to labour under the yoke of our own disunity, caused by the puffed-up pride of those who were lucky to enjoy better opportunities in life than their less fortunate brothers; we have experienced the slow and painful progress of constitutional changes by which, from councils on which Africans were either absent or merely nominated, this august House has evolved through the exercise by the enfranchised people of their democratic right to a voice in their own affairs and in so doing they have shown their confidence in their own countrymen by placing on us the responsibility of our country's affairs.

And so through the years, many have been laid to final rest from the stresses and dangers of the national struggle and many, like our illustrious friends of the Opposition who, notwithstanding the fact that we may differ on many points, have also contributed a share to the totality of our struggle. (Cheers.) And we hope that whatever our differences, we shall today become united in the demand for our country's freedom.

As I said earlier, what we ask is not for ourselves on this side of the House, but for all the Chiefs and people of this country—the right to live as free men in the comity of nations. Were not our ancestors ruling themselves before the white man came to these our shores? I have earlier made reference to the ancient history of our more distant forebears in Ghana. To assert that certain people are capable of ruling themselves while others are not yet 'ready', as the saying goes, smacks to me more of imperialism than of reason. Biologists of repute maintain that there is no such thing as a 'superior' race. Men and women are as much products of their environment—geographic, climatic, ethnic, cultural, social—as of instincts and physical heredity. We are determined to change our environment, and we shall advance in like manner.

According to the motto of the valiant *Accra Evening News*, 'We prefer self-government with danger to servitude in tranquillity'. Doubtless we shall make mistakes as have all other nations. We are human beings, and hence fallible. But we can try also to learn from the mistakes of others so that we may avoid the deepest pitfalls into which they have fallen. Moreover, the mistakes we may make will be our own mistakes, and it will be our responsibility to put them right. As long as we are ruled by others we shall lay our mistakes at their door (laughter) and our sense of responsibility will remain dulled. Freedom brings responsibilities, and our experience can be enriched only by the acceptance of these responsibilities.

In the two years of our representative Government, we have become most deeply conscious of the tasks which will devolve upon us with self-rule. But we do not shrink from them; rather are we more than ever anxious to take on the reins of self-government. And this, Mr Speaker, is the mood of the Chiefs and people of this country at this time; on the fundamental choice between colonial status and self-government, we are unanimous. And the vote that will be taken on the Motion before this Assembly will proclaim this to the world.

Honourable Members, you are called, here and now, as a result

of the relentless tide of history, by Nemesis, as it were, to a sacred
charge, for you hold the destiny of our country in your hands. The
eyes and ears of the world are upon you; yea, our oppressed brothers
throughout this vast continent of Africa and the New World are
looking at you with desperate hope, as an inspiration to continue
their grim fight against cruelties which we in this corner of Africa,
have never known! Cruelties which are a disgrace to humanity, and to
civilization which the white man has set himself to teach us! At this
time, history is being made; a colonial people in Africa has put forward the first definite claim for independence. An African colonial
people proclaim that they are ready to assume the stature of free men
and to prove to the world that they are worthy of the trust.

I know that you will not fail those who are listening for the mandate that you will give to your Representative Ministers. For we are
ripe for freedom, and our people will not be denied. They are conscious that the right is theirs, and they know that freedom is not
something that one people can bestow on another as a gift. They
claim it as their own and none can keep it from them.

And while yet we are making our claim for self-government, I want
to emphasize, Mr. Speaker, *that self-government is not an end in
itself.* It is a means to an end, to the building of the good life to the
benefit of all, regardless of tribe, creed, colour or station in life. Our
aim is to make this country a worthy place for all its citizens, a country that will be a shining light throughout the whole continent of
Africa, giving inspiration far beyond its frontiers. And this we can do
by dedicating ourselves to unselfish service to humanity. We must
learn from the mistakes of others so that we may, in so far as we can,
avoid a repetition of those tragedies which have overtaken other human societies.

We must not follow blindly, but must endeavour to create. We
must aspire to lead in the arts of peace. *The foreign policy of our
country must be dedicated to the service of peace and fellowship. We
repudiate the evil doctrines of tribal chauvinism, racial prejudice and
national hatred.* We repudiate these evil ideas because in creating that
brotherhood to which we aspire, we hope to make a reality, within the
bounds of our own small country, of all the grandiose ideologies
which are supposed to form the intangible bonds holding together
the British Commonwealth of Nations in which we hope to remain.
We repudiate racial prejudice and national hatred, because we do not
wish to be a disgrace to these high ideals.

Her Majesty, Queen Elizabeth the Second has just been crowned
—barely one month ago—the memory is still fresh in our minds; the
Queen herself has not forgotten the emotions called forth as she first

felt the weight of the Crown upon her head; the decorations in London streets are hardly down; the millions of words written about the Coronation and its meaning will endure for centuries; the prayers from millions of lips are still fresh; the vows of dedication to duty which the Queen made are a symbol of the duties devolving on the Commonwealth. And so, we repudiate the evil doctrines which we know are promulgated and accepted elsewhere as the truth.

To Britain this is the supreme testing moment in her African relations. When we turn our eyes to the sorry events in South, Central and East Africa, we are cheered by the more cordial relationship that exists between us and Britain. We are now asking Her Majesty to allow that relationship to ripen into golden bonds of freedom, equality and fraternity, by complying without delay to our request for self-government. We are sure that the British Government will demonstrate its goodwill towards the people of the Gold Coast by granting us the self-government which we now so earnestly desire. We enjoin the people of Britain and all political parties to give our request their ardent support.

The self-government which we demand, therefore, is the means by which we shall create the climate in which our people can develop their attributes and express their potentialities to the full. As long as we remain subject to an alien power, too much of our energies is diverted from constructive enterprise. Oppressive forces breed frustration. Imperialism and Colonialism are a two-fold evil. This theme is expressed in the truism that 'no nation which oppresses another can itself be free'. Thus we see that this evil not only wounds the people which is subject, but the dominant nation pays the price in a warping of their finer sensibilities through arrogance and greed. Imperialism and Colonialism are a barrier to true friendship. For the short time since we Africans have had a bigger say in our own affairs, the improved relations between us and the British have been most remarkable. Today there exists the basis of real friendship between us and His Excellency the Governor, Sir Charles Arden-Clarke, and the *ex-officio* Ministers of Defence and External Affairs, of Finance and of Justice. I want to pay tribute to these men for their valuable co-operation in helping us to make a success of our political advance. (Hear!—) I feel that they have done this, firstly because as officers in the British Colonial Service, it is their duty to guide the subject territory in the attainment of self-government in accordance with the expressed aim of British Colonial policy and, secondly, because we have by our efforts in managing our own affairs, gained their respect, and they are conscious of the justice of our aspirations.

Let me recall the words of the great Casely Hayford, which he spoke in 1925:

'It must be recognized that co-operation is the greatest word of the century. With co-operation we can command peace, goodwill and concord. Without; chaos, confusion and ruin. But there can really be no co-operation between inferiors and superiors. Try as they may, there must come a time when the elements of superiority will seek to dictate, and the inferior ones will resent such dictation. It logically follows, therefore, that unless an honest effort is made to raise the inferior up to the prestige of the superior and the latter can suffer it, all our talk of co-operation is as much empty gas . . .'

Unless, therefore, our claim to independence is met now, the amicable relations which at present exist between us and the British may become strained. Our Chiefs and people will brook no delay. But I feel confident that our claim, because of the reasons I have already given, will be accepted and our amity towards Britain will be deepened by our new association.

The strands of history have brought our two countries together. We have provided much material benefit to the British people, and they in turn have taught us many good things. We want to continue to learn from them the best they can give us and we hope that they will find in us qualities worthy of emulation. (Hear!—) In our daily lives, we may lack those material comforts regarded as essential by the standards of the modern world, because so much of our wealth is still locked up in our land; but we have the gifts of laughter and joy, a love of music, a lack of malice, an absence of the desire for vengeance for our wrongs, all things of intrinsic worth in a world sick of injustice, revenge, fear and want.

We feel that there is much the world can learn from those of us who belong to what we might term the pre-technological societies. These are values which we must not sacrifice unheedingly in pursuit of material progress. That is why we say that self-government is not an end in itself.

We have to work hard to evolve new patterns, new social customs, new attitudes to life, so that while we seek the material, cultural and economic advancement of our country, while we raise their standards of life, we shall not sacrifice their fundamental happiness. That, I should say, Mr Speaker, has been the greatest tragedy of Western society since the Industrial Revolution.

In harnessing the forces of nature, man has become the slave of the machine, and of his own greed. If we repeat these mistakes and suffer the consequences which have overtaken those that made them, we shall have no excuse. This is a field of exploration for the young men and women now in our schools and colleges, for our sociologists and economists, for our doctors and social welfare workers, for our engineers and town planners, for our scientists and our philosophers.

Mr Speaker, when we politicians have long passed away and been forgotten, it is upon their shoulders that will fall the responsibility of evolving new forms of social institutions, new economic instruments to help build in our rich and fertile country a society where men and women may live in peace, where hate, strife, envy and greed shall have no place. (Hear!—)

Mr Speaker, but we can only meet the challenge of our age as a free people. Hence our demand for our freedom, for only free men can shape the destinies of their future.

Mr Speaker, Honourable Members, we have great tasks before us. I say, with all seriousness, that it is rarely that human beings have such an opportunity for service to their fellows.

Mr Speaker, for my part, I can only re-echo the words of a great man:

'Man's possession is life, and since it is given him to live but once, he must so live as not to be smeared with the shame of a cowardly existence and trivial past, so live that dying he might say: all my life and all my strength were given to the finest cause in the world —the liberation of mankind.' (Hear! Hear! Hear!)

Mr Speaker, 'Now God be thank'd. Who has match'd us with His Hour!'

APPENDIX IV

EXTRACT FROM THE GOLD COAST (CONSTITUTION) ORDER IN COUNCIL, 1954[1]

At the Court of Saint James, the 29th day of April, 1954.
Present,
Her Majesty Queen Elizabeth The Queen Mother
Her Royal Highness The Princess Margaret
Lord Privy Seal   Mr Selwyn Lloyd
Viscount Simon   Sir Thomas Dugdale
Miss Horsbrugh   Mr Hopkinson

Whereas Her Majesty, in pursuance of the Regency Acts, 1937 to 1953, was pleased, by Letters Patent dated the twentieth day of November, 1953, to delegate to Her Majesty Queen Elizabeth The Queen Mother, Her Royal Highness The Princess Margaret, His Royal Highness The Duke of Gloucester, Her Royal Highness The Princess Royal and the Earl of Harewood, or any two or more of them, as Counsellors of State, full power and authority during the period of Her Majesty's absence from the United Kingdom to summon and hold on Her Majesty's behalf Her Privy Council and to signify thereat Her Majesty's approval of anything for which Her Majesty's approval in Council is required:

Now, therefore, Her Majesty Queen Elizabeth The Queen Mother and Her Royal Highness The Princess Margaret, being authorized thereto by the said Letters Patent, and in pursuance of the powers conferred upon Her Majesty by the British Settlements Act, 1887 and 1945 (a), the Foreign Jurisdiction Act, 1890 (b), and of all other powers in that behalf, do hereby, by and with the advice of Her Majesty's Privy Council, on Her Majesty's behalf order, and it is hereby ordered, as follows:

[1] Statutory Instruments, 1954, No. 551.

[PART I OMITTED]

PART II

THE EXECUTIVE

4. There shall be a Cabinet of Ministers in and for the Gold Coast of not less than eight persons, being Members of the Assembly, appointed from time to time in accordance with the provisions of this Part of this Order.

5.—(1) The Cabinet of Ministers shall be the principal instrument of policy and shall perform such functions and duties, and exercise such powers, as may from time to time be prescribed by or under this Order, any other Orders of Her Majesty in Council or, subject to the provisions of this Order and of any such other Orders, by or under any other law in force in the Gold Coast:

Provided that the Cabinet shall not exercise any powers in relation to the subjects set out in the Second Schedule to this Order.

(2) The Ministers shall be collectively responsible to the Assembly.

6.—(1) The Governor shall exercise all functions conferred upon him by this Order or by any other law in force in the Gold Coast in accordance with any Instructions under Her Majesty's Sign Manual and Signet, and subject thereto—

(a) the Governor shall obtain, and act in accordance with, the advice of the Cabinet in the exercise of all such functions other than functions which he is by this Order or by any such law, as the case may be, directed or empowered to exercise in his discretion or after consultation with, or on the advice or recommendation of, any person or authority other than the Cabinet; and,

(b) where the Governor is by this Order or by any other law in force in the Gold Coast directed to exercise any function on the advice of any person or authority other than the Cabinet, he shall exercise such function in accordance with such advice; and

(c) where the Governor is by this Order or by any other law in force in the Gold Coast directed to exercise any function on the recommendation of any person or authority he shall not exercise that functions except in accordance with such a recommendation, but may accept the recommendation or

refer it back for further consideration by such person or
authority.

(2) Nothing in subsection (1) of this section shall apply to matters for which provision is made by sections 7, 14 and 44 of this
Order.

7.—(1) The Ministers, one of whom shall be styled 'the Prime
Minister', shall be appointed and may be dismissed by the Governor,
by Instrument under the Public Seal.

(2) In the matter of the appointment and dismissal of Ministers the Governor shall, subject to the provisions of section 16 of
this Order, act in accordance with the constitutional convention applicable to the exercise of such function in the United Kingdom by
Her Majesty:

Provided that no act or omission on the part of the Governor
shall be called in question in any Court of law or otherwise on the
ground that the foregoing provisions of this subsection have not
been complied with.

8.—(1) Whenever the office of Prime Minister has become vacant
and a person has been appointed to be Prime Minister in accordance
with the provisions of section 7 of this Order, the offices of all the
other Ministers shall become vacant.

(2) The office of a Minister shall in any case be vacant—

(a) if he shall cease to be a Member of the Assembly, or

(b) if a Minister shall be absent from the Gold Coast without
    written permission given by the Governor acting on the ad-
    vice of the Prime Minister:

Provided that, if a Minister shall cease to be a Member of the
Assembly by reason of a dissolution thereof, he shall not on that
account vacate his ministerial office until such time as the Governor
shall have appointed a Prime Minister in accordance with the provisions of section 7 of this Order.

(3) A Minister may by writing under his hand, addressed to the
Governor, resign his ministerial office, and upon the receipt of such
resignation by the Governor the office of such Minister shall become
vacant.

(4) The Governor may, by Instrument under the Public Seal,
declare a Minister to be by reason of illness temporarily incapable
of discharging his functions as a Minister: and thereupon such Minister shall not discharge any of the functions of his office or sit or
vote in the Cabinet until he is declared in manner aforesaid again
to be capable of discharging his said functions.

9. Every Minister shall, before entering on the duties of his
office, take and subscribe before the Governor the official oath or

make before the Governor the appropriate affirmation in lieu thereof in accordance with the provisions of the Oaths Ordinance or any Ordinance repealing and re-enacting with or without modification, or amending, the provisions of that Ordinance.

10. Ministers shall take precedence amongst themselves, as Her Majesty may specially assign and, if precedence be not so assigned, as follows:

First, the Prime Minister.

Secondly, the other Ministers according to the length of time for which they have been continuously Ministers, Ministers who have been continuously in such office for the same length of time taking precedence according to age.

Any interval between the vacation by a Minister of his office in consequence of a dissolution of the Assembly and the date of his appointment as a Minister upon the first formation of the Cabinet following such dissolution shall not be taken into account in determining the length of time for which a person shall have been continuously a Minister.

11. The Prime Minister shall, so far as is practicable, attend and preside at all meetings of the Cabinet and in the absence of the Prime Minister such Minister as the Prime Minister shall appoint shall preside:

Provided that whenever the Governor attends a special meeting of the Cabinet summoned under the provisions of the proviso to subsection (1) of section 13 of this Order he shall preside thereat.

12. Subject to the provisions of subsection (2) of section 13 of this Order, the Cabinet shall not be disqualified for the transaction of business by reason of any vacancy among the Ministers; and any proceedings of the Cabinet shall be valid notwithstanding that some person who was not entitled to do so sat or voted in the Cabinet or otherwise took part in the proceedings.

13.—(1) The Cabinet shall be summoned by the Prime Minister or, in the absence of the Prime Minister, by such Minister as the Prime Minister shall appoint:

Provided that the Governor, acting in his discretion, may summon and attend a special meeting of the Cabinet whenever he shall think fit.

(2) No business except that of adjournment shall be transacted in the Cabinet if objection is taken by any Minister present that there are less than four Ministers present besides the person presiding.

14. Where any matter is dependent upon the decision of the Cabinet, any decision shall be regarded as the decision of the Cabi-

net if a majority of votes of the persons present and voting is cast in its favour. Ministers shall have an original vote and, if upon any question the votes shall be equally divided, the person presiding may exercise a casting vote.

15. There may be established, by or in pursuance of any Instructions under Her Majesty's Sign Manual and Signet and subject to the provisions of any such Instructions, a Committee of the Cabinet to exercise such functions, in such manner, as may be prescribed by or in pursuance of any such Instructions.

16.—(1) The Prime Minister may by directions in writing—

(a) charge any Minister with the responsibility for any department or subject other than the subjects set out in the Second Schedule to this Order; and

(b) revoke or vary any directions given under this subsection.

(2) The Prime Minister may retain in his charge any department or subject other than the subjects set out in the Second Schedule to this Order.

(3) Responsibility for a department or subject retained by the Prime Minister or assigned to a Minister under this section shall, unless the responsibility does not by its nature relate to Togoland, extend to Togoland under the United Kingdom Trusteeship, but—

(a) the responsibility of the Governor under section 17 of this Order shall not thereby be affected; and

(b) all functions relating to Togoland exercisable by the Prime Minister or other Minister, by virtue of the provisions of this subsection shall, in so far as they affect the responsibility of Her Majesty's Government in the United Kingdom in respect of Togoland by virtue of the Trusteeship Agreement approved by the General Assembly of the United Nations on the thirteenth day of December, 1946, be exercised in accordance with and subject to such directions (if any) as the Governor, acting in his discretion, may address to the Prime Minister or other Minister, as the case may be.

(4) A Minister shall, while charged with the responsibility for any department or subject under the provisions of subsection (1) of this section, be styled a Minister with portfolio.

(5) A Minister who is not charged with responsibility for any department or subject aforesaid, shall be styled a Minister without portfolio.

17. The Governor, acting in his discretion, shall be responsible for the subjects set out in the Second Schedule to this Order, and for matters which affect the responsibility of Her Majesty's Government in the United Kingdom in respect of Togoland under United

Kingdom Trusteeship by virtue of the Trusteeship Agreement approved by the General Assembly of the United Nations on the thirteenth day of December, 1946.

18.—(1) The Attorney General shall be vested with responsibility for the initiation, conduct and discontinuance of prosecutions for criminal offences triable in Courts constituted under the provisions of the Courts Ordinance or any Ordinance repealing and re-enacting with or without modification, or amending, the provisions of that Ordinance.

(2) The assignment to a Minister of responsibility for the department of the Attorney General shall confer responsibility only for submitting to the Cabinet questions referring to that department and conducting Government business relating to that department in the Assembly, and shall have effect without prejudice to the provisions of subsection (1) of this section.

19.—(1) The Governor, acting on the advice of the Prime Minister, may, from among the Members of the Assembly, appoint Ministerial Secretaries to assist the Ministers in the exercise of their ministerial duties and may likewise at any time revoke the appointment of a Ministerial Secretary:

Provided that the number of Ministerial Secretaries shall not at any time exceed the number of Ministers.

(2) Any Ministerial Secretary may at any time resign his office by notice in writing addressed to the Governor, and upon the receipt of such resignation by the Governor the office of such Ministerial Secretary shall become vacant.

(3) No person shall continue to hold the office of Ministerial Secretary if he shall cease to be a Member of the Assembly:

Provided that if a Ministerial Secretary shall cease to be a Member of the Assembly by reason of a dissolution thereof, he shall not on that account vacate his office of Ministerial Secretary until such time as the Governor shall have appointed a Prime Minister in accordance with the provisions of section 7 of this Order.

(4) A person appointed to be a Ministerial Secretary shall, before entering on the duties of his office, take and subscribe before the Governor the official oath or make before the Governor the appropriate affirmations in lieu thereof in accordance with the provisions of the Oaths Ordinance or any Ordinance repealing and re-enacting with or without modification, or amending, the provisions of that Ordinance.

20.—(1) There shall be for each Ministry a Permanent Secretary who shall be a person who is a public officer.

(2) Each Permanent Secretary shall, subject to the general direc-

tion and control of his Minister, exercise supervision over the department or departments for which his Minister is responsible.

(3) For the purposes of this section the department of the Attorney General and the Auditor-General, and the office of the Secretary to the Cabinet and of the Clerk to the Assembly shall be deemed not to be departments of Government.

21.—(1) There shall be a Secretary to the Cabinet who shall be a person who is a public officer.

(2) The Secretary to the Cabinet shall have charge of the Cabinet office and shall, in accordance with such instructions as may be given to him by the Prime Minister, arrange the business for, and keep the minutes of, meetings of the Cabinet, and convey the decisions of the Cabinet to the appropriate person or authority.

(3) The Secretary to the Cabinet shall transmit to the Governor all Cabinet agenda and papers at the same time as he submits such agenda and papers to Ministers and shall transmit to the Governor, immediately following every meeting of the Cabinet, a record of all decisions and conclusions of the Cabinet reached at that meeting.

PART III

TRANSITIONAL PROVISIONS

22. Whenever the Governor shall have occasion, before the commencement of Part II of this Order, to exercise any function conferred upon him by any other part of this Order, then unless the function is one which he is by this Order directed or empowered to exercise in his discretion or in accordance with the advice or on the recommendation of, or after consultation with, any person or authority other than the Cabinet, he shall, in the exercise of the function, consult with the Executive Council constituted under the provisions of the existing Orders in such circumstances and under such conditions as may be prescribed by such provisions of the existing Instructions as may at that time have effect and shall, subject to those provisions of the existing Instructions, act in accordance with the advice of such Executive Council in any matter which he is by this section obliged to consult with such Executive Council.

23. For the avoidance of doubts it is hereby declared that, upon the date of the commencement of Part II of this Order, the appointment of Prime Minister, of other Ministers and of the Governor's Secretary and Secretary to the Executive Council, made under the

provisions of the existing Orders and in force immediately before such commencement, shall determine.

PART IV

LEGISLATIVE ASSEMBLY

24. There shall be a Legislative Assembly in and for the Gold Coast, which shall consist of a Speaker and of one hundred and four Members.

25.—(1) The Speaker shall be a person, not being either the holder of any public office or a Minister or Ministerial Secretary, elected by the Members of the Assembly.

(2) The election of the Speaker shall take place before the despatch of any other business at the first sitting of the Assembly after the date of the commencement of this Part of this Order and thereafter at the first sitting after every dissolution of the Assembly.

(3) A person holding office as Speaker may, by writing under his hand addressed to the Governor, resign the office of Speaker; and upon receipt of such resignation by the Governor the office of Speaker shall become vacant.

(4) A person holding office as Speaker shall, unless he earlier resigns his office, vacate his office on the dissolution of the Assembly.

(5) Whenever the office of Speaker shall become vacant otherwise than as a result of a dissolution of the Assembly, the Assembly shall, at its first sitting after the occurrence of the vacancy, elect another person to be Speaker.

(6) A person shall, if qualified, be eligible for re-election to the office of Speaker from time to time.

26.—(1) The Assembly shall—

(a) at its first sitting in every session, and
(b) at its first sitting after the occurrence of a vacancy in the office of Deputy Speaker,

or as soon thereafter as may be convenient, elect as Deputy Speaker of the Assembly one of its own Members, who shall not be a Minister or Ministerial Secretary.

(2) A person shall, if qualified, be eligible for re-election to the office of Deputy Speaker from time to time.

(3) The Deputy Speaker shall, unless he earlier vacates his office under the provisions of this Order, hold office until some other person is elected a Deputy Speaker under paragraph (a) of subsection (1) of this section.

(4) (*a*) A person shall vacate the office of Deputy Speaker—

(i)   upon ceasing to be a member of the Assembly; or

(ii) upon becoming a Minister or Ministerial Secretary.

(*b*) The Deputy Speaker may by writing under his hand addressed to the Speaker or, in the absence of the Speaker or if there shall be no Speaker, to the Clerk of the Assembly, resign his office; and upon receipt of such resignation by the Speaker or by the Clerk of the Assembly, as the case may be, the office of Deputy Speaker shall become vacant.

27. In any election of a Speaker or a Deputy Speaker the votes of the Members of the Assembly shall be given by ballot in such manner as not to disclose how any particular Member shall have voted.

28.—(1) The Members of the Assembly shall be—

(i)   ninety-seven Rural Members, of whom thirty-nine shall represent rural electoral districts in the Colony other than the Trans-Volta/Togoland Region; thirteen shall represent rural electoral districts in the Trans-Volta/Togoland Region; nineteen shall represent rural electoral districts in Ashanti; and twenty-six shall represent rural electoral districts in the Northern Territories and Northern Togoland; and

(ii) seven Municipal Members of whom three shall represent municipal electoral districts in the municipal area of Accra; one shall represent the electoral district of Cape Coast; two shall represent municipal electoral districts in the municipal area of Kumasi; and one shall represent the municipal electoral district of Sekondi-Takoradi.

(2) Subject to the provisions of this Order, rural and municipal electoral districts shall be defined by, and the Rural and Municipal Members of the Assembly shall be elected in accordance with, provision made under section 49 of the existing Orders or under section 35 of this Order.

29. Subject to the provisions of section 30 of this Order, any person who—

(*a*) is either a British subject or a British protected person; and

(*b*) is of the age of twenty-five years or upwards; and

(*c*) is able to speak and, unless incapacitated by blindness or other physical cause, to read the English language with a degree of proficiency sufficient to enable him to take an active part in the proceedings of the Assembly;

shall be qualified to be elected as a Member of the Assembly, and no other person shall be qualified to be so elected or, having been so elected, shall sit or vote in the Assembly.

30. No person shall be qualified to be elected as a Member of the Assembly who—

(a) is, by virtue of his own act, under any acknowledgment of allegiance, obedience or adherence to a foreign Power or State; or

(b) holds or is acting in any public office; or

(c) holds the office of Speaker; or

(d) is a party to, or a partner in a firm, or a director or manager of a company, which is a party to, any contract with the Government of the Gold Coast for or on account of the public service, and has not, within one month before the day of election, published in the English language in the *Gazette* a notice setting out the nature of such contract, and his interest, or the interest of any such firm or company, therein; or

(e) is an undischarged bankrupt, having been adjudged or otherwise declared bankrupt under any law in force in any part of Her Majesty's dominions; or

(f) being a person possessed of professional qualifications, is disqualified (otherwise than at his own request) in any part of Her Majesty's dominions, from practising his profession by order of any competent authority made in respect of him personally:

Provided that if five years or more have elapsed since the disqualification referred to in this paragraph, the person shall not be disqualified for membership of the Assembly by reason only of the provisions of this paragraph; or

(g) is a person adjudged to be of unsound mind or detained as a criminal lunatic under any law in force in the Gold Coast; or

(h) has, in any part of Her Majesty's dominions, been sentenced to death or to imprisonment (by whatever name called) for a term exceeding twelve months, or has been convicted of any offence involving dishonesty, and has not been granted a free pardon:

Provided that if five years or more have elapsed since the termination of the imprisonment or, in the case of conviction of an offence involving dishonesty in respect of which no sentence of imprisonment has been passed, since the conviction, the person shall not be disqualified from membership of the Assembly by reason only of such sentence or conviction; or

(i) is not qualified to be registered as an elector under the provisions of any law for the time being in force in the Gold Coast; or

(j) is disqualified for election by any law for the time being in force in the Gold Coast by reason of his holding, or acting in, any office the functions of which involve any responsibility for, or in connection with, the conduct of any election, or any responsibility for the compilation or revision of any electoral register; or

(k) is disqualified for membership of the Assembly by any law for the time being in force in the Gold Coast relating to offences connected with elections.

31.—(1) Every Member of the Assembly shall in any case cease to be a Member at the next dissolution of the Assembly after he has been elected or previously thereto if his seat shall become vacant under the provisions of this Order.

(2) The seat of a Member of the Assembly shall become vacant:—

(a) upon his death; or

(b) if he shall be absent from two consecutive meetings of the Assembly, without having obtained from the Speaker, before the termination of either of such meetings, permission to be or to remain absent therefrom; or

(c) if he shall cease to be a British subject, or shall cease to be a British protected person without becoming a British subject; or shall take any oath, or make any declaration or acknowledgment, of allegiance, obedience or adherence to any foreign Power or State; or shall do, concur in or adopt any act done with the intention that he shall become a subject or citizen of any foreign Power or State; or

(d) if he shall be appointed to, or to act in, any public office; or

(e) if he shall be elected to be Speaker; or

(f) if he shall become a party to any contract with the Government of the Gold Coast for or on account of the public service, or if any firm in which he is a partner, or any company of which he is a director or manager, shall become a party to any such contract, or if he shall become a partner in a firm, or a director or manager of a company, which is a party to any such contract:

Provided that, if in the circumstances it shall appear to them to be just so to do, the Assembly may exempt any Member from vacating his seat under the provisions of this paragraph, if such Member shall, before becoming a party to such contract as aforesaid or before, or as soon as practicable after, becoming otherwise interested in such contract (whether as partner in a firm or as director or manager of a company), disclose to the Speaker the nature of such contract and his interest or the interest of any such firm or company therein; or

(g) if he shall be adjudged or otherwise declared bankrupt under any law in force in any part of Her Majesty's dominions; or

(h) if he shall, in any part of Her Majesty's dominions, be sentenced by a court to death or to imprisonment (by whatever name called) for a term exceeding twelve months, or be convicted of any offence involving dishonesty; or

(i) if he shall become subject to any of the disqualifications specified in paragaphs (f), (g), (i), (j) or (k) of section 30 of this Order.

(3) A Member of the Assembly may by writing under his hand addressed to the Speaker, resign his seat in the Assembly, and upon receipt of such resignation by the Speaker or Deputy Speaker the seat of such Member shall become vacant.

(4) Any person whose seat in the Assembly has become vacant may, if qualified, again be elected as a Member of the Assembly from time to time.

32. All questions which may arise as to the right of any person to be or remain a Member of the Assembly shall be referred to and determined by the Supreme Court of the Gold Coast in accordance with the provisions of any law in force in the Gold Coast.

33.—(1) Whenever the seat of a Member of the Assembly becomes vacant under the provisions of subsections (2) or (3) of section 31 of this Order, the Speaker shall, by writing under his hand, report such vacancy to the Governor.

(2) As occasion may require, a report under subsection (1) of this section may be made by the Deputy Speaker.

34. Whenever the seat of a Member of the Assembly becomes vacant an election shall be held to fill the vacancy in accordance with the provisions of this Order.

35. Subject to the provisions of this Order, provision may be made, by or in pursuance of any law enacted under this Order, for the election of Members of the Assembly including (without prejudice to the generality of the foregoing power) the following matters, that is to say—

(a) the qualifications and disqualifications of electors;

(b) the registration of electors;

(c) the ascertainment of the qualifications of electors and of candidates for election;

(d) the division of the Gold Coast into electoral districts for the purposes of elections;

(e) the holding of elections;

(f) the determination of all questions which may arise as to the right of any person to be or remain a Member of the Assembly; and

(g) the definition and trial of offences relating to elections and the imposition of penalties therefor, including disqualification for membership of the Assembly, or for registration as an elector, or for voting at elections, of any person concerned in any such offence.

PART V

LEGISLATION AND PROCEDURE IN ASSEMBLY

36.—(1) Subject to the provisions of this Order, it shall be lawful for the Governor, with the advice and consent of the Assembly, to make laws for the peace, order and good government of the Gold Coast:

Provided that should any such law be repugnant to any provision of the Trusteeship Agreement approved by the General Assembly of the United Nations on the thirteenth day of December, 1946, in respect of Togoland under United Kingdom Trusteeship, such law shall to the extent of such repugnancy, but not otherwise, be void.

(2) No such law shall make persons of any racial community liable to disabilities to which persons of other such communities are not made liable.

(3) Any laws made in contravention of subsection (2) of this section shall to the extent of such contravention, but not otherwise, be void.

37. Subject to the provisions of this Order, the Governor and the Assembly shall, in the transaction of business and the making of laws, conform as nearly as may be to the directions contained in any Instructions under Her Majesty's Sign Manual and Signet which may from time to time be addressed to the Governor in that behalf.

38.—(1) Subject to the provisions of this Order and of any Instructions under Her Majesty's Sign Manual and Signet, the Assembly may from time to time make, amend and revoke Standing Orders for the regulation and orderly conduct of its own proceedings and the despatch of business, and for the passing, intituling and numbering of Bills, and for the presentation thereof to the Governors for assent.

(2) The first Standing Orders of the Assembly shall, subject to the provisions of this Order, be the Standing Orders of the Legislative Assembly constituted under the existing Orders and in force at the time of the revocation of the existing Orders, and may be amended or revoked by the Assembly under subsection (1) of this section.

39. The Speaker, or in his absence the Deputy Speaker, or in their absence a Member of the Assembly (not being a Minister or Ministerial Secretary) elected by the Assembly for the sitting, shall preside at the sittings of the Assembly.

40. The Assembly shall not be disqualified for the transaction of business by reason of any vacancy among the Members thereof, including any vacancy not filled at a General Election; and any proceedings therein shall be valid notwithstanding that some person who was not entitled so to do sat or voted in the Assembly or otherwise took part in the proceedings.

41. No business except that of adjournment shall be transacted in the Assembly if objection is taken by any Member present that there are less than twenty-five Members present besides the Speaker or Member presiding.

42.—(1) Save as otherwise provided in this Order, all questions proposed for decision in the Assembly shall be determined by a majority of the votes of the Members present and voting; and if, upon any question before the Assembly, the votes of the Members shall be equally divided the motion shall be lost.

(2) (a) The Speaker shall have neither an original nor a casting vote; and

(b) any other person, including the Deputy Speaker, shall, when presiding in the Assembly, have an original vote but no casting vote.

43.—(1) Save as is provided in subsections (2), (3) and (6) of this section, and subject to the provision of this Order and of the Standing Orders of the Assembly, any Member may introduce any Bill, or propose any motion for debate in, or may present any petition to, the Assembly, and the same shall be debated and disposed of according to the Standing Orders of the Assembly.

(2) Except with the recommendation or consent of the Governor signified thereto, the Assembly shall not proceed upon any Bill, motion or petition which, in the opinion of the Speaker or Member presiding, would dispose of or charge any public revenue or public funds of the Gold Coast, or revoke or alter any disposition thereof or charge thereon, or impose, alter or repeal any rate, tax or duty.

(3) With respect to a Bill or motion which, in the opinion of the Speaker or of the Attorney-General, would effect any alteration in the salary, allowances or conditions of service of any public officer, or in the law, regulations or practice governing the grant of leave, passages or promotion applicable to any such officer or the payment of pensions, gratuities or other like allowances applicable to any such officer or his widow, children, dependants or personal representatives, the following provisions shall have effect:—

(a) except with the recommendation or consent of the Governor, acting in his discretion, signified thereto, the Assembly shall not proceed upon any such Bill or motion;

(b) if the Governor, acting in his discretion, shall consider that any alteration effected by any such Bill would prejudicially affect any public officer, he shall reserve that Bill for the signification of Her Majesty's pleasure;

(c) unless the Governor, acting in his discretion, shall by writing under his hand otherwise direct, no such motion, other than a motion relating to a Bill, shall take effect until the expiration of a period of three days from the date upon which it shall have been carried; and if the Governor, acting in his discretion, shall within that period certify by writing under his hand that any alteration which would be effected by such motion would prejudicially affect any public officer, such motion shall not take effect unless and until it shall have been approved, in the case of a public officer not in the local service, by a Secretary of State and, in the case of a public officer in the local service, by the Governor, acting in his discretion.

(4) For the purposes of this section, the local service shall consist of such persons as may be determined by or in pursuance of any order made by the Governor, acting in his discretion.

(5) An order made under subsection (4) of this section may be varied or revoked by a subsequent order made in like manner.

(6) Except with the recommendation or consent of the Governor, acting in his discretion, signified thereto, the Assembly shall not proceed upon any Bill or motion which, in the opinion of the Speaker, or the Attorney-General relates to or affects any subject the responsibility for which is vested in the Governor or any matter the responsibility for which is vested in the Attorney-General by virtue of the provisions of sections 17 and 18 of this Order respectively.

(7) The Governor, acting in his discretion, may—

(a) send by message to the Speaker the draft of any Bill or

motion which it appears to him should be introduced or proposed in the Assembly; and

(b) in the same or a later message require that the Bill or motion shall be introduced or proposed not later than a date specified in such message;

and if such requirement is not complied with, the Bill or motion shall be deemed for all purposes to have been introduced or proposed in the Assembly on the date so specified.

44.—(1) Subject to the provisions of subsection (2) of this section, if the Governor shall consider that it is expedient in the interests of public order, public faith or good government (which expressions shall, without prejudice to their generality, include the responsibility of the Gold Coast as a territory within the British Commonwealth of Nations, and all matters pertaining to the creation or abolition of any public office or to the salary or other conditions of service of any public officer) that any Bill introduced, or any motion proposed, in the Assembly should have effect, then, if the Assembly fail to pass such a Bill or motion within such time and in such form as the Governor may think reasonable and expedient, the Governor at any time which he shall think fit, may, notwithstanding any provisions of this Order or of any Standing Orders of the Assembly, declare that such Bill or motion shall have effect as if it had been passed by the Assembly, either in the form in which it was so introduced or proposed or with such amendments as the Governor shall think fit which have been proposed in the Assembly or in any Committee thereof; and thereupon the said Bill or motion shall have effect as if it had been so passed, and, in the case of any such Bill, the provisions of this Order relating to assent to Bills and disallowance of laws shall have effect accordingly.

(2) The Governor shall not make any declaration under this section except in accordance with the following conditions, that is to say:—

(a) the question whether the declaration should be made shall first be submitted in writing by the Governor to the Cabinet and if upon the question being so submitted to it, the Cabinet shall resolve that the declaration be made, the Governor may make the declaration;

(b) if, when the question whether the declaration should be made is submitted to it as aforesaid, the Cabinet shall not within such time as the Governor may think reasonable and expedient resolve that the declaration be made, then—

(i) the Governor may submit the said question to a Secretary of State and may make the declaration if, upon the question being so submitted to him, a Secretary of State authorises the Governor to make the declaration; or

(ii) the Governor may make the declaration without submitting the said question to a Secretary of State, if in the Governor's opinion urgent necessity requires that the declaration be made without obtaining the authority of a Secretary of State; in which case he shall, at the time of making the declaration, certify in writing that urgent necessity requires that the declaration be made without obtaining such authority.

(3) (a) Whenever the Governor, in accordance with the provisions of paragraph (b) of subsection (2) of this section, shall submit to a Secretary of State the question whether a declaration should be made, or shall make a declaration without submitting the said question to a Secretary of State, he shall inform the Cabinet in writing of his reasons for so doing.

(b) Whenever the Governor shall make a declaration under this section, other than a declaration made with the authority of a Secretary of State, he shall forthwith report to a Secretary of State the making of, and the reasons for, the declaration and, in the case of a declaration made in accordance with the provisions of subparagraph (ii) of paragraph (b) of subsection (2) of this section, the grounds of urgency.

(4) If any Member of the Assembly objects to any declaration made under this section, he may, within seven days of the making thereof, submit to the Governor a statement in writing of his reasons for so objecting; and a copy of such statement shall, if furnished by such Member, be forwarded by the Governor as soon as practicable to a Secretary of State.

(5) Any declaration made under this section, other than a declaration relating to a Bill, may be revoked by a Secretary of State, and the Governor shall cause notice of such revocation to be published in the *Gazette*; and from the date of such publication any motion which shall have had effect by virtue of the declaration shall cease to have effect; and the provisions of subsection (2) of sections 38 of the Interpretation Act, 1889, shall apply to such revocation as they apply to the repeal of an Act of Parliament.

45.—(1) No Bill shall become a law until either the Governor shall have assented thereto in Her Majesty's name and on Her Majesty's behalf and shall have signed the same in token of such assent, or Her Majesty shall have given her assent thereto through a Secretary of State.

(2) When a Bill is presented to the Governor for his assent, he shall, acting in his discretion but subject to the provisions of this Order and of any Instructions addressed to him under Her Majesty's Sign Manual and Signet or through a Secretary of State, declare that he assents, or refuses his assent, thereto, or that he reserves the Bill for the signification of Her Majesty's pleasure:

Provided that the Governor shall reserve for the signification of Her Majesty's pleasure—

(a) any Bill by which any provision of this Order is revoked or amended or which is in any way repugnant to, or inconsistent with, the provisions of this Order; and

(b) any Bill which determines or regulates the privileges, immunities or powers of the Assembly or of its Members;

unless he shall have been authorised by a Secretary of State to assent thereto.

(3) A law assented to by the Governor shall come into operation on the date of its publication in the *Gazette*, or, if it shall be enacted either in such law or in some other law (including any law in force on the date of the commencement of this Part of this Order), that it shall come into operation on some other date, on that date.

(4) A Bill reserved for the signification of Her Majesty's pleasure shall become a law so soon as Her Majesty shall have given Her assent thereto through a Secretary of State and the Governor shall have signified such assent by Proclamation published in the *Gazette*. Every such law shall come into operation on the date of such Proclamation or, if it shall be enacted, either in such law or in some other law (including any law in force on the date of the commencement of this Part of this Order), that it shall come into operation on some other date, on that date.

46.—(1) Any law to which the Governor shall have given his assent may be disallowed by Her Majesty through a Secretary of State.

(2) Whenever any law has been disallowed by Her Majesty, the Governor shall cause notice of such disallowance to be published in the *Gazette*.

(3) Every law so disallowed shall cease to have effect as soon as notice of such disallowance shall be published as aforesaid; and thereupon any enactment repealed or amended by, or in pursuance of, the law disallowed shall have effect as if such law had not been made. Subject as aforesaid, the provisions of subsection (2) of section 38 of the Interpretation Act, 1889, shall apply to such disallowance as they apply to the repeal of an Act of Parliament.

47. Except for the purpose of enabling this section to be complied with, no Member of the Assembly shall sit or vote therein until he shall have taken and subscribed before the Assembly the Oath of Allegiance or have made before the Assembly the appropriate affirmation in lieu thereof as provided in the Oaths Ordinance or any Ordinance repealing and re-enacting, with or without modification, or amending, the provision of that Ordinance:

Providing that if, between the time when a person becomes a Member of the Assembly and the time when the Assembly next meets thereafter, a meeting takes place of any Committee of the Assembly of which such person is a member, such person may, in order to enable him to attend the meeting, and take part in the proceedings, of the Committee, take and subscribe the said oath or make the appropriate affirmation before a Judge of the Supreme Court of the Gold Coast; and the taking and subscribing of the oath, or the making of the appropriate affirmation, as the case may be, in such manner shall suffice for all purposes of this section. In any such case the Judge shall forthwith report to the Assembly through the Speaker or, as occasion may require, through the Deputy Speaker that the person in question has taken and subscribed the said oath or made the affirmation before him.

48. It shall be lawful, by laws enacted under this Order, to determine and regulate the privileges, immunities and powers of the Assembly and its Members; but no such privileges, immunities or powers shall exceed those of the Commons' House of Parliament of the United Kingdom or of the Members thereof.

49.—(1) There shall be a session of the Assembly once at least in every year, so that a period of twelve months shall not intervene between the last sitting of the Assembly in one session and the first sitting thereof in the next session.

(2) The first session of the Assembly shall commence within three months after the date of the commencement of this Part of this Order.

(3) The sessions of the Assembly shall be held in such places and shall commence at such times as the Governor may from time to time by Proclamation or notice in the *Gazette* appoint.

50.—(1) The Governor, after consultation with the Prime Minister, may at any time, by Proclamation published in the *Gazette*, prorogue or dissolve the Assembly.

(2) The Governor shall dissolve the Assembly at the expiration of four years from the date of the return of the first writ at the last preceding general election, if it shall not have been sooner dissolved.

51. There shall be a general election at such time within two

months after the date of the commencement of this Part of this Order and thereafter within two months after every dissolution of the Assembly, as the Governor shall by Proclamation published in the *Gazette* appoint.

PART VI

THE PUBLIC SERVICE

52.—(1) The appointment, promotion, transfer, termination of appointment, dismissal and disciplinary control of public officers (other than the Deputy Governor, Judges of the Supreme Court, judicial officers and the Auditor-General) is hereby vested in the Governor acting in his discretion.

(2) The Governor, acting in his discretion, may, by regulations published in the *Gazette*, provide for the delegation to any public officer, subject to such conditions as may be prescribed in any such regulations, of any of the powers vested in the Governor by subsection (1) of this section.

(3) The exercise of his powers under subsection (2) of this section, the Governor shall not delegate to any public officer the power to appoint, promote or transfer to any public office which carries an initial salary exceeding four hundred and thirty pounds *per annum* or to dismiss from or terminate an appointment to any public office which carries a salary exceeding four hundred and thirty pounds *per annum*.

(4) The Governor shall, before exercising the powers conferred upon him by subsection (1) of this section in relation to the appointment or promotion to a special post, consult with the Prime Minister. For the purpose of this subsection the expression "special post" means the post of Permanent Secretary and posts of a corresponding or higher grade in the public service.

(5) The Governor shall, before exercising the power conferred on him by subsection (1) of this section to terminate the appointment of, or dismiss, or inflict any other punishment on, a public officer on the grounds of any act done or omitted to be done by that officer in the exercise of a judicial function conferred upon him, consult with the Judicial Service Commission.

(6) For the purposes of this section the expression "transfer" means a transfer involving an increase of salary.

53.—(1) There shall be, in and for the Gold Coast, a Public Service Commission (hereafter in this Part of this Order referred to as "the Commission") and, subject to the provisions of subsection (3) of this section, the Commission shall consist of such persons as the Governor, after consultation with the Prime Minister, shall appoint.

(2) The Governor, after consultation with the Prime Minister, may terminate the appointment of any member of the Commission and, subject as aforesaid, the members of the Commission shall hold office upon such terms and conditions as may be prescribed by regulations made under section 55 of this Order.

(3) No person shall be appointed as, or shall remain, a member of the Commission if he is or becomes a Member of the Assembly.

54.—(1) The Governor, acting in his discretion, may refer to the Commission for their advice any question relating to the appointment (including promotion and transfer) or termination of appointment or to the dismissal or other disciplinary control of public officers or of any public officer (other than Judges of the Supreme Court, judicial officers and the Auditor-General) or to any other matter which, in his opinion, affects the public service.

(2) It shall be the duty of the Commission to advise the Governor on any question which he shall refer to it in accordance with the provisions of this section, but the Governor shall not be required to act in accordance with the advice given to him by the Commission.

55. Subject to the provisions of this Order, the Governor, acting in his discretion, may make regulations for giving effect to sections 53 and 54 of this Order, and in particular and without prejudice to the generality of the foregoing power may by such regulations make provision of all or any of the following matters, that is to say:—

(a) the tenure of office and terms of service of members of the Commission;

(b) the organisation of the work of the Commission and the manner in which the Commission shall perform its functions;

(c) consultation by the Commission with persons other than members of the Commission;

(d) the appointment, tenure of office and terms of service of staff to assist the Commission in the performance of its functions;

(e) the delegation to any member of the Commission of all or any of the powers or duties of the Commission;

(f) the definition and trial of offences connected with the functions of the Commission and the imposition of penalties for such offences:

Provided that no such penalty shall exceed a fine of one hundred pounds and imprisonment for a term of one year;

(g) the protection and privileges of members of the Commission in respect of the performance of their duties and the privilege of communications to and from the Commission or its members in case of legal proceedings.

56. On the date appointed, under the provisions of subsection (2) of section 2 of this Order, for this section to come into operation the provisions of Part I of the Third Schedule to this Order shall apply.

57.—(1) All pensions, gratuities or other like allowances which have been or which may be, granted to any persons who have been, and have ceased to be, public officers at any time before the date appointed under the provisions of subsection (2) of section 2 of this Order for the commencement of the provisions of Part IV of this Order, or to the widows, children, dependants or personal representatives of such persons, shall be governed by the law under which they were granted, or, if granted after that day, by the law in force on that day, or, in either case, by any law made thereafter which is not less favourable.

(2) All pensions, gratuities and other like allowances which may be granted to persons who are public officers on the aforesaid date, or to the widows, children, dependants or personal representatives of such persons, shall be governed by the law in force on that day or by any law made thereafter which is not less favourable.

(3) Any pension, gratuity or other like allowance which may be granted to any person who may be appointed to be a public officer after the aforesaid date, or to the widow, children, dependants or personal representatives of any such person shall be governed by the law in force on the day on which such person is so appointed or by any law made thereafter which is not less favourable.

(4) Where any person is entitled to exercise an option for his case to be governed by one or two or more laws, the law specified by him in exercising such option shall, for the purposes of this section, be deemed to be more favourable than the other law or laws.

58.—(1) The provisions contained in the Fourth Schedule to this Order shall have effect with respect to the public service and retirement therefrom and to the grant of compensation, pensions, gratuities and other like allowances.

(2) Notwithstanding the revocation of the existing Orders an officer having rights immediately before such revocation under the provisions of Section 71 of the Gold Coast (Constitution) Order in Council, 1950(g), shall retain such rights as if that section continued to have effect.

59. There shall be charged on and paid out of the general revenue

and assets of the Gold Coast all compensation, pensions, gratuities and other like allowances granted in accordance with the provisions of section 58 of this Order, and all other pensions, gratuities and other like allowances granted in respect of public service.

PART VII

THE JUDICATURE

60.—(1) The Chief Justice of the Supreme Court of the Gold Coast shall be appointed by the Governor after consultation with the Prime Minister; Judges of the Supreme Court other than the Chief Justice shall be appointed by the Governor acting after consultation with the Judicial Service Commission.

(2) A Judge of the Supreme Court shall not be removable except by the Governor on an address of the Assembly carried by not less than two-thirds of the Members thereof, praying for his removal on the ground of misbehaviour or of infirmity of body or mind.

(3) The maximum age for the retirement of Judges of the Supreme Court shall be sixty-two years:

Provided that the Governor, acting in his discretion, may permit a Judge of the Supreme Court, who has reached the age of sixty-two years, to continue in office for a period not exceeding twelve months.

(4) Any Judge of the Supreme Court may resign his office by writing under his hand addressed to the Governor.

(5) Notwithstanding the foregoing provisions of this section the Chief Justice and other Judges of the Supreme Court appointed before the date on which this section comes into operation and in office on that date shall continue in their offices on the terms and conditions on which they held office immediately before that date and the rights and privileges which they enjoyed before that date by virtue of their offices shall continue to appertain to them and their rights and privileges shall not be adversely affected by the provisions of this section.

(6) The salaries of Judges of the Supreme Court shall be determined by the Assembly and shall be charged on the general revenue and assets of the Gold Coast and shall not be diminished during their terms of office.

61.—(1) There shall be a Judicial Service Commission which shall consist of—

(a) the Chief Justice;

(b) the Attorney General;

(*c*) the senior Puisne Judge;

(*d*) the Chairman of the Public Service Commission; and

(*e*) a person who is, or shall have been, a Judge of the Supreme Court, appointed by the Governor, acting in his discretion.

(2) In subsection (1) of this section the expression "senior" means senior according to the date of substantive appointment by the Governor, or, if in any case two persons were appointed substantively on the same date, according to age.

(3) The Governor, acting after consultation with the Judicial Service Commission, may make regulations in regard to the exercise by the Commission of any of its functions.

(4) The Governor, acting in his discretion, may appoint a secretary to the Judicial Service Commission.

62.—(1) The appointment, promotion, transfer, termination of appointment, dismissal and disciplinary control of judicial officers is hereby vested in the Governor acting after consultation with the Judicial Service Commission.

(2) Any judicial officer may resign his office by writing under his hand addressed to the Governor.

(3) Subject to the provisions of section 58 of this Order every judicial officer appointed before the date on which this section comes into operation and in office on that date shall continue in office as if he had been appointed under the provisions of this section.

(4) In this section the expression "appointment" includes an acting or temporary appointment, and the expression "transfer" means a transfer involving an increase of salary.

63. On the date appointed, under the provisions of subsection (2) of section 2 of this Order, for this section to come into operation the provisions of Part II of the Third Schedule to this Order shall apply.

64. Every person who, otherwise than in the course of his duty, directly or indirectly, by himself or by any other person, in any manner whatsoever, influences or attempts to influence any decision of the Judicial Service Commission or of any member thereof shall be guilty of an offence and shall be liable to a fine not exceeding one hundred pounds or to imprisonment for a term not exceeding one year or to both such fine and imprisonment:

Provided that nothing in this section shall prohibit any person from giving a certificate or testimonial to any applicant or candidate for any judicial office.

PART VIII

FINANCE

65.—(1) The Minister responsible for finance shall cause to be prepared annually estimates of revenue and expenditure for public services during the succeeding financial year which, when approved by the Cabinet, shall be laid before the Assembly.

(2) The proposals for all expenditure contained in the estimates (other than statutory expenditure) shall be submitted to the vote of the Assembly by means of an Appropriation Bill, which shall contain estimates under appropriate heads for the several services required.

(3) Whenever—

(a) any expenditure is incurred or is likely to be incurred in any financial year upon any service which is in excess of the sum provided for that service by the Appropriation Ordinance relating to that year, or

(b) any expenditure (other than statutory expenditure) is incurred or is likely to be incurred in any financial year upon any new service not provided for by the Appropriation Ordinance relating to that year,

a Supplementary Appropriation Bill, which shall contain that expenditure under appropriate heads, shall be introduced in the Assembly.

(4) Statutory expenditure, which shall not be submitted to the vote of the Assembly, for the purposes of this section means—

(a) the expenditure charged on the general revenue and assets of the Gold Coast by virtue of the provisions of section 59, subsection (6) of section 60 and subsection (4) of section 67 and, after the commencement of section 56 of this Order, subsection (7) of section 52 of this Order;

(b) the interest on the public debt, sinking fund payments and the costs, charges and expenses incidental to the management of the public debt (which is hereby also charged upon the general revenue and assets of the Gold Coast); and

(c) such other expenditure as may by law be charged upon the general revenue and assets of the Gold Coast and in such law be expressly stated to be statutory expenditure.

(5) The Assembly may assent or refuse its assent to any head of estimate or expenditure contained in an Appropriation or Supplementary Appropriation Bill but may not vote an increased amount, a reduced amount or an alteration in its destination.

66.—(1) No expenditure shall be met from the general revenue and assets of the Gold Coast except upon the authority of a warrant under the hand of the Minister responsible for finance.

(2) Subject to the provisions of subsection (3) of this section no such warrant shall be issued unless such expenditure has been authorised for specified public services for the financial year to which the warrant relates by resolution of the Assembly or of a Committee thereof appointed for that purpose by the Assembly, or by any law.

(3) If an Appropriation Bill has not become a law by the first day of the year to which it relates, the Minister responsible for finance may, with the prior approval of the Cabinet, unless the Assembly shall already have made provision therefor, authorise the meeting of such expenditure from the general revenue and assets of the Gold Coast as he may consider essential for the continuance of the public services shown in the estimates until the Appropriation Bill becomes law:

Provided that the expenditure so authorised for any service shall not exceed one quarter of the amount voted for that service in the Appropriation Ordinance for the preceding year.

67.—(1) There shall be an Auditor-General who shall be appointed by the Governor, after consultation with the Prime Minister, and who shall not be removable except by the Governor or an address of the Assembly carried by not less than two-thirds of the Members thereof, praying for his removal on the grounds of misbehaviour or of infirmity of body or mind.

(2) The maximum age for the retirement of the Auditor-General shall be fifty-five years.

(3) The Auditor-General may resign his office by writing under his hand addressed to the Governor.

(4) The salary of the Auditor-General shall be determined by the Assembly, shall be charged on the general revenue and assets of the Gold Coast and shall not be diminished during his term of office.

68.—(1) The accounts of all departments and offices of Government, including the offices of the Clerk to the Assembly, the Secretary to the Cabinet, the Public Service Commission and the Judicial Service Commission, and of the Supreme Court, shall be audited by the Auditor-General who, with his deputies, shall at all times be entitled to have access to all books, records or returns relating to such accounts.

(2) The Auditor-General shall report annually to the Assembly on the exercise of his functions under this Order.

PART IX

MISCELLANEOUS

69.—(1) Any person who—

(a) having been elected as a Member of the Assembly but not having been, at the time when he was so elected, qualified to be so elected, shall sit or vote in the Assembly, or

(b) shall sit or vote in the Assembly after his seat therein has become vacant or he has become disqualified from sitting or voting therein,

knowing, or having reasonable grounds for knowing, that he was so disqualified, or that his seat has become vacant, as the case may be, shall be liable to a penalty not exceeding twenty pounds for every day upon which he so sits or votes.

(2) The said penalty shall be recoverable by action in the Supreme Court of the Gold Coast at the suit of the Attorney-General.

70. On the commencement of Part II of this Order all functions which at the date of such commencement shall be vested by any law in force in the Gold Coast in the Governor in the Executive Council, howsoever the association of the said Council with the Governor may be described in any such law, shall, so far as the same shall continue in existence and be capable of being exercised after the said date and save as otherwise provided by any law made under this Order, be vested in the Governor, and the provisions of subsection (1) of section 6 of this Order shall apply accordingly to the exercise of such functions.

71. Notwithstanding the revocation of the existing Orders the provisions of Part I of the Second Schedule of the Gold Coast (Constitution) Order in Council, 1950, in force immediately before the revocation of the existing Orders shall, in so far as they relate to the constitution of the Joint Provincial Council and the recognition of Paramount Chiefs, continue in force unless and until it shall be otherwise provided by any law made under this Order.

72.—(1) If any difficulty shall arise in bringing into operation any of the provisions of this Order or in giving effect to the purposes thereof, a Secretary of State may, by Order, make such provisions as seems to him necessary or expedient for the purpose of removing the difficulty and may by such Order amend or add to any provision of this Order:

Provided that no Order shall be made under this section later than the first day of July, 1955.

(2) Any Order made under this section may be amended, added to, or revoked by a further Order, and may be given retrospective effect to a date not earlier than the date of this Order.

(3) This section shall come into operation on the day after the day on which this Order shall have been laid before both Houses of Parliament.

73.—(1) Her Majesty hereby reserves to Herself, Her Heirs and Successors power, with the advice of Her or Their Privy Council, to amend, add to or revoke this Order as to Her or Them shall seem fit.

(2) Nothing in this Order shall affect the power of Her Majesty in Council to make laws from time to time for the peace, order and good government of the Gold Coast.

W. G. Agnew.

The First, Second, Third and Fourth Schedules
to the above Order-in-Council are omitted.

APPENDIX V

DECISIONS OF THE ASIAN-AFRICAN CONFERENCE—
1955

The Asian-African conference, convened by the Governments of Burma, Ceylon, India, Indonesia and Pakistan, met in Bandung from the 18th to 24th of April, 1955.

In addition to the sponsoring countries, the following twenty-four countries participated in the conference:

Afghanistan, Cambodia, People's Republic of China, Egypt, Ethiopia, Gold Coast, Iran, Iraq, Japan, Jordan, Laos, Lebanon, Liberia, Libya, Nepal, the Philippines, Saudi Arabia, Sudan, Syria, Thailand, Turkey, Democratic Republic of [North] Vietnam, State of Viet-nam and Yemen.

The Asian-African conference considered the position of Asia and Africa and discussed ways and means by which their peoples could achieve the fullest economic cultural and political co-operation.

A. ECONOMIC CO-OPERATION

1. The Asian-African conference recognized the urgency of promoting economic development in the Asian-African region. There was general desire for economic co-operation among the participating countries on the basis of mutual interest and respect for national sovereignty.

The proposals with regard to economic co-operation within the participating countries do not preclude either the desirability or the need for co-operation with countries outside the region, including the investment of foreign capital.

It was further recognized that assistance being received by certain participating countries from outside the region through international or under bilateral arrangements had made a valuable contribution to the implementation of their development programmes.

2. The participating countries agree to provide technical assistance to one another, to the maximum extent practicable, in the form of:

Experts, trainees, pilot projects, and equipment for demonstration purposes;

Exchange of know-how, and establishment of national and—where possible—regional training and research institutes for imparting technical knowledge and skills in co-operation with the existing international agencies.

3. The Asian-African conference recommended:

The early establishment of a special United Nations fund for economic development;

The allocation by the International Bank for Reconstruction and Development of a greater part of its resources to Asian-African countries;

The early establishment of an international finance corporation, which should include in its activities the undertaking of equity investment; and

Encouragement of the promotion of joint ventures among Asian-African countries in so far as this will promote their common interest.

4. The Asian-African conference recognized the vital need for stabilizing commodity trade in the region.

The principle of enlarging the scope of multilateral trade and payments was accepted. However, it was recognized that some countries would have to take recourse to bilateral trade arrangements in view of their prevailing economic conditions.

5. The Asian-African conference recommended that collective action be taken by participating countries for stabilizing international prices of and demand for primary commodities through bilateral and multilateral arrangements, and that as far as practicable and desirable they should adopt a unified approach on the subject in the United Nations Permanent Advisory Commission on International Commodity Trade and other international forums.

6. The Asian-African conference further recommended:

Asian-African countries should diversify their export trade by processing their raw materials whenever economically feasible before export; intra-regional trade fairs should be promoted and encouragement be given to the exchange of trade delegations and groups of business men; exchange of information and of samples should be encouraged with a view to promoting intra-regional trade; and normal facilities should be provided for the transit trade of landlocked countries.

7. The Asian-African conference attached considerable importance to shipping and expressed concern that shipping lines reviewed from time to time their freight rates often to the detriment of participating countries.

It recommended a study of this problem and collective action thereafter to put pressure on the shipping lines to adopt a more reasonable attitude.

8. The Asian-African conference agreed that encouragement should be given to the establishment of national and regional banks and insurance companies.

9. The Asian-African conference felt that exchange of information on matters relating to oil, such as remittance of profits and taxation, might finally lead to the formation of a common policy.

10. The Asian-African conference emphasized the particular significance of the development of nuclear energy for peaceful purposes for Asian-African countries.

The conference welcomed the initiative of the powers principally concerned in offering to make available information regarding the use of atomic energy for peaceful purposes;

Urged the speedy establishment of an international atomic energy agency which should provide for adequate representation of the Asian-African countries on the executive authority of the agency; and

Recommended that Asian and African governments take full advantage of the training and other facilities in the peaceful uses of atomic energy offered by the countries sponsoring such programmes.

11. The Asian-African conference agreed to the appointment of liaison officers in participating countries, to be nominated by their respective national governments, for the exchange of information and matters of mutual interest.

It recommended that fuller use should be made of the existing international organizations, and participating countries who were not members of such international organizations but were eligible should secure membership.

12. The Asian-African conference recommended that there should be prior consultation of participating countries in international forums with a view, as far as possible, to furthering their mutual economic interest. It is, however, not intended to form a regional bloc.

B.   CULTURAL CO-OPERATION

1. The Asian-African conference was convinced that among the most powerful means of promoting understanding among nations is

the development of cultural co-operation. Asia and Africa have been the cradle of great religions and civilizations which have enriched other cultures and civilizations while themselves being enriched in the process.

Thus the cultures of Asia and Africa are based on spiritual and universal foundations. Unfortunately, cultural contacts among Asian and African countries were interrupted during the past centuries.

The people of Asia and Africa are now animated by a keen and sincere desire to renew their old cultural contacts and develop new ones in the context of the modern world. All participating governments at the conference reiterated their declaration to work for closer cultural co-operation.

2. The Asian-African conference took note of the fact that the existence of colonialism in many parts of Asia and Africa, in whatever form it may be, not only prevents cultural co-operation but also suppresses the national cultures of the peoples.

Some colonial powers have denied their dependent peoples basic rights in the sphere of education and culture, which hampers the development of their personality and also prevents cultural intercourse with other Asian and African peoples.

This is particularly true in the case of Tunisia, Algeria and Morocco, where the basic right of the people to study their own language and culture has been suppressed.

Similar discrimination has been practised against African and Coloured people in some parts of the Continent of Africa.

The conference felt that these policies amount to a denial of the fundamental rights of man, impede cultural advancement in this region and also hamper cultural co-operation on the wide international plan.

The conference condemned such a denial of fundamental rights in the sphere of education and culture in some parts of Asia and Africa by this and other forms of cultural suppression.

In particular, the conference condemned racialism as a means of cultural suppression.

3. It was not from any sense of exclusiveness or rivalry with other groups of nations and other civilizations and culture that the conference viewed the development of cultural co-operation among Asian and African countries.

True to the age-old tradition of tolerance and universality, the conference believed that Asian and African cultural co-operation should be developed in the larger context of world co-operation.

Side by side with the development of Asian-African cultural co-operation the countries of Asia and Africa desire to develop cultural contacts with others. This would enrich their own culture and would also help in the promotion of world peace and understanding.

4. There are many countries in Asia and Africa which have not yet been able to develop their educational, scientific and technical institutions.

The conference recommended that countries in Asia and Africa which are more fortunately placed in this respect should give facilities for the admission of students and trainees from such countries to their institutions.

Such facilities should also be made available to the Asian and African people in Africa, to whom opportunities for acquiring higher education are at present denied.

5. The Asian-African conference felt that the promotion of cultural co-operation among countries of Asia and Africa should be directed towards:

(a) The acquisition of knowledge of each other's country;

(b) Mutual cultural exchange and,

(c) Exchange of information.

6. The Asian-African conference was of the opinion that at this stage the best results in cultural co-operation would be achieved by pursuing bilateral arrangements to implement its recommendations and by each country taking action on its own wherever possible and feasible.

C. HUMAN RIGHTS AND
SELF-DETERMINATION

1. The Asian-African conference declared its full support of the fundamental principles of human rights as set forth in the Charter of the United Nations and took note of the Universal Declaration of Human Rights as a common standard of achievement for all peoples and all nations.

The conference declared its full support of the principle of self-determination of peoples and nations as set forth in the Charter of the United Nations and took note of the United Nations resolutions on the right of peoples and nations to self-determination, which is a prerequisite of the full enjoyment of all fundamental human rights.

2. The Asian-African conference deplored the policies and practices of racial segregation and discrimination which form the basis of government and human relations in large regions of Africa and in other parts of the world.

Such conduct is not only a gross violation of human rights but also a denial of the fundamental values of civilization and the dignity of man.

The conference extended its warm sympathy and support for the courageous stand taken by the victims of racial discrimination, especially by the peoples of African and Indian and Pakistani origin in South Africa; applauded all those who sustained their cause; reaffirmed the determination of Asian-African peoples to eradicate every trace of racialism that might exist in their own countries; and pledged to use its full moral influence to guard against the danger of falling victims of the same evil in their struggle to eradicate it.

3. In view of the existing tension in the Middle East caused by the situation in Palestine and of the danger of that tension to world peace, the Asian-African conference declared its support of the rights of the Arab people of Palestine and called for the implementation of the United Nations resolutions on Palestine and of the peaceful settlement of the Palestine question.

D.   PROBLEMS OF DEPENDENT PEOPLE

1. The Asian-African conference, in the context of its expressed attitude on the abolition of colonialism, supported the position of Indonesia in the case of West Irian [Dutch New Guinea] on the relevant agreements between Indonesia and the Netherlands.

The Asian-African conference urged the Netherlands Government to re-open negotiations as soon as possible to implement their obligations under the above-mentioned agreements and expressed the earnest hope that the United Nations could assist the parties concerned in finding a peaceful solution to the dispute.

2. In view of the unsettled situation in North Africa and of the persisting denial to the peoples of North Africa of their right to self-determination, the Asian-African conference declared its support of the rights of the people of Algeria, Morocco and Tunisia to self-determination and independence and urged the French Government to bring about a peaceful settlement of the issue without delay.

E. PROMOTION OF WORLD PEACE
AND CO-OPERATION

1. The Asian-African conference, taking note of the fact that several states have still not been admitted to the United Nations, considered that for effective co-operation for world peace membership in the United Nations should be universal, called on the Security Council to support the admission of all those states which are qualified for membership in terms of the Charter.

In the opinion of the Asian-African conference the following countries which were represented in it—Cambodia, Ceylon, Japan, Jordan, Laos, Libya, Nepal, and unified Vietnam—were so qualified.

The conference considered that the representation of the countries of the Asian-African region on the Security Council in relation to the principle of equitable geographical distribution was inadequate.

It expressed the view that as regards the distribution of the non-permanent seats, the Asian-African countries which, under the arrangement arrived at in London in 1946, are precluded from being elected, should be enabled to serve on the Security Council so that they might make a more effective contribution to the maintenance of international peace and security.

2. The Asian-African conference, having considered the dangerous situation of international tension existing and the risks confronting the whole human race from the outbreak of global war in which the destructive power of all types of armaments including nuclear and thermonuclear weapons would be employed, invited the attention of all nations to the terrible consequences that would follow if such a war were to break out.

The conference considered that disarmament and the prohibition of production, experimentation and use of nuclear and thermonuclear weapons of war are imperative to save mankind and civilization from the fear and prospect of wholesale destruction.

It considered that the nations of Asia and Africa assembled here have a duty towards humanity and civilization to proclaim their support for the prohibition of these weapons and to appeal to nations principally concerned and to world opinion to bring about such disarmament and prohibition.

The conference considered that effective international control should be established and maintained to implement such prohibition and that speedy and determined efforts should be made to this end. Pending the total prohibition of the manufacture of nuclear and thermonuclear weapons, this conference appealed to all the powers concerned to reach agreement to suspend experiments with such weapons.

The conference declared that universal disarmament is an absolute necessity for the preservation of peace and requested the United Nations to continue its efforts and appealed to all concerned speedily to bring about the regulation, limitation, control and reduction of all armed forces and armaments including the prohibition of the production, experimentation and use of all weapons of mass destruction and to establish effective international control to this end.

3. The Asian-African conference supported the position of the Yemen in the case of Aden and the southern parts of Yemen known as the protectorates and urged the parties concerned to arrive at a peaceful settlement of the dispute.

F.   DECLARATION OF PROBLEMS OF DEPENDENT PEOPLES

The Asian-African conference discussed the problems of dependent peoples and colonialism and the evils arising from the subject. To what is stated in the following paragraph, the conference is agreed:

1. In declaring that colonialism in all its manifestations is an evil which should speedily be brought to an end;

2. In affirming that the subjection of peoples to alien subjugation, domination and exploitation constitute a denial of fundamental human rights, is contrary to the Charter of the United Nations and is an impediment to the promotion of world peace and co-operation;

3. In declaring its support of the cause of freedom and independence for all such peoples; and

4. In calling upon the powers concerned to grant freedom and independence to such peoples.

G.   DECLARATION OF PROMOTION OF WORLD PEACE AND CO-OPERATION

The Asian-African conference gave anxious thought to the question of world peace and co-operation. It viewed with deep concern the present state of international tension with its danger of an atomic world war.

The problem of peace is correlative with the problem of international security. In this connection all states should co-operate especially through the United Nations in bringing about the reduction of armaments and the elimination of nuclear weapons under effective international control.

In this way international peace can be promoted and nuclear energy may be used exclusively for peaceful purpose. This would help answer the needs, particularly of Asia and Africa, for what they urgently require are social progress and better standards of life in larger freedom.

Freedom and peace are interdependent. The right of self-determination must be enjoyed by all peoples and freedom and independence must be granted with the least possible delay to those who are still dependent peoples.

Indeed all nations should have the right freely to choose their own political and economic systems and their own way of life in conformity with the purposes and principles of the Charter of the United Nations.

Free from distrust and fear and with confidence and goodwill towards each other, nations should practise tolerance and live together in peace with one another as good neighbours and develop friendly co-operation on the basis of the following principles:

1. Respect for the fundamental human rights and for the purposes and principles of the Charter of the United Nations.

2. Respect for the sovereignty and territorial integrity of all nations.

3. Recognition of the equality of all races and of the equality of all nations, large and small.

4. Abstention from intervention or interference in the internal affairs of another country.

5. Respect for the right of each nation to defend itself singly or collectively in conformity with the Charter of the United Nations.

6a. Abstention from the use of arrangements of collective defence to serve the particular interests of any of the big powers.

6b. Abstention by any country from exerting pressures on other countries.

7. Refraining from acts or threats of aggression or the use of force against the territorial integrity or political independence of any country.

8. Settlement of all international disputes by peaceful means such as negotiation, conciliation, arbitration or judicial settlement, as well as other peaceful means of the parties' own choice in conformity with the Charter of the United Nations.

9. Promotion of mutual interest and co-operation.

10. Respect of justice and international obligations.

The Asian-African conference declares its conviction that friendly co-operation in accordance with these principles would effectively contribute to the maintenance and promotion of international peace and security while co-operation in the economic, social and cultural fields would help bring about the common prosperity and well-being of all.

The Asian-African conference recommended that the full sponsoring countries should consider the next meeting of the conference in consultation with other countries concerned.

INDEX

GEORGE PADMORE was born Malcolm Nurse in the West Indies, and he adopted his *nom de guerre* when he joined the Communist Party. He rose to become the foremost black figure in the Communist International—the Comintern—and his career culminated in his being commissioned into the Red Army as a colonel. He traveled extensively in Africa in an effort to create the nucleus of a Comintern-directed African leadership. Subsequently, as head of the African Bureau of the Comintern in Germany, he organized an International Conference of black workers in Hamburg. When it dawned on him that Stalin and his satraps looked upon black men as political pawns of Soviet power politics, to be maneuvered in Russian interests alone, he broke with the Kremlin. George Padmore became Kwame Nkrumah's Adviser on African Affairs in 1957. He died in 1959.